Thor's Microsoft® Security Bible

Thor's Microsoft® Security Bible
A Collection of Practical Security Techniques

Timothy "Thor" Mullen

Jeffrey W. Brown, Technical Editor

AMSTERDAM • BOSTON • HEIDELBERG • LONDON
NEW YORK • OXFORD • PARIS • SAN DIEGO
SAN FRANCISCO • SINGAPORE • SYDNEY • TOKYO
Syngress is an imprint of Elsevier

SYNGRESS.

Acquiring Editor: Angelina Ward
Development Editor: Heather Scherer
Project Manager: André Cuello
Designer: Dennis Schaefer

Syngress is an imprint of Elsevier
225 Wyman Street, Waltham, MA 02451, USA

Notices
Knowledge and best practice in this field are constantly changing. As new research and experience broaden our
understanding, changes in research methods or professional practices may become necessary. Practitioners and
researchers must always rely on their own experience and knowledge in evaluating and using any information or
methods described herein. In using such information or methods they should be mindful of their own safety and the
safety of others, including parties for whom they have a professional responsibility.

To the fullest extent of the law, neither the Publisher nor the authors, contributors, or editors assume any liability
for any injury and/or damage to persons or property as a matter of products liability, negligence or otherwise, or
from any use or operation of any methods, products, instructions, or ideas contained in the material herein.

Windows is a registered trademark of Microsoft Corporation in the United States and other countries.
Microsoft does not endorse this publication and no affiliation is implied nor should be inferred.

Library of Congress Cataloging-in-Publication Data
Application submitted

British Library Cataloguing-in-Publication Data
A catalogue record for this book is available from the British Library.

ISBN: 978-1-59749-572-1

Printed in the United States of America
11   12   13   14   10   9   8   7   6   5   4   3   2   1

Working together to grow
libraries in developing countries

www.elsevier.com | www.bookaid.org | www.sabre.org

ELSEVIER   BOOK AID International   Sabre Foundation

For information on all Syngress publications visit our website at www.syngress.com

Contents

About the Author

Timothy Mullen is a Principal Security Architect for a worldwide, multibillion-dollar commerce platform and is rumored to operate somewhere in the vicinity of Seattle, Washington. Also known as "Thor," he is the founder of the "Hammer of God" security co-op group. He is a member of American Mensa, is a Microsoft Certified Trainer, has Microsoft Engineer certifications in all remotely recent operating systems, and has been awarded Microsoft's "Most Valuable Professional" (MVP) award in Windows Enterprise Security four years running.

TECHNICAL EDITOR

Jeffrey W. Brown (CISSP-ISSMP, CISM, CRISC, PMP) is a senior information security professional with more than 14 years' experience defining and implementing enterprise security programs to meet business, regulatory, compliance, and information security requirements for top Fortune 500 companies. He is currently a Global Information Security Program Manager at GE Capital, where he manages the development and implementation of global information security and IT risk initiatives. His industry experience includes membership on advisory boards and participation in industry associations including ISSA, ISACA, and The Technology Manager's Forum. He is also a governing member of the New York CISO Executive Summit. Jeff was a member of the SANS *Windows Security Digest* Editorial Board and has been a participant in several SANS Step-by-Step guides including *Windows NT Security Step-by-Step* and *Securing Windows 2000 Step-by-Step*. He has been an author and contributor for several publications, including *Mission Critical Internet Security* (Syngress), and holds a BA and an MS from Pace University.

Introduction

What is security? Is it a mindset? Is it a measurable and actionable posture or position? Or is it a bit of both? People, as a race, learn from doing; they learn by example. Ingrained into our psyche is a process that builds new information upon previous knowledge as we learn. As Isaac Newton said, "If I have seen further than others, it is by standing on the shoulders of giants." Basically, we bring in a foundation of old information as we process new information.

But this does not always work in our favor, particularly in the area of technology. Technology has a way of exposing the flaws in past ways of thinking by filling in the gaps between human assumptions. Technology answers many of the questions that, frankly, were previously answered by ad-libs. I think the relationship between science and religion also exemplifies this quite well. As more technological advances are made, more things about the world that were previously explained by divine intervention, or magic if you will, are demystified. The people who came up with these answers were revered as some manner of guru and were held in a position of regard. Some were indeed gifted and contributed to the well-being of others with their insight and wisdom. And some were a bunch of jackleg gurus making up stories in the absence of wisdom, insight, and altruism—or they were simply snake oil salesmen. My intent is not to be prophetic, but rather to make the suggestion that we need to focus on making clear distinctions between the lessons that history holds that provide true value to information security (infosec) and the ones that are simply a bunch of crap.

A security strategy needs to plan for and respond to incidents as moving targets on a sliding scale. Vectors and targets will change as technology changes, and as revenue sources for criminals dry up, new ones will be scouted out. Attacks against users and modes of behavior in a home-usage environment will migrate to mobile scenarios as both individuals and businesses conduct more and more business via cell phone. But while the attacks change with the targets, what remains constant are the fundamental building blocks of security, which I believe are security in depth and least privilege. The reason for this is because I have been writing about this subject for decades now and these two security concepts have remained as reliable and dependable as they were years ago.

I think the security industry has been trending in a direction that is actually counterintuitive to its raison d'être. It is getting further away from actual infosec and closer to the marketing of a three-ring circus. Today, it seems to be all about flash and ego. If you look at any popular security conference, the main theme is not actually security, but rather *anti-security*: how to hack this, how to attack that, and how to break into whatever else. As time has gone on, the attacks have become more convoluted and complex and even those attacks that have the least possibility of occurring are now presented as everyday threats. It seems like presenters nowadays are not showing you how to be more secure; they are showing you how brilliant they are. If they can come up with some crazy method of doing something, then they must be geniuses, and as such, you should buy whatever it is they are selling.

Researchers only want to find bugs and report them so that they get noticed, not because they are "forcing companies to secure their products," as is so often claimed. They want the issues they find to be as bad as they can possibly be, and, in searching for the worst-case scenario, they often overlook the simpler points of logic, like setting permissions on a vector to prevent exploitation. For the most part, the content I now see being sold as sound security advice is pretty lame. The most trivial of security issues are being portrayed as critical security vulnerabilities. One may argue that it is this level of public scrutiny that has led the industry to be as secure as it is, and there is some merit to that. However, the amount of really smart people seems to continually shrink while the number of snake oilers is increasing.

To be fair, I have seen some really interesting, even fascinating, methods of attacking systems that are amazingly clever; however, their application to real-world business is far removed. If we use the circus analogy, it is like those acrobats who do handstands on each other's heads while flipping around and landing with a foot in each of the other guy's hands. It is truly remarkable and takes an incredible amount of practice and skill, but they are not really *doing* anything. Sure, it is art and there is value in the entertainment, but at the end of the day from a production standpoint, these guys have not created a single thing. It is, quite literally, all for show.

This is why I have always presented information security from a defensive point of view. Every training event I have lead and every session I have presented was based on the concept of "do this to protect yourself from that." And to me, that is where the value is. I take five minutes of someone's time to show them a setting that will prevent the attacks illustrated in five hours of ethical hacking training. It just seems like the natural way to approach things.

So, as funny as it may sound, not getting hacked is boring. Watching failed attack after failed attack is not very interesting. And this is why security does not sell. Watching the acrobatics creates as much security as an open door, yet we feel our money is well spent because it keeps our attention. This book is about using the building blocks of security to improve your security posture. It is about deploying solutions with security in depth in an environment of least privilege. And it is about using what you already have to attain that security posture rather than having to continue spending money on new security products. I wanted to approach this book differently than other infosec books that focus on aspects of a single application, and I wanted to present the material in a way different from the typical academic approach to writing. I think I have accomplished both. For one, this book is in the first person—it is me talking to you. This is basically a collection of ideas and methods that I have used to create security in a particular way, and it comes naturally to me to deliver the information as if we were sitting across from each other. To get the security points across, I use a word problem format and create various business scenarios that we will need to figure out. This is more in line with how things work in the real world. For instance, you do not just secure SQL Server. You can read about it and practice it, but, in the end, you are really securing the process you have built around SQL Server. So in these stories the plot is a business project we have been tasked with, and the characters are different products and product features working together to get the job done.

It is important to understand that the stories are not just about the scenario, but, like other bibles out there, they each carry a lesson. As you read about how to write a particular piece of code or create a user in a particular way to do something specific, I would like for you to consider how the same concepts could be applied to other things. By way of example, you will see a scenario later in this book about logging firewall proxy data to a SQL server, and how the SQL server is running in the context of a low-privileged user, and how to ensure that the connection is always encrypted so the data integrity is guaranteed. While the project may be to create autonomous log monitoring in order to automatically enforce access rules, you will be able to use the exact same process to ensure data from any given application is encrypted in transit when logged to SQL. In other words, there is always more to the story than the story itself.

Speaking of which, we will now cover a bit of what is actually in the book. In addition to the chapters herein, you will have some video presentation of run-throughs from the book content along with code samples and projects on the companion media. We shall cover a wide range of topics, ideas, and processes here. I will illustrate how to create the autonomous traffic monitor I wrote of earlier, how to compile and report on traffic from a country-by-country geolocation standpoint, how to set up a secure external web proxy, how to cover RDP security, how to set up remote security logging in a least privilege and secure way, and how to create and maintain service users with associated tricks, traps, and more.

I try to present each story/project in a sequential manner, consistent with how you would build a project when venturing out on your own. That is, I try to mimic the experience you might have when trying to figure out things by yourself. I like the organic approach to solving projects because many times certain aspects of a project do not make themselves known until you come upon them. Of course, some of my opinions on life, the universe, and everything will also be intertwined within. So I thank you for supporting the Hammer of God research facilities by purchasing this book and, without further ado, let us begin.

Chapter

Securely Writing Web Proxy Log Data to SQL Server and Programmatically Monitoring Web Traffic Data in Order to Automatically Inject Allow/Deny Rules into TMG

INFORMATION IN THIS CHAPTER:

- Implementation
- Securely Logging Data to SQL
- Designing the Workflow
- Execution

PRODUCTS, TOOLS, AND METHODS:

- Active Directory (AD)
- MS SQL Server
- Internet Security and Acceleration (ISA) Server/TMG[1] Windows Firewall with Advanced Security
- TMG Logging to SQL Server
- Least Privilege Service User

---

[1]From this point forward, only TMG will be discussed, though many options may be used in ISA Server as well.

- SQL Common Language Runtime (CLR) to Replace xp_cmdshell
- AD Permissions Delegation
- Organizational Units
- TMG Deny Rules
- Computer Certificates
- AppLocker

INTRODUCTION

The purpose of this process example is to securely combine the logging features of Microsoft's Threat Management Gateway (TMG) with the power of SQL Server to monitor user traffic with the goal of determining if the user has violated corporate (or other) web browsing policies by way of checking the destination uniform resource identifier (URI) called by the browser against a blacklist of predetermined sites. We will then block that user using dynamically managed AD group membership in an automated fashion. These techniques can also be applied to different scenarios, so take note of those that you can port over to other applications and configurations.

In this example, we will configure TMG to log web proxy data to a SQL database using integrated machine credentials and then create a SQL job to monitor entries in the log in order to trigger an event where the SQL service will update user group information for an AD global group that has been preconfigured as the target of a DENY rule in TMG.

In other words, SQL will monitor the TMG logs practically in near-real-time and look for destination sites in the logs that match a list of admin-defined blacklisted sites. When it finds a user that has broken a policy (for example, visiting ESPN during work hours), it will automatically execute a command to add that user to a global group that has been denied outbound access in TMG. When the rule is matched, rather than the default TMG access error page, the user will be redirected to an internal web page where they will be greeted by Quake Arena's DENIED.wav file and a spinning skull graphic telling him that he is a loser, to pack his things, and to report to the front desk. I have actually deployed this method into a production environment at a corporation I worked for previously, and the results were well worth the issues it created with Human Resources. You, of course, will have to make that determination on your own.

At each step, we will be consciously aware of what process environment we can create using security in depth and using least privilege where possible. While these illustrations are just examples of the integration possibilities available, I will try to make each as complete as possible insofar as working code is concerned. When I present ideas, they are complete, tested, and operational—unlike security by theory, which is not worth the HTML it is written in. As always, these processes can be applied to a multitude of different security processes with varied end results.

SCOPE AND CONSIDERATIONS

I have seen many SQL environments where scheduled jobs would run as administrator and drop down to the command interpreter via the ever popular *xp_cmdshell* extended system stored procedure in order to interact directly with the operating system (OS) or file system. Years back, there were not many reliable solutions for doing this other than xp_cmdshell, and people were not as worried about security then as we are now. For similar solutions, I would typically see SQL set up for mixed mode authentication, using a database source name (DSN) on the TMG box to connect to the SQL server with stored credentials that post log records, and with the SQL Server service running in a privileged context so it could directly alter group membership in AD and do something like execute a net user command via the previously mentioned xp_cmdshell.

There are consequences to this type of configuration when it creates a vulnerability that allows an attacker to execute code in the context of the service account, or when SQL injection vectors allow for attacker-defined scripts to be injected into the SQL code. If xp_cmdshell was enabled, injecting Transact-SQL (T-SQL) in order to drop down to the command (cmd) prompt and add users to the local administrators group was trivial. It was also easy to build cmd scripts one line at a time with *echo ftp > getit. cmd* in order to begin building an ftp connection script, and then continuing on with *echo open >> getit.cmd* and so on so you could execute the connection script and have the server download your favorite toolset. Afterward, you could execute server-side tools so you could make direct connections to it, steal data, and so on. You can see how dangerous this can be, and though xp_cmdshell is disabled by default on SQL Server now, people still leverage the power of xp_cmdshell to do their dirty work. We will not be doing that, of course. We will actually walk through three progressive examples of bad, better, and even better so that the benefits of our final method, SQL CLR, are clearly illustrated.

Secure Process Prerequisites

This exercise has two prerequisites. We first need the SQL Server service running as least privileged user as discussed in Chapter 5, "The Creation and Maintenance of Low Privileged Service Users." To summarize the takeaways from that chapter, our *MSSQLSERVICE* service should be running as a domain user (*HAMMEROFGOD\SQLUser*), which is in turn a member of the *HAMMEROFGOD\gServiceUsers*[2] global group. This user/group has no rights other than those granted during the assignment of the user during the installation of SQL Server. More specifically, the user is *not* part of any other built-in group, and has explicitly been removed from the default domain users group. As also discussed in Chapter 5, Windows Authentication (or Integrated Windows Authentication) will be used because of its inherited security benefits like account lockout and password complexity enforcement.

Secondly, in order for TMG to properly log the name of the Windows user in the web proxy log, we must ensure that our outbound Internet access rule requires authentication. All browser requests, even when a proxy is configured, are initially made in the context of an anonymous user. If the access rule for TMG's outbound Internet access is configured to allow all users, then the anonymous request will succeed, the access will be granted, and the log file will look something like (snipped):

```
ClientIP      ClientUserName   DestHost        DestHostIP
3232235829    anonymous        www.bing.com    3232235786
```

Notice that the client username is anonymous, as you would expect from an all-users TMG rule. Note also that the client IP and destination host IP are notated in long integer format. This is normal, and I will show you how to write a scalar function for easy conversion to dot-decimal notation in Chapter 3, "Analyzing and Blocking Malicious Traffic Based on Geolocation." Figure 1.1 illustrates what your TMG rule should look like. You can, of course, base the authentication on any other local or domain-based grouping. As long as you do not allow all users, TMG will force authentication for the rule.

It is important to understand that this does *not* change the default behavior of your browser. Internet Explorer (IE), for example, will still continue to attempt an anonymous connection initially. TMG will deny this request and challenge IE for credentials, which it will then provide to TMG either by integrated authentication or by displaying a credential logon dialog

■ **FIGURE 1.1** TMG Access Rule Showing Outbound HTTPS Access for Authenticated Users

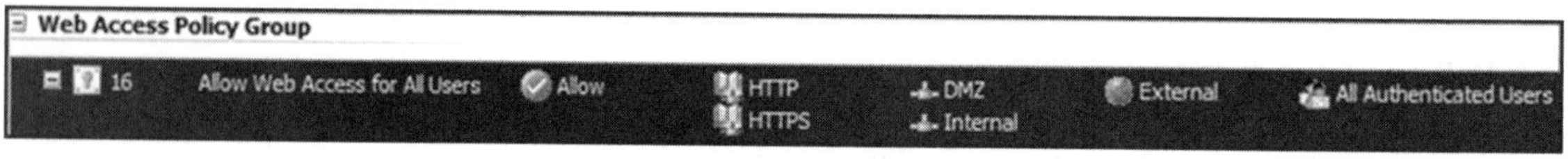

⊟ Web Access Policy Group					
⊟ ❓ 16 Allow Web Access for All Users	✓ Allow	🌐 HTTP 🌐 HTTPS	⊥ DMZ ⊥ Internal	🌐 External	👥 All Authenticated Users

---

[2] I prepend my global groups with a *g* so that they are all sorted together.

(depending on how you have configured your browser and domain). Your log will now look something like this:

```
ClientIP     ClientUserName    DestHost       DestHostIP
3232235829   anonymous         www.bing.com   3232235786
3232235829   HAMMEROFGOD\thor  www.bing.com   3232235786
```

For purposes of reporting, you can either delete the log entries for the anonymous users in the database itself, simply remove them from your query criteria, or not include them in the first place, whichever works best for your environment. I personally delete the anonymous requests records because I require authentication for all web access in my environment and am not concerned with the attempts. This may not work in your environment, or you might find that parsing source client data (browser types, for example) is helpful in weeding out rogue access attempts on your network.

IMPLEMENTATION

Assuming the preceding prerequisites are met, we will continue with the process. Since we will be blocking all attempts for external access based on group membership, we need to create a target global group to act as a container to move users into and out of when we deny them access and subsequently reenable access—after they have been sufficiently pummeled and ridiculed by the IT staff in the parking lot.

The important point here is that for our autonomous traffic analysis system to work, the SQL Server database engine (specifically the SQL Server Agent in this case) will have to perform the group membership assignment transaction itself. This will be executed within the context of our HAMMEROFGOD \SQLUser account since the SQL Server Agent runs under that context. In our example, a scheduled SQL job will be doing the heavy lifting. While we could certainly execute the job in an escalated privileged account context, that would be lazy and potentially dangerous because the process could be hijacked to perform other functions. We will, of course, have a structure in place to minimize any potential attack of that sort (defense in depth), but we should minimize such opportunities for attack whenever possible. We will use delegation control in AD to specifically grant the SQL user the rights to read members and write members to the organizational unit containing the global group that will contain the denied user membership. Since you delegate control at the organizational unit (OU) level as opposed to the group specifically, we will need to create the OU, and then create the group within that OU where we ultimately want the delegated control target to have membership management capabilities. Figure 1.2 shows the organizational attributes suggested.

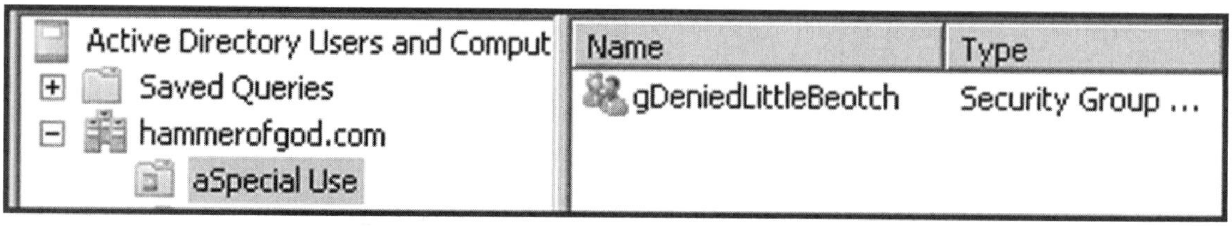

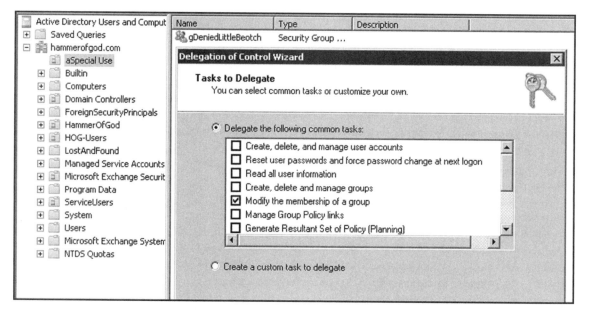

■ **FIGURE 1.2** The aSpecial Use OU Container with the gDeniedLittleBeotch Group as a Member

Delegating Rights to Users

The *aSpecial Use* organizational unit was created, and then the *gDeniedLittleBeotch* global group was created within it. At this point, the gDeniedLittleBeotch group has no members, which is fine. While we are here, we will take advantage of the previously mentioned and very powerful aspect of AD called delegation of control. We will delegate control of this OU to the HAMMEROFGOD\SQLUser account, allowing it to manage group membership, and *only* group membership, of the aSpecial Use OU.

■ **FIGURE 1.3** Permission Delegation for the aSpecial Use OU to Be Able to Modify the gServiceUsers Group

Right-click the OU and select **Delegate Control** to bring up a wizard that we can use to easily set the rights we want imposed on the selected OU to the users we choose. As seen in Figure 1.3, the selection we want is **Modify the membership of a group** so that the SQLUser account can manage group membership of objects contained in the aSpecial Use OU. Once this is selected, SQLUser will be able to add members to, and remove members from, the gDeniedLittleBeotch group (and any other groups that we put into the aSpecial Use OU).

This selection in the wizard will write two specific permissions to the OU, which you can view, as shown in Figure 1.4, by opening the security properties of the OU and selecting **Advanced**.

The read members and write members permissions are the true resultant permissions applied to the OU for the selected group or user. You could have

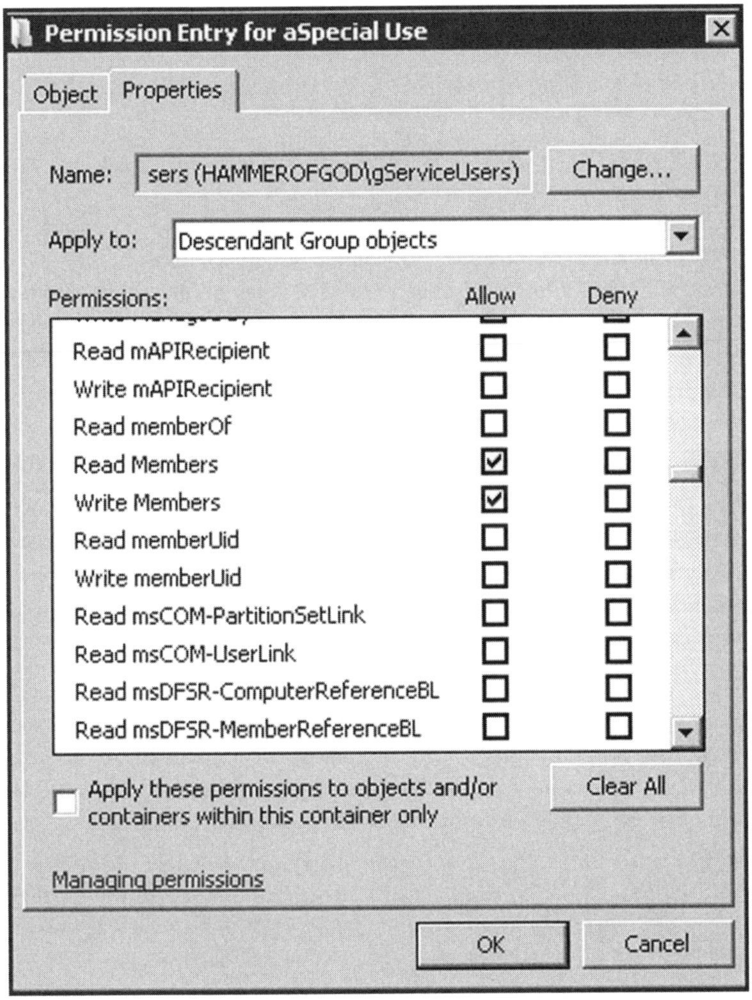

■ **FIGURE 1.4** Detailed Advanced Permissions Applied to the gServiceUsers Group in the aSpecial Use OU

also simply selected the OU's permissions and manually applied the **Read** and **Write** options for the SQL user, but the wizard makes it easier.

WARNING

As with all delegation, you will want to make sure you properly document changes made to OU and other AD permissions, as there is no simple way of knowing that you have changed the default permissions on an OU unless you use a third-party application or do a verbose Lightweight Directory Access Protocol (LDAP) dump. You might think running the Delegation of Control Wizard would bring up the last permissions selected, but it does not. It is simply an interface to make changes to permissions and does not retrieve any data. If you go nuts delegating control to lots of users and groups to lots of OUs and do not document it properly, you will find your auditing process tedious.

Everything is ready to go as far as AD is concerned. We have got a container for our bad users, we have delegated authority for the user to alter group membership, and all we have to do now is tie that group to a deny rule in TMG. This is done by creating a local group in TMG comprised of the Windows AD group. Simply navigate to the **Users** tab of your TMG toolbox window, and **Add** a new group, making sure to add in the Windows group of gDeniedLittleBeotch, as shown in Figure 1.5.

TMG Access Rules

Now that our local user set is created and linked to the Windows global group, we need to create a deny rule that is applied to that user. I have positioned it on the top so that it gets imposed first, right above my blackout rule for all Russia and China traffic (covered in more depth in Chapter 3, which focuses on geolocation). Your rule should look like the one in Figure 1.6.

This will result in all denied users (members of the gDeniedLittleBeotch group) to be denied all outbound access from the internal network to the external network. When you deploy this rule set into production, make sure you have properly configured your outbound access authentication model with your entire policy in mind; otherwise, you could end up blocking all traffic for everyone who does not authenticate. My example in Figure 1.6 showing the deny rule in the first position will probably be problematic in a production environment, so again, the authentication model and access rule priority will have to be configured to support this. We are now finished with the groups and rules for AD and TMG.

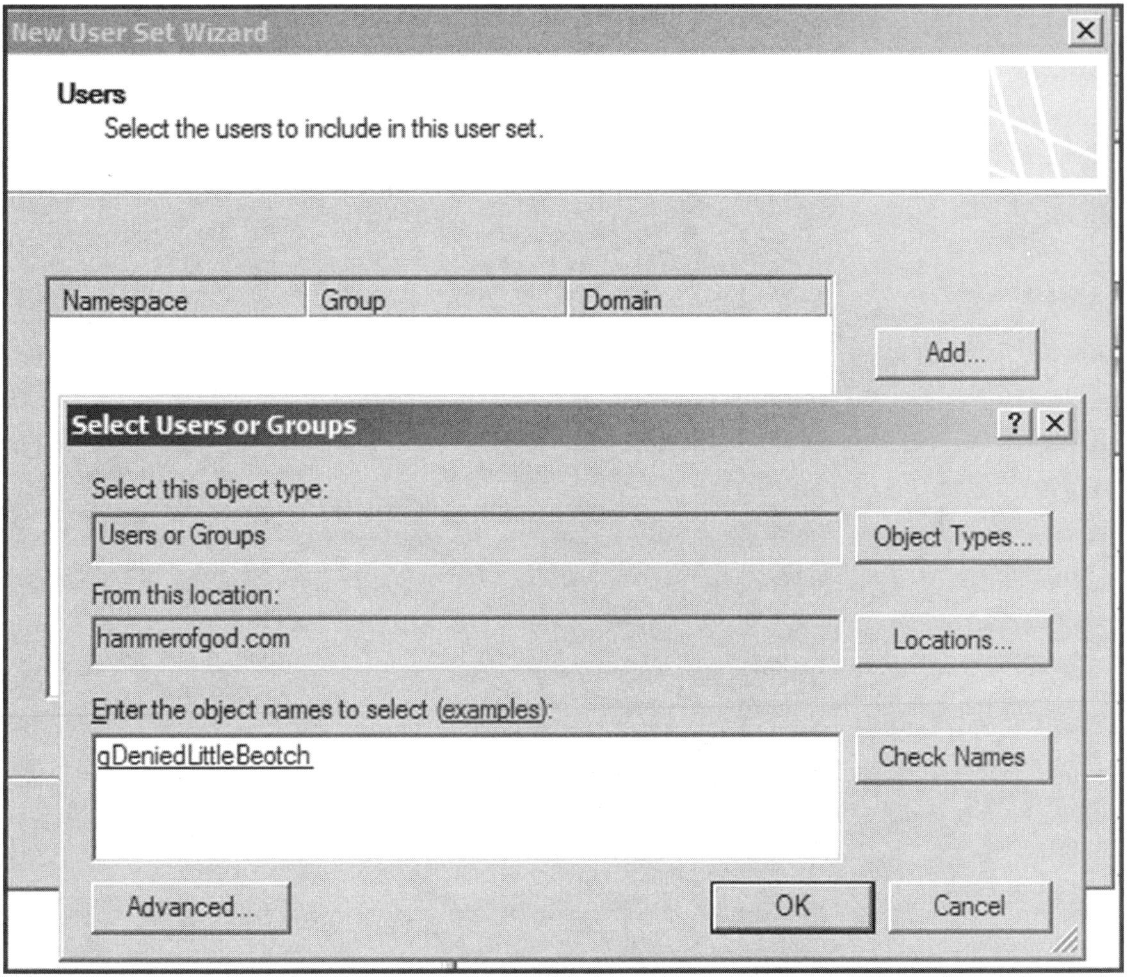

■ FIGURE 1.5 Adding Your AD Group to the TMG Users Object

■ FIGURE 1.6 Placement of the Deny Rule

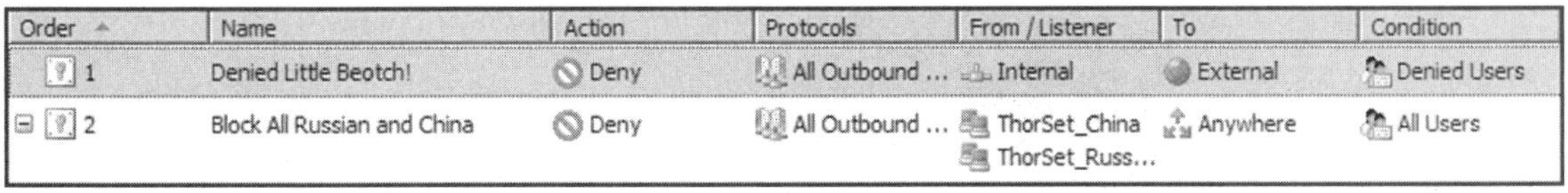

Order ▲	Name	Action	Protocols	From / Listener	To	Condition
📄 1	Denied Little Beotch!	⊘ Deny	All Outbound ... Internal	External	Denied Users
⊟ 📄 2	Block All Russian and China	⊘ Deny	All Outbound ... ThorSet_China ThorSet_Russ...	Anywhere	All Users

SECURELY LOGGING DATA TO SQL

Now we need to configure TMG to log proxy data to SQL. TMG and ISA Server ship with the SQL scripts needed to create the *WebProxyLog* table structure, and it is important for you to use the right script for the version you have. If you have previously created log data in ISA Server on SQL and have migrated to TMG, you will need to update the table structure to match the definitions in the TMG w3proxy.sql file located in the TMG program files folder because TMG adds new elements to the log data. The following SQL code snip creates the tables needed. This will not do you much good printed in a book since you will need the files off your install of TMG,[3] but you can see some of the fields it will create:

```
CREATE TABLE WebProxyLog (
  [ClientIP] uniqueidentifier,
  [ClientUserName] nvarchar(514),
  [ClientAgent] varchar(128),
  [ClientAuthenticate] smallint,
  [logTime] datetime,
  [service] smallint,
  [servername] nvarchar(32),
  [referredserver] varchar(255),
  [DestHost] varchar(255),
  [DestHostIP] uniqueidentifier,
  [DestHostPort] int,
  [processingtime] int,
  [bytesrecvd] bigint,
  [bytessent] bigint,
  [protocol] varchar(13),
  [transport] varchar(8),
  [operation] varchar(24),
  [uri] varchar(2048),
  [mimetype] varchar(32),
  [objectsource] smallint,
  [resultcode] int,
  [CacheInfo] int,
  [rule] nvarchar(128),
  [FilterInfo] nvarchar(256),
  [SrcNetwork] nvarchar(128),
```

---

[3]These files are included on the companion media for this book.

```
[DstNetwork] nvarchar(128),
[ErrorInfo] int,
[Action] varchar(32),
[GmtLogTime] datetime,
[AuthenticationServer] varchar(255),
[ipsScanResult] smallint,
[ipsSignature] nvarchar(128),
[ThreatName] varchar(255),
[MalwareInspectionAction] smallint,
[MalwareInspectionResult] smallint,
[UrlCategory] int,
[MalwareInspectionContentDeliveryMethod] smallint,
[UagArrayId] varchar(20),
[UagVersion] int,
[UagModuleId] varchar(20),
[UagId] int,
[UagSeverity] varchar(20),
[UagType] varchar(20),
[UagEventName] varchar(60),
[UagSessionId] varchar(50),
[UagTrunkName] varchar(128),
[UagServiceName] varchar(20),
[UagErrorCode] int,
[MalwareInspectionDuration] int,
[MalwareInspectionThreatLevel] smallint,
[InternalServiceInfo] int,
[ipsApplicationProtocol] nvarchar(128),
[NATAddress] uniqueidentifier,
[UrlCategorizationReason] smallint,
[SessionType] smallint,
[UrlDestHost] varchar(255),
[SrcPort] int
)
GO
```

You will need to create a database first, and then run the w3proxy.sql code while attached to that database in order to create the table. This is not all. We also have to ensure that the TMG instance has the necessary permissions to write to the table and to execute the post stored procedures it also creates, or else it will fail. This means that a logon must be created in SQL Server and assigned the necessary rights; however, the TMG service runs as a network service. You may be tempted to create a local SQL user and switch SQL to mixed mode, and then use a DSN to connect, but that is neither necessary nor desirable. Remember that SQL authentication is much weaker than Integrated Windows Authentication, so logon or account policies are not applied, and any logon attempts lockout or password complexity requirements will have to be home grown into your SQL install.

Creating the TMG Server User Account in SQL

Even though the TMG service runs as a network service and not as a proper user, it can, as the name implies, create a network connection in the context of the machine itself. To take advantage of this, we will not create a logon for a user in SQL, but, rather, one for the machine. This is done the same way you would create a user: Simply enter the domain\[*machine name*] with a *$* to specify a machine name as in HAMMEROFGOD\TMG$ and as reflected in Figure 1.7.

Once the user is created, you can assign the necessary permissions with the following SQL code or via the user interface. Note that in SQL 2008, creating the user logon and granting permissions is not enough; you must also grant the user connect rights as well.

```
--Give the machine (computer) account the rights it
--needs to connect to the database and post data into the tables.
--use TMSB
grant connect to "hammerofgod\tmg$"
exec sp_addrolemember 'db_datareader','hammerofgod\uag$'
exec sp_addrolemember 'db_datawriter','hammerofgod\uag$'
grant select,insert,update on dbo.WebProxyLog to "hammerofgod
--\uag$"
--above grant is redundant given role additions, but can be
--explicitly
--executed if one does not want to grant role membership
grant execute on dbo.sp_batch_discard to "hammerofgod\uag$"
grant execute on dbo.sp_batch_insert to "hammerofgod\uag$"
```

■ **FIGURE 1.7** Entering a Computer System Name as a SQL Logon

Login name:	HAMMEROFGOD\TMG$
⊙ Windows authentication	

TIP

There are other ways to set permissions, such as making the user a role member that suits your needs as noted in the preceding comments, but I prefer to set just the minimum permissions required. You do not actually have to set update permissions because TMG will only be logging to the table, but you might want to perform some sort of post-log updates to the table as we will be doing later in this example.

Configuring Logging Options

The WebProxyLog table has been created along with the TMG machine's logon and permissions set. Now we simply configure TMG to log to our SQL server, but first make sure that your SQL Server firewall is configured to allow TCP 1433 in. Windows Server 2008 turns the firewall on by default, so you will need to create an exception in your **Domain and Private** profile. If you know that all units connecting will be domain members, you can select **Domain** only. The exception rule on SQL in your Windows Firewall with Advanced Security should look similar to Figure 1.8.

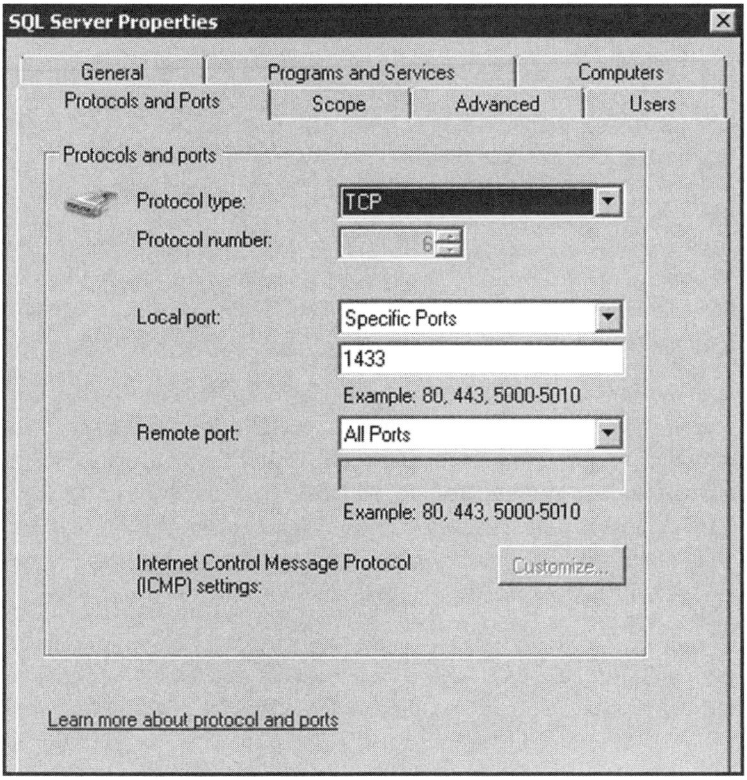

■ **FIGURE 1.8** Creating a Rule for SQL Server in the Windows Firewall

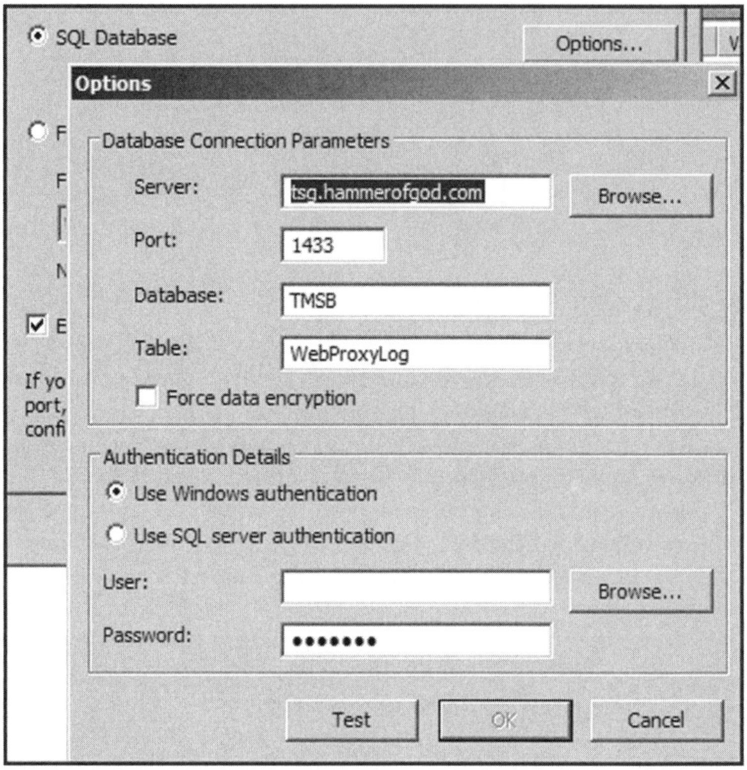

■ **FIGURE 1.9** TMG's SQL Logging Parameters

Now we are ready to configure TMG logging. Under **Logging and Reports**, choose **Configure Web Proxy Logging**. Select the **SQL Database** radial button and **Options**. Your configuration should resemble Figure 1.9.

We will leave **Force data encryption** cleared on purpose, and will discuss why in a moment. If you have not thought of it already, it will come to you after accepting the preceding settings. TMG will need a rule to allow SQL traffic from the local interface to the SQL server itself. Fortunately, the TMG interface is smart enough to know that, and upon selecting SQL logging, it presents you with the dialog box pictured in Figure 1.10.

Notice that you are prompted to create a system policy rule and not just an access rule. This is important—system policy rules remain enforced should the TMG firewall service itself stop. This is a TMG failsafe that does not allow any connections through the firewall other than those in the system policy. If something traffic-based is causing issues, you want to make sure

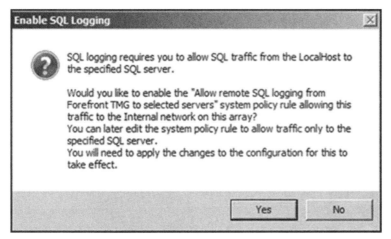

■ **FIGURE 1.10** TMG's Dialog Box Regarding Automatic Rule Creation for SQL Logging

that TMG can continue to log traffic. This is also why you will want remote access and Remote Desktop Protocol (RDP) rules for TMG access to be in your system policy; if the firewall service is shut down, you need to be able to remote in and figure out why.

Testing the Connection

With the system policy rule created, we are ready to test the connection. Note that since we are using Integrated Windows Authorization, we do *not* need to specify a username, and we want this because it is more secure. If you have done everything correctly, you will see a screen similar to Figure 1.11.

Our connection to the database works, and we can start logging web proxy entries to our SQL database. So, let us revisit why we did not select the **Force data encryption** flag.

Securing the SQL Communications Channel

In general, we want to encrypt data in transit whenever possible, particularly if the process does not add too much of an administrative or process overhead. The process of forcing encryption can be relatively straightforward as it relates to SQL connections; however, a few things should be considered, particularly in this environment. We will start with the basic encryption components involved in SQL connections. SQL server protocol encryption is certificate-based. In its simplest form, SQL protocol encryption can be accomplished by configuring the SQL instance to use a certificate and by having the client trust the issuing certificate authority. In other words, the server supporting the secure connection must have an appropriate

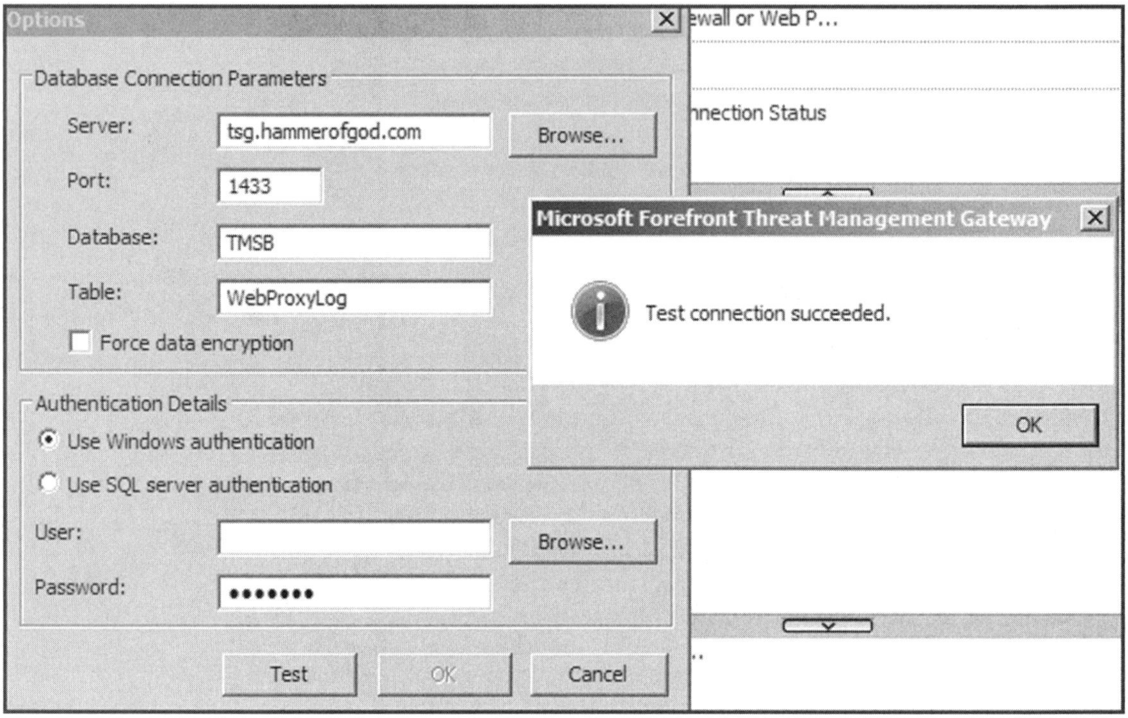

Options [X]

Database Connection Parameters

Server: tsg.hammerofgod.com [Browse...]

Port: 1433

Database: TMSB

Table: WebProxyLog

☐ Force data encryption

Authentication Details

◉ Use Windows authentication

◯ Use SQL server authentication

User: [Browse...]

Password: ••••••••

[Test] [OK] [Cancel]

Microsoft Forefront Threat Management Gateway [X]

ⓘ Test connection succeeded.

[OK]

■ **FIGURE 1.11** A Successful Test of the TMG to SQL Logging Connection

certificate, and the client must trust the authority that issued the certificate. The actual issuance process can be a bit more complicated though.

The general issuance of certificates in our environment is handled by a group policy object (GPO) specifying auto-enroll parameters. As described in the same chapter, we have a Microsoft Enterprise Root Certificate Authority integrated with AD. Our test lab environment does not have subordinate authorities, though based on your needs, you will probably deploy them in your infrastructure. I placed the auto-enroll policy in my default domain policy, as reflected in Figure 1.12, and will proceed under the assumption that you have done the same or have similar solutions in place.

Certificate Enrollment and Configuration

The auto-enroll policy ensures that all users and computers on the domain are issued certificates by our Certificate Authority (CA). This also places the CA signing certificate in the Trusted Enterprise Certificates store, thus automatically setting up and configuring the domain certificate trust chain. With this structure in place, we can immediately begin to deploy certificate-based encryption solutions.

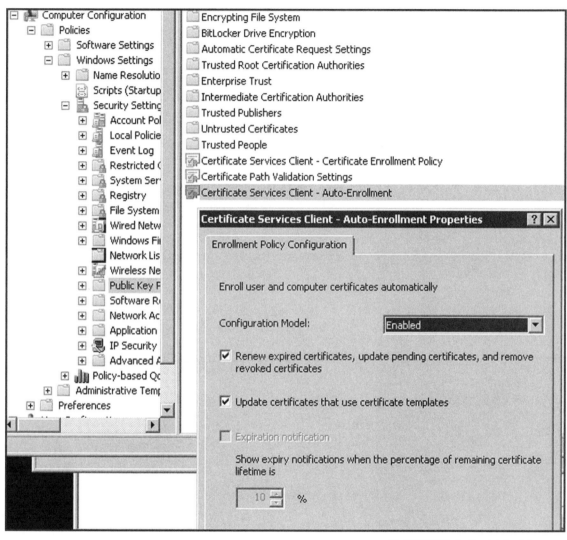

■ **FIGURE 1.12** Enabling Auto-Enroll for Certificates in AD

In regard to TMG, you may have to do a bit of legwork in order to properly install enterprise root certificates, especially if you deployed your certificate enrollment policy after you installed TMG, because automatic certificate enrollment and certificate request operations work via Distributed Component Object Model (DCOM)/Remote Procedure Call (RPC). TMG does not play well with RPC, and has a default behavior of strict RPC compliance in the system policy. Now, assume that you are one of the many people who joined your TMG box to the domain, installed TMG, and then later decided to roll out a certificate enrollment policy. You will, of course, want the TMG box to also be part of the certificate trust infrastructure, but you may find that your certificates did not get installed the way you thought they would. Inevitably, this will be due to RPC being filtered by the firewall, which is a good thing. If your TMG server enrolled certificates prior to your installation or otherwise already has the proper certificates in place, then you may skip the following step.

TMG Specific Enrollment

First, open the **System Policy Editor**, and click **Active Directory**, then clear the **Enforce strict RPC compliance** box as shown in Figure 1.13.

■ **FIGURE 1.13** System Policy for AD Connections and RPC Compliance

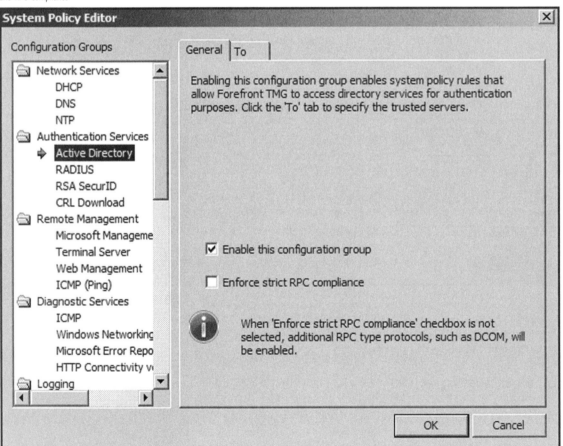

Completing only the preceding step has yielded different results in my tests, and I have never been able to figure out why, so you are not done yet. While writing this and re-creating these steps in my lab, I created and set the group policy for auto-enroll, and only after running the *GPUPDATE* cmd on TMG was I able to receive the Enterprise CA certificate in my Trusted Enterprise Root Certificates store, but I still did not receive my computer certificate in the Personal store. Manual attempts to request the certificate resulted in a failure noting the cause as, "RPC server is unavailable." A temporary allow all rule from the TMG local host to internal (or the AD controllers and CA) was necessary for the entire process to work, but I have honestly had varying results with this while building production TMG systems. The allow all rule is a horrible solution, even if the box is built offline. Note that you must click **Enforce strict RPC compliance** to turn it off of the temporary rule and select **Configure RPC**. You can now clear strict RPC enforcement for the rule. When the new settings have been applied, you should be able to perform a *GPUPDATE* and/or manually request a computer certificate via the Certificates Manager in the Microsoft Management Console (MMC). Once your certificates are in place, be sure to go back and delete or disable your allow all rule. As an alternative to the iffy allow all rule, you can opt for turning off the firewall service during your initial certificate enrollment (this has always worked for me).

NOTE

Anytime I select a onetime use rule or one that is only used intermittently, I name it appropriately. Onetime rules have *DELETE ME* in the name, and temporary but reusable rules typically have something like *(Normally disabled)* in the name so they are easily spotted later if you forget to clean up after yourself.

We have got our certificates in place on TMG, and your SQL box should already have them pushed down from your GPO. If not, go to the Certificates MMC and request a computer certificate or have an otherwise appropriate certificate in place with the right trusts.

We are almost done. We will be logging on to SQL Server soon and will be able to build queries and base automated responses on the logs. There are still a few more steps though, and they are important. Even though our certificates are in place and the trusts are established, we cannot force protocol encryption yet. If we try, we will get the message shown in Figure 1.14.

This is because SQL still does not know how to encrypt the connection. We must assign the certificate previously created to the SQL instance in

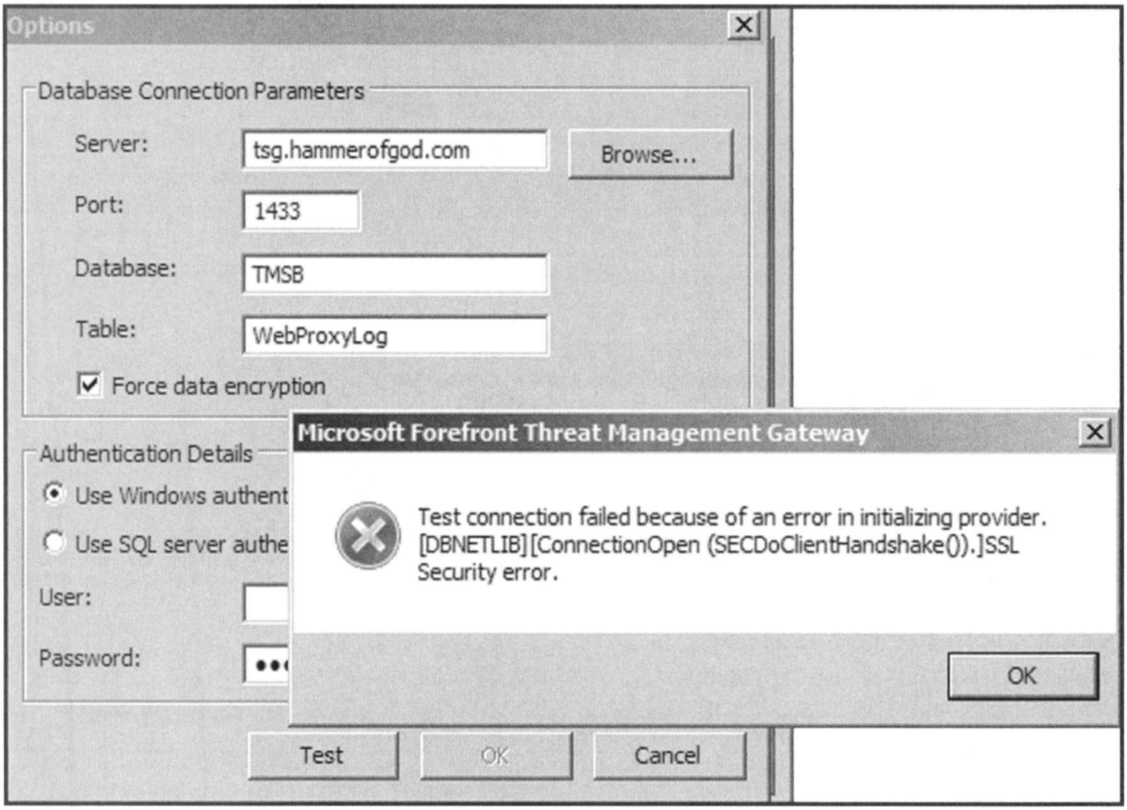

FIGURE 1.14 Forced Data Encryption Fail

the SQL Configuration Manager (SCM). While in SCM, expand **SQL Server Network Configuration** to expose your instances. Right-click the instance (in our case, the default instance of MSSQLSERVER) and expose the properties. Here you will see a **Certificate** tab where you can select a server certificate to use for encryption. If you do not see any certificates here, then you do not have the proper server certificates. Once you apply the certificate, you will get a message telling you that you must restart the SQL Server service in order for changes to be applied, as shown in Figure 1.15.

Troubleshooting

Everything is fine now, right? Unfortunately, it is not. If we try to restart the SQL Server service, we will get the error shown in Figure 1.16 as it starts back up, assuming you have configured it as previously discussed.

No one likes service startup errors, and this type is the worst. It basically says, "Something went wrong, but we have no idea what it is, so here is

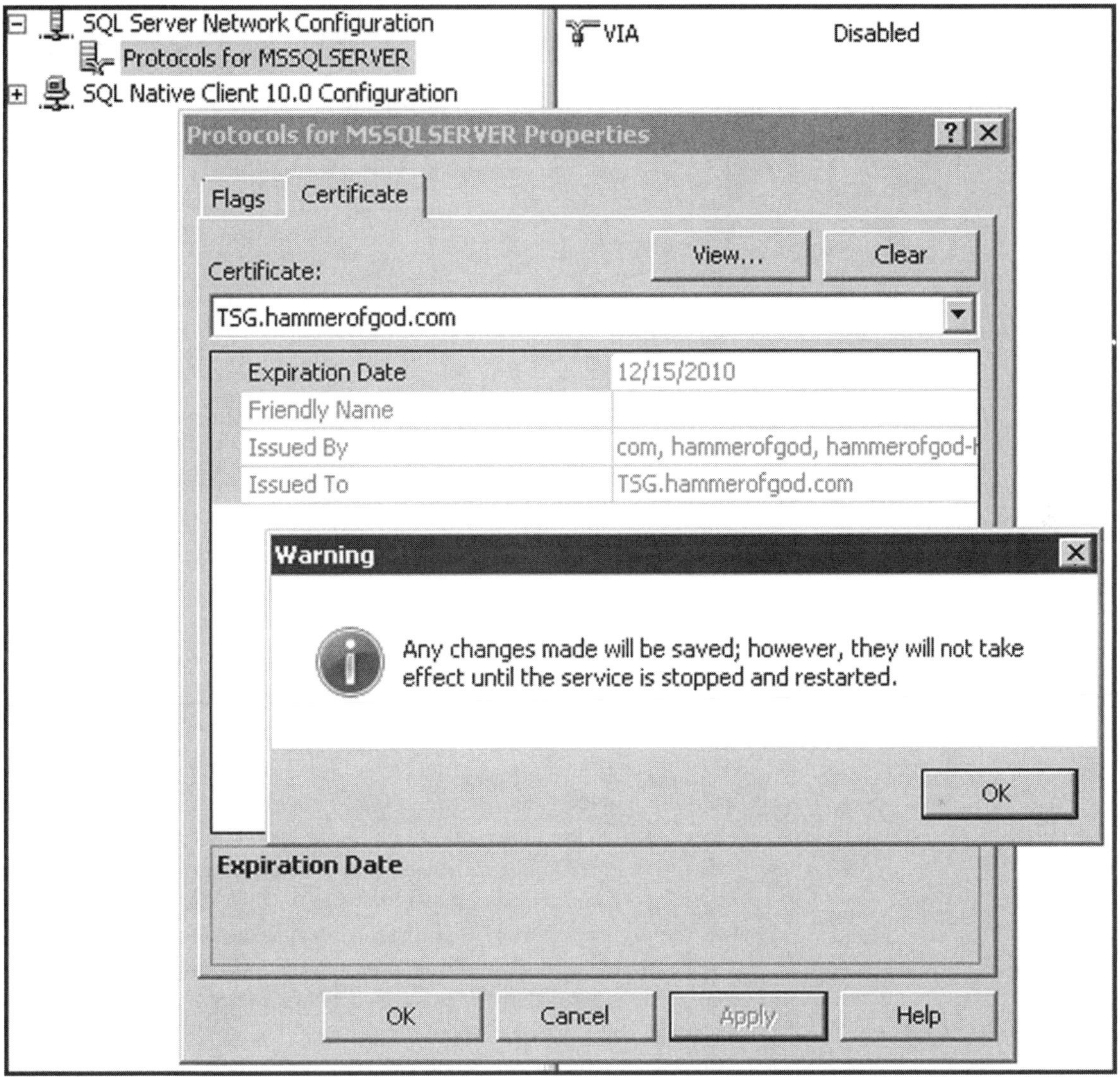

■ **FIGURE 1.15** Assigning SQL Certificate for Protocol Encryption

a random number we generated to make you feel better while you call some-one else who cares." Looking in the System Event Log does not, of course, give you any additional information, it just says the same thing. There is nothing to be found in searches about error code -2146885628 on Bing or Google, so this is a "you're on your own" error. The cause of this error ac-tually makes me chuckle a bit, as I have seen many references in numerous forums about how to configure SQL to use certificates for connection secu-rity, but I have never seen anything about this error. I find it funny that none

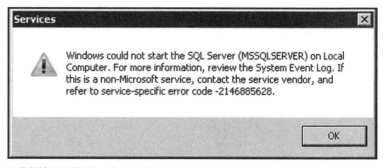

FIGURE 1.16 SQL Server Restart Fail

of the security documents out there seem to address running SQL Server in a more secure environment, because if they did, they would have seen this error. Obviously this has something to do with the assignment of the certificate, since that is all we did.

One thing you *could* do is take the -2146885628 and convert it to hexadecimal code, which yields 0x80092004. This might give you better results in your search, or you can use the Err.exe tool to look it up. This can be found at http://blogs.msdn.com/alexdan/archive/2008/02/28/looking-up-error-codes-with-err-exe.aspx. Thanks to Jim Harrison of Microsoft for pointing me in the direction of that little trick.

If it has not become clear yet, this error is caused by a simple certificate permissions problem. The certificate created is a MACHINE certificate, and in order for us to use the certificate for server encryption, the system service must have access to the certificate's private key. Since we are running the SQL Server service under the HAMMEROFGOD\SQLUser account, and not the local system, the service user cannot read the private key, and it crashes. Better error control should be in place for a service-dependent setting like this, particularly since we are not forcing encryption from the server side, but that is the way it goes. Apparently, in all the examples you see of people using encryption, the SQL Service is running as a local system or as an administrator, which I find unfortunate. The solution to this error is quite easy though. Depending on what version of Windows you are running, you will be able to choose a certificate in your Certificates MMC. Right-click it and then select **Manage Private Keys** to set permissions. The **FindPrivateKey** Software Development Kit (SDK) tool (which replaces **CertKeyFileTool**) should also let you set permissions on the private key of a certificate. Obviously, the **Manage Private Keys** method is much simpler. By default, only SYSTEM and administrators have rights to the private key of the computer certificate, as shown in Figure 1.17.

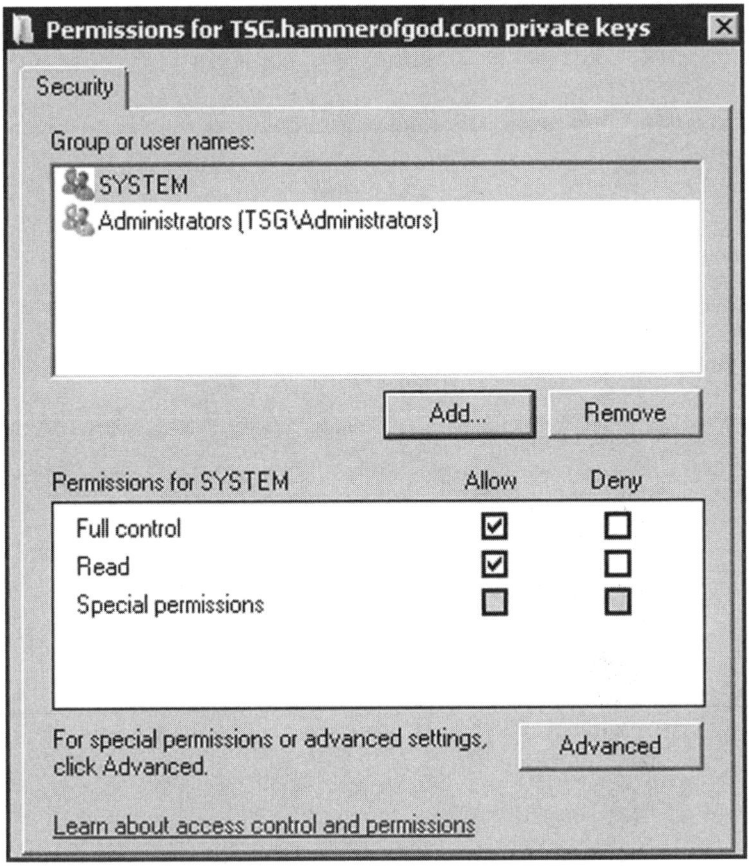

■ FIGURE 1.17 Default Permissions for Private Keys

To finish, we need to set the private key permissions for the HAMMEROFGOD \SQLUser by setting the permissions to **Read**, as shown in Figure 1.18.

Testing and Verification

Now that the SQLUser account has rights to read the private keys of the certificate selected in the protocol setup for the instance SQL Server that it is running under, we can try to start the service again.

And it *will* start right up (see Figure 1.19). So the certificate has been selected, the certificate permissions have been set, and the service has been restarted. Now we shall see how the test responds with the **Force data encryption** option selected this time, as shown in Figure 1.20.

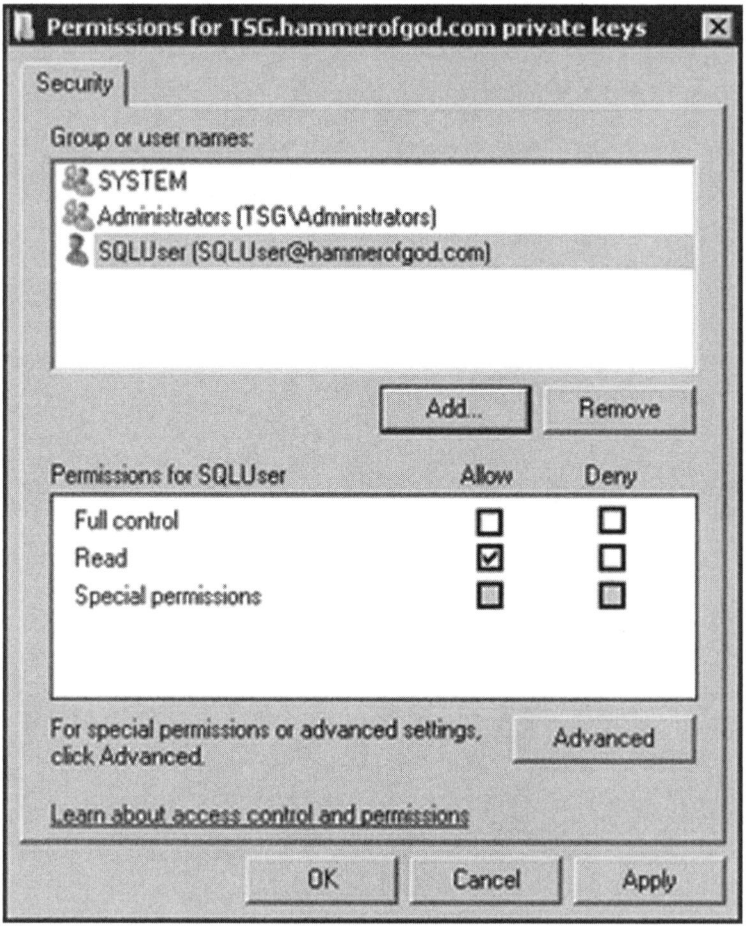

■ **FIGURE 1.18** Setting Read Permissions to the SQL/User on the Private Key

■ **FIGURE 1.19** Successful Startup of the SQL
Server Service

Success, as expected. Now all log data sent via the SQL connection will be encrypted in transit, and the integrity of that data is ensured. We have finally done everything we need to do in order to get TMG securely logging web proxy log data to our SQL server. Now we can carve out the processes involved in getting SQL to analyze log data and respond to particular results.

I like to represent something as workable and usable as possible in these process examples; they should be models that you can actually use with little modification to at least get the process up and running. I would also like to illustrate how we might handle ideas conceptualized after we have the processes in place so as to better represent real-world environments. So let us give a little thought to how we will go about blocking users and the mechanisms we will put in place to perform the processing. The process must function properly, but we also want it to be secure.

Our goal here will be to create a list of blocked sites that we will compare against the log entries to see if people are violating policy by visiting them during work hours. We could certainly enter them as blocked URLs in TMG and even set a schedule for them, but that is not nearly as fun as scaring them with an audio file chastising "DENIED!" and a spinning skull appearing on their screen. Of course, we could do that with TMG as well, but this is about policy enforcement and effective communication. More importantly, it is a mechanism by which we can illustrate the nuts and bolts in more complex solutions. This is, of course, still just an example, so you will have to adapt this to your own usage.

DESIGNING THE WORKFLOW

Now we shall discuss the structure that will allow you to define the criteria that will execute the blocking transaction, the context in which that execution shall occur, and some methods to track the results of the functions we will use. The first decision to make is what data elements to use to base our blocking transaction on. Since we have all the raw data from the logs, we are really only limited to our imagination. This example uses only the web proxy log, but you could use the firewall log as well, and base your decision on any number of elements such as protocol, log time, destination address, websites visited, source/destination network, source application or mime type, and even aggregated data, such as total requests to a host within a certain time frame. For ease of implementation, we shall use the destination web address as previously stated.

The Blacklist Table

The first thing we need is a table containing the URLs of websites we will check against, which is easy enough. We should also have a table that contains the users we want to block and where the records will be inserted from the log. A history would also be useful to track results. Finally, we have to determine exactly *how* to execute the transaction to alter AD group membership.

You could of course post any other data you wish, but remember not to alter the actual WebProxyLog table itself. Doing so will make the bulk insert function fail (unless you alter it, too), so it is best to create your own table for users, tracking, history, and so on, and leave the structure of WebProxyLog alone. That being said, it would be nice to have a mechanism that tracks when a log record has been processed so that we can eliminate it from subsequent processing, and this can be done with a linked table, or in my case, using a data element already in the table to act as a flag field: *ClientAuthenticate*. ClientAuthenticate is not used in my environment, and I have some flexibility to use that field as my flag for processed records because it is a small integer data type. This is important because once we nail someone for visiting a site and thump his

SQL.TMSB - dbo.DeniedHosts	SQLQuery1.sql - ...OFGOD\thor (56))*	
	ID	DestHost
	1	www.myspace.com
	3	www.ihatebacon.com
	5	www.facebook.com/group.php?gid=2233628500
▶*	*NULL*	*NULL*

■ **FIGURE 1.21** A Simple DeniedHosts Table

nose, we do not want that log record to be used to nail him again. The default value for ClientAuthenticate is *0*, so we will just change it once we process the data without having to worry about linking to other tables for record status. We will match on the host names www.myspace.com, www.ihatebacon.com, and a bacon hater page on www.facebook.com, as displayed in Figure 1.21.

For added security, we will not select comparison data, or rather *JOIN* on, from the actual WebProxyLog table. We will instead use a view to limit the data that our procedures will have access to. The following T-SQL code will create our view and assign the *SELECT* permission to the SQL user (which may or may not be necessary based on your overall permissions for the SQL user):

```
CREATE VIEW [dbo].[vDenyLog]
AS
SELECT ClientUserName, DestHost
FROM dbo.WebProxyLog
WHERE (ClientAuthenticate = 0) AND (NOT (ClientUserName =
-- N'anonymous'))
GO
Grant select on dbo.vDenyLog to "hammerofgod\sqluser"
GO
```

The user interface view of the *vDenyLog* will look like the one shown in Figure 1.22.

We have got a nice tight view of the data we want from the logs now. The *INNER JOIN* command will link the URL in the logs to the denied URL list. If there is a match, the records will show up in the record set. If no match exists, no record set is created. So basically, if no users have visited any sites

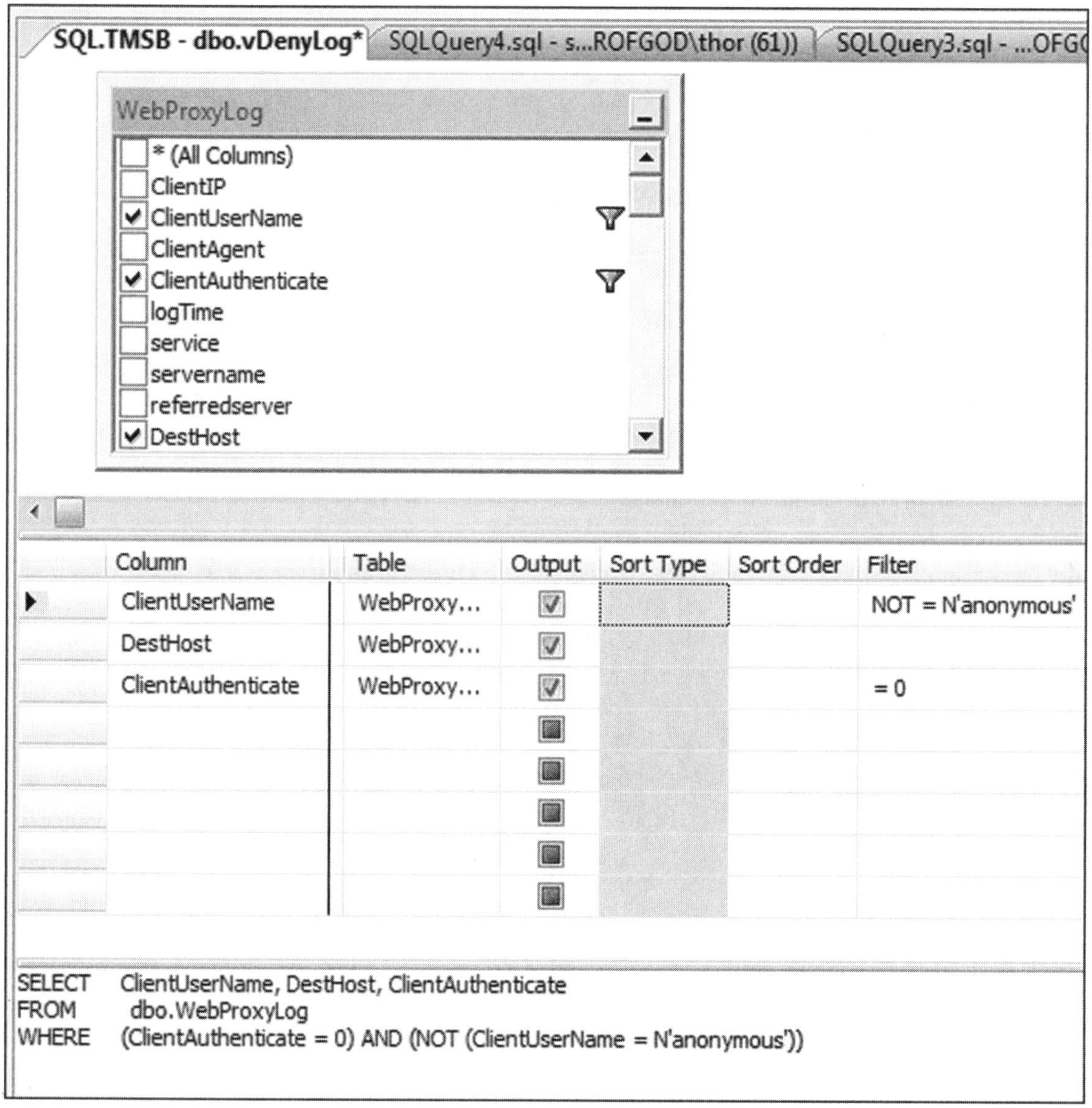

SQL.TMSB - dbo.vDenyLog*	SQLQuery4.sql - s...ROFGOD\thor (61))	SQLQuery3.sql - ...OFGC

WebProxyLog

- [ ] * (All Columns)
- [ ] ClientIP
- [x] ClientUserName
- [ ] ClientAgent
- [x] ClientAuthenticate
- [ ] logTime
- [ ] service
- [ ] servername
- [ ] referredserver
- [x] DestHost

Column	Table	Output	Sort Type	Sort Order	Filter
ClientUserName	WebProxy...	☑			NOT = N'anonymous'
DestHost	WebProxy...	☑			
ClientAuthenticate	WebProxy...	☑			= 0
		☐			
		☐			
		☐			
		☐			
		☐			

```
SELECT   ClientUserName, DestHost, ClientAuthenticate
FROM     dbo.WebProxyLog
WHERE    (ClientAuthenticate = 0) AND (NOT (ClientUserName = N'anonymous'))
```

■ **FIGURE 1.22** SQL Layout for the vDenyLog View

that match the sites currently listed in the DeniedHosts table at the time the query is executed, no records will appear; otherwise, a record for each instance of a log entry in WebProxyLog will be returned.

We do not need all the records that match in this example—just one record will do the job. We just want the name of the person we are going to nail, so our usage requires a distinct list of users to be compiled. We could certainly build the view using *DISTINCT*, but let us just use a stored procedure to do that in case we want more flexibility out of the view:

```
CREATE PROCEDURE [dbo].[sp_GetDistinctDenyUsers]
AS
BEGIN
  SET NOCOUNT ON;
--I'm "cheating" here since I know the DOMAIN\ is 12 char long,
--and I
--don't want to have to parse out the "HAMMEROFGOD\" bits from the
--"HAMMEROFGOD\Username" ClientUserName field. You need to
--either parse
--out the \ or cheat too.
  SELECT DISTINCT RIGHT(ClientUserName,LEN
--(ClientUserName)-12) from vDenyLog
END
```

We now find ourselves at a fork in the logic where we must make a critical decision. I am striving for this book to provide real-world challenges where the process examples represent situations and scenarios that you will face in your own production environment. I find that security guides too often present situations tailored to the disposition of the author and not to those in the field. Hopefully this example will have some applicable meaning to you.

We currently have the log structure set up in a secure environment and the capability of pulling out records and logically determining if the names of users meet specific criteria—in this case, visiting the sites on the black list. Our permissions are in place (the delegated permissions for the SQL user), the data is in place, and we are ready to go. The question here is *how* exactly do we execute the command to add them to the gDeniedLittleBeotch group? What process physically connects to AD and executes the membership addition transaction?

EXECUTION

Outside of access to log data, we want MS SQL to identify a user based on some event in the logs, and to then add the offending user to an AD group. When the user becomes a member of the specific group, then his access to the Internet will be blocked by TMG with an authenticated deny-all rule.

SQL xp_cmdshell

I have already covered the basics of why xp_cmdshell is bad, but I want to properly define the issues. The enabling of xp_cmdshell is a simple SQL Server–based setting: It is either enabled for the server or it is not. You can turn it on or off with *sp_configure*, but it operates at the server level and you cannot select particular databases to enable it for. When you combine this with a high-privileged user (like *LocalSystem*) you have opened up a serious security issue because there are multiple points in SQL in which someone might be able to drop down to the command shell and do whatever they want. The extent of damage is contingent upon user permissions and vector disposition (allowing service account or user access for instance), but we will look at it as an overall, high-impact security hole. The following is an example of using xp_cmdshell.

```
ALTER PROCEDURE [dbo].[sp_DenyUsers]
@UName nvarchar(50) = 0,
@Action nvarchar(10)
AS
BEGIN
Declare @SQL nvarchar(255)
if @Action = '' select @action = 'add'
Select @SQL = 'net group gDeniedLittleBeotch ' + @UName + ' /'
--+@action+ ' /domain '
        SET NOCOUNT ON;
 select @SQL
 Exec xp_cmdshell @SQL
END
```

We pass through the user we want to add and the type of action we want: add or remove. This will be the overall trigger for this procedure, and we will just pass along the input variables upon execution. All of our examples will use this logic. Once we get the permissions set up properly (covered later in this chapter), this approach will work just fine. It is labeled bad because it presents a very high level of risk to enable.

SQL CmdExec

A more secure way of executing OS commands is by using *CmdExec* inside a SQL job. CmdExec is similar to xp_cmdshell in its ability to execute OS commands, but it references one particular command to run specifically rather than an unrestricted overall shell as xp_cmdshell provides. This is a better approach, but it still creates issues since the target executable (an actual EXE or *batch/cmd* file) can be tampered with to allow an attacker to replace that target executable with one of their own. A batch file would work, but we would be limited to what OS commands can do. As in the previous code snippet, *net group* would also do the job, but batch files are trivial to change to do whatever you want them to. When some type of shell access is required, I like to limit exposure as much as possible by writing my own EXE to do exactly what I want rather than executing multiple batch commands. The benefit of developing your own code is that you are completely flexible in your approach. The downside (to some) is that you have to code up your application. Here is an example of code that accomplishes what we want by accepting input variables of username and action type and handling the rest.

```csharp
// Timothy Thor Mullen
// Add Users to Deny Group C#
// Thor's Microsoft Security Bible

using System;
using System.Collections.Generic;
using System.Linq;
using System.Text;
using System.DirectoryServices;
using System.Data.SqlClient;

namespace AddUsersToGroup
{
  class MainClass
  {
  static void Main(string[] args)
  {
// Set dummy user and action for execution with no arguments
when run from console for testing
// We'll use the same program to add and remove users, so let's
set defaults for testing here.

  Console.WriteLine("AddUsertoDeniedGroup v1.1");
  Console.WriteLine("Thor's Microsoft Security Bible");
  Console.WriteLine("Usage:");
  Console.WriteLine("AddUsers-C Username Operation");
  Console.WriteLine("Operation is:");
  Console.WriteLine("'add' to check for existing records,");
  Console.WriteLine("'remove' to remove a user, and");
  Console.WriteLine("'forceadd' to add a user regardless of
--disposition.");
  Console.WriteLine("");
  Console.WriteLine("No flags runs default test user of
--'JoeMamma' 'Remove'");
  Console.WriteLine("and should return error of 'There is no
--such object on the server.'");
```

```
string strUser = "JoeMamma";
string strOperation = "Remove";

strUser = "Thor";
strOperation = "Add";

if (args.Length != 0)
{
strUser = Convert.ToString(args[0]);
strOperation = Convert.ToString(args[1]);
}
```

// Keep the strUser string a separate variable than the "CN="
string.

```
    string CNstrUser = ("CN=" + strUser);
```

// Build data connection to SQL Server and retrieve a distinct
list of users from the vDenyLog view.

// When possible, I like to combine functions into single
instances of code so that I don't have to repeat myself.

// The main purpose of the code is to loop through the database
results for people we want to add to the group.

And we might as well use the same code to remove them from the
group if we want. Since removal means

  a recordset won't be returned, we'll leave the code unmodi-
fied and force a record return with

//a simple select statement. So just check the strOperation and
set the commandtext accordingly.

//I'd also like to be able to forceadd a user from a commandline
in the absence of records just in case

//I feel like screwing with someone, so I'll accept the super-
secret "forceadd" flag too.

```
  using (SqlConnection connectionDenyUsers = new
--SqlConnection("Data Source=sql.hammerofgod.com;Initial
--Catalog=TMSB;Integrated Security=True"))
  {
  connectionDenyUsers.Open();


  using (SqlCommand commandDenyUsers = new SqlCommand
--("sp_GetDistinctDenyUsers", connectionDenyUsers))
  {
  if (strOperation.ToLower() == "remove") commandDenyUsers.
--CommandText = "select '" + strUser + "'";

  if (strOperation.ToLower() == "forceadd")
  {
```

```
commandDenyUsers.CommandText = "select '" + strUser + "'";
strOperation = "add";
}

SqlDataReader readerDenyUsers = commandDenyUsers.
--ExecuteReader();

try
{
// Build AD connection, create the user object find it in AD,
and create the group object for the

/gDeniedLittleBeotch directory, and iterate through the
group object to check for membership

DirectoryEntry ad = new DirectoryEntry("LDAP://OU=HOG-
--Users,DC=hammerofgod,DC=com");
DirectoryEntry denyGroup = new DirectoryEntry("LDAP://
--CN=gDeniedLittleBeotch,OU=aSpecial Use,DC=hammerofgod,
--DC=com");

//Let's grab the reader object and loop through all the users
we're going to nail

while (readerDenyUsers.Read())
{

CNstrUser = ("CN=" + Convert.ToString(readerDenyUsers[0]));
strUser = Convert.ToString(readerDenyUsers[0]);
DirectoryEntry denyUser = ad.Children.Find(CNstrUser,
--"user");
ad.Dispose();
bool isMember = false;

// This method uses the properties to retrieve the entire user
distinguished name and convert it to
// common name.
foreach (object member in denyGroup.Properties["member"])
{
string memberDN = Convert.ToString(member);
string memberCN = memberDN.Substring(0, CNstrUser.Length);
if (CNstrUser.ToLower()==memberCN.ToLower()) isMember=true;
}
// Make sure the user you test with has permissions to alter
the group membership.
// The SQL box will ultimately do this for us.
try
```

```
{
if (isMember == true && strOperation.ToLower() == "remove")
denyGroup.Invoke(strOperation, new Object[] { denyUser.
--Path.ToString() });
else if (isMember == false && strOperation.ToLower() ==
--"add")
denyGroup.Invoke(strOperation, new Object[] { denyUser.
--Path.ToString() });
}
catch (DirectoryServicesCOMException cex)
{
Console.WriteLine(cex.Message);
}

// only clear the flag if the user was added to the group;
removals should leave the log as it was.
// If for some reason, you want to clear the log once you remove
them (logically, nothing else should be in there,
// but you never know) to start "fresh" remove the add condition.

if (strOperation.ToLower() == "add")
{
commandDenyUsers.CommandText = ("sp_ClearDenyUserLogFlag
--'" + strUser + "'");
readerDenyUsers.Dispose();
readerDenyUsers = commandDenyUsers.ExecuteReader();
}
denyUser.Dispose();
}
readerDenyUsers.Dispose();
connectionDenyUsers.Dispose();
ad.Dispose();
denyGroup.Dispose();

}
catch (DirectoryServicesCOMException cex)
{
Console.WriteLine(cex.Message);
}

}
}
}
}
}
```

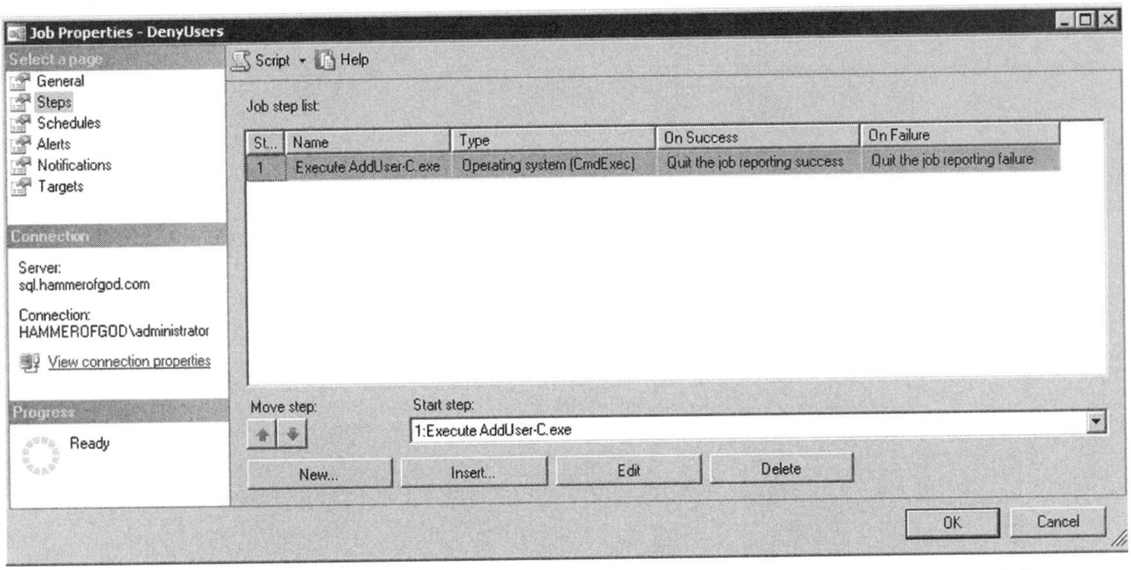

■ **FIGURE 1.23** CmdExec in Job Properties

This is simple enough code, and it does just what it is supposed to do. We basically connect to AD, create a user and group objects, populate them, and use *invoke* to add or delete a user from the deny group. This can then be compiled to an EXE and used as part of a scheduled job that executes the application, passing the proper variables to effect the user's group membership. This presumes some sort of *SELECT* statement to get the names you want to delete from the logs, as shown in Figure 1.23.

Now all you have to do is schedule the job for an appropriate time interval, and that part is done.

SQL CLR

SQL CLR is a powerful tool when it comes to creating your own procedures and functions available within SQL, where T-SQL does not give you the flexibility, scalability, or standards compliance you need. Organizations with a strict Software Development Lifecycle (SDL) policy often require that xp_cmdshell be disabled completely, and that the use of CmdExec be limited and thoroughly reviewed since both represent execution branches to a process where SQL does not have control. CLR allows you to write your own functions in Visual Studio and deploy them to SQL where they are registered as assemblies and made available as functions you can call directly from a stored procedure. I have found CLR to be an excellent alternative to control branching where it is appropriate. In the context of this project, choosing CLR as a solution also serves as an excellent example because it will require that we examine the pros and cons about which direction we will go on a final decision. It allows us to practice what real security is—risk management.

Visual Studio C# SQL CLR projects using any of the supported .NET libraries are easy to code. You create your functions, test, and deploy the CLR to SQL. In fact, this is exactly what we will do in order to convert the *uniqueID* IP values to integers when we get to Chapter 3, which is about geolocation. With our project here, it will not be quite that easy. I purposefully chose this particular project example for CLR because it requires directory services. This is not a problem in itself, but it will require some trade-offs in design. Only certain assemblies have been approved for use with SQL Server CLR. *System.DirectoryServices* is not one of them. You can browse through the default SQL components available for reference by following the **Add References** dialogs. If the assembly you want is not there, then you will have to manually reference the library with *USING*, as illustrated in the following code. Only then will the code build, but we are not ready to deploy the CLR project yet. First, we will take a look at what the previous *AddUsers-C* code looks like within the structure of a SQL CLR project:

```
// Timothy Thor Mullen
// Add Users to Deny Group C# SQL CLR Procedure
// Thor's Microsoft Security Bible
//
using System;
using System.Collections.Generic;
using System.Data;
using System.Data.SqlClient;
using System.Data.SqlTypes;
using Microsoft.SqlServer.Server;
using System.Linq;
using System.Text;
using System.DirectoryServices;

public partial class UserDefinedFunctions
{
  [Microsoft.SqlServer.Server.SqlFunction]
  public static SqlString AddDenyUsers(SqlString SQLstrUser,
  --SqlString SQLstrOperation)
  {
  //set dummy user and action for execution with no args

  string strUser = Convert.ToString(SQLstrUser);
  string strOperation = Convert.ToString(SQLstrOperation);
```

```
// Keep the strUser string a separate variable than the
CN= string.
string CNstrUser = ("CN=" + strUser);
try
{
// build ad connection, create the user object and find it in
ad, create the group object for dir
// gDeniedLittleBeotch, and iterate through the group object
to check for membership

        DirectoryEntry ad = new DirectoryEntry("LDAP://
        --OU=HOG-Users,DC=hammerofgod,DC=com");
        DirectoryEntry denyUser = ad.Children.Find
        --(CNstrUser, "user");
        DirectoryEntry denyGroup = new DirectoryEntry
        --("LDAP://CN=gDeniedLittleBeotch,OU=aSpecialUse,
        --DC=hammerofgod,DC=com");
bool isMember = false;

// this method uses the Properties property to retrieve the
entire user DN and convert to CN
foreach (object member in denyGroup.Properties["member"])
{
string memberDN = Convert.ToString(member);
string memberCN = memberDN.Substring(0, CNstrUser.
--Length);
if (CNstrUser.ToLower() == memberCN.ToLower()) isMember =
--true;
}

try
{
if (isMember == true && strOperation.ToLower() ==
--"remove")
denyGroup.Invoke(strOperation, new Object[] { denyUser.
--Path.ToString() });
else if (isMember == false && strOperation.ToLower() ==
--"add")
denyGroup.Invoke(strOperation, new Object[] { denyUser.
--Path.ToString() });
}
catch (DirectoryServicesCOMException cex)
{
Console.WriteLine(cex.Message);
}
```

```
denyGroup.Close();
denyUser.Close();
ad.Close();
}
catch (DirectoryServicesCOMException cex)
{
Console.WriteLine(cex.Message);
}

return new SqlString("ret");
}
};
```

While this code will compile and run, you will not be able to deploy it to your SQL box since there is no corresponding DirectoryServices assembly registered (by default). We will have to add the DirectoryServices assembly (a DLL file) manually. Attempting to deploy the previous code without the manual registration will produce an error similar to this:

```
Deploy error SQL01268: .Net SqlClient Data Provider: Msg 6503,
Level 16, State 12, Line 1 Assembly 'system.directoryservices,
version=2.0.0.0, culture=neutral, publickeytoken=b03f5f7f11
d50a3a.' was not found in the SQL catalog.

ALTER DATABASE TMSB SET TRUSTWORTHY ON
```

This will simply indicate that the content of the database you are using (in this case *TMSB*) should be trusted by SQL. This posture is easily maintained by controlling access to the database as you would normally do, so I consider the risk of trusting the database in this scenario low.

We can now add the DirectoryServices assembly using:

```
CREATE ASSEMBLY DirectoryServices from
'C:\Windows\Microsoft.NET\Framework64\v2.0.50727\System.
DirectoryServices.dll' with PERMISSION_SET = UNSAFE
```

The main thing to understand here is that DirectoryServices is not cleared or supported by SQL at this point in Visual Studio 2010. As such, you will see the following warning generated:

```
Warning: The Microsoft .NET Framework assembly 'system.
directoryservices, version=2.0.0.0, culture=neutral,
publickeytoken=b03f5f7f11d50a3a, processorarchitecture=
msil.' you are registering is not fully tested in the SQL Server
hosted environment and is not supported. In the future, if you
```

upgrade or service this assembly or the .NET Framework, your
CLR integration routine may stop working. Please refer to SQL
Server Books Online for more details.

This means that you need to ensure you properly test and perform code
analysis on your production code to minimize the creation of resource
allocation issues. In my example, I had to set the DirectoryServices permissions to UNSAFE. The UNSAFE permissions set represents the least
restricted access model for SQL assemblies, and is less secure. A CLR
assembly can have a safety assignment (by user) of SAFE, EXTERNAL,
or UNSAFE. Safe assemblies can only access localized SQL functions
and objects. External assemblies can access other objects beyond the
SQL instance, such as other local system and network resources. This
is why external assemblies must be digitally signed in order to function.
Assemblies marked as unsafe are unrestricted, meaning they can do
whatever they want, and can even call unmanaged code. Unsafe assemblies can be very dangerous from a security perspective, and should
only be used when you can trust the code, which we can do with the
DirectoryServices library.

In order for EXTERNAL or UNSAFE assemblies to be processed, they
must have a digital key created and then be signed by that key during the
build process. This is no problem if you are the one who owns the code.
If you do not own the code, then you can also process EXTERNAL
and UNSAFE assemblies if the database instance itself is modified
from its default untrustworthy status using *ALTER DATABASE SET
TRUSTWORTHY ON.*

If the nature of the code you are running creates risk in regard to the
database being trustworthy or the DirectoryServices DLL file being registered as UNSAFE (along with our AddDenyUser function), then you
will have to weigh the risks of this environment versus the risks of
leveraging CmdExec. I am curious as to what decision you will make
and why. We can now deploy the assembly and will receive something
similar to:

```
------ Build started: Project: AddUsersC-CRL, Configuration:
Release Any CPU ------
  AddUsersC-CRL -> U:\Users\Finkelstein.the.Gunman\
Documents\Visual Studio 2010\Projects\Archive\AddUsers-C-
CLR\SQLJihad\bin\Release\AddUsersCCLR.dll
------ Deploy started: Project: AddUsersC-CRL, Configuration:
Release Any CPU ------
Build started 1/16/2011 8:54:22 PM.
```

```
SqlClrDeploy:
  Beginning deployment of assembly AddUsersCCLR.dll to server
sql.hammerofgod.com : TMSB
  The following error might appear if you deploy a SQL CLR
project that was built for a version of the .NET Framework that
is incompatible with the target instance of SQL Server: "Deploy
error SQL01268: CREATE ASSEMBLY for assembly failed because
assembly failed verification". To resolve this issue, open the
properties for the project, and change the .NET Framework
version.
  Deployment script generated to:
  U:\Users\Finkelstein.the.Gunman\Documents\Visual Studio
2010\Projects\Archive\AddUsers-C-CLR\SQLJihad\bin\
Release\AddUsersCCLR.sql

  Creating [AddUsersCCLR]...
  Creating [dbo].[AddDenyUsers]...
  The transacted portion of the database update succeeded.
  Deployment completed

Build succeeded.

Time Elapsed 00:00:12.26
========== Build: 1 succeeded or up-to-date, 0 failed,
0 skipped ==========
========== Deploy: 1 succeeded, 0 failed, 0 skipped ==========
```

We are now ready to call AddDenyUsers (*user*, *add*) in our stored procedure to manage the group management process without branching to any command interpreters. This illustrates a far greater level of security than any of the previous examples of how a typical solution may be implemented.

Alternatives

Though not mentioned yet, SQL would employ a SQL Agent Job to check the logs and execute the group modification transaction. I think it should run every couple of minutes for the previous CLR function. We will keep that structure in place, and simply move the function to an external application rather than within SQL itself. The CmdExec command allows us to execute external commands in singularity during a job run. This differs from xp_cmdshell in that SQL specifically executes one command directly, and does not invoke an overall command shell and then pass parameters in through it. CmdExec does not require xp_cmdshell, though it does require system administrator permissions to run. While we could indeed use CmdExec to execute a batch file that runs net group commands as we discussed earlier, I feel uneasy about that since the batch file itself could be modified to do whatever someone wanted it to do, and I do not know how easy it would be to alter. Instead, we will be executing a procedure that calls our AddDenyUser function as part of its operation. Now, if you chose to use CmdExe instead, you will want to think about the fact that all an attacker would have to do is replace the EXE file with something nasty, and you will be compromised. We will indeed address that with AppLocker, the successor to Software Restriction Policies that is now available in Windows 7 and Server 2008 R2, later in this chapter.

So what we have done is build a data reader for the results of the *sp_GetDistinctDenyUsers* procedure, created our AD object, looped through the data results, grabbed the username we are going to nail, looked it up in the group to see if it exists, and if so, executed the **Invoke** AD method to add the user to the gDeniedLittleBeotch group. Once they are added to the group, TMG will immediately begin applying the deny rule to them. Also note the execution of the *sp_ClearDenyUserLogFlag* procedure. This procedure sets the ClientAuthenticate small integer to *1*, with the logic being that if we are going to deny the user, it does not really matter what site(s) matched up, just that sites *did* create a record.

At the time of this writing, SQL 2008 on Server 2008 R2 installed version 3.5 of the .NET framework by default. Make sure when you compile your executable that you have selected the proper .NET version before building your EXE file, otherwise it will not run properly, if at all, when you copy it over to the SQL box.

With this code compiled, we now have to build the job to execute the program and we will be good to go.

The following code will create our job owned by administrator, but that runs within the context of the SQLUser account. More specifically, it is set to run in the context of the SQL Server Agent Service, which is running as SQLUser.

```
USE [msdb]
GO
/****** Object: Job [DenyUsers] Script Date: 12/12/2112
12:12:12 ******/
BEGIN TRANSACTION
DECLARE @ReturnCode INT
SELECT @ReturnCode = 0
/****** Object: JobCategory [[Uncategorized (Local)]]]
Script Date: 12/12/2112 12:12:12 ******/
IF NOT EXISTS (SELECT name FROM msdb.dbo.syscategories WHERE
name=N'[Uncategorized (Local)]' AND category_class=1)
BEGIN
```

```
EXEC @ReturnCode = msdb.dbo.sp_add_category @class=N'JOB',
@type=N'LOCAL', @name=N'[Uncategorized (Local)]'
IF (@@ERROR <> 0 OR @ReturnCode <> 0) GOTO QuitWithRollback
END
DECLARE @jobId BINARY(16)
EXEC @ReturnCode = msdb.dbo.sp_add_job @job_name=N'
DenyUsers',
                @enabled=1,
                @notify_level_eventlog=0,
                @notify_level_email=0,
                @notify_level_netsend=0,
                @notify_level_page=0,
                @delete_level=0,
                @description=N'Check ISA/TMG logs for records
where users have violated policy and add them to the gDenie
dLittleBeotch group for denied access to the Internet.',
                @category_name=N'[Uncategorized (Local)]',
                @owner_login_name=N'HAMMEROFGOD\administrator',
@job_id = @jobId OUTPUT
IF (@@ERROR <> 0 OR @ReturnCode <> 0) GOTO QuitWithRollback
/****** Object: Step [Execute AddUser-C.exe] Script Date:
12/12/2112 12:12:12 ******/
EXEC @ReturnCode = msdb.dbo.sp_add_jobstep @job_id=@jobId,
@step_name=N'Execute AddUser-C.exe',
                @step_id=1,
                @cmdexec_success_code=0,
                @on_success_action=1,
                @on_success_step_id=0,
                @on_fail_action=2,
                @on_fail_step_id=0,
                @retry_attempts=0,
                @retry_interval=0,
                @os_run_priority=0, @subsystem=N'CmdExec',
                @command=N'c:\clr\AddUsers-C.exe',
                @flags=0
IF (@@ERROR <> 0 OR @ReturnCode <> 0) GOTO QuitWithRollback
EXEC @ReturnCode = msdb.dbo.sp_update_job @job_id = @jobId,
@start_step_id = 1
IF (@@ERROR <> 0 OR @ReturnCode <> 0) GOTO QuitWithRollback
EXEC @ReturnCode = msdb.dbo.sp_add_jobschedule @job_id=
@jobId, @name=N'Run every couple of minutes',
                @enabled=1,
                @freq_type=4,
```

```
          @freq_interval=1,
          @freq_subday_type=4,
          @freq_subday_interval=2,
          @freq_relative_interval=0,
          @freq_recurrence_factor=0,
          @active_start_date=20100207,
          @active_end_date=99991231,
          @active_start_time=0,
          @active_end_time=235959,
          @schedule_uid=N'5178b009-6b48-46e6-93bf-
f812a9620c6e'
IF (@@ERROR <> 0 OR @ReturnCode <> 0) GOTO QuitWithRollback
EXEC @ReturnCode = msdb.dbo.sp_add_jobserver @job_id =
@jobId, @server_name = N'(local)'
IF (@@ERROR <> 0 OR @ReturnCode <> 0) GOTO QuitWithRollback
COMMIT TRANSACTION
GOTO EndSave
QuitWithRollback:
 IF (@@TRANCOUNT > 0) ROLLBACK TRANSACTION
EndSave:

GO
```

Now this job will run every two minutes and check against our database log for violations and automatically deny bad users outbound access, which is quite cool. You can of course set it to run in whatever interval meets your expectation of near-real-time. To look at the deny rule itself, see Figure 1.24.

While the default action is simply to deny the request with a standard TMG error, as mentioned, I have chosen to redirect to a custom HTML file that results in the page in Figure 1.25 being displayed, with an intentionally loud sound clip from Quake Arena that says "DENIED!" I have watched it scare the ever-loving crap out of people, and it is totally worth setting people up to see the result.

You can alter the process to meet whatever criteria you wish, but you get the point.

Leveraging AppLocker

We are almost there! We could leave things as they are, but this is a perfect opportunity to use AppLocker to shore up the security around our custom EXE file if we took that route instead of SQL CLR. We will simply go to **Local Security Policy, Application Control, Policies, AppLocker**

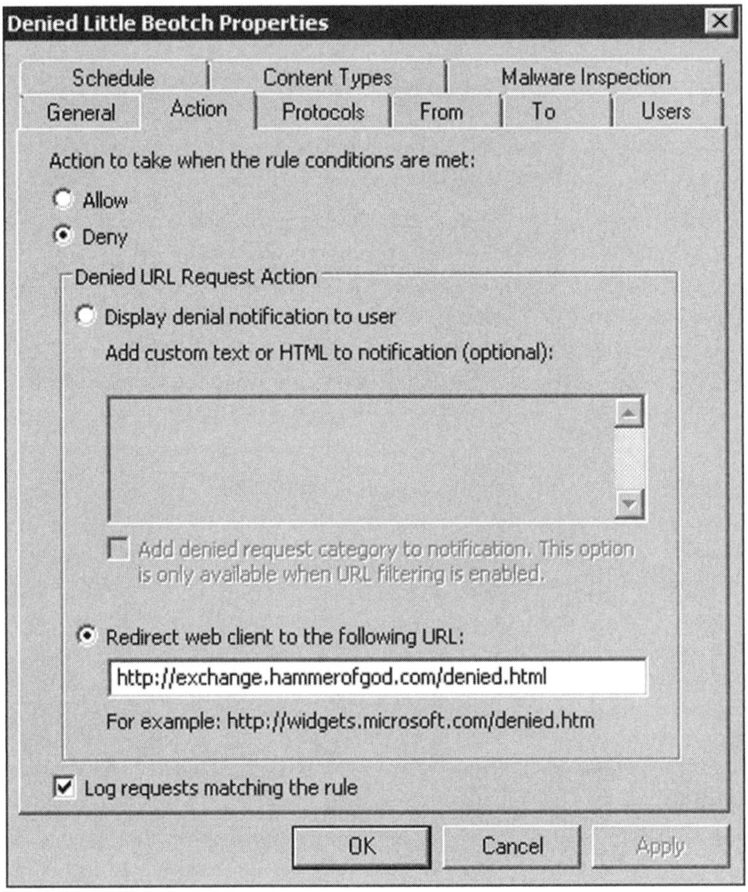

■ FIGURE 1.24 Properties of the Deny Rule

and create the allow policy for AddUsers-C.exe via file hash. This process is covered in depth in the chapter, "Client Security," including the use of digital certificates to sign code for validation. Figure 1.26 shows what the policy will look like.

We always want to test to make sure our policies work, so copy calc.exe over to our c:\clr directory on the SQL box. I know it is not really CLR, but the directory was already there! We will execute AddUsers-C.exe, which we know will try to remove JoeMamma if no parameters are given, and JoeMamma does not exist, resulting in a message saying, "There is no such object on the server." We will copy calc.exe over it, replacing our AddUsers-C code. Figure 1.27 displays what happens when we try to execute it.

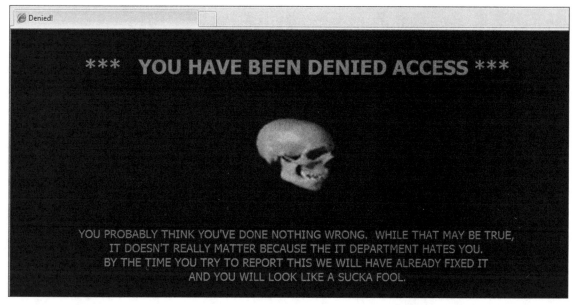

	Action	User	Name	Condition
Security Settings	Allow	Everyone	(Default Rule) All files located in the Progr...	Path
⊞ Account Policies	Allow	Everyone	(Default Rule) All files located in the Windo...	Path
⊞ Local Policies	Allow	BUILTIN\Administrators	(Default Rule) All files	Path
⊞ Windows Firewall with Advanced Security	Allow	Everyone	AddUsers-C.exe	File Hash
Network List Manager Policies				
⊞ Public Key Policies				
⊞ Software Restriction Policies				
⊟ Application Control Policies				
⊟ AppLocker				
Executable Rules				

■ **FIGURE 1.26** Showing the Executable Rules for the EXE File

As you can see, even as administrator, the AddUsers-C.exe runs fine as long as the hash matches the one created in the policy. Once we copy calc.exe over it (replacing it), it just returns without executing (same as calc.exe does). Personally, I like the silent exit back to prompt without the tell-tale error message, "The hash of this file does not match that in AppLocker Policy," but I can see how no error message might make it harder to troubleshoot. Just know that when your AppLocker hash does not match, the executable will not run. Copying back our original code puts it right back in working order. This prevents anyone from inserting Trojans in our code. Woot!

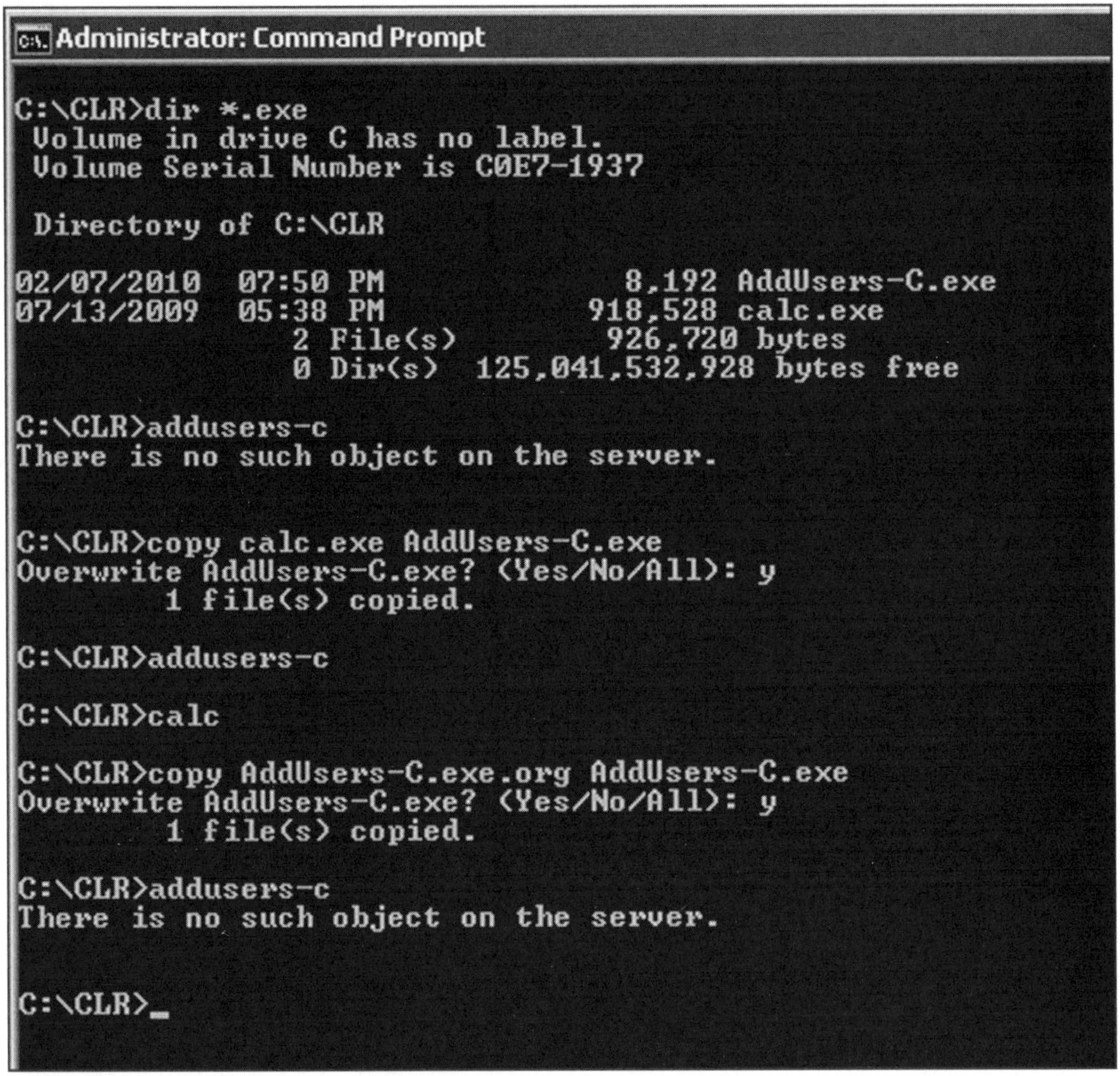

```
C:\. Administrator: Command Prompt

C:\CLR>dir *.exe
 Volume in drive C has no label.
 Volume Serial Number is C0E7-1937

 Directory of C:\CLR

02/07/2010  07:50 PM              8,192 AddUsers-C.exe
07/13/2009  05:38 PM            918,528 calc.exe
               2 File(s)         926,720 bytes
               0 Dir(s)  125,041,532,928 bytes free

C:\CLR>addusers-c
There is no such object on the server.


C:\CLR>copy calc.exe AddUsers-C.exe
Overwrite AddUsers-C.exe? (Yes/No/All): y
        1 file(s) copied.

C:\CLR>addusers-c

C:\CLR>calc

C:\CLR>copy AddUsers-C.exe.org AddUsers-C.exe
Overwrite AddUsers-C.exe? (Yes/No/All): y
        1 file(s) copied.

C:\CLR>addusers-c
There is no such object on the server.


C:\CLR>_
```

■ **FIGURE 1.27** Executing the Replaced
AddUsers-C Code

■ **SUMMARY**

We have got a very secure overall solution in place here. The SQL service is running as a very low privileged user, a certificate is used by the ISA Server to encrypt data logged from the firewall to the SQL box, the SQL account is limited to group management only via delegated permissions, and a job calling a specific executable is utilized, using the CmdExec directive to execute code that is validated by its hash. Nice and tight.

Chapter 2

Internet Information Server (IIS) Authentication and Authorization Models, and Locking Down File Access with EFS and WebDAV

INFORMATION IN THIS CHAPTER:

- RSA and AES
- Building the Web Application Structure
- Security in Depth
- Securing Access with WebDAV
- Conclusion

PRODUCTS, TOOLS, AND METHODS:

- Internet Information Server (IIS)
- WebDAV
- New Technology File System (NTFS)
- Encrypting File System (EFS)
- Custom Application Pools

INTRODUCTION

Microsoft's Encrypting File System technology is one of the strongest yet most underutilized security features that I have seen in my many years of working with Microsoft infrastructures and enterprise deployments. I have very rarely seen it used in enterprise or even medium-sized environments, and when I have, it has been in isolated instances where individuals or teams took it upon themselves to implement EFS-based security controls. This is not entirely without justification. EFS is easy for individuals to set up and use autonomously, but the proper deployment of EFS in large environments requires careful planning around certificate and recovery agent management, backup and restoration, and access model implementation. The consequences of improperly rolling out EFS can be serious: You can lose access to your data. To be more specific, inadequately designed EFS controls can result in files being encrypted on the file system that, based on a failure scenario, can prevent the decryption of files even though you may have physical access to them.

EFS, in its simplest form, is a Windows OS–based feature that allows a user (administrator or otherwise) to set a folder, or an individual file, to have its contents encrypted. Encrypting at the folder level is the typical method of using EFS as it guarantees that any file added to the encrypted folder is automatically encrypted. While you can certainly select an individual file and encrypt it, the examples used in this chapter will be based on folders that are created in a directory structure, and the folder itself marked for encryption. As mentioned, when a folder is set to be encrypted, all files created within that folder will be encrypted by their respective owners. Setting a folder to be encrypted is quite simple; you just pull up the **Advanced Attributes** of a folder and select **Encrypt contents to secure data**, as shown in Figure 2.1.

EFS is a user-based encryption control. Basically, the way it works is that when a user requests that a file or folder be encrypted, an EFS certificate is generated for the user and its private key is stored in the user's profile. The public key is stored with the files created by that user, and only that user can decrypt the file. Because of this, a recovery agent certificate is typically associated with a different user account, and that user's public key is also embedded in the file. This way, if the user loses the certificate used to encrypt the file, the recovery agent user, or more specifically the holder of the associate private key, can also decrypt the file. In the same way that the recovery agent public key is automatically stored with the encrypted file, you can also assign other users' public keys to a file, allowing them to decrypt it as well. This allows one file to be shared among multiple users while remaining encrypted on the file system. When an EFS certificate is either distributed by your CA or created automatically when an EFS operation is requested for the first time in a domain environment, the public key of the user's certificate is stored in AD. This is true for the recovery agent certificate as well, and in fact is how the public key is automatically included with EFS files

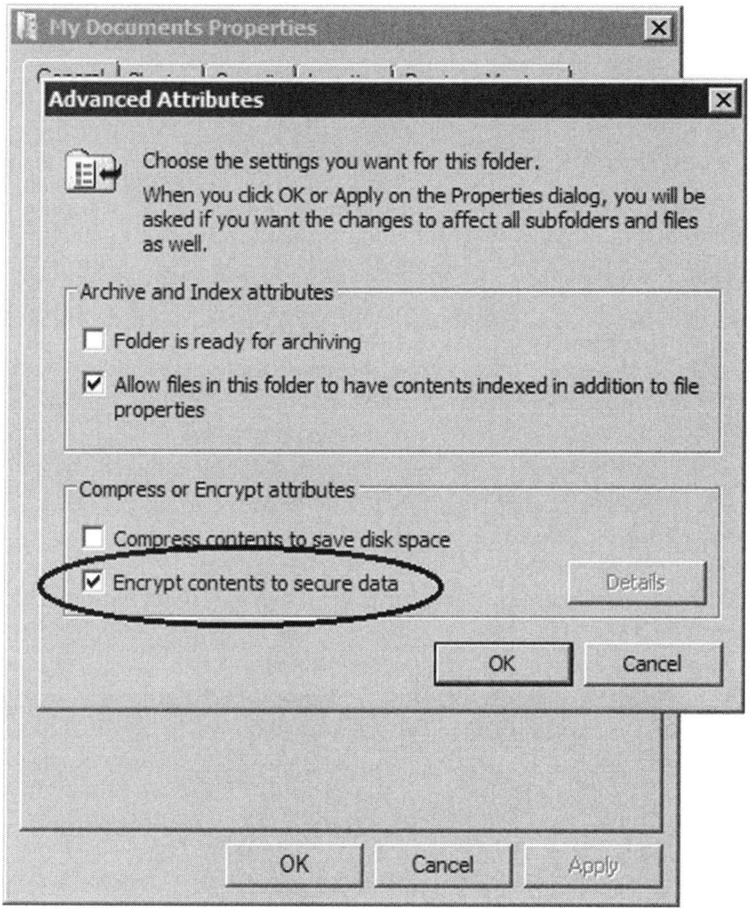

■ **FIGURE 2.1** EFS Dialog Box Selection

created in a domain: It is pulled directly from AD based on the policy settings for the EFS file recovery group policy object. I will elaborate more on this later.

Let us take a moment to actually detail the encryption process. When it comes to multiple users sharing an encrypted file, knowing how this works at the file and encryption process level will help give you a better understanding of how EFS works in an enterprise or smaller AD environment. There is nothing magical about an EFS certificate. It is simply an X.509 certificate with a private/public key pair generated by the Rivest, Shamir, and Adleman (RSA) algorithm, with EFS as a key usage, as seen in Figure 2.2.

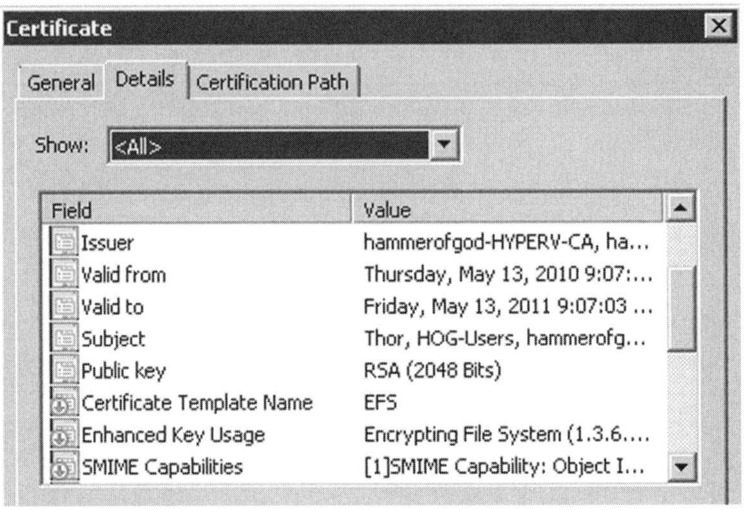

■ **FIGURE 2.2** EFS Certificate Details

When the certificate is created for the user, the RSA algorithm is used to generate public and private keys that are stored in the user certificate. Only the public key is stored in AD. Data is encrypted with the public key, and decrypted with the private key. That is why the public key is public, so that other users can encrypt data for you, but only the person holding the private key can decrypt it. Not even the person encrypting the data with the public key can decrypt it once it is encrypted.

Most people I have spoken with about encryption seem to be under the impression that the RSA keys are used to encrypt and decrypt the actual data in an encrypted file. This applies to any RSA-based encryption by the way, not just EFS. What actually happens is that before the file is encrypted, a cryptographically strong random key is generated. In this case, it is based on the default Advanced Encryption Standard (AES) cipher. It is actually this key that the RSA algorithm encrypts, and not the data. The public RSA key is used to encrypt the AES key, which is used to encrypt the actual data.

RSA AND AES

RSA is an asymmetric encryption algorithm. That means that one key encrypts the data, and another different key decrypts it. The calculations involved in this type of encryption are not trivial. They are actually processor intensive, and much slower than symmetric ciphers which encrypt and decrypt with the same key. The public RSA key is used to encrypt the AES key, and the holder of the private key uses it to decrypt the AES key, which is then used to decrypt the file. Each time you add a user to the list of users who can encrypt the file, new AES keys are generated, and each user's public key is used to encrypt a version of the AES key that they, and only they, can decrypt.

The reason for this is because the current implementations of the RSA cipher are restricted in the amount of data they can encrypt based on key length. A 1024-bit RSA key can encrypt about 116 bytes of data. That is not much. A 2048-bit RSA key can encrypt about 245 bytes. Again, this is because the encrypted data must be generated with the public key in such a way that only the private key can decrypt it. AES, however, does not have a limit. That key is used to encrypt data in blocks, and as such, any length file stream can be fed into an AES cryptographic service provider and the resulting ciphertext streamed to a file. This type of encryption scheme introduces two attack vectors: one against the RSA key, and one against the AES key. If I can crack the AES key, then it does not matter how strong the RSA key was that encrypted it. That is why cryptographically strong keys are used. An example of a base64-encoded RSA 2048-bit encrypted AES 256-bit key is:

```
f570+Lw5e7ZPmrvAmM4j5ykL6vUbjoo8jWMAOXY4uRgtqVJBiKmAjbEzN
C7q21E5deKfjFkDt2sYqYDE6TODRwUOS1wrlivXqVVVkvyOS/62cBeLP
Eitl0FoVnGPKbhOfDlujTsp9yw1Z9N2APLwh/Zyzgp8GAK2nZvzBt6oE
Vjtvz1K1GxZYGg4QxZ7AWAIfAU2eXTpoHC/wuYSed3EV62or8pYnFHen
NF94sLdqZcOBmE2tatXhCTUN/mTgaMqZJuuTIPRd+dHVMBeVYDw8v4sD
oPN2DwjDJvSdAnu59rQohnYHEtHTb9ssW8fKVAWN+ZCDIaPC69dKq672
C6q4A==
```

The key itself is much smaller than that (256 bits), but you get the picture. If you were to simply use *bananadog* as a password from which to generate the AES key, a brute force attack against this would be far easier than against a cryptographically strong key that is not based on a password combination. The RSA key will be substantially harder to crack at 2048 bits. The following is a purposefully tiny example of a base64-encoded, encrypted RSA 2048-bit private key, from which the public key can be derived in the C# implementation of the RSA Cryptographic Service Provider:

```
5vp34TOnlwDQyOLuu/gK8Idj4mBeKYEa93aZJGdO9P2WWyiR4BcdOBtQ
geqetW5A9xhYRLpAw2AG69x0e7wNmkjptQt456nyLhaedGBR+b3HrsyN
Ug9wgcx7Lc+2JtdFuhDGA/Qj3DwbwL90rz8hzFbQKDY2SElDesEZs2Kd
jncYWPJvQzmWDeMsMtKPFnOfhLz67s9CUUtEHAOuNnEWvGnJgvUWhvAB
XEXh/nYRL+qDvTbdetR5c/fOVFj5TLkFei15LKXibpPqR2J726fGXlzt
PrxSzK/O2yDy20TjhyeJTSv60cVDhOCetlRv/LRPDE/eH5NqWDi+6kv7
3GgxyPPV+1dVzhpM347p6D7Rf1R5Qea9wupC8JqbqYJegIMpiBjERqAl
rszbBDLygQrRnA45j2BsClIsWjMYTimpBtClfvFIhzCDCrqQyxgvOrE2
PMIxxOefxkwBFHekKqATGybmROoIiayp3LkNLDJve4KZ9TCSAlRVee3k
4xT8GgccuaNXn7JR207x7kS5SSpz33xOKde20kMp8eFxuWQ7K4pqNo7j
z5EVosyxrE2+SabSyHCrdwKlemSdOOauYovOSPvfMtsEifSWnvR5lfwv
```

HDz3XWRwmFdWxb//sCUgzbMEuJAQYIC1J6HbkYe5EBTqmVPP+BfGOGTw
miZd6yaVFAOiwy5nETttpkCyjJeM+bdBoPjWSG4tdfVs6nUzgR5e4kez
I1Mtt17IyIPdmvMrDvDnZsLLCKnMs1Big5aFk1EI9KgnX1r68dF8NW12
H9obE9x7sFTv1nPhbkAkF/eOwziJmh2A9DJVnuH8TA08ddWoghUVf34x
N8SqJxVGUo3mk/H3vgE9ioELE2VjWGOiIzxmhUq5HSZA2uD+PJ3CODt
8n68Nx40dWexCYRDr15TKLh2Heo3CwJAyemZy/OED9s3YNC2cMLYcfOIe
ffGSiOVGeC/rhhN+6jy8QRODOg/nUZSTGNZ57E+80hfBhkHnF3fJsjAB
pm6iK+GF7PoC8jAY4xxUrsY3uee05+CvUMPZuI2eQO8VjD/jbC4ezqye
TQzq4Xd7Wy3TOAep+EKJyesW1CyVeVny3B1BBkDunHeEHU3J+35mUMAd
+6mThixCpKuS4t80qTrG3Sk1vqtfPsHKRnVbBO3hkRmFcUJaITsOP3o2
VvZLibPw+2wCoToBBvd8op8n+O3Kxd59rZu66ThJGRFtQDaqUtfSnU8k
hNZ9j3V6btOEJ26kGCAaOO3bNOdLh1XSRkutpzO1yrA704QvyEO1cN/
FPA7IYnFJxB6mWdPqnZJWR8aK/ObYM1oiYBOS1FDbuHUVOukeNPzgok/
jDBPjPEEGZNcLT1qw17mYrOks9IxRnih6oUnOT1OwVJI9rj7pSu1BtaSH
tm/PCtbZK+RIxWkpsp35mgWkN6f3CYZSXJzB6CD7CmvWOujwuatqOp+
XzwBegxEu7fcyj5kh6NO9F7GJ7WTOkr6DNn+AGjOOIeHH9xjraLGIGTAU
QEkKq1qUn5ovz+XTtRH18kUatTeX6V+mdKTVArvcwaMzAdGFePUAdWUo
XCWCRNY38BqNTADYFfkwbrOi3KdwPdrnA7MW2/jZ/FZ+NsPUYwsZ/7f4
Cn1PIF7jMipZFEc3CNwcr+2R34hn2UUsI48Pr1UuO1tndfYZS7vp94fu
tBr6RhrKkUsIGCLmWfZbcGoXPhqalnBiiUojFc3OoJdz+yf7dVik03sd
yR45ICFzPaYUD9GYBTWs3OAqGvU71xT3jPXXFtrO+2iGykZL6sCMGrS5
znc+2xmGa7LvKxf3bUeGR4vzsIB8/YLI8zdfo/GOnIHxegj75YWVmD+
LOChRvJLkOYbiPmdQLCgjNn1avITkhjOs16Nv3zZBB1GsZeNLmiOKuvME
IjwGhgEGFHgm6srntSsUEo8cCFWDBi7QLI5eOOy9Y5VunpdBORMCh1h6
LTFvLVruKapH95nOkCdNUAn3XCrtLwie7LmAjWO233e3bfpnwFRpoc1p
rjJfkBB1JVQMsFg8++OLJQRoLbHzRaYHvOZIcTcLFooQWYLpkOhx8cZ+
3loSP6NbOh1RTWnvxPQCnOd6z79nyJzWE1J5+XwPf8PZk/YmTjLVilDs
QRnxkH6wXkTPfywsh7yOzLYprOYEKTAUUi7EXv/RPnZ5gr6BYc2ndNhZ
tOxACszs3hHJUCy2rmXREVQnGBWRub2ukmFZ5Og6o9GTPOTNww6I/JPm
ablFTqMHa6wgOrv9RoMEhXihKsl014OUhM1zCNU4zFWPFwObwAhDp+fd
pzE7FluvIGrZDjhgiuOMAF2EGcRz3EhB/qHIdDGHZRIvCSyo4/VKHvtP
pr1s25jAD8w3vuz+EJfp5PLaYxt90h5gxOTcz5sT+AwwZ5TwrLkYcBt3
WKQxrzKqcMVdV88vf2C6+gcBpUv8RR1JjaLFdVaNfnZZfL9efYLjAxLL
RxBK52krJwnVPUza6mDCOb/tV3oGanO7bXJXfQLQms3dk2xDuLc1jF+
yP2qgQXv8v1aeZEQT9mduynoEyNT4PioKncwaONkBH4mCEFTrtkvBt8Of
BOL8m4rgImOoYmyXvMOubA+3Casjru2CZGJ1wi9yVCZtha+Qe+t6fE8
cf3PiBu7DnOM7ItIBaOgoBqXMyyep3mFXa32VwxC3ULIIJiE32J+fwNs
yZnSFhchwGQCpdEeuJ9Jz/k+OKDPcBKbWsMtXaiMpqJJ9Spv9fMeRsKe
y8KGh4noZ6Gf79/IMHs8priwPh18pwb69Nc/gYEa+HtN11LsJdaZQfs8
ycq1Eabff27ro76oI4eM8bpbGYdB7em4OIJNXStbMX75NDd4PMN1YQMi
JTpxRnMFeZhGRUothgUx1DxRuo7Q5G155IXHocwOCJDOViJDrLEIOnOV
1hnwzZGinUkurK83qR3AVgSOmzoenRBmGxax48IVi5kHmXt7o8Hk8PcC
R5hx1+uEoYjdjf1GW3awQqUPNPrG8+k+9pa6yd08cuwb8vBFF19xxUTA
LyUqd57E9SSMY8MMFYFsp9aT1vV14XCf1VQ7abv5NO7fwoL3TJa3v1FB
SaoOH359cmt77xLfhE/rF9VWxA2/OOoz9eLM3j4q7YSGMjJVowz5V/Og
PRT6hEZfKiI2fBEckUVSjbzBhE/HN+wLMgKBYSYcNcE3k3C1F157QWFv/
VpT7XHe6p43mKNQAhRjjH2VcrHYs4OmiVfojVc+GhO+sMLeLO95Nrok
TMZbQmeadNNV8IN5Mt6iZwOhdzePUQ40+v8bmPe8c1EAaSJOG4Bgc1rv
hoxK4UPJ1G3PwunQJMHwKHHfM6ZD3TUOjexX1x3ya7fGJ4s359InYYSC

```
n3XlsWbcu4ibctYkOjbVTjPk34rcqwst+9ES3c6l3c8ik2sbqhc3lCNO
kdPyonGKOfLMV2ovKPSCcPfaJOACKnDh6pdwBBKBsVPOqI49zJUZNuuu
hOF+HeTjBn68eiuaduvsEXKp5yxBPzx+7Ced4lopL6pnM+549iHA+Idk
/VsG9FCbheLSEcUlptJWscPbGQSKRGXF/bL1AvERNnjmypVRU+8+gH15
qV66EGP+cBt6ETjTMWstLbvO4F7DhR3UlboXEpeYSa2LOpMIQmLQsWK5
n8uAumgDwDE5EIHKoXOXOHqd7Q+6BdzKx/DJQxc91hZQnX5GNM7ZOoAi
OQhdflClOFwAshFukK+aSD28oLV68UL3mEsGkGW1OS9kfA6wwhPwDhWo
rx3NHkz49GfdSAUOKUE9YtTBoFW4rTVLmhaMN1zNWISnauTowMMyLYlw
UW5VE3H1Yxez4h6RhP1ESmabPGuOsjqhIvVZC5b3ErjM7HX9uI2TVOZM
lojAlcQpsZ3s/zPsLTdJ1FtUZyOkRJlR2CoeM5HhFzvROjOc4SCchzGz
i+dVky+MEouGhaWILCIj5gkx7y5CEln3wwpOlV8iv6eWxw/pXdSoxmLf
iR/IVGtLCZhAJtoNKIzCxUUNEujGkC+ISfLSsWnHCpiqlpSHw1GYyRCJ
pO1p4m/z3zq8PCm6yCPtTm49I1SHCIPnwOu6jcDhX9ROTZnmnx+FVfIF
alYeHsJXt17J87OOvjVNlPQL47X1GXOAHY8P4He827PltCqubJ/UmDrK
Wj/OndxDVOq7AI6d3WUrO5FUt2sFG6SRG6Zat8+rd3tONIITZTL3w/jv
9hOOdXp+S3vTMHEcQc9YT+3t/MO8v7gzdW2QbPuiQnB+Ldpjy3UpegYa
4b1Q5ixRsqP85f2NMMZCl7Iepna+oXgWzO4iPo9ud9EI+gXwOl8tSya6
uvpB/EsliIyBhoJ7iONl8+X9EqgOljpsGDTJCf3ystO/WMgenQplUpQ4
9BdVO3iKhk6N3bP+dZ6qOB4vdUkNb+S+4wuTSKdCXi4Rl04t+/5xNjkH
71Kg6TFkSH/hykHwh6LLIzf2gD/kJKDgOrLd/CHrD82/aaOp7Aitwcgp
</EncPrivateKey><KeyHash>8k9pOOZLN8zNUYkx7xH8zNdqctqXkn/
LV6EQLruN6JY=</KeyHash><KeyNaCl>MuIDM+EhC/21c1rzE6Y3nQ==
```

That will take some time to brute force, and is commonly referred to as a BAN, or big ass number. Currently, even considering Moore's Law, factoring an RSA 2048-bit key is considered computationally infeasible, meaning that we will all have window seats in The Restaurant at the End of the Universe by the time it is cracked. However, that is today. Who knows what tomorrow shall bring. The model can be represented by the diagram in Figure 2.3.

AES is listed as the symmetric encryption algorithm; however, different ciphers can be configured, including Elliptic Curve Encryption. For file-by-file–based encryption in a public environment, I have designed and coded a free encryption Windows application that I call *Thor's Godly Privacy* (TGP).

TIP

I have not liked the Gnu Privacy Guard standard for various reasons, nor its commercial counterpart Pretty Good Privacy, so I wrote TGP using a different method of communicating encrypted data as well as distributing keys. You can find out more at my website: www.hammerofgod.com/tgp.aspx.

EFS Planning and Troubleshooting

One of the most common issues I have seen and heard about regarding EFS is the proper management of certificates and recovery plans. I do not want to spend too much more time on what I consider the administration of EFS

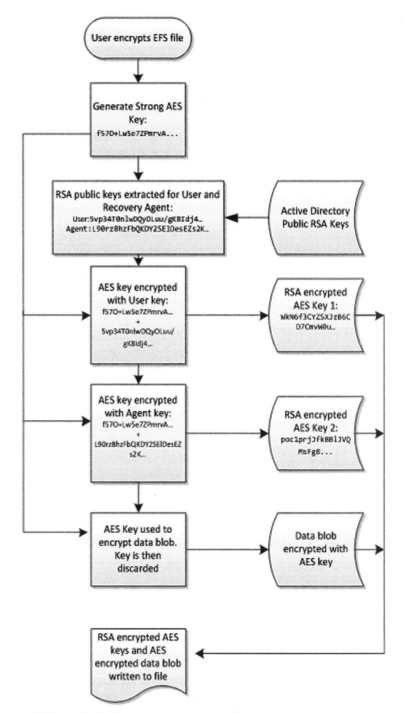

■ **FIGURE 2.3** The Workflow of an RSA Asymmetric and AES Symmetric Encryption Model

since it is time for us to get into the more interesting things we can do, but I will take a moment more to illustrate how a recovery issue can be created without an administrator realizing it.

BEST LAID PLANS

Let me tell you a short story. You have got a domain that has grown organically along with the organization, and administrators have come and gone, but policy dictates that the domain and enterprise administrator accounts be carefully controlled and managed. This does not always happen of course, but let us assume it has in this case. EFS has already been used in the past and any examination of EFS files looks fine. For example, you have your own EFS directory where everything is encrypted, and have a file named SplinterCell.txt outlining all the steps needed to walk through the game successfully. The EFS access properties should look as they do in Figure 2.4.

This all looks good, but suppose your system crashes and you have to rebuild a new one. Further, suppose all your data is on a separate drive from the system and you only back up that drive to make things easier. You get your

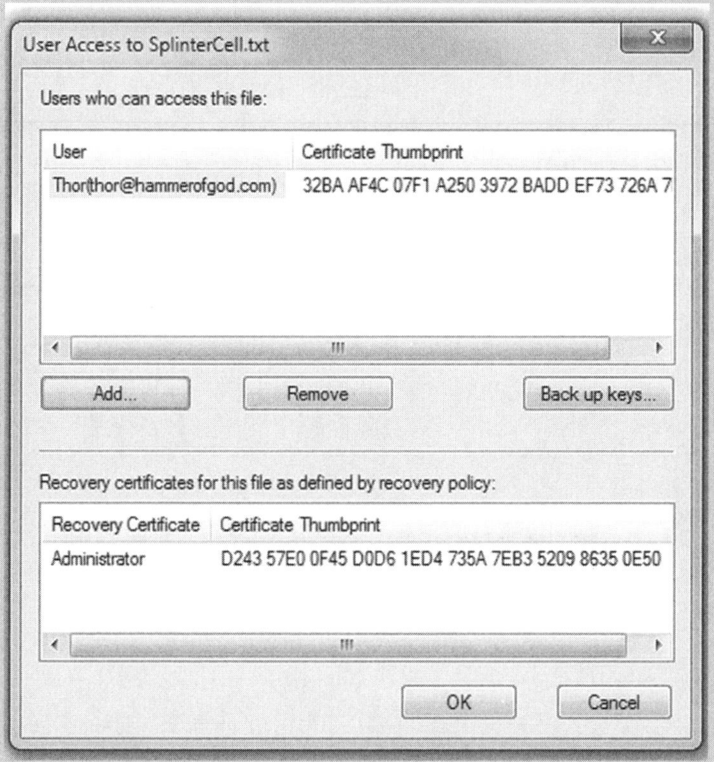

User Access to SplinterCell.txt

Users who can access this file:

User	Certificate Thumbprint
Thor(thor@hammerofgod.com)	32BA AF4C 07F1 A250 3972 BADD EF73 726A 7

[Add...] [Remove] [Back up keys...]

Recovery certificates for this file as defined by recovery policy:

Recovery Certificate	Certificate Thumbprint
Administrator	D243 57E0 0F45 D0D6 1ED4 735A 7EB3 5209 8635 0E50

[OK] [Cancel]

■ **FIGURE 2.4** EFS User Access Properties Dialog Box

new system up and running, plug in your data drive, go to access SplinterCell.txt, and get the dialog shown in Figure 2.5.

You cannot open the file, nor can you open *any* of your other encrypted files. You can view the EFS properties of the file and see who can access it, which is shown in the diagram in Figure 2.3. The user can access the file, and we see that the administrator is the recovery agent. You then realize that the EFS certificate containing the private key used to encrypt that file was in the profile on your old system, which went to see the great hard drive in the sky when it crashed. Any new encrypted files you create will generate a new EFS certificate (the first time EFS is requested), and that certificate will be used going forward. But that does not help you out here. Basically, you are hosed. You then go to the administrator knowing you are going to have to beg for help in getting your data recovered. You hand over your drive. He plugs it in, logs in as the domain administrator, goes to open up SpinterCell.txt, and is greeted with the dialog box in Figure 2.6.

The admin checks the file again, and sees that the administrator account is indeed the recovery agent, but nothing he does will open the file. He decides to match the certificate thumbprint in the EFS properties to that of the domain administrator account's certificate, as shown in Figure 2.7.

The administrator says "uh-oh," because the thumbprints are different, and that is not good. It is not the right certificate. Yet plain as day, you both see the thumbprint of the certificate as *defined by recovery policy*. The administrator fires up the Group Policy Management Editor and searches out the hive for the applicable GPO in **Computer | Windows Settings | Security Settings | Public Key Policies** and checks the EFS entry. He sees the certificate referenced in the GPO (top left in the diagram in Figure 2.3), opens it, and pulls up the **Certificate Properties** shown in Figure 2.8.

Whew! The thumbprints match! Seeing the private key symbol of a golden key on the certificate relieves the administrator. All he has to do now is export the certificate with its private key and install it on his system, and he can restore the data. He will be a hero, and the user will have to worship him forever, but when he goes to export the file, he sees the screen displayed in Figure 2.9.

"Uh-oh." There is no private key. Nor should there be; it is on the user's system where the certificate was created, but the admin has one more trick up his

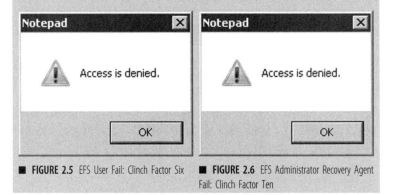

■ **FIGURE 2.5** EFS User Fail: Clinch Factor Six   ■ **FIGURE 2.6** EFS Administrator Recovery Agent Fail: Clinch Factor Ten

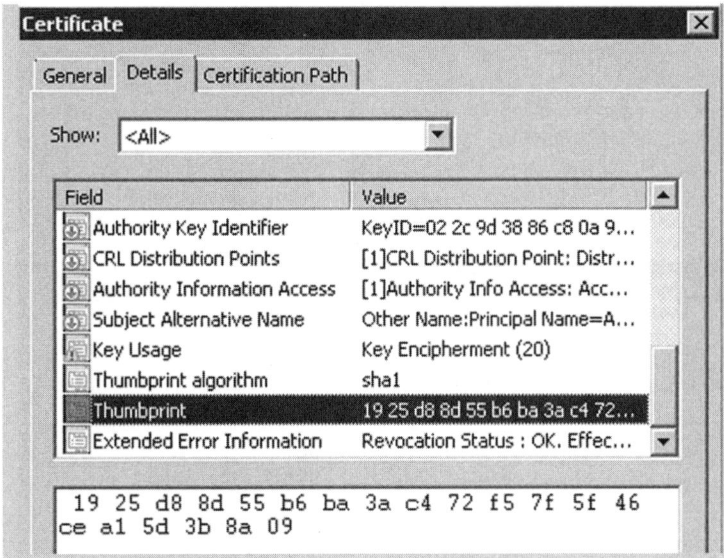

■ FIGURE 2.7 Domain Administrator Certificate Thumbprint

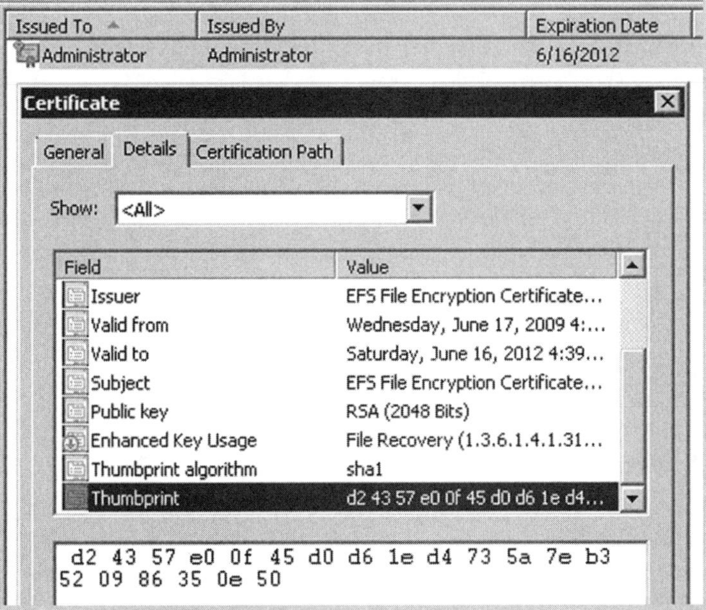

■ FIGURE 2.8 Properties for the Administrator Certificate Entry for the File Recovery Agent

sleeve. Since they have their own Microsoft Certificate Services installed, all he has to do is pull up a list of all the certificates issued and match the thumbprint to find out what administrator user account it was in the hopes of tracking down the proper certificate. So he goes into the CA management console and sorts all the issued certificates by thumbprint, as shown in Figure 2.10.

"Uh-oh." There is no *d2 43 57 e0 0f 45 d0 d6 1e d4 73 5a 7e b3 52 09 86 35 0e 50* thumbprint entry. There is no user holding that certificate because this CA *did not issue it*. You are now completely screwed. Your data is encrypted with keys that do not exist anywhere within your infrastructure, and there is no way to get it back. There is not some super elite hack or backdoor I am going to reference, and there is no last-ditch Hail Mary that will enable the administrator to recover the data. It is not a very happy ending.

■ **FIGURE 2.9** Export Private Key from Recovery Policy Entry Fail

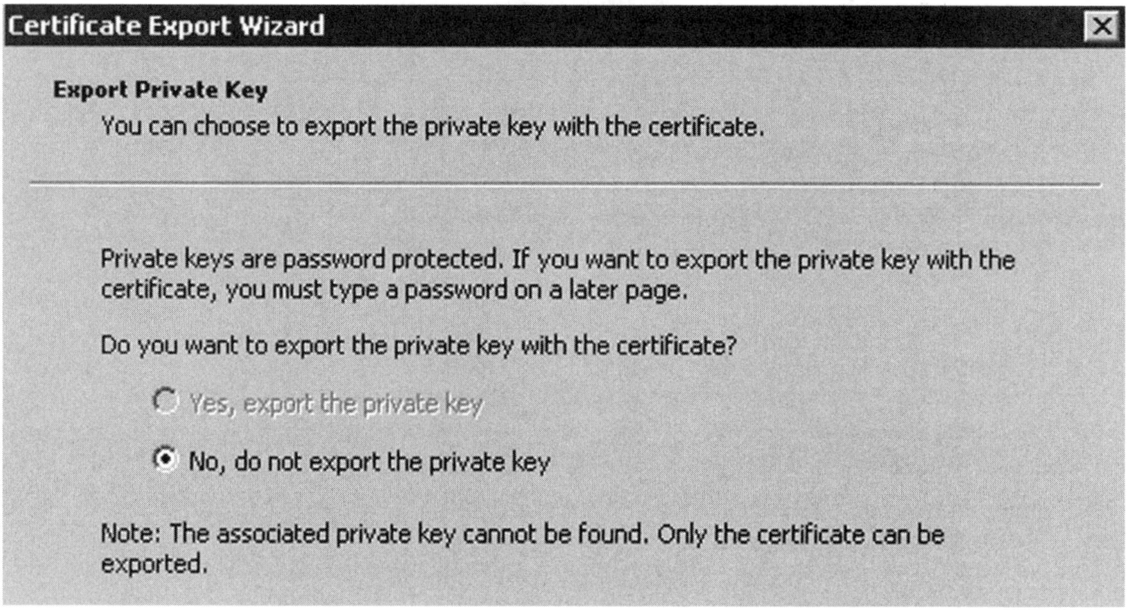

Certificate Export Wizard ✕

Export Private Key
You can choose to export the private key with the certificate.

Private keys are password protected. If you want to export the private key with the certificate, you must type a password on a later page.

Do you want to export the private key with the certificate?

○ Yes, export the private key

◉ No, do not export the private key

Note: The associated private key cannot be found. Only the certificate can be exported.

■ **FIGURE 2.10** Snippet of Certificates Issued by CA and Sorted by Certificate Hash (Thumbprint)

Certificate Effective Date	Certificate Expiration Date	Certificate Hash ▲
2/28/2010 1:56 PM	2/28/2011 1:56 PM	cd 3a 98 cc 10 f6 8a 9d 94 1b e8 5a 6a 0d 1d 27 83 c8 00 8d
12/15/2009 3:08 PM	12/15/2011 3:18 PM	cf 66 68 b4 7b 73 e3 e2 5c 8e 1b 51 82 17 b6 54 7e 54 51 14
12/15/2009 3:05 PM	12/15/2011 3:15 PM	d0 72 a5 fb 65 08 11 e0 6d ef 53 d1 89 c1 70 10 f1 cb 97 0d
12/30/2009 8:21 PM	12/30/2010 8:21 PM	d0 7a 75 85 1f 6a bb c4 b1 93 76 f0 12 49 72 35 13 38 d0 fa
12/17/2009 7:10 PM	12/17/2010 7:10 PM	d1 44 0a 06 0d 2b d2 0c 00 76 63 10 3b e7 1d 6e ab 8f 50 c0
1/17/2011 2:57 AM	1/17/2012 2:57 AM	d7 22 12 9b 49 79 76 58 a2 e8 00 17 1a fc 3c 2d 9b 85 75 8f
2/16/2011 4:25 PM	2/16/2012 4:25 PM	d9 12 ae 0a 20 25 5a d5 63 a4 46 64 9e 24 62 6c ca 77 b0 e0
2/15/2011 7:18 AM	2/15/2012 7:18 AM	da e9 e8 f0 73 f8 ca 17 8e 5c 70 61 42 26 a3 3d 1c 77 7b 8e
12/26/2009 10:03 PM	12/26/2010 10:03 PM	dd b4 36 89 d9 7f da 96 a6 87 0c c8 72 f4 40 77 b6 89 a2 47
11/19/2010 3:37 AM	11/19/2011 3:37 AM	e0 2e f7 10 16 be 2b 01 74 61 63 0c 77 8a e6 30 2e 01 06 55
12/26/2010 7:25 PM	12/26/2011 7:25 PM	e1 ba 84 5b cd 60 85 1e 07 b9 2e 8e f8 d3 e8 ab c3 00 7f b1
12/15/2009 2:24 PM	12/15/2010 2:24 PM	e4 73 2d 7b 29 ef 13 32 d8 33 93 ee 7b da 2b 58 fc 0d 57 f2

Postmortem Use Case Analysis

Here is what happened. When the domain was created, the recovery certificate was created for the administrator on the first domain controller created. It was then stored in the certificate store of that administrative user and a copy of its public key certificate was stored in AD, set as the recovery agent certificate. Administrators need to be aware of this when they first roll out EFS. It is fine to add other domain controllers, but if something happens to the system where the first domain controller was rolled out, then the default recovery certificate is gone. When you begin deploying EFS, it is important to create a number of trusted accounts for recovery agents appropriate for your environment, and to back up the certificates with their private key and store them in a secure location.

It is time to build an operational example around leveraging EFS together with IIS to greatly increase the security posture around an extremely common use case: web-based file access.

It may be surprising that I chose such a mundane and common function to build an example around, but it was deliberate. Security is not about being sexy. I certainly could have come up with some incredibly complex, intricate network design with overlapping boxes and interwoven lines pointing to other interwoven lines and overlapping boxes. It would be extremely hard to build, and I could try to convince you that the difficulty in deploying the model equated to the same level of security, and then leave it up to you to figure out a maintenance plan claiming that administration was out of scope for this book. And it is. I do not talk about administration or operations much; this is supposed to be a security bible after all. Doing that would be a cop-out, and then you would never try to use the model. Security should be simple and sustainable. That is not to say that examples in this book are all simple and easy to configure. They are not. But the basic premise should be to design infrastructure security controls that can be documented and deployed with repeatable results.

BUILDING THE WEB APPLICATION STRUCTURE

Using this type of basic functionality as an example should also make it easier to apply the same type of logic and design to other applications for EFS. The goal in this example is for an external source (although an internal one will work as well) to be able to access data files over HTTPS in a secure way. Files will not only be accessed locally on the web server, but we also need to configure a virtual directory for access to other file servers via the web host. This makes things more difficult to configure, but it mirrors the actual deployment requirements we will have in production. Accessing files on the web server itself is trivial. When we need to access other resources on other servers, however, we have to consider authentication methods, application pool user context, and internal share design. We will also address scenarios where Kerberos authentication delegation is required and the pros and cons of authorizing a server to delegate authentication is in the bonus content.

We will take iterative steps to make this happen because different IIS authentication mechanisms work in different ways with different features. In my experience, understanding IIS authentication is actually where many people get confused and make mistakes when designing access models, so the intent of this example is to walk through one design and then build upon that design with another and see what we have to do in order to accommodate the feature requirements. At each iterative step, we will use examples that illustrate where authentication mechanisms work and where they do not. Knowing what does not work is as valuable as knowing what does.

Access Overview

We will be building web services to access data in a virtual directory where the user will log on to get access to the virtual directory. I want to start with a straightforward example with what I consider a typical use case, highlighting the hows and whys of authentication and application pool context for the website application based on our access requirements. EFS will not be introduced at this point. While this is a simple configuration, the details of the context of authentication can be a little confusing for those not entirely familiar with IIS authentication. In fact, I have seen instances where people have deployed sites with sweeping, overprivileged access rights because they did not fully understand the model. Figure 2.11 illustrates the simple design we will accomplish as our first step.

Web Access and Authentication

Our goal is to provide the authenticated users with access to files via HTTPS from the Internet. In this example, we will be giving two users, let us call them Steve and Greg, access to some files via their web browsers. Both will have to log on to view their respective directories and files, but we do not want Steve to be able to view Greg's content, and we certainly do not want Greg to have access to Steve's content. There will be a web server that the users will hit, which is configured with virtual directories pointing to a network folder that each user has on a separate file server. Having the virtual directory on a different server is significant, as you will see.

We will be working with three logon contexts here: the users themselves (Steve and Greg), the World Wide Web Publishing Service (IIS), and the

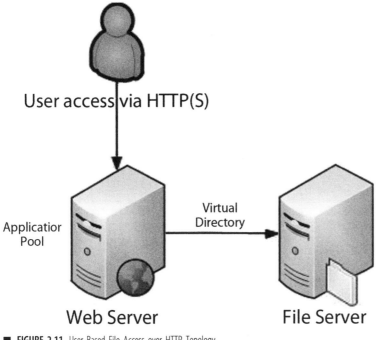

User access via HTTP(S)

Application Pool

Virtual Directory

Web Server

File Server

■ **FIGURE 2.11** User-Based File Access over HTTP Topology

account identity that our website (or website application) application pool will run in. An application pool isolates website application processes from each other and allows specific configuration parameters to be set differently among pools. When you create a website in IIS, it will be assigned an application pool automatically, the *DefaultAppPool*, running as a default identity called, appropriately enough, the *ApplicationPoolIdentity*.

I point all this out because even though the IIS service itself runs as Local System, the website we will be using actually runs under the context of a different identity as specified earlier. Not only is this more secure, but it allows you to assign different identities to different application pools for different purposes. Examples may be the separation of roles between one application and another in regard to the data the account can access, and the rights the account has.

If we were storing files directly on the web server, then our job would be easy as we could use the default website and application pool settings. We would just create our site, allow directory browsing to the folders we wanted, require authentication to those folders, and set the proper NTFS permissions for the users. Figure 2.12 shows what that configuration would look like.

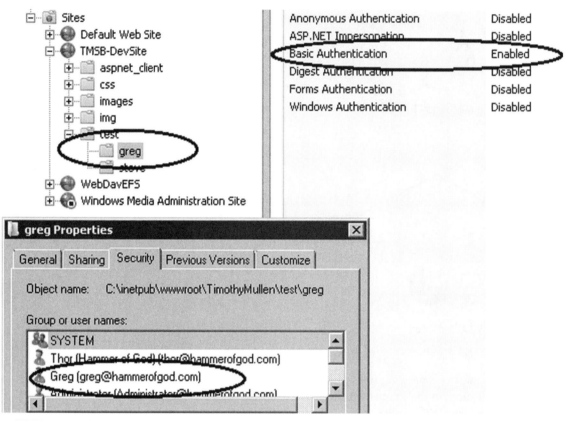

■ **FIGURE 2.12** IIS Website Configuration Showing Local Directory, Authentication, and Permissions for the greg Directory

Testing Access

When Greg goes to his directory URL, he is prompted to log in, after which he will see a screen similar to Figure 2.13.

Now Greg sees his MIDI files and can download what he needs. The same configuration applies for Steve, shown in Figure 2.14.

Testing access gives the results shown in Figure 2.15.

And there, as expected, we see Steve's documents, including the manual for the telescope he borrowed from me and never returned. In this IIS authentication model, two different entities needed to be given permissions to view the steve and greg directories. The Windows user accounts had to be given permission to access and read the files in their respective directories. The default *ApplicationPoolIdentity* identity actually already had the appropriate permissions to read the directories, and not only the steve and greg directories, but the entire website file structure.

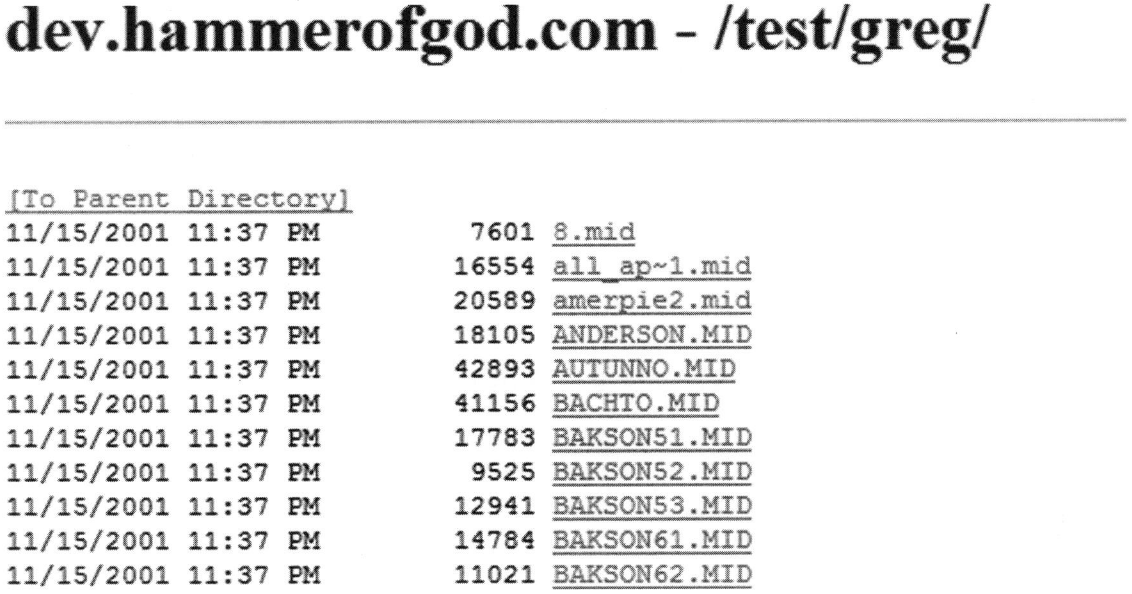

dev.hammerofgod.com - /test/greg/

```
[To Parent Directory]
11/15/2001 11:37 PM          7601 8.mid
11/15/2001 11:37 PM         16554 all_ap~1.mid
11/15/2001 11:37 PM         20589 amerpie2.mid
11/15/2001 11:37 PM         18105 ANDERSON.MID
11/15/2001 11:37 PM         42893 AUTUNNO.MID
11/15/2001 11:37 PM         41156 BACHTO.MID
11/15/2001 11:37 PM         17783 BAKSON51.MID
11/15/2001 11:37 PM          9525 BAKSON52.MID
11/15/2001 11:37 PM         12941 BAKSON53.MID
11/15/2001 11:37 PM         14784 BAKSON61.MID
11/15/2001 11:37 PM         11021 BAKSON62.MID
```

■ **FIGURE 2.13** Directory Browsing Enabled View of the greg Directory

Application Pools

By default, your website directory will be given read access by way of the *IIS_USRS* group that is automatically created when IIS is installed. In turn, this group will be populated by built-in application pool accounts created under the *IIS APPPOOL* principal account that is also created during the install of IIS. These take the form of *IIS APPPOOL\DefaultAppPool* and *IIS APPPOOL\Classic .NET AppPool* in the same way that *NT AUTHORITY* principal account members are created, such as *LOCAL SERVICE* and *NET-WORK SERVICE*, when the OS is installed. Note that this is different than versions of IIS prior to 7.0 where an actual *IUSR_MACHINE* user account was created. This account is also included in the *EVERYONE* group context when used on the local server. That is to say, if you have permissions on a resource located on the web server itself, and those permissions are set to EVERYONE, then the IIS APPPOOL users will be matched as part of that group during authorization.

Our test site here, as previously mentioned, is running as the DefaultAppPool account pool. This account pool is set to use the default ApplicationPoolIdentity identity. Figure 2.16 shows the Application Pool feature view in IIS.

This application pool must be able to at least read the directory structure of our website, or the site will not function. The application pool permissions

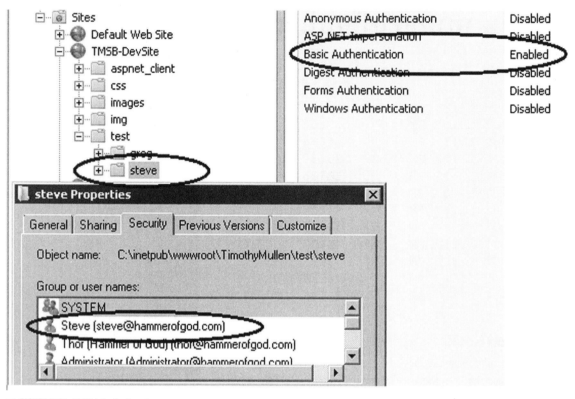

■ **FIGURE 2.14** IIS Website Configuration
Showing Local Directory, Authentication, and
Permissions for the steve Directory

■ **FIGURE 2.15** Directory Browsing Enabled View
of the steve Directory

dev.hammerofgod.com - /test/steve/

```
[To Parent Directory]
 9/17/2009   6:28 AM       3557515 CelestronNexStar8se.pdf
11/7/2007   8:22 AM         67959 linuxadminmanual.pdf
 1/4/2006  11:40 PM       6162631 Netgear FVX538 Manual.pdf
 2/25/2011   7:31 PM         <dir> NexStar 8 se
 2/25/2011   7:44 PM           261 web.config
```

Application Pools

This page lets you view and manage the list of application pools on the server. Application pools are associated with worker proce
provide isolation among different applications.

Filter:	▼ 🔍 Go ▼ 🔍 Show All	Group by:	No Grouping	▼	
Name ▲	Status	.NET Framewo...	Managed Pipeline Mode	Identity
ASP.NET v4.0	Started	v4.0	Integrated	ApplicationPoolIdentity
ASP.NET v4.0 Classic	Started	v4.0	Classic	ApplicationPoolIdentity
Classic .NET AppPool	Started	v2.0	Classic	ApplicationPoolIdentity
DefaultAppPool	Started	v2.0	Integrated	ApplicationPoolIdentity

■ FIGURE 2.16 Application Pool Details Showing the DefaultAppPool and ApplicationPoolIdentity

are applied at the base level irrespective of what type of authentication you will require users to have to access the website. As seen in Figures 2.11 and 2.12, authentication to a website by actual users can be based on a number of methods: Anonymous Authentication, ASP.NET Impersonation, Basic Authentication, Digest Authentication, Forms Authentication, and Windows Authentication.

Application Pool Access Structure

The DefaultAppPool is authorized to read the file structure of the website based on operating system NTFS permissions at the file level. However, your users must be authenticated to access the site—the difference being that users are authenticated by the IIS service. Once the users are authenticated through IIS by way of the application pool, they must then also be authorized to access portions of the site via NTFS permissions. Consider it like a pipeline: The application pool creates the pipe between the user and the resource based on the authentication model, and once that pipeline is established, the user context is passed through to the resource because we have chosen **Basic Authentication**. If we had used **Anonymous Authentication**, then all user interaction would be handled within the context of the application pool identity. The Basic Authentication model is illustrated in Figure 2.17.

The separate permissions for Greg and Steve prevent each user from accessing the other's content. From a management and administration standpoint, specifying users directly in a permissions structure is not recommended; group permissions are far more flexible and allow for access control by way of group membership management. Additionally, setting permissions on each subdirectory for each user would be an arduous process in a user environment of significance, but I used this example because it better illustrated the way access control can be accomplished with different user contexts. If Steve were to navigate directly to Greg's folder after

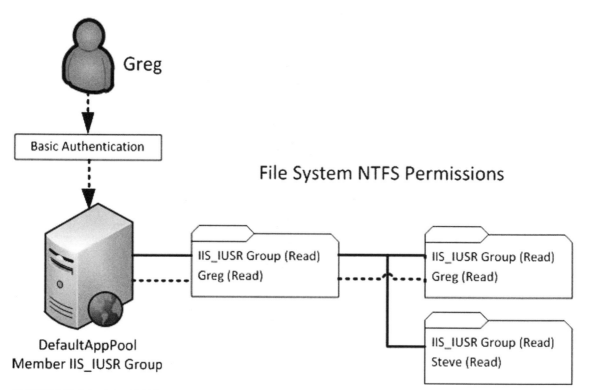

File System NTFS Permissions

logging in to his own content, the application pool's pipe would allow Steve to actually reach the resource, but the request would fail since his user account has no permissions to do so. As such, Steve would be challenged for a set of different credentials to access the folder, as illustrated in Figure 2.18.

Authentication Considerations

Up to this point, we have used HTTP to log on and view files. This is noted in the dialog box in Figure 2.18 by the warning about passwords being sent in an insecure manner. This is because we are using Basic Authentication and it transmits the credentials in the clear or unencrypted. Someone sniffing the network connection could see these credentials (in Chapter 4, titled "Creating an Externally Accessible Authenticated Proxy in a Secure Manner," see Figure 4.4 for further explanation). You cannot use Windows authentication over the Internet to access these resources as we did with TMG, so it is important to remember this. Let me clarify that statement. More specifically, you cannot use Windows authentication via HTTP with IE by default. Specifically configured domain members could use Windows

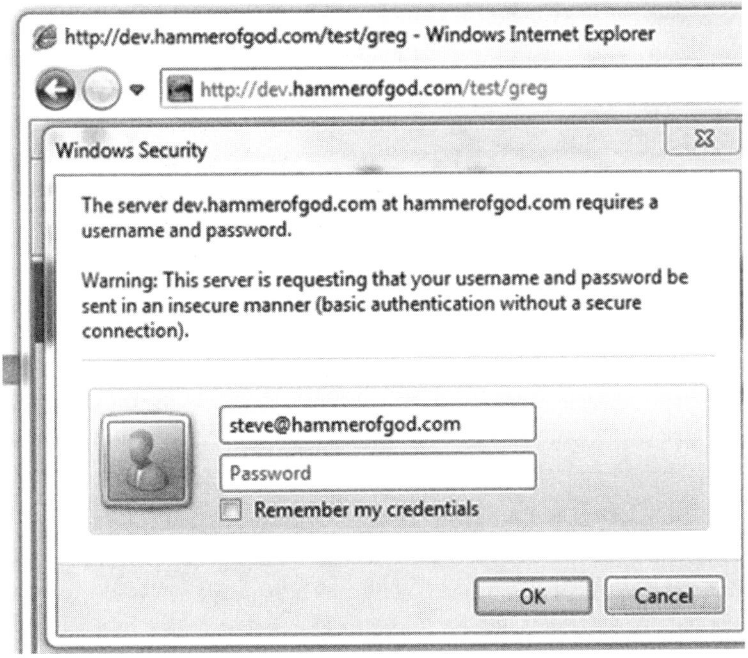

■ **FIGURE 2.18** Steve Is Challenged for New Credentials When Trying to Access Greg's Content

authentication over HTTP, but this should only be used if you are forced to. Remember, security is about risk management. There will be times where we simply have to do something in a way that is not as secure as it could be, and such a use case is discussed in the aforementioned chapter, but for purposes of this chapter we will not consider Windows Authentication over HTTP as an option. For review, Figure 2.19 shows what the clear logon looks like to a packet sniffer.

This is why one should use an SSL tunnel (HTTPS) when authenticating users via HTTP Basic Authentication wherever and whenever possible.

■ **FIGURE 2.19** Network Capture of Basic Authentication over HTTP

```
Authorization: Basic
  Authorization:   Basic Z3J1Z0BoYW1tZXJvZmdvZC5jb206R3J1Z01zQUNyaW1pbmFsKg==
    WhiteSpace:
    BasicAuthorization:
      Scheme: Basic
      Realm: greg@hammerofgod.com:GregIsACriminal*
```

ACCESSING REMOTE FILES

In summary, so far we have set up a web server running under the DefaultAppPool application pool where we used Basic Authentication to require logon. The users logging on were limited to what directories they could use by setting NTFS permissions on those directories. And finally, the files accessed were on the local file system of the web server along with the normal website files. The users' folders were both subfolders of a folder called *test* directly off the web root.

More EFS is coming soon, but for now we need to configure our web application to accommodate a more realistic requirement of users accessing files on a file server located elsewhere in the network as originally illustrated in Figure 2.10. This step will require changes in our authentication model, and we will utilize this change to illustrate a way of leveraging EFS for additional access control.

Virtual Directories

Continuing with the same access model, let us say that Steve and Greg have their own user folders on an internal file server that is not accessible from the Internet. We have the same directory structure similar to what we had before on the local web server. We will call this internal file server the *remote server* since it is remote from the web server's point of view. As mentioned earlier, assigning permissions on a group basis offers more flexibility, so we will change our approach now. With that in mind, we will create a global group called *gShared* and populate that group with the accounts that can access the user folders share we need to create on the remote server. This will prove to be a wise move later, but for now, gShared only has Greg and Steve as members (see Figure 2.20).

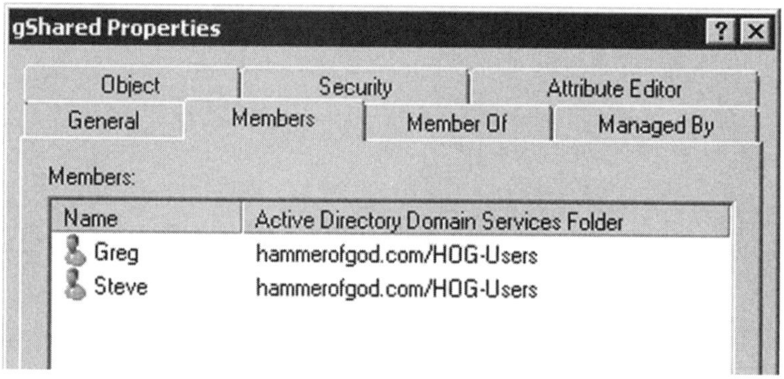

■ **FIGURE 2.20** gShared Global Group Membership

We share the users directory on the remote server and add the gShared group permissions to read. Note that at this time Greg, Steve, and anyone else we add to the group will have access to each other's files. The NTFS permissions are applied to the directory file structure based on the users you choose to share with. Note that earlier versions of Windows treated share permissions separately as it did with NTFS permissions. This model makes things far easier to manage and understand. From the remote server, we share the users directory as demonstrated in Figure 2.21.

This will result in propagating the users folder with the NTFS permissions shown in Figure 2.22.

From our web server, we will now create a virtual directory that links to the newly created users share on the remote server, as shown in Figure 2.23.

When we create the virtual directory shown in Figure 2.23, we see the users virtual directory (indicated with the shortcut icon) and verify the directory structure by drilling down through the file structure as shown in Figure 2.24.

Testing Access

We can now see the entire directory for both users: Steve's telescope information, and Greg's music folder, which, not surprisingly, contains Yanni. The files are still set to allow the gShared group read access, and we have even left the Anonymous Authentication method enabled which was

■ **FIGURE 2.21** Sharing the Users Folder on the Remote Server

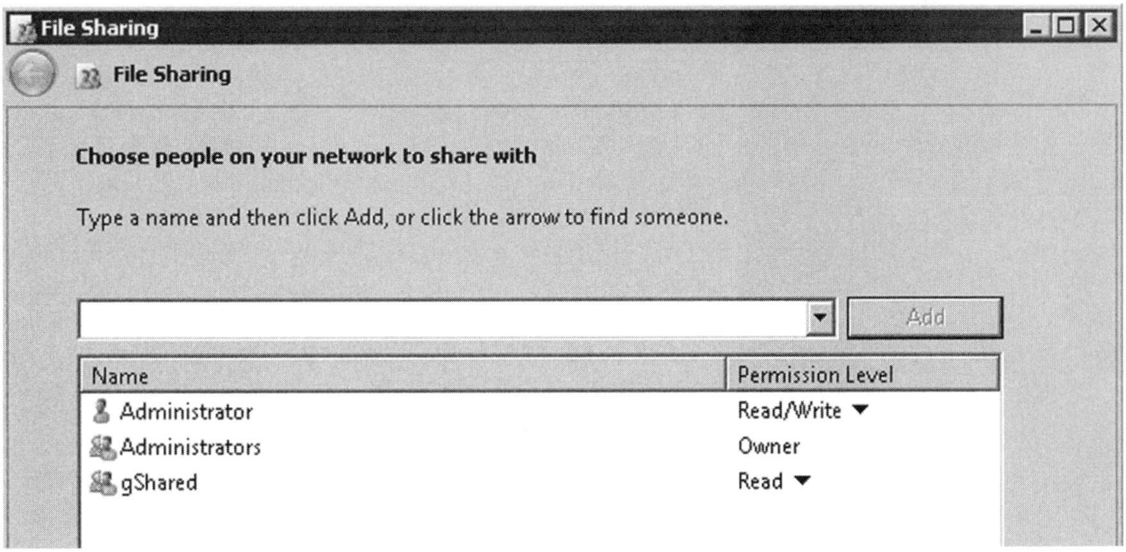

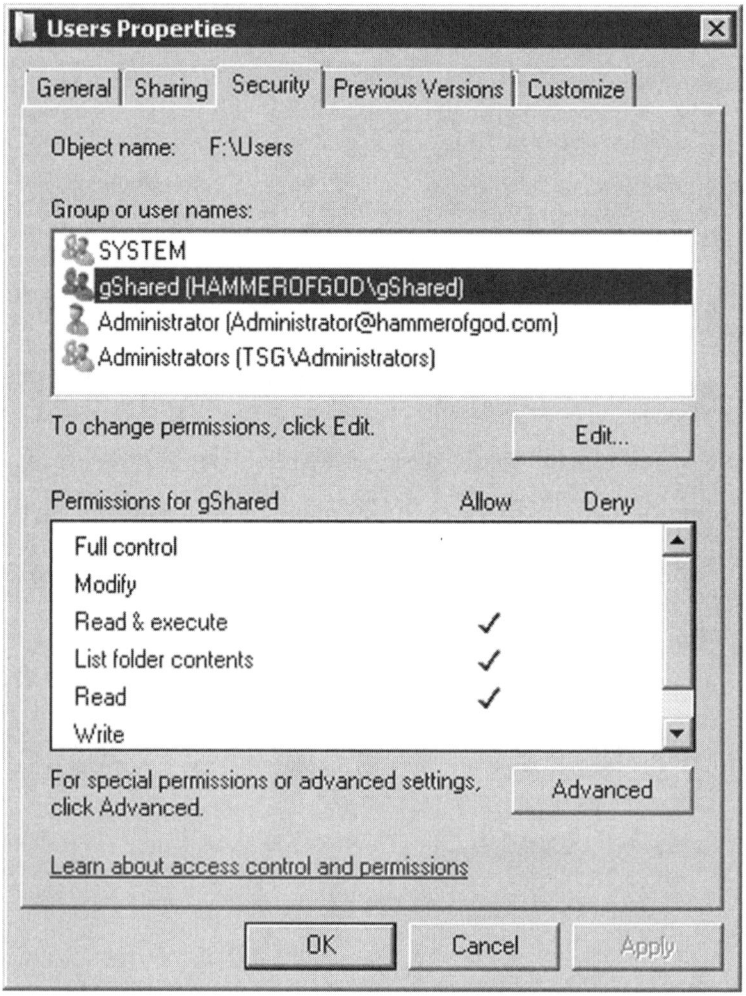

■ **FIGURE 2.22** NTFS Permissions Set from Sharing the Users Folder on the Remote Server

inherited from the root to test. This is another iterative step: We add controls one at a time so that troubleshooting is easier. The fewer variables we start out with the better. Do not forget to enable **Directory Browsing** so that the user can see a list of the files via the browser. So let us test access externally. Figure 2.25 shows the results of that test.

So apparently Anonymous Authentication did not work. We turn on **Basic Authentication** so that we can explicitly log on as the user, as shown in Figure 2.26.

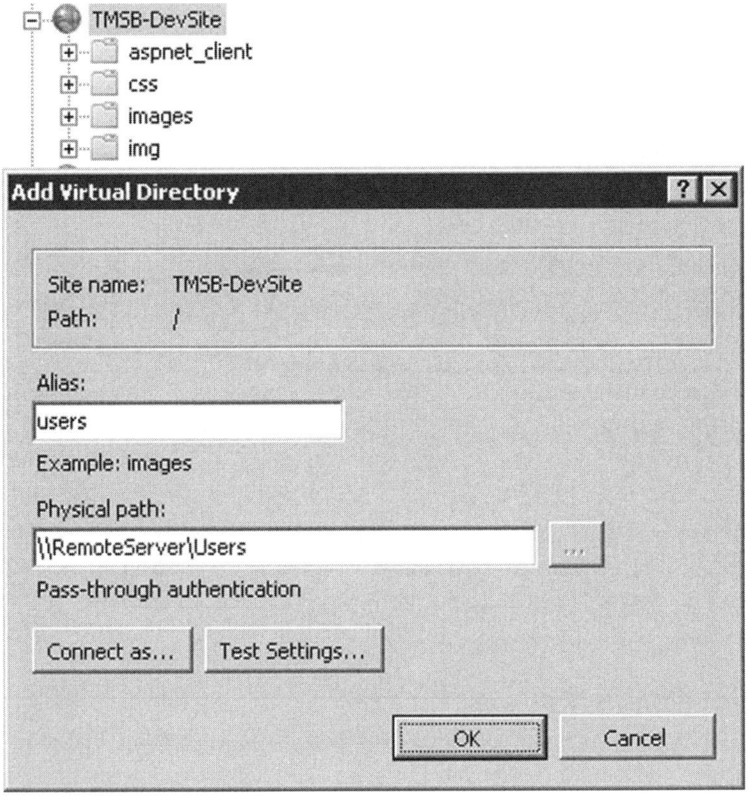
TMSB-DevSite
aspnet_client
css
images
img
Add Virtual Directory
Site name: TMSB-DevSite
Path: /
Alias:
users
Example: images
Physical path:
\\RemoteServer\Users
Pass-through authentication
Connect as...
Test Settings...
OK
Cancel

■ **FIGURE 2.23** Create a Virtual Directory in IIS to the Remote Server with an Alias of users

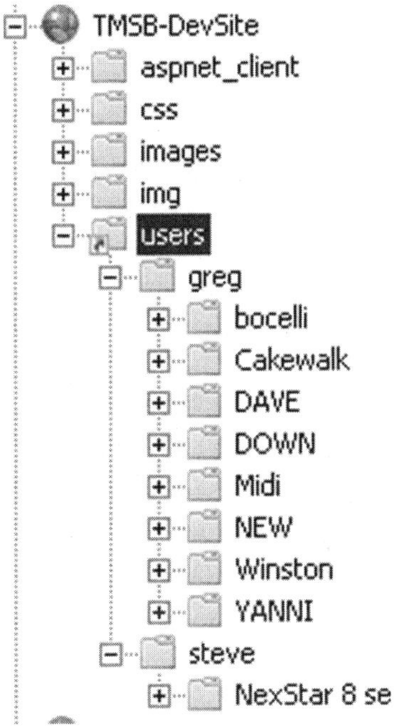
TMSB-DevSite
aspnet_client
css
images
img
users
greg
bocelli
Cakewalk
DAVE
DOWN
Midi
NEW
Winston
YANNI
steve
NexStar 8 se

■ **FIGURE 2.24** Validated Directory Structure of users Virtual Directory

■ **FIGURE 2.25** The Dreaded Internal Server Error When Requesting the Virtual Directory List

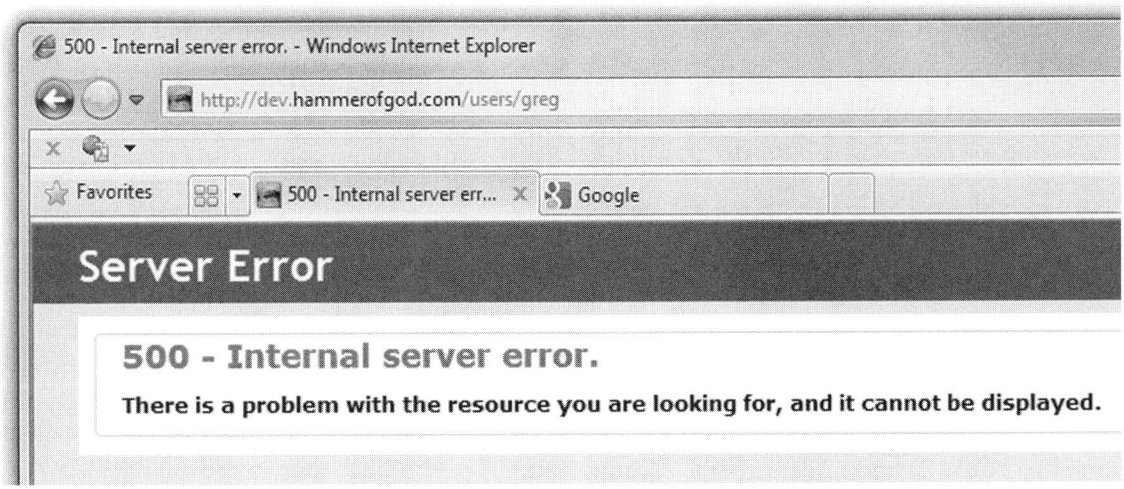
500 - Internal server error. - Windows Internet Explorer
http://dev.hammerofgod.com/users/greg
Favorites
500 - Internal server err...
Google
Server Error
500 - Internal server error.
There is a problem with the resource you are looking for, and it cannot be displayed.

Authentication

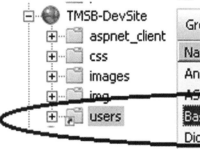

Group by: No Grouping	
Name ▲	Status
Anonymous Authentication	Disabled
ASP.NET Impersonation	Disabled
Basic Authentication	Enabled
Digest Authentication	Disabled
Forms Authentication	Disabled
Windows Authentication	Disabled

■ **FIGURE 2.26** Explicitly Setting Basic Authentication to Troubleshoot the 500 - Internal Server Error Message

Unfortunately, this does not fix anything. We are tipped off to the problem however by noticing that even though we set Basic Authentication, we were never asked to log on and a 500 error was immediately generated.

Troubleshooting

The DefaultAppPool:ApplicationPoolIdentity context is being used to attempt to create the pipe we talked about earlier, and the remote server does not know anything about that identity, so it denies access. We are not able to grant IIS APPPOOL\DefaultAppPool access to the users directory because the only place that user identity lives is on the local web server. There is no way to explicitly reference the account on the remote server even if we wanted to. Secondarily, Basic Authentication did not affect access because the authentication requirements are only established after the application pool creates the pipe to the resource, based on the user context permissions. In this case, the application pool could not query the resource to find out what its permissions were in the first place and it has to be able to do this.

Here is a list of a few immediate solutions to fix this problem along with any associated concerns:

1. You could keep the DefaultAppPool configuration the way it is and explicitly configure the virtual directory to use a specific user account to access the resource instead of using the application pool context. In other words, you can assign a user to the pipe for the virtual directory. This user account would have to be given permissions to read the users share but this is easily accomplished by adding the user to the gShared group.

The issue here is that you have to set the user context for directory access. Every file accessed via this virtual directory will be as if it was that user. Since the user has to have read access to the directory structure to function, there is no way to require authentication to the resource as it is already authenticated explicitly.

2. You could edit the DefaultAppPool and specify that the application pool explicitly use a particular user context. You have the same user restrictions as that stated earlier, but virtual directories could use the application pool context and not a specific user as outlined in the first solution.

This would allow for pass-through authentication, where the application pool user establishes the pipe, yet a logon is required for the end user to access that pipe (based on the NTFS permissions). This may create an issue with other applications already using the DefaultAppPool; it depends entirely upon your environment.

3. You could create a new application pool specifying a user account context for the application pool to run in. This would be the same as the second solution, except that it is not the default application pool. This is really the best way to go. You will have a custom application pool that is isolated from all other processes and pools. You can do what you want without affecting other applications, and you limit the user account to only the application bound to the application pool.

If you have not guessed by now, we are going to go with the third solution. This will give us the greatest flexibility. All we have to do now is determine what account we are going to use. I am going to refer to this type of account as a *service account* since it will be assigned to a process and not a user; you can do it however you want to, of course. I always limit the scope of access for service accounts so that I can tightly control what assets they can reach in the event of a breach that yields execution capabilities in the context of the service user. This is the concept of least privilege. You give a process the authorization to perform its required functions and nothing more. Processes executing in a high-privileged context are dangerous, as they can be leveraged to do things they normally would not be able to do, like adding users, creating files, or accessing groups of assets.

The Service User

We need to keep the concept of least privilege in mind when we create the user for the application pool. A good example of least privilege would be removing newly created service accounts from the default domain users group once they have been set up. The domain users group is widely used by many administrators to give both read and write access to resources when they are users authenticated by the domain. Our user account does not need this type of access, so we will pull them out the moment we create it. To make this process easy and to better track service users, I create a global group for service users and populate that group with service accounts. That way I can create access rules specific to service users. In this example, I will be using *gServiceUsers*. Not exactly creative, but it is self-explanatory. This overall least privilege process is covered in detail in the Chapter 5, titled "The Creation and Maintenance of Low-Privileged Service Users." Detailed suggestions regarding service account creation and administration are also discussed there, including password expiration policies and lockout considerations for service accounts.

My service account user will end up being a very low-privileged user that is a member of gServiceUsers, and only gServiceUsers. A user must have a primary group set in AD, and this is the domain users group by default. The other reason to create a separate gServiceUsers group is so you can add them to the service group, set the service group as the primary group, and then delete their membership from domain users. You cannot remove the user from domain users until you do this.

Pursuant to the instructions in the chapter about service users, we will end up with a lowly user. I will call the account *MyWebApp*, which is so far only a member of the gServiceUsers group. This is shown in Figure 2.27.

Create a new application pool in IIS and edit the advanced settings to change the default entry of ApplicationPoolIdentity to specify the MyWebApp custom account to be used as the application pool identity. This is illustrated in Figure 2.28.

Now that we have changed the application pool identity as reflected in Figure 2.28, we are all set. Take note of the fact that the custom account

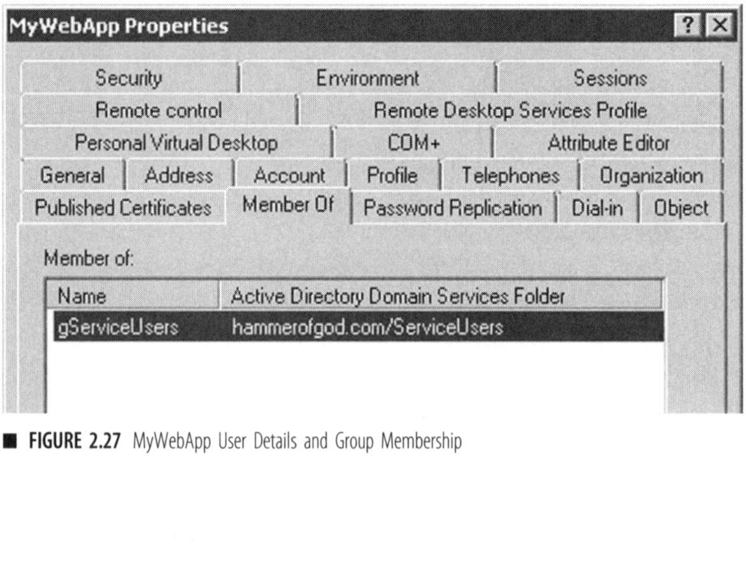

■ FIGURE 2.27 MyWebApp User Details and Group Membership

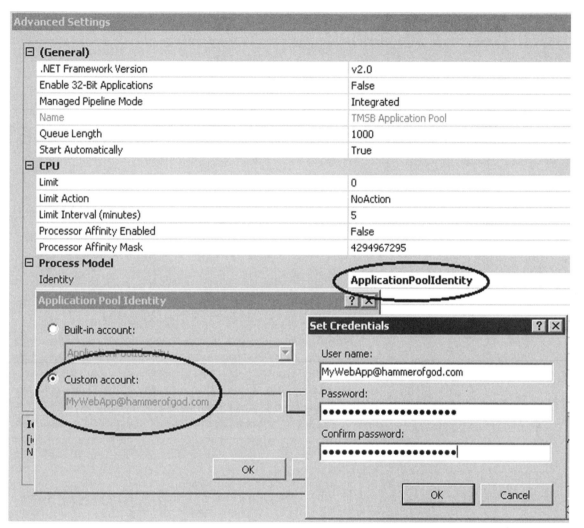

■ **FIGURE 2.28** TMSB Application Pool Advanced Settings Showing the Default ApplicationPoolIdentity Being Changed to the MyWebApp Custom User Account

credentials have to be entered here and are stored by IIS. If you change the password of the account in AD without changing the password stored here, your application will stop working. The passwords are not synchronized.

All that is left to do is to add the MyWebApp service account to the gShared group that is already configured to have read access, and our site is ready to go. Since the gShared group already contains Steve and Greg, this is a simple way of ensuring that all the parties involved have read access (see Figure 2.29).

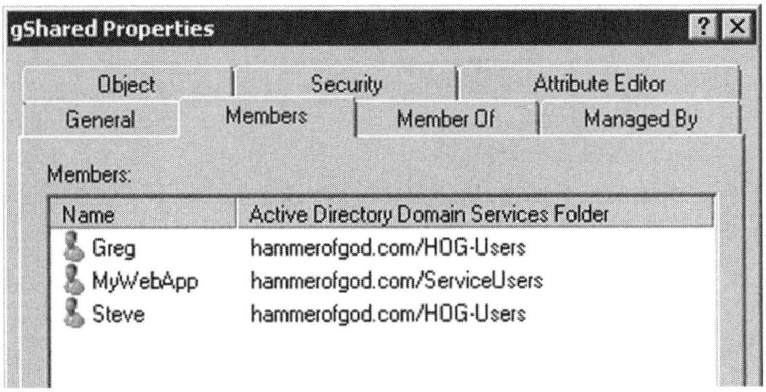

■ **FIGURE 2.29** Updated gShared Group Containing the Users and Service Account That Must Access the Remote Server Users Share

Note that this example access policy will still give Steve and Greg access to each other's files, but we know how to change permissions to accommodate access requirements as shown in Figures 2.12 through 2.14.

It is important that we have a web application that is configured to allow for easy access to virtual directories on other servers within the context of a user account that is very limited in authorization scope. This is a Good Thing. Since existing share structures will already have access permissions in place that meet your needs, these shares can be extended to external users for remote read access by simply including the MyWebApp user, the gShared group, or the equivalent group in read access. We may now consider our milestone reached as outlined in Figure 2.11. Yippee!

However, as is typically the case in IT security, the extension of functionality often inherits an expanded scope of risk. And this case is no different. We no longer have a user context limited to local-server-only file access where granted. We now have a web application using a domain account that, by design, can read files and folders on other servers (again, where granted). Sure, the localized IIS APPPOOL\DefaultAppPool could also reach network shared where EVERYONE or authenticated users are granted access if the web server is a domain member, but this is an actual domain user. Does that make this a poor solution? Not at all. If you want a web application to have access to virtual directories on other servers, then it has to be able to read the data. In configuring this solution, we have performed our due diligence in design and deployed the account while considering the concept of least privilege.

SECURITY IN DEPTH

We should look at another postulate of IT security: *security in depth*. In its simplest form, security in depth is simply a serialized approach to building defenses so that if one particular defense fails, another mechanism is there to impede the progress of an attacker. Bank security controls are a good example of security in depth. There are locked doors, cameras, and guards. The guards are armed. There is a safe on a timer and limited access to its contents. The tellers have limited cash on hand and ink bombs. And of course the tellers are armed with utterly crappy attitudes which should make thieves not even want to bother in the first place.

There is another fundamental aspect of bank security: It never costs more than the value of the safe's contents. If it does, then someone is not doing their job.

In that respect, our jobs are the same. Before we set out to secure something, we need to have insight into the value of what we are securing. The data must be quantified before controls can be qualified. Security professionals who not only command technology, but who can also embrace the total cost of ownership of their systems and procedures are very valuable assets to a company. As such, utilizing existing technologies and features is a key to your success, and that is what I like to talk about in this book.

Leveraging EFS

This now seems like a perfect time to introduce EFS into our model. The configurations can become complex at this point, so it is critical to understand the ramifications of each particular feature configuration. As we did with our first milestone, we will continue to take iterative steps toward our final goal, and not only will we continue to support secure remote access to files over HTTP, but we will roll out a feature that will allow our users to have full read and write access to their files right in Windows Explorer from anywhere they want, all over HTTP, and all in a secure manner. I believe you will find it to be quite cool.

We left Greg and Steve with the ability to access their internal files externally should they need a secure mechanism to retrieve files. It is hardly a dazzling feature, but at least we have started the application off the right way. We are again in a situation where configuring a real-world implementation that does not require a tremendous amount of administration has introduced some concerns. Greg and Steve obviously need read-write access to their shares, so we gave the gShared group read-write access. Not only did this give them both access to each other's files (which is quite common in businesses), but since the MyWebApp user is part of that group, it also has read-write access.

This presents us with an interesting decision to make regarding administration. It is far easier to have a users directory where we set group permissions to, but that does not conform to least privilege standards. There really is not a right or wrong way—just a way that gives you the most benefit at the least cost. Even if we carved out each user's permissions per directory and limited the MyWebApp user to read only, that user still has read rights to all the files by operational requirement. One might think that you can drill down to the MyWebApp user and limit the rights to list folder contents only, but that gets tricky quickly. The application pool needs full read access to any directory with a web.config file, and if it ever hits a web.config that it cannot read, or any other file that it actually has to read the contents of, your app will immediately throw a server error exception. That being said, you can actually manually set the rights to list folder contents only for the user on directories that only need the files listed, which is the case for directory browsing. In production though, you will most likely have to live with read permissions.

EFS and the Service User

This becomes a real-world threat when an error in a web application or some other vulnerability allows an attacker to execute functions in the context of the web application. If an attacker found such a security hole, then he would be able to read whatever files the MyWebApp user had access to. This is why it is important to properly configure the permissions of service users: The scope *should* be limited to explicit assignment of permissions. Regardless, the users directory would be open for read access and that could be dangerous. So we are going to explore another route.

If we leverage EFS properly, we can enforce transparent encryption of all user files per user. When this is done, no matter who has access permissions to the files themselves, they will never be able to view their contents unless they have the private key certificate, which the MyWebApp user will not be able to get. The application of this goes far beyond simple web access to files. This can be deployed in any number of environments. As it relates to our example, the application pool will be able to fully perform its required function, but all encrypted files will be completely secured from it. The added benefit of this is a direct administration benefit because we can leave top level users directory permissions set to read-write at the gShared group level, but still protect all user files from information disclosure to the MyWebApp user as well as all other users—and that is sweet.

Setting up EFS on the Share

When deploying EFS strategies, one of the first things I have found helpful to understand is exactly where data gets encrypted. By that I mean, which physical asset is applying the cipher algorithm during the encryption process. It may be a bit counterintuitive, but when files are encrypted with EFS locally and within file shares, they are encrypted by the target system. If you encrypt a file on a local hard drive, your system is the target system, so it performs the encryption. However, if you encrypt a file on a share or, more appropriately, if you create a file or copy a file into an encrypted folder on a share, then the file is actually encrypted and decrypted by the remote server. It may seem odd that with something so personal as user-based encryption the target server does the encryption for shares, but that is the way it works. When I say personal I mean a process where a particular user's EFS certificate must be used to encrypt and decrypt data, but where that processing happens on a machine other than the one the user is logged into. Again, this specifically applies to remote Server Message Block (SMB) shares, and with that come some design and security considerations.

> **NOTE**
> Certificates are required to use EFS. A public key is used to encrypt data, and the associated private key is used to decrypt it. I will refer to actions that require a file to be encrypted or decrypted as a *crypto order*, except where I want to specifically note encryption or decryption.

Encryption and Decryption

When a client requests that a file be encrypted, the encrypting system looks for an appropriate certificate to encrypt the data for that user. If it has a valid certificate (cert) somewhere in its certificate store, then that cert is used. If not, one is created for the user and stored. I will be speaking in terms of domain operations where certificate services have been installed, but in the absence of a proper Public Key Infrastructure (PKI) ad hoc certificates will be created for you. If you do not leverage your own certificate services, then key distribution and creation can become an arduous process. Certificate Services are included as a role in Windows Server, so this should not be an issue for you. When a client requests decryption of a file, the process is a bit different. The system serving the crypto order will look for a private key certificate to decrypt the file. If it cannot find one, the decryption fails.

If you think about that for a moment, an interesting challenge may come to mind. You might be thinking, "OK, the files get encrypted with my public key, and that makes sense because the public key can be sent anywhere, but if the remote server performs the crypto order, and I own the private certificate to decrypt it, how does the remote server get the private key to do that?" Congratulations if that is indeed what you were thinking. You have won a cookie! Feel free to go get it, and the rest of us will just wait here. Do not worry if you did not consider that. It is something you would have discovered anyway, so we will approach this in the same way I first did, which was to learn it the hard way.

Thinking back to our users share, we have folders and files for Greg and Steve already in place. If I interactively log on to the server hosting the share, I can certainly go to each users' directory and mark it for encryption. However, if I do that, the files will become encrypted with the administrator account (or whatever account I used that has the proper permissions to do so), and that will not work all that well. I cannot create a new directory, mark it for encryption, and copy the user files into it, because they would then also become encrypted with the administrator account.

The first thing you might try is to simply have the user go to the share, and encrypt their folder themselves, but Figure 2.30 shows what happens when Steve tries that.

In this case, we get a nice friendly message telling us that the server hosting the share must be trusted for delegation. This message may be different depending on the version of your client.

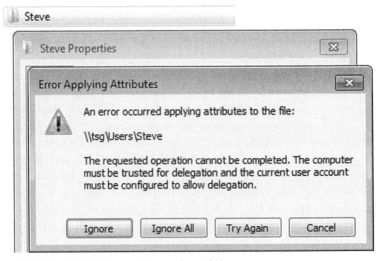

■ **FIGURE 2.30** EFS Fails Applying Attributes to Remote Folder

The reason we get this error is the basis of the answer for the cookie prize. When Steve asks to encrypt the folder on the share, the remote server gets the crypto order. It tries to encrypt the file, but finds that there is not a key anywhere for it to use. If Steve was on his own computer and encrypting something for the first time (as we are in this case on the remote server), then he would request a cert, and the CA would give it to him. While Steve is indeed logged on as Steve on his computer, he is only remotely connected to the share based on authorization. Steve asks the remote server to encrypt the file for him as if it were him, but when the remote server attempts to get an EFS cert on Steve's behalf, the operation fails because the server is not trusted to do so. When Steve asks for a cert himself, the CA knows it is Steve because Steve authenticated himself when he did so, but when the remote server goes to the CA and requests on Steve's behalf, the CA denies it because it does not trust the remote server.

Delegation

What has to happen here is that the remote server has to be specifically configured as a trusted entity to act on Steve's behalf, kind of like a power of attorney that allows someone to act on your behalf as if they were you. The process of configuring a server to be a trusted entity in order to act on behalf of other users is called *delegation*.

The server you want to trust, in this case the one hosting the users share, is the delegate. The delegate is trusted to act on behalf of users to services on other systems. In this case, the remote server has to be able to get an EFS certificate on behalf of a user, and use that certificate to encrypt files.

Establishing delegation is fairly straightforward. You retrieve the properties for the computer you want to make a delegate, and select the **Delegation** tab, as shown in Figure 2.31.

That is the simplest way to do it. Set the server for delegation, and off you go. Now if Steve were to navigate to his folder on the users share and set it for encryption, it would work. The crypto order is placed, the remote server requests a certificate on behalf of Steve, gets it, and then encrypts the files for Steve. Presto.

Delegation and Certificates

If Steve were to open up his Certificates MMC and look for the EFS cert on his system, he would not find it because he did not ask for it. The remote server did, and the certificate lives there. If Steve got a cert, it would be in his personal certificates. When the remote server requested a certificate on Steve's

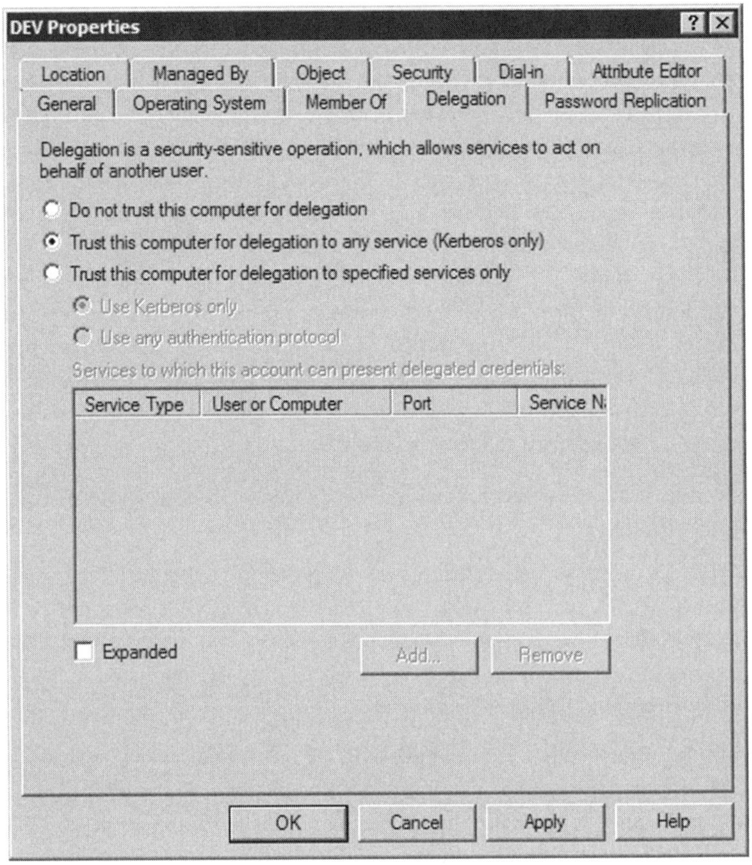

■ FIGURE 2.31 Configuring DEV as a Delegate to Any Service

behalf, that certificate was generated and returned back to the system. The remote system is not Steve (or logged in as Steve), so it needs to be able to always get to the certificate to encrypt data for Steve. This is in the *Other People* certificate store for the local machine. The private key required to decrypt the files when requested lives in protected storage on the server.

If you go to the remote server and check out the certificates for the local computer, you will find the cert that was created in Other People, as shown in Figure 2.32.

If we pull up the details of a file Steve remotely encrypted in the users share, we see the confirmation message in Figure 2.33.

From now on, anytime Steve wants to access the encrypted file on his share, it will be automatically decrypted when he requests it, and automatically

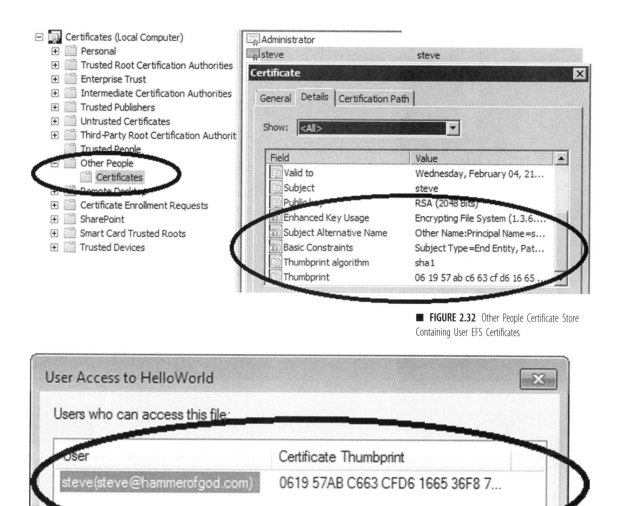

■ **FIGURE** 2.32 Other People Certificate Store Containing User EFS Certificates

■ **FIGURE** 2.33 Confirmation of Certificate Thumbprint on EFS File Matching EFS Cert on Server

encrypted when he saves it. Nice, eh? In fact, since the cert is now on the server, delegation is no longer required to perform crypto orders. It would be required for new user requests where certificates did not exist, but once the certificate is on the server, you are good to go.

Delegation Authentication in Action

Auto-encryption of user files is now set up on the internal share for users. As you will remember, this share is also a virtual directory accessible via our website. What is cool about it is that since we configured our web virtual directory to use pass-through authentication under the application pool user context of our MyWebApp user, the user context is passed through to the remote share via the virtual directory when users log on to the website to access files. This means that when Steve logs on via the web interface and selects his file, the web app will pass the authentication request on the remote server through the virtual directory where the request will be parsed as Steve's. The remote server will then identify the crypto order, search for an appropriate certificate for Steve, find it in the Other People store, decrypt the requested file, and pass the decrypted data to the web server all transparently.

Even though Steve is logging on to web access remotely, on any system, when he goes to pull up the HelloWorld.txt file he previously encrypted, the decrypted version is given, as shown in Figure 2.34.

Note that the textual contents of the file were displayed since the web server parses .txt files as content files in the same way it would server-side HTML files; other files would generate a download dialog box. So if the web server was somehow compromised, even if an attacker took full control over the MyWebApp user, they could not get the contents of the users' files. Even if the attacker gained administrative control of the web server, they could not get to the users' files. Yet the users enjoy seamless access to their files in a very secure way.

You can actually use this type of access control to provide dual-factor authentication for specific files via the web browser when you want to protect them from your normal user account. I do this by creating another special use user specifically for encryption. The user does not have to be part of a group or given any other rights. This user encrypts the file that I want to encrypt within my normal directory structure. When I navigate to that file and request it, I am prompted for a set of credentials to open the file since my user context cannot access it. I simply use my encryption user to gain access

■ **FIGURE 2.34** Web Access to Encrypted HelloWorld.txt File Stored on Remote Users Share via Web Virtual Directory

to the file. It gives me an extra layer of protection should my user account become compromised.

Delegation and Data in Motion

Regarding access and crypto orders, it is important to understand that when a client saves a file in an encrypted share, the cleartext data is sent to the server over SMB, and it is encrypted on the server. The same is true for decryption—when you request a file, the server will decrypt it, and send you the cleartext data back over SMB. This is also true for the remote web call—when the web server passes the request down the virtual directory pipe, the remote server will decrypt the file (for example, HelloWorld.txt) and send the decrypted bits back to the web server where it is displayed to the user. Even if the user is viewing the file over HTTPS, the remote-server-to-web-server communication via virtual directory is sent in the clear. You should know this.

Similar to the SplinterCell.txt example, the retrieved file looks like Figure 2.35 over the wire even though it is encrypted on the users share.

Again, when the data is being transmitted via shares or via the virtual directory web access, it is decrypted first. EFS is only providing security of access and encryption at rest.

The Dangers of Delegation

Delegation can be dangerous. Just as when you give power of attorney to someone, you have got to explicitly trust that person in every way. They could get married, commit crimes, confess to others, quit jobs, and so forth, all in your name. Giving anyone blanket power to act on your behalf is something you should not do trivially. The same goes for trusting a computer for delegation. In the configuration in Figure 2.31, **Trust this computer for delegation to any service (Kerberos only)** is selected. This is equivalent to power of attorney because now this computer could authenticate to any other service on any other server on your behalf when you make a request to it. You may only intend for it to ask for a certificate on your behalf, but if someone owned that box, they could redirect that request to wherever they wanted on your behalf.

Consider this scenario: We have got the users directory on the remote server, which is trusted for delegation in order to allow remote EFS generation by clients. Suppose there is also a simple website running on that system that allows users to do something mundane, like a daily company quote, and it is running under the default application pool context. Now think about what could be done if an attacker, or even a malicious internal user, gained access

Hex Details																
⌞⌝ Decode As ‖ ☰ Width ▾														Prot Off: 20 (0x14)		

```
0100  20 20 20 0D 0A 20 20 20 20 20 20 20 20 20 20 20   ..
0110  20 20 20 20 4D 20 20 20 0D 0A 0D 0A 0D 0A 0D 0A       M   ........
0120  2A 2A 4F 72 69 67 69 6E 61 6C 20 61 72 74 20 62   **Original art b
0130  79 20 57 75 6C 66 3B 20 4D 6F 64 69 66 69 65 64   y Wulf; Modified
0140  20 62 79 20 6D 65 0D 0A 0D 0A 0D 0A 2A 2A 2A 2A    by me......****
0150  2A 2A 2A 2A 2A 2A 2A 2A 2A 2A 2A 2A 2A 2A 2A 2A   ****************
0160  2A 2A 2A 0D 0A 0D 0A 0D 0A 20 20 20 20 20 49 4E   ***......      IN
0170  54 52 4F 44 55 43 54 49 4F 4E 0D 0A 0D 0A 0D 0A   TRODUCTION......
0180  2A 2A 2A 2A 2A 2A 2A 2A 2A 2A 2A 2A 2A 2A 2A 2A   ****************
0190  2A 2A 2A 2A 2A 2A 2A 0D 0A 0D 0A 0D 0A 54 68 61   *******......Tha
01A0  6E 6B 73 20 66 6F 72 20 63 6C 69 63 6B 69 6E 67   nks for clicking
01B0  20 74 68 65 20 46 41 51 2E 20 57 65 6C 63 6F 6D    the FAQ. Welcom
01C0  65 20 62 61 63 6B 20 74 6F 20 74 68 65 20 49 6E   e back to the In
01D0  74 65 72 6E 61 74 69 6F 6E 61 6C 20 53 75 70 65   ternational Supe
01E0  72 20 0D 0A 53 70 79 20 53 70 65 63 74 72 75 6D   r ..Spy Spectrum
01F0  2E 20 49 20 77 69 6C 6C 20 65 78 70 6C 61 69 6E   . I will explain
0200  20 68 6F 77 20 74 6F 20 61 63 68 69 65 76 65 20    how to achieve
0210  31 30 30 25 20 43 6F 6D 70 6C 65 74 69 6F 6E 20   100% Completion
0220  66 6F 72 20 61 6C 6C 20 0D 0A 4C 65 76 65 6C 73   for all ..Levels
0230  20 6F 66 20 53 43 3A 43 54 20 57 49 54 48 4F 55    of SC:CT WITHOU
0240  54 20 6B 69 6C 6C 69 6E 67 20 61 6E 79 20 65 6E   T killing any en
0250  65 6D 79 20 73 65 6E 74 72 69 65 73 20 66 6F 72   emy sentries for
0260  20 53 4F 4C 4F 20 4D 4F 44 45 2E 0D 0A 0D 0A 49    SOLO MODE.....I
0270  20 77 69 6C 6C 20 70 72 65 73 65 6E 74 20 79 6F    will present yo
0280  75 20 77 69 74 68 20 45 56 45 52 59 20 61 6C 74   u with EVERY alt
```

■ **FIGURE 2.35** Network Capture of EFS File Being Retrieved from Storage

to that server. He could, by design, redirect requests made by users to any other service. The *Windows Impersonation Context* class specifically provides this functionality. The following .NET code is a simple example of redirecting an authenticated request (any request at all) to another function under impersonation.

```
protected void Shiny(object sender, EventArgs e)
{

string host = Request.ServerVariables["REMOTE_HOST"];
string adhost = "WinNT://" + host + ",computer";
System.Security.Principal.WindowsImpersonationContext
--impersonationContext;
impersonationContext = ((System.Security.Principal.
--WindowsIdentity)User.Identity).Impersonate();


Response.Write(System.Security.Principal.WindowsIden
--tity.GetCurrent().Name + "<br/>");
```

```
try
{
DirectoryEntry AD = new DirectoryEntry(adhost);
DirectoryEntry grp = AD.Children.Find("Administrators", "group");
String userPath = String.Format("WinNT://{0}/{1},user", "hammerofgod","haxx0r");

if (grp != null) { grp.Invoke("Add", new object[] { userPath }); }

}
catch (Exception ex)
{
Response.Write(ex.Message);
}
impersonationContext.Undo();
}
```

■ **CODE 4.1** Impersonation code redirecting authenticated requests

This code would take any connection made to the web server and use the security context of that connection to launch another distinct process. If the site is set for integrated authentication (most internal sites are) then this would be silent. The attacker could alter the quote-of-the-day code to include this, or a totally separate link could be distributed that simply pulled up a photo. Then each time a connection was made, the system would attempt to add the haxx0r user to the administrators group. Anyone with high privileges who visited the site would execute this code. It is for this reason that default high-privileged accounts like the domain administrator cannot be delegated by default. More than likely you would see code that pulled up payroll information, but any initiated connection could be made to do anything the attacker wanted. Calls from the system would be authorized to execute on behalf of the users since the system is trusted for delegation.

None of this represents any sort of vulnerability or security hole in itself and this functionality does not represent a design flaw; impersonation is a required function in a volume of applications. It simply represents the need to ensure that controls set on a server that is trusted for delegations are properly designed with this risk in mind.

This is also why you see so many security people recommending against mixing roles on a domain controller. If an attacker could alter code on a web service, SQL service, or any other service on a domain controller, then they could automatically perform impersonation. You do not have to delegate a domain controller since it is already the authoritative authentication controller. For instance, if you created a share on a domain controller for

EFS usage as we did for the users directory, you would not have to delegate the server to support remote encryption of files. It would just immediately work. Attackers would not have to dump AD accounts or try to crack NT LAN Manager (NTLM) authentication of any of that—they would just redirect requests.

Limiting Delegation

With this in mind, let us revisit the delegation configuration of the DEV host where we allowed delegation to any service. This is good timing because I was actually starting to get a little freaked out for having to leave it like that until we got to this point.

The rules of least privilege dictate that we only provide delegation rights to the specific servers required, and only to the specific services on those servers needed to perform the necessary functions. As such, in order for EFS to work on remote shares, our remote server needs to delegate to Common Internet File System (CIFS) and LDAP services on a controller, as well as to act on behalf of a user for protected storage requests. We will now limit, or constrain, delegation of requests from DEV to reflect this, as shown in Figure 2.36.

Make no mistake, even with constrained delegation you still need to ensure that access to the server is very carefully controlled and that additional roles supported by the server are deployed with this in mind.

Checkpoint

We are almost there! So, time for a little review. We have got a share on a remote server where user files are automatically and transparently encrypted with EFS supported by constrained Kerberos delegation. We then have a web application running an application pool in the context of a low-privileged user with pass-through authentication to the users share by way of a virtual directory. Files on the users directory are protected from other users and the application pool users, even though a single group is used to manage overall access rights to the directory. Thus, we have security and manageability. A win–win.

SECURING ACCESS WITH WebDAV

We are now poised to execute our final iterative step to finish the configuration and hit pay dirt. Up until this point, Steve and Greg have had full access to files via a share internally where data is encrypted automatically, and read access to those files has been extended to them over the web should they

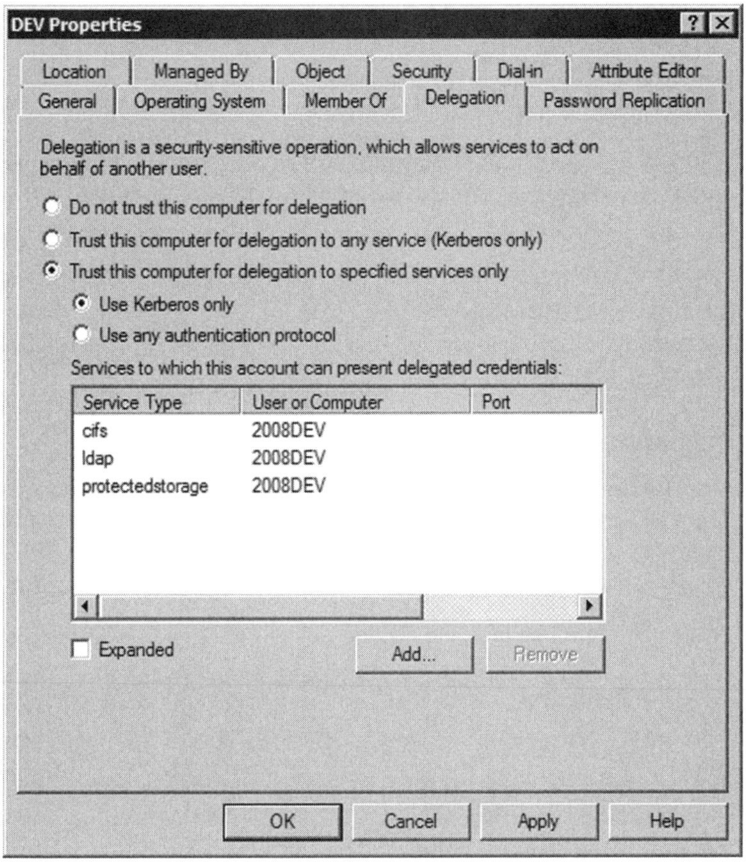

■ **FIGURE 2.36** Constrained Kerberos Delegation to the Required Services on the Required Server

ever need to grab a file. And while read access to files in a secure method from anywhere is a nice feature, it really does not quite serve our overall needs. Having to log on to the web server to get these files is a little bit complicated for our users. What would be great is if we could use the web interface to actually map drive letters to our share from wherever we wanted to while still taking advantage of transparent encryption. What would be even better is if we could do that in a way so that we do not have to delegate authentication. That would be perfect. Now it is time for the big chapter finale.

Installing WebDAV

With just a few more steps, we can extend the configuration of our solution to include the functionality of full SMB-like access using only HTTP. We will do this using the WebDAV protocol. We have done a lot of really good work setting up our web application and internal EFS structure, so we shall keep it the way we have it. We will just enable WebDAV authoring on this particular site, and with all the architecture work already done, this will be surprisingly simple.

WebDAV is a service included with the Web Server Role, and it can be installed by adding a role service from the Server Manager Web Server Role MMC, as shown in Figure 2.37.

WebDAV is enabled at the site level, not the content level. However, you can fully restrict what content different users have access to via **Authoring Rules** where you can configure different levels of access for different groups to different content.

Configuring WebDAV

The easiest way to enable WebDAV is to simply have an authoring rule where all users have access to all content, and where read, write, and source access are given. We embrace least privilege though, so after we enable WebDAV on our site we will create the authoring rule shown in Figure 2.38.

This authoring rule allows the members of our gShared group to access all content with read and write permissions. If we only wanted users to be able to access a class of file, like documents and spreadsheets, we could limit those by noting the acceptable file types in the **Specify Content** option.

Read and write access should be enough for you, unless you actually need your users to be able to run EXE files remotely. It is fine if you do, but do not specify it if you do not need to.

■ **FIGURE 2.37** Installing the WebDAV Publishing Service on Your Web Server Role

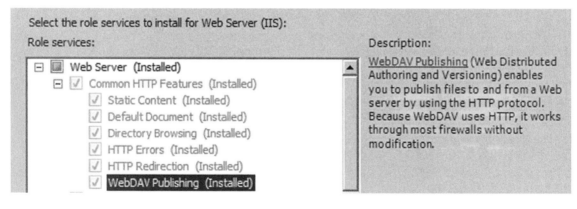

Select the role services to install for Web Server (IIS):

Role services:

Description:

- ⊟ ▣ Web Server (Installed)
  - ⊟ ☑ Common HTTP Features (Installed)
    - ☑ Static Content (Installed)
    - ☑ Default Document (Installed)
    - ☑ Directory Browsing (Installed)
    - ☑ HTTP Errors (Installed)
    - ☑ HTTP Redirection (Installed)
    - ☑ WebDAV Publishing (Installed)

WebDAV Publishing (Web Distributed Authoring and Versioning) enables you to publish files to and from a Web server by using the HTTP protocol. Because WebDAV uses HTTP, it works through most firewalls without modification.

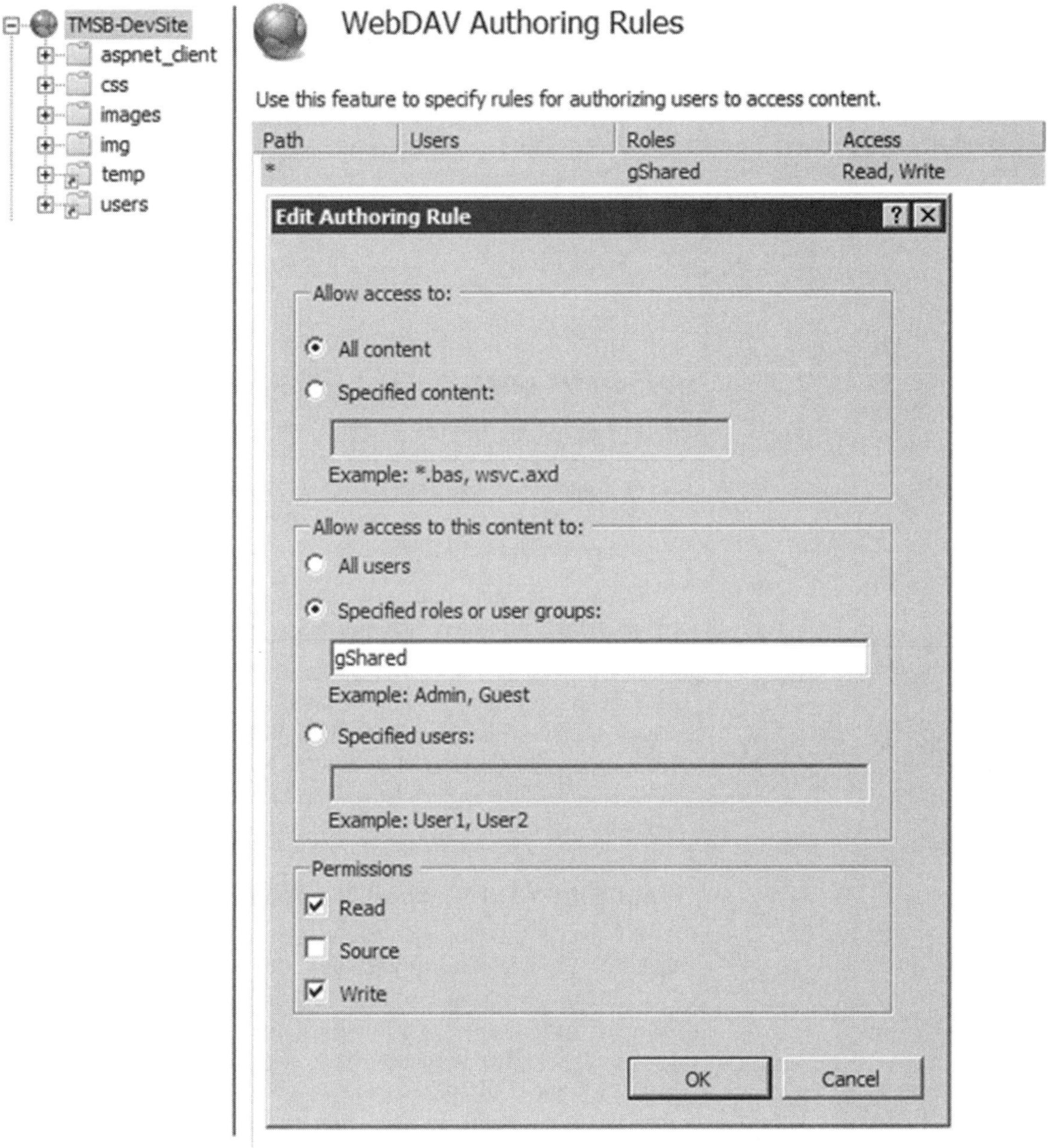

TMSB-DevSite
- aspnet_client
- css
- images
- img
- temp
- users

WebDAV Authoring Rules

Use this feature to specify rules for authorizing users to access content.

Path	Users	Roles	Access
*		gShared	Read, Write

Edit Authoring Rule ? ✕

Allow access to:

- ⦿ All content
- ○ Specified content:

  [   ]

  Example: *.bas, wsvc.axd

Allow access to this content to:

- ○ All users
- ⦿ Specified roles or user groups:

  [gShared   ]

  Example: Admin, Guest
- ○ Specified users:

  [   ]

  Example: User1, User2

Permissions

- ☑ Read
- ☐ Source
- ☑ Write

[OK] [Cancel]

■ **FIGURE 2.38** WebDAV Authoring Rule

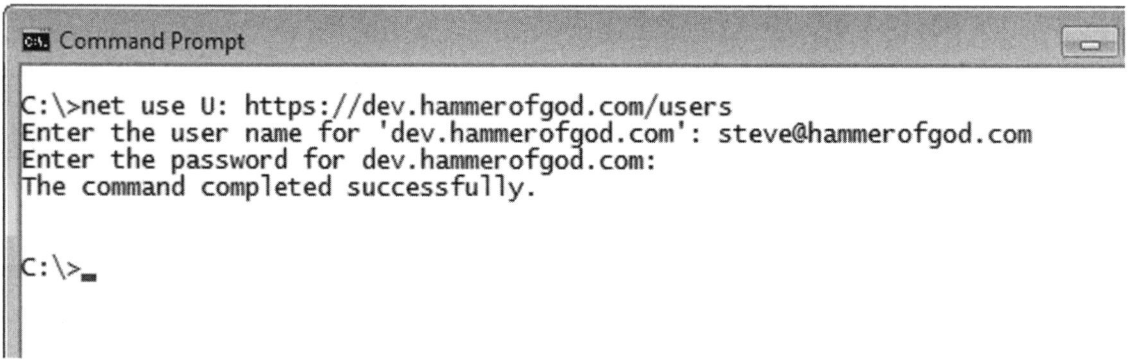

```
Command Prompt                                                    ─

C:\>net use U: https://dev.hammerofgod.com/users
Enter the user name for 'dev.hammerofgod.com': steve@hammerofgod.com
Enter the password for dev.hammerofgod.com:
The command completed successfully.


C:\>_
```

■ **FIGURE 2.39** Successful Net Use of U: Drive to WebDAV Share over HTTPS

Remote WebDAV Drive Mapping Goodness

Once this has been properly configured, you will have the capability of remotely mapping a drive letter to your published users directory in the context of an appropriate user directly over HTTPS. If you are in a coffee shop somewhere and want access to your files, then a simple *net use* command is all you need, as shown in Figure 2.39.

With this drive letter mapped, you can simply access your files as you would any other drive, no matter where you are, as shown in Figure 2.40.

We have hit pay dirt. You can configure direct file access in programs or do anything else you could do with a mapped drive. In addition, WebDAV-aware applications can make use of specific WebDAV functionality like file locking and synchronization. For instance, Microsoft Word is WebDAV aware, and you will notice that file save operations change to reflect connections with web folders.

WebDAV and EFS—Look Ma, No Delegation

There is more to this than just a fantastic remote access experience. I have used HTTPS for the connection, and that is the preferred way of doing this from a security standpoint. If you use HTTPS, the local WebDAV redirector will allow connections with Basic or Windows Authentication. Conversely, if you must use HTTP to connect, by default the redirector will not allow Basic Authentication for security reasons. In addition to these features, when we deploy web folders in this manner, we no longer have the delegation requirement as we did with SMB share access. The WebDAV redirector allows for complete server-side encryption at rest, as well as for EFS encryption in transit. This happens outside of any HTTPS connection and it is completely managed by the WebDAV server and client redirector. It is an incredibly powerful feature and adds an unparalleled level of security.

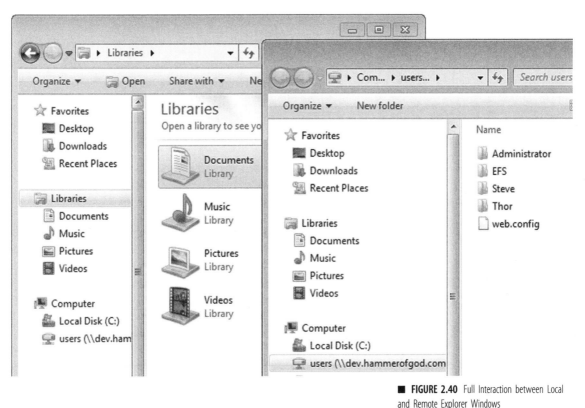

■ **FIGURE 2.40** Full Interaction between Local and Remote Explorer Windows

Even if there was HTTPS-to-HTTP redirection somewhere for, say, an intrusion detection system, the data files themselves would stay encrypted by WebDAV.

WebDAV and EFS—Data in Motion

Figure 2.41 shows a packet capture of a client accessing one of their Word document EFS files over HTTP in a WebDAV folder.

That, my friends, is about as cool as you can get. Before the WebDAV server sends the data back to the client, the server and client negotiate an encrypted session between themselves. The WebDAV server will decrypt the EFS file into cleartext and this text is then re-encrypted based on this negotiation. This would be a perfect solution for allowing onetime client access to required files in a secure manner or for remote projects where people require access. Having the ability to copy and paste, or just load files remotely, work on them, and save them back to an encrypted share is awesome.

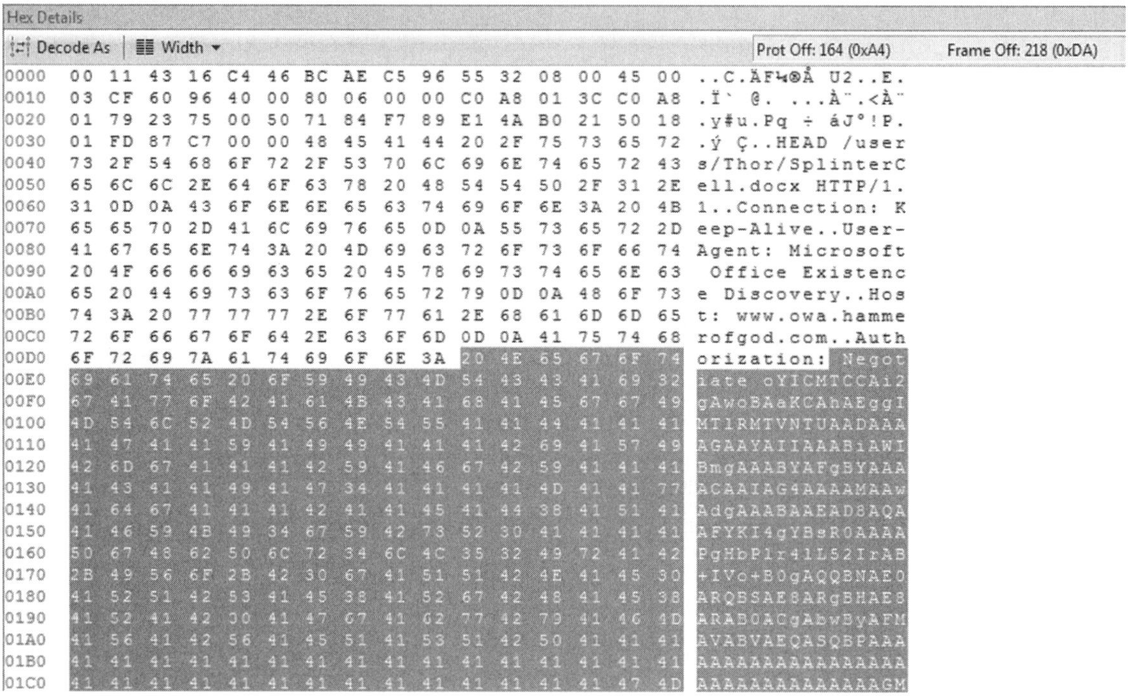

FIGURE 2.41 Network Capture of a Client-Server Negotiated Encrypted File over HTTP via WebDAV

CONCLUSION

So that about does it. There is one quick thing you should know though. In regard to remote file access over WebDAV and encryption, the files that the web server is configured to handle will be copied over, but they will not be encrypted in transit. In other words, you noticed earlier that when I accessed a text file via the directory index, it did not ask me to download it, but rather it rendered the text file in my browser. This is because the web server reads TXT files as content files it should publish via HTTP, as opposed to something like a DAT file that it would prompt the user to download. Like I said, the files will still be transferred over, but the automatic encryption in transit will not take place. We shall now look at our SplinterCell.txt file again, rather than a DOCX file, and see what happens (Figure 2.42).

Again, this is why if you just pipe everything through HTTPS, you have nothing to worry about. That is the skinny on authentication, authorization, and encryption.

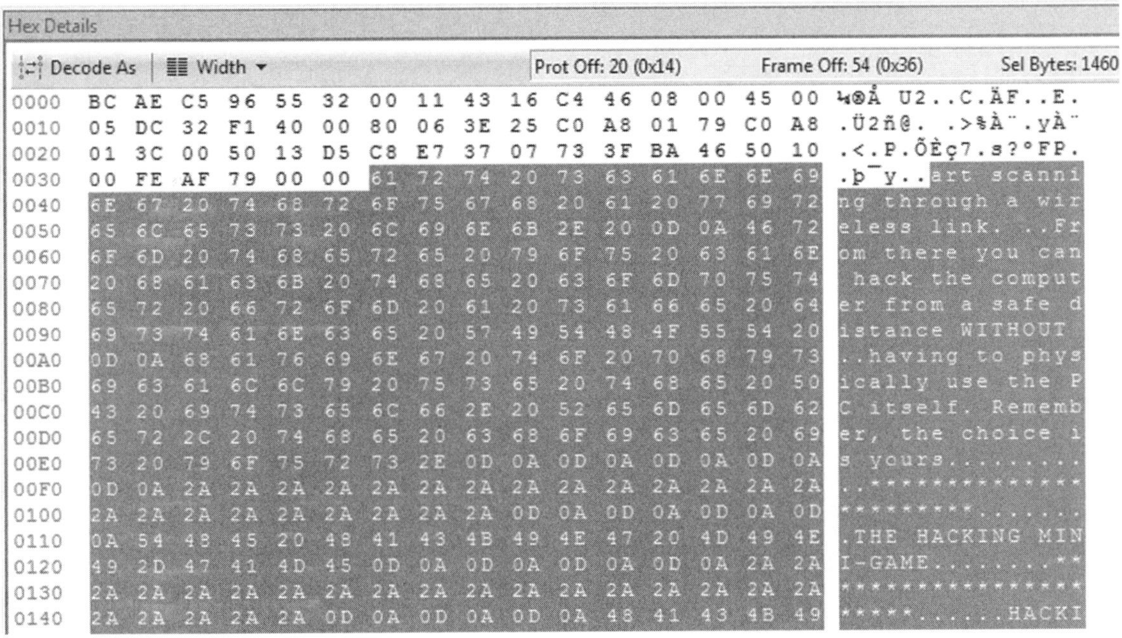

■ **FIGURE 2.42** Example of Web Content File Being Transferred in Clear via WebDAV over HTTP

■ SUMMARY

In this chapter, we explored many examples of least privilege and security in depth. We outlined low-privileged uses in application pools, limited permissions on network-based virtual directories, securing access with EFS, how to properly deploy EFS, and the considerations you need to take into account when doing so. We covered Kerberos constrained delegation, and finally, we outlined how to provide secure access to remote drive letter maps while using EFS to ensure that data is encrypted at rest as well as in transit.

Analyzing and Blocking Malicious Traffic Based on Geolocation

INFORMATION IN THIS CHAPTER:

- Research and Due Diligence
- Implementing a Solution
- Integrating with TMG

PRODUCTS, TOOLS, AND METHODS:

- MS SQL Server
- TMG
- Visual Studio (C#/Visual Basic for Applications)
- TMG Logging to SQL Server
- SQL CLR
- TMG Deny Rules

INTRODUCTION

Years back, while working on a research project involving SQL Slammer and the persistence of vulnerable installations around the globe, I started paying particular attention to the trending of attacks originating from and associated with vulnerabilities within different countries. In this particular case, China headed the list with the most attacks originating within its borders. This piqued my interest not only in quantifying attacks targeted at age-old vulnerabilities, but also in looking further into instances where an individual country was more exposed than others, and where more attacks were sourced for any particular vulnerability.

Further research increased my interest and prompted the writing of an article[1] where I floated the concept of designing security controls around the actual source of the attacks rather than the vector that an attack was trying to leverage. I have published different aspects of this overall approach around the Internet in the past few years, and have continued to focus on how applicable this control would be in a production network, mostly by way of collecting as much data as I could and analyzing it in different ways as the opportunities presented themselves. As such, I have included some of that new data here along with some interesting code and tools to freshen up the project and present it here.

> **NOTE**
>
> This is where my obligatory disclaimer comes in. The aforementioned article prompted its share of contemptuous and critical e-mails where people thought I had some position about China specifically. I do not. I do not care if the traffic is coming from Disneyland. If it is attacking my network, I am going to block it. As such, nothing in the following chapter is motivated by any political, religious, racial, or other ideal or prejudice. Processes discussed and opinions reached are based on technical and statistical research. No other bias is intended nor should be inferred.

RESEARCH AND DUE DILIGENCE

When you are considering the implementation of a security control, having a basis of research from which to make decisions is extremely important, if not critical. Of course, what a basis consists of is up to you. Personally, my mind was made up from the initial results of my Slammer traffic captures. I saw that China sourced a level of malicious traffic that I did not have any production reasons to process, so I blocked the entire country. However, it would have been irresponsible of me to move forward without performing due diligence in research and data collection. Based on the analysis of many different attacks, vulnerabilities, and overall junk traffic, this decision has turned out to be valuable to me. Even with substantial data to support the quantification of traffic from China and other countries of interest, I felt like I had to better qualify the statistics by getting data from sources where actual attack information was being compiled. In other words, just knowing how much traffic was coming from countries I was concerned with was not enough; I wanted to know what the content of the traffic itself was, and what current trend of threat those attacks represented. After some conversations with other colleagues in the industry, I was fortunate enough to get in touch

---

[1]www.symantec.com/connect/articles/blocking-traffic-country-production-networks

with some nice folks with the Honeynet Project, a leading international security research organization, who provided me with data for April of 2009 of attacks against a honeypot in Hawaii. There were almost 13,000 attacks categorized by type, such as mass mailing worms, attacks against P2P networks, protocol anomalies, and Denial of Service (DoS) attacks. They were also rated by severity and impact. Low-severity and impact attacks were numerous and interesting, but I wanted to focus on the high-severity attacks which were likely to succeed based on Honeynet's rating. I further limited the attacks to DoS attacks to level the playing field against OS types, patch levels, and so on. I ended up with 2,527 high-risk/success attacks that I subsequently broke down by country of source, as shown in Figure 3.1.

I found the results compelling. They are ranked highest to lowest and read left to right, so the USA is first, China is second, Japan is third, and so on. Almost 30 percent of the attacks were sourced from China, with over 50 percent coming from countries that I might very well be able to block. I have to say that I did feel a bit sorry for France, who could only muster a single successful attack, but I will leave any further significance of that statistic for you to infer.

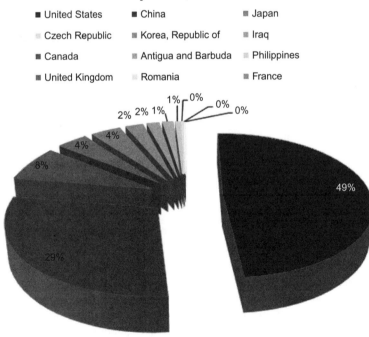

"Likely Successful" Attacks

- United States   - China   - Japan
- Czech Republic   - Korea, Republic of   - Iraq
- Canada   - Antigua and Barbuda   - Philippines
- United Kingdom   - Romania   - France

2527 High-Risk Attacks, Hawaii Honeynet, April 2009

■ **FIGURE 3.1** Likely Successful High-Risk Attacks by Country (Ratings by Honeynet)

Research Findings

This is the type of data that allows you to make intelligent decisions about controls that can be put around traffic. A control illustrates direct value when 30 percent of malicious traffic, traffic actually qualified as a would-be successful attack, can be significantly reduced just by geographically filtering traffic at your border.

In June of 2008, I published a paper on www.SecurityFocus.com providing some initial figures for various standard traffic patterns like HTTP and Simple Mail Transfer Protocol (SMTP) from different countries as well. That research also provided some interesting statistics around sources of SMTP, HTTP, FTP, SSH, and so on. During the preparation of this book, I wanted to be able to work with current data for examples of parsing and manipulating log data, so I initiated a full traffic capture and analysis project on July 19, 2010, which ran uninterrupted until February of 2011. Hammer of God is just a simple little domain I own, but I have had it for over a decade, so I get my fair share of spam just like everyone else. And though I have got various implementations of spam filtering, I wanted to see just how much SMTP traffic I was getting. Figure 3.2 shows the results. I was surprised by this research as well.

There is no business or personal reason for me to get e-mail from the Russian Federation. Yet, in about seven months, I blocked over 1 *billion* SMTP connection attempts to my network. And of the countries listed, I really only need e-mail from a few of them. In total, I blocked over 9 billion SMTP connections alone to my relatively tiny network. Those packets never even made it through to my mail gateway; they were immediately and silently dropped at the border.

In my opinion, this level of research and analysis is more than sufficient to warrant consideration of implementation into production environments where appropriate.

IMPLEMENTING A SOLUTION

Some of you do not have a business model that supports country blocking and some of you do. Irrespective of your disposition, I wanted to outline a process by which you could leverage a few technologies from which to perform data analysis, and to have the ability to take action should you decide to implement this control. It may be in the form of blocking SMTP from a particular set of countries, or web traffic from others, or blacklisting all traffic from any particular source.

So we will now get started.

1/29/2011 2:00:04 AM

SourceCountry	DstPort	Count
Russian Federation	25	1080700
India	25	909634
Brazil	25	572700
Viet Nam	25	539937
Ukraine	25	466390
Indonesia	25	374473
Korea Republic of	25	336197
China	25	319347
France	25	232864
Romania	25	198408
Colombia	25	194663
Argentina	25	189289
Pakistan	25	181994
United States	25	177374
Taiwan; Republic of China (ROC)	25	170022
Italy	25	166182
Spain	25	152217
Kazakhstan	25	145305

■ **FIGURE 3.2** Hammer of God's Top 20 SMTP Sources by Country (Spelling from Original Source)

In simple terms, we want to capture traffic, figure out what country it came from, analyze it to meet our needs, and then form rules to take the appropriate actions we want. In this example, I am using TMG, which already has logging capabilities in place for all aspects of IP traffic we need. The most obvious project dependency we have is a source for country-by-country IP ranges in order to identify the country based on IP. In the beginning, I spent a substantial amount of time aggregating IP source data from several sources until I decided to use a single source of data from WebNet77,[2] but your sources are up to you.

Now we shall get into the tech of how to make this happen. Figure 3.3 illustrates an overall workflow diagram of our process to work from.

Log Traffic

Before we tackle figuring out how to identify the traffic source, we need to ensure that we are logging the raw data in a suitable environment. As I try to do whenever possible, this is a case where we can build upon the logging setup and design already discussed in the book. Please see the first chapter, "Securely Writing Web Proxy Log Data to Structured Query Language (SQL) Server and Programmatically Monitoring Web Traffic Data in Order to Automatically Inject Allow/Deny Rules into Threat Management Gateway (TMG)," for complete instructions on how to get TMG logging in a manner conducive to this project if you have not already.

Figure 3.4 shows WebNet77's comma delimited download.

> **NOTE**
> An IPv4 address[3] is simply a dot notation of octets that represent an integer value from 0 to 4,294,967,295 or 0.0.0.0 to 255.255.255.255, or x00000000 to xFFFFFFFF. Hex dotted notation works as well in the form of FF.FF.FF.FF, which directly converts to 255.255.255.255, which in turn converts to 4,294,967,295 decimal in the form of $256^3.256^2.256^1.256^0$. This is important to know when you begin to work with the logging of IP addresses and the subsequent mapping of an IP address to a record containing a range of IPs as in Figure 3.4.

Data Functions

In human-readable reports, the IP address is typically in dotted notation, while system-based log values and database fields typically work with integers. For instance, in both ISA Server and TMG, IP address records in a monitoring

---

[2]http://software77.net/geo-ip/

[3]www.subnetmask.info/

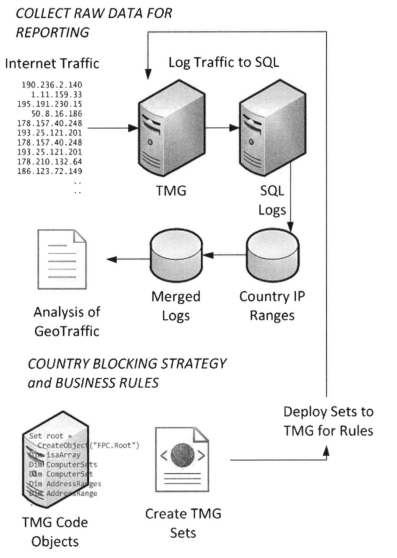

COLLECT RAW DATA FOR
REPORTING

Internet Traffic

```
190.236.2.140
  1.11.159.33
195.191.230.15
  50.8.16.186
178.157.40.248
193.25.121.201
178.157.40.248
193.25.121.201
178.210.132.64
186.123.72.149
     ..
     ..
```

Log Traffic to SQL

TMG

SQL
Logs

Analysis of
GeoTraffic

Merged
Logs

Country IP
Ranges

COUNTRY BLOCKING STRATEGY
and BUSINESS RULES

Deploy Sets to
TMG for Rules

```
Set root =
  CreateObject("FPC.Root")
Dim isaArray
Dim ComputerSets
Dim ComputerSet
Dim AddressRanges
Dim AddressRange
```

TMG Code
Objects

Create TMG
Sets

■ **FIGURE 3.3** Workflow: Log Traffic, Process Source Country, Report, Determine Rule Set Actions, Deploy Computer Sets to TMG, and Create Appropriate Rules

session will be displayed in dot notation even though the address is being stored differently: ISA Server logs store the IP as an integer value while TMG stores it as a *uniqueidentifier* data type. See Figure 3.13 for further information.

You will need dotted notation as you look at reports and later when you programmatically create TMG computer set objects, but you will use integers

BegIP	EndIP	Type	Assigned	Country2	Country3	Country
0	16777215	iana	410227200	ZZ	ZZZ	Reserved
16777216	16777471	apnic	1272931200	AU	AUS	Australia
16843008	16843263	apnic	1264118400	AU	AUS	Australia
16909056	16909311	apnic	1264118400	AU	AUS	Australia
17039360	17039615	apnic	1272931200	AU	AUS	Australia
17367040	17432575	apnic	1276128000	MY	MYS	Malaysia
17435136	17435391	apnic	1272931200	AU	AUS	Australia
17498112	17563647	apnic	1276646400	KR	KOR	Korea Republic of
17563648	17825791	apnic	1273536000	CN	CHN	China
17825792	18087935	apnic	1273622400	KR	KOR	Korea Republic of
18153472	18219007	apnic	1276646400	JP	JPN	Japan
18219008	18350079	apnic	1273017600	IN	IND	India

■ **FIGURE 3.4** WebNet77 Sample Comma Delimited IpToCountry Rows

when you log and compare records. I will of course include some code I have written to do this for you, but first we will have a quick math lesson so we know what is happening as we convert back and forth. Borrowing from examples used in one of my previous articles, we will take the IP address 203.83.16.1, which was last seen somewhere in Papua New Guinea. Starting with the base octet form of $256^3.256^2.256^1.256^0$, we will extrapolate each decimal equivalent out respectively, resulting in 16777216.65536.256.0, as odd as that may look. With that base, we multiply each octet by the base and add them together, yielding:

$$(16,777,216 * 203) + (65,536 * 83) + (256 * 16) + (1)$$

which equals

$$(3405774848) + (5439488) + (4096) + (1)$$

This finally results in the integer 3,411,218,433 (shown with comma separators obviously). To reverse the process and create a dotted octet notation from an integer, we cast the integer as a binary SQL data type (hex), carve it up into octets, and convert back to decimal separated by a period. 3411218433 converted to hex is xCB531001, dotted out to CB.53.10.01, and finally to 203.83.16.1, which is a good bit easier to do than the other way around.

Before we can use this, we need to import the IpToCounty data into SQL. This is done easily enough by opening the CVS file downloaded from WebNet77 in Excel, saving it as a workbook, and then importing it into the log database similar to that described in figure 3.5. The IpToCountry table already has the big integer (BIGINT) data types specified for the

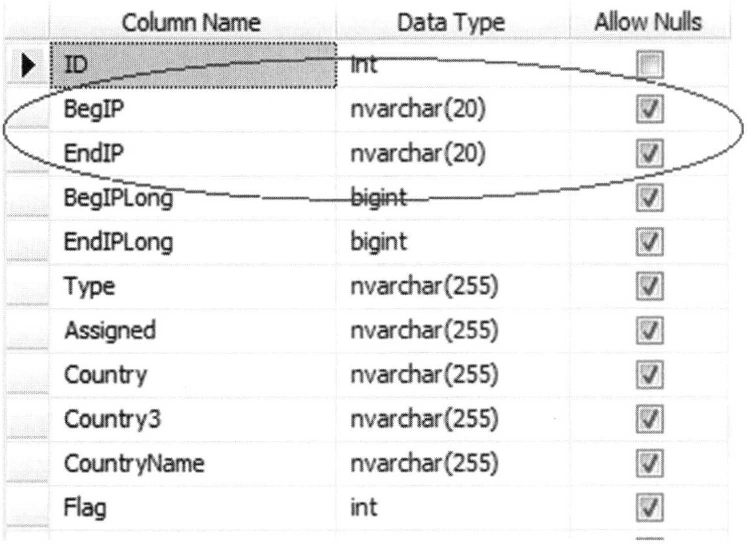

Column Name	Data Type	Allow Nulls
ID	int	☐
BegIP	nvarchar(20)	☑
EndIP	nvarchar(20)	☑
BegIPLong	bigint	☑
EndIPLong	bigint	☑
Type	nvarchar(255)	☑
Assigned	nvarchar(255)	☑
Country	nvarchar(255)	☑
Country3	nvarchar(255)	☑
CountryName	nvarchar(255)	☑
Flag	int	☑

■ **FIGURE 3.5** IpToCountry Table with Dot Notation Fields Added

integer values, so we just have to add a couple of fields for the dot notation as shown in Figure 3.5.

> **NOTE**
> Be sure that when you create this table you configure *BIGINT* data types, and not just *INT* data types. The INT data type can only store values 2,147,483,648 through 2,147,483,647 and requires four bytes. These four bytes *could* represent 4294967294 integers, but only if they are unsigned. The INT will only let you store up to IP 127.255.255.255, which will bite you moving forward. BIGINT might take up twice as much storage, but it is easier to work with. Of course, if you are worried about storage, then you will have to work with four-byte binary data or muck about with negative numbers.

With the IpToCountry data imported into our SQL log database and the *BegIP* and *EndIP* character fields added, we get a list of all the Papua New Guinea records, similar to what is shown in Figure 3.6.

Note that the BegIP and EndIP columns are null, as they should be. We now need to update those fields by converting the *BegIPLong* and *EndIPLong* integer fields to dot notation. At this point, we will convert the manual process we did earlier into a SQL scalar-value function to do it for us. This function takes a BIGINT input parameter, converts it to variable length binary data (varbinary), parses it out as described earlier, and returns the dot notation.

```
SET ANSI_NULLS ON
GO
SET QUOTED_IDENTIFIER ON
GO
-- ===========================================
-- Author:      Timothy "Thor" Mullen
-- Description: Convert Long Int to IP Address
-- ===========================================
CREATE FUNCTION [dbo].[fn_SQLLong2String]
(
      @LongIP bigint
)
RETURNS varchar(20)
AS
BEGIN
      declare
      @bin varbinary(4),
      @ip varchar(15)
select @bin = cast(@LongIP as varbinary(4))
select @ip = cast(convert(int,substring(@bin,1,1)) as
-- varchar(3)) + '.'
+cast(convert(int,substring(@bin,2,1)) as varchar(3)) + '.'
+cast(convert(int,substring(@bin,3,1)) as varchar(3)) + '.'
+ cast(convert(int,substring(@bin,4,1)) as varchar(3))

RETURN @IP
END
```

■ **CODE SAMPLE 3.1** fn_SQLLong2String: T-SQL to Convert Integer (Long) to Dotted IP

Figure 3.7 shows the successful results of the function.

With this simple function, we can now update all 100,000+ records of our IpToCountry table with this one SQL command, as shown in Figure 3.8.

At this point, you may be asking yourself why we need the dot notation IP address in this table. We have got the beginning and ending integer equivalence, and if our base logging data type is based on integers in ISA Server (again, TMG uses a uniqueidentifier, which we will discuss), why would we need the dot notation? We need the dot notation because at some point we will be exporting this data to TMG in the form of a computer set, and the computer set input mechanism is by beginning and ending IP address in dot notation, not integer. So this step

```
select * from IpToCountry where CountryName like 'Papua%' order by BegIPLong
```

	BegIP	EndIP	BegIPLong	EndIPLong	Type	Assigned	Country2	Country3	CountryName	Flag
1	NULL	NULL	247482368	247483391	apnic	1.28442e+009	PG	PNG	Papua New Guinea	NULL
2	NULL	NULL	460984320	460988415	apnic	1.28589e+009	PG	PNG	Papua New Guinea	NULL
3	NULL	NULL	2013061120	2013065215	apnic	1.20571e+009	PG	PNG	Papua New Guinea	NULL
4	NULL	NULL	2096152576	2096160767	apnic	1.19439e+009	PG	PNG	Papua New Guinea	NULL
5	NULL	NULL	3029793792	3029794815	apnic	1.25297e+009	PG	PNG	Papua New Guinea	NULL
6	NULL	NULL	3389018112	3389018367	apnic	7.32845e+008	PG	PNG	Papua New Guinea	NULL
7	NULL	NULL	3389071360	3389079551	apnic	7.41917e+008	PG	PNG	Papua New Guinea	NULL
8	NULL	NULL	3389124608	3389128703	apnic	8.05507e+008	PG	PNG	Papua New Guinea	NULL
9	NULL	NULL	3392439552	3392439807	apnic	1.2795e+009	PG	PNG	Papua New Guinea	NULL
10	NULL	NULL	3392831488	3392832511	apnic	1.18031e+009	PG	PNG	Papua New Guinea	NULL
11	NULL	NULL	3392995328	3392995583	apnic	7.98336e+008	PG	PNG	Papua New Guinea	NULL
12	NULL	NULL	3395272704	3395276799	apnic	1.06021e+009	PG	PNG	Papua New Guinea	NULL
13	NULL	NULL	3399860224	3399864319	apnic	1.18031e+009	PG	PNG	Papua New Guinea	NULL
14	NULL	NULL	3400265728	3400267775	apnic	1.11586e+009	PG	PNG	Papua New Guinea	NULL
15	NULL	NULL	3411218432	3411220479	apnic	1.13754e+009	PG	PNG	Papua New Guinea	NULL

■ **FIGURE 3.6** Listing of All Papua New Guinea Records in New Table

is required if we are to build sets from this data. It is also human-readable, which helps as you scan through records trying to manually match dot notation entries to a range. And to me, it just looks more natural to have the dot notation included, as demonstrated in Figure 3.9.

Again, the dot notation does not help us match a country to a record; the BegIPLong and EndIPLong integer values do that. But as far as having a table that allows us to look up a country based on its (converted) IP address, we have everything we need.

Linking the Data

For those of you not explicitly familiar with SQL Server and T-SQL in general, the query method used to find records within this table structure may be a bit counterintuitive, but it is fairly straightforward. We have the beginning integer and ending integer for a given range along with the country name in the table. Given an integer representation of an IP (in this example, 3411218433), we can determine which country it is from with a query or procedure that finds the records where the value is between the two ranges, as Figure 3.10 illustrates.

We simply provide the value, and tell SQL to find the record where that value is between the BegIPLong and EndIPLong values. It is not exactly

```
SELECT dbo.fn_SQLLong2String(BegIPLong), BegIPLong
FROM IpToCountry WHERE CountryName like 'Papua%'
ORDER BY BegIPLong
```

	(No column name)	BegIPLong
1	14.192.72.0	247482368
2	27.122.16.0	460984320
3	119.252.224.0	2013061120
4	124.240.192.0	2096152576
5	180.150.252.0	3029793792
6	202.0.80.0	3389018112
7	202.1.32.0	3389071360
8	202.1.240.0	3389124608
9	202.52.133.0	3392439552
10	202.58.128.0	3392831488
11	202.61.0.0	3392995328
12	202.95.192.0	3395272704
13	202.165.192.0	3399860224
14	202.171.240.0	3400265728
15	203.83.16.0	3411218432

■ **FIGURE 3.7** Successful Results of the fn_SQLLong2String Function Test

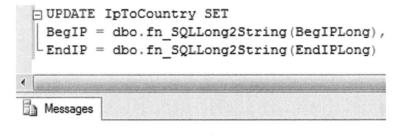

```
UPDATE IpToCountry SET
BegIP = dbo.fn_SQLLong2String(BegIPLong),
EndIP = dbo.fn_SQLLong2String(EndIPLong)
```

Messages

`(106591 row(s) affected)`

■ **FIGURE 3.8** Output of Command to Update All IpToCountry Records with Beginning and Ending IP Dot Notation

the most performance-optimizing structure we could use, but given our options, it is what we have to work with.

So we can take an integer and convert it to an IP, but now we need to be able to parse out a dot notation IP address and convert it to an integer. This is for cases where we only have dotted IP or when we just want to test. In order to do this efficiently, we will build another function and then use that function inside

```
SELECT BegIP,EndIP,BegIPLong,EndIPLong,CountryName
FROM IpToCountry WHERE CountryName like 'Papua%'
```

Results | Messages

	BegIP	EndIP	BegIPLong	EndIPLong	CountryName
1	14.192.72.0	14.192.75.255	247482368	247483391	Papua New Guinea
2	27.122.16.0	27.122.31.255	460984320	460988415	Papua New Guinea
3	119.252.224.0	119.252.239.255	2013061120	2013065215	Papua New Guinea
4	124.240.192.0	124.240.223.255	2096152576	2096160767	Papua New Guinea
5	180.150.252.0	180.150.255.255	3029793792	3029794815	Papua New Guinea
6	202.0.80.0	202.0.80.255	3389018112	3389018367	Papua New Guinea
7	202.1.32.0	202.1.63.255	3389071360	3389079551	Papua New Guinea
8	202.1.240.0	202.1.255.255	3389124608	3389128703	Papua New Guinea
9	202.52.133.0	202.52.133.255	3392439552	3392439807	Papua New Guinea
10	202.58.128.0	202.58.131.255	3392831488	3392832511	Papua New Guinea
11	202.61.0.0	202.61.0.255	3392995328	3392995583	Papua New Guinea
12	202.95.192.0	202.95.207.255	3395272704	3395276799	Papua New Guinea
13	202.165.192.0	202.165.207.255	3399860224	3399864319	Papua New Guinea
14	202.171.240.0	202.171.247.255	3400265728	3400267775	Papua New Guinea
15	203.83.16.0	203.83.23.255	3411218432	3411220479	Papua New Guinea

■ **FIGURE 3.9** List of Papua New Guinea IP Ranges Including Dot Notation

```
SELECT CountryName FROM IpToCountry
WHERE 3411218433 between BegIPLong and EndIPLong
```

Results | Messages

	CountryName
1	Papua New Guinea

■ **FIGURE 3.10** Find Country Based on Integer IP Address Integer Value

```
SET ANSI_NULLS ON
GO
SET QUOTED_IDENTIFIER ON
GO
-- ========================================
-- Author:        Timothy "Thor" Mullen
-- Description:    Convert IP dot notation to integer
-- ========================================
CREATE FUNCTION [dbo].[fn_SQLString2Long]
(
@ip CHAR(15)
)
RETURNS BIGINT
AS
BEGIN
 DECLARE @rv BIGINT,
 @o1 BIGINT,
 @o2 BIGINT,
 @o3 BIGINT,
 @o4 BIGINT,
 @base BIGINT
 SELECT
 @o1 = CONVERT(BIGINT, PARSENAME(@ip, 4)),
 @o2 = CONVERT(BIGINT, PARSENAME(@ip, 3)),
 @o3 = CONVERT(BIGINT, PARSENAME(@ip, 2)),
 @o4 = CONVERT(BIGINT, PARSENAME(@ip, 1))
 IF (@o1 BETWEEN 0 AND 255)
 AND (@o2 BETWEEN 0 AND 255)
 AND (@o3 BETWEEN 0 AND 255)
 AND (@o4 BETWEEN 0 AND 255)
 BEGIN
 SET @rv = (@o1 * 16777216 ) +
 (@o2 * 65536) +
 (@o3 * 256) +
 (@o4)
 END
 ELSE
 SET @rv = -1
 RETURN @rv
END
```

■ **CODE SAMPLE 3.2** fn_SQLString2Long: T-SQL to Convert Dotted IP to Integer (Long)

a stored procedure. This is where we will take apart the dot notation's $256^3.256^2.256^1.256^0$ decimal equivalence to derive the integer shown in Code Sample 3.2.

It seems like quite a bit of code just to convert an IP to an integer, and it is, but that happens to be the way T-SQL works. The process required to convert TMG's uniqueidentifier to an integer is even more complicated, but we have better solutions for that coming up.

Testing the function, we should see results similar to those shown in Figure 3.11.

In the same way that we retrieved the Papua New Guinea record by explicitly providing the integer value in Figure 3.10, we can now substitute the function to find the same record, as demonstrated in Figure 3.12.

Process Source Country

Now that the two-way conversion functionality exists, we can easily get whatever country-based information we want from the logs based on what our needs are. However, now is the time for you or your database administrators to make some design decisions. Deriving the country from stored integer values in reports or data sets is going to have significant performance issues. If you only have the raw integer IP data stored, and if every time you wish to reference the country you have to derive it by including the country

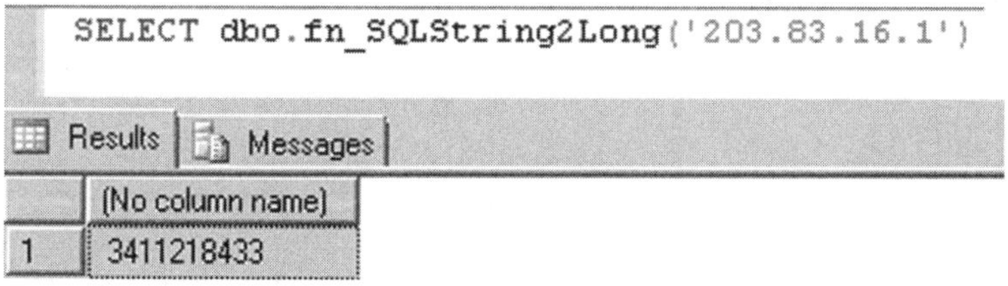

```
SELECT dbo.fn_SQLString2Long('203.83.16.1')
```

	Results	Messages
	(No column name)	
1	3411218433	

■ **FIGURE 3.11** Successful Test of IP-to-Integer Function

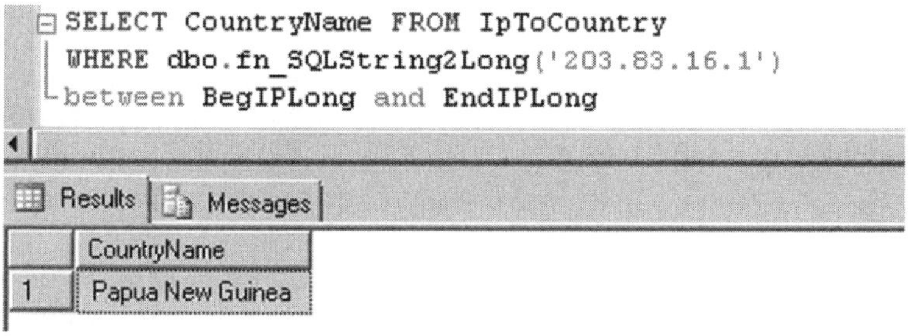

```
SELECT CountryName FROM IpToCountry
WHERE dbo.fn_SQLString2Long('203.83.16.1')
between BegIPLong and EndIPLong
```

	Results	Messages
	CountryName	
1	Papua New Guinea	

■ **FIGURE 3.12** Find Country Based on Integer IP Address Integer Value Using Our IP String-to-Integer Function

lookup in a subquery, then each record in your result set will have to be evaluated and matched. Depending on your environment, that may be acceptable, but for my purposes, no.

I opted for the data separation and parsing model where I created a customized table containing the relevant log data I wished to retain, and populated that table with data and associated country lookup information via a scheduled SQL job that runs each night. Since my logs collect all inbound and outbound connections, there is a tremendous amount of traffic that does not relate to this particular function. However, I want to keep that data. So, I designed a process where the data I want was taken out of the TMG firewall logs, posted to my reporting table, parsed out, and updated. That way I can do whatever I want with that table without affecting other data sets. One thing to remember is that if you change the actual TMG WebProxyLog and FirewallLog table structures stored in SQL, you will have to change the procedures TMG uses to post data to those tables during the logging process. I recommend against that. Try to keep the logging process as simple and uncomplicated as you can. Actually changing how the data gets logged can be risky and you could introduce problems that you won't be aware of, which could include failing to log at all. This process could end up being a good example of how trying to implement a valuable security feature ended up causing more problems than you had in the first place—and nobody wants to be That Guy.

INTEGRATING WITH TMG

Now is a good time to address a TMG-specific logging element we must solve for. Again, while we have everything we need to actually create TMG-based Computer Set objects to block or allow traffic at the firewall, the current functions we have implemented at this point can only support linkage to ISA Server log formats since ISA Server logs the integer of the IP address and TMG logs IP as a uniqueidentifier data type, or a Global Unique Identifier (GUID) as it is also generally referred to. The purpose of the GUID function is to be able to create a data element that is guaranteed to be a universally unique value no matter who generates it or when, which is done by using CPU clock and network interface controller variables. In that sense, it is really a UUID, but it is called *global* instead of *universal*. The part we care about here is a 16-byte (stored) binary value formatted field in the format of 00000001-FFFF-0000-0000-000000000000. TMG presumably uses this new format to support IPv6 logging, but that is not for me to say. Regardless, it is a new logging format and we have to be able to convert it to both integer and dotted IP in order to leverage our required functionality. Even though a uniqueidentifier data type is used, TMG is only storing the IP, which is neither a unique ID nor a GUID. However, for simplicity's sake, I will refer to the format as *GUID* from here on out to avoid confusion.

Decisions, Decisions...

As is typically the case, we will see that the decisions we are about to make regarding something as inane as converting data types can have an impact on our overall security. I think you should pay particular attention to these next couple of steps since one contains a simple nuance—and a perfectly valid command structure—which could weaken our security posture.

First, you should treat this like you would any other development project and get down to the business of converting the data. An actual GUID would use the entire data type space with a value like 6F9619FF-8B86-D011-B42D-00C04FC964FF. However, when TMG logs the IPv4 address with a GUID data type, it only uses the first 4 bytes of field for the IP, sets the second 2 bytes to FFFF, and fills the remaining 10 bytes with 0s. Our earlier example of 203.83.16.1, which is CB531001 in hex, would be logged as CB531001-FFFF-0000-0000-000000000000 in the TMG GUID format.

Figures 3.13a and 3.13b show a comparison of ISA Server and TMG logs for IP address storage.

As you can see, insofar as TMG and the IP address are concerned, we only have to concern ourselves with the first four bytes of the GUID. To be pedantic, we are actually going to be working with the first eight characters of the GUID as string *nvarchar* data when we convert it and not actually the first four bytes of data, because the GUID field itself is a uniqueidentifier data type and its binary output is different. If you look at the binary output of the GUID field value of 6F9619FF-8B86-D011-B42D-00C04FC964FF, as stored in SQL, you will see 0xFF19966F868B11D0B42D00C04FC964FF. You will notice the reverse (little endian[4]) storage of the first eight bytes which is something you might want to be aware of in the future. But for our purposes this does not matter since the output of the GUID is text in this example.

■ **FIGURE 3.13A** A Log Snip from ISA Server

servername	logTime	protocol	SourceIP	SourcePort	DestinationIP	DestPort
ISA	2/10/11 2:00 AM	TCP	2943609376	4773	2912994203	25
ISA	2/10/11 2:00 AM	TCP	2935870990	58877	2912994203	443
ISA	2/10/11 2:00 AM	TCP	1231072257	58851	2912994203	443

A

---

[4]Little endian stores low order bits in the lowest memory address, or little end, first. Big endian is the opposite.

serve rname	logTime	protocol	SourceIP	Source Port	DestinationIP	DestPort
TMG	2/10/11 2:00 AM	TCP	AF73EA20-FFFF-0000-0000-000000000000	4773	ADA0C39B-FFFF-0000-0000-000000000000	25
TMG	2/10/11 2:00 AM	TCP	AEFDD60E-FFFF-0000-0000-000000000000	58877	ADA0C39B-FFFF-0000-0000-000000000000	443
TMG	2/10/11 2:00 AM	TCP	4960A001-FFFF-0000-0000-000000000000	58851	ADA0C39B-FFFF-0000-0000-000000000000	443

B

■ **FIGURE 3.13B** A Log Snip from TMG

From here, we just need to parse out the first four bytes of the GUID, and convert that to an integer in order to find the source country. If you want to view the dot notation, then you will have to write a converter for that as well. Of course, we could just convert the GUID to an integer and use our existing fn_SQLLong2String function to convert it again.

As most people do, we would probably do a search on the Internet for a solution that someone else has already done the legwork on. Before long we would come across the public domain example[5] shown in Code Sample 3.3.

```
CREATE FUNCTION [dbo].[fnIpAddressToText]
(
@Ipv6Address [uniqueidentifier]
)
RETURNS varchar(40) AS
BEGIN
DECLARE @strInAddress varchar(40)
DECLARE @strOutAddress varchar(40)
SET @strInAddress = LOWER(CONVERT(varchar(40),@Ipv6Address))
SET @strOutAddress = ''
IF (SUBSTRING(@strInAddress, 10, 4) = 'ffff')
BEGIN
-- ipv4 (hex to int conversion)
DECLARE @IsNum int, @ZERO int, @IsAlpa int
set @ZERO = ASCII('0')
set @IsNum = ASCII('9')
set @IsAlpa = ASCII('a')-10
DECLARE @intH int, @intL int

SET @intH = ASCII(SUBSTRING(@strInAddress, 1, 1))
IF (@intH <= @IsNum) SET @intH = @intH-@ZERO ELSE SET @intH =
-- @intH - @IsAlpa
SET @intL = ASCII(SUBSTRING(@strInAddress, 2, 1))
```

■ **CODE SAMPLE 3.3** fnIpAddressToText: Public Example of Converting TMG GUID to Dotted IP

(continued)

---

[5]Multiple sources found.

```
IF (@intL <= @IsNum) SET @intL = @intL-@ZERO ELSE SET @intL = @intL-@IsAlpa
SET @strOutAddress = CONVERT(varchar(3), @intH * 16 + @intL) + '.'

SET @intH = ASCII(SUBSTRING(@strInAddress, 3, 1))
IF (@intH <= @IsNum) SET @intH = @intH-@ZERO ELSE SET @intH = @intH-@IsAlpa
SET @intL = ASCII(SUBSTRING(@strInAddress, 4, 1))
IF (@intL <= @IsNum) SET @intL = @intL-@ZERO ELSE SET @intL = @intL-@IsAlpa
SET @strOutAddress = @strOutAddress + CONVERT(varchar(3), @intH * 16 + @intL) + '.'

SET @intH = ASCII(SUBSTRING(@strInAddress, 5, 1))
IF (@intH <= @IsNum) SET @intH = @intH-@ZERO ELSE SET @intH = @intH-@IsAlpa
SET @intL = ASCII(SUBSTRING(@strInAddress, 6, 1))
IF (@intL <= @IsNum) SET @intL = @intL-@ZERO ELSE SET @intL = @intL-@IsAlpa
SET @strOutAddress = @strOutAddress + CONVERT(varchar(3), @intH * 16 + @intL) + '.'

SET @intH = ASCII(SUBSTRING(@strInAddress, 7, 1))
IF (@intH <= @IsNum) SET @intH = @intH-@ZERO ELSE SET @intH = @intH-@IsAlpa
SET @intL = ASCII(SUBSTRING(@strInAddress, 8, 1))
IF (@intL <= @IsNum) SET @intL = @intL-@ZERO ELSE SET @intL = @intL-@IsAlpa
SET @strOutAddress = @strOutAddress + CONVERT(varchar(3), @intH * 16 + @intL)
END
ELSE
BEGIN
-- ipv6
SET @strOutAddress = @strOutAddress + SUBSTRING(@strInAddress, 1, 4) + ':'
+ SUBSTRING(@strInAddress, 5, 4) + ':'
+ SUBSTRING(@strInAddress, 10, 4) + ':'
+ SUBSTRING(@strInAddress, 15, 4) + ':'
+ SUBSTRING(@strInAddress, 20, 4) + ':'
+ SUBSTRING(@strInAddress, 25, 4) + ':'
+ SUBSTRING(@strInAddress, 29, 4) + ':'
+ SUBSTRING(@strInAddress, 33, 4)
END
-- guid sample '6F9619FF-8B86-D011-B42D-FFF34FC964FF'
RETURN @strOutAddress
END
```

■ **CODE SAMPLE 3.3—cont'd**

Code Sample 3.3 looks good, and in testing we see that it works. You might also notice that the developer used the exact same example GUID that I have used, which means that they did their homework first and snagged it from the MS Developer Network (MSDN) example you find when searching for the GUID uniqueidentifier. It also goes the extra step and parses out the full GUID text into IPv6 colon notation which is an added bonus.

```
select dbo.fnIpAddressToText('6F9619FF-8B86-D011-B42D-00C04FC964FF'),
dbo.fnIpAddressToText('ADA0C39B-FFFF-0000-0000-000000000000')
```

	(No column name)	(No column name)
1	6f96:19ff:8b86:d011:b42d:00c0:4fc9:64ff	173.160.195.155

■ **FIGURE 3.14** Example IPv6 and IPv4 Output of the fnIpAddressToText Function

While the functions in Figure 3.14 may work just fine, a developer may find it too complicated and processor intensive. There is also the overhead of the developer figuring out exactly what someone else did and why they did it so they can not only fully understand the function, but also be able to test and troubleshoot it. I know that does not always happen, but it should.

Keeping It Simple(r)

The "Keep It Simple, Stupid" model would rather rudely dictate that we choose a simpler and easier-to-understand solution. Since we only need the IPv4 address, and all we care about is the first eight characters, the code shown in Code Sample 3.4 would do what we need more efficiently.

```
CREATE PROCEDURE [dbo].[sp_UID2IP]
        @UIDLong uniqueidentifier
AS
BEGIN
        SET NOCOUNT ON;
declare @UID nvarchar(10),
                @Hex1 nvarchar(5),
                @Hex2 nvarchar(5),
                @Hex3 nvarchar(5),
                @Hex4 nvarchar(5),
                @SQL nvarchar(1000),
                @Param nvarchar(100),
                @IP nvarchar(16)

set @UID = LEFT(@UIDLong,8)
select
@Hex1 = '0x'+substring(@UID,1,2), @Hex2 = '0x'+substring
-- (@UID,3,2),
@Hex3 = '0x'+substring(@UID,5,2), @Hex4 = '0x'+substring
-- (@UID,7,2)
```

■ **CODE SAMPLE 3.4** sp_UID2IP: T-SQL Procedure to Convert TMG GUID to Dotted IP

(continued)

```
Set @SQL = N'Select
CONVERT(nvarchar(3),(CONVERT(int,' + @Hex1+ '))) + CHAR(46) +
CONVERT(nvarchar(3),(CONVERT(int,' + @Hex2+ '))) + CHAR(46) +
CONVERT(nvarchar(3),(CONVERT(int,' + @Hex3+ '))) + CHAR(46) +
CONVERT(nvarchar(3),(CONVERT(int,' + @Hex4+ ')))'
Set @Param = N'@Result nvarchar(16) output'
Exec master.dbo.Sp_executesql @SQL, @Param, @IP Output
END
```

■ **CODE SAMPLE 3.4—cont'd**

If we test the output, we get the results shown in Figure 3.15.

In this example, we take advantage of embedded CONVERT directives to convert the embedded converted values directly into a dotted IP address. Since we know that we are working with hex data that we wish to convert to integers to represent each octet, we can leverage the syntax of prepending *0x* to character data to directly convert hex to integer. In other words, we may think of *CB* as hex data that represents *203*, however to SQL it is just a couple of characters. Telling SQL to convert *0xCB* to an integer explicitly tells it to treat the character data as hexadecimal input. No matter how geeky it may sound, little things like that make me happy. In fact, I like it so much (I am role playing now) that I do not mind concatenating string data together into the *@SQL* variable so that I can build a customized string to execute with the *Sp_executesql* system stored procedure. Not only is it flexible and fast, but prepending *0x* to character data in a one-line, doubled-down back-to-back series of convert statements wins me geek points.

But it also opens up the possibility that a SQL injection vulnerability could be introduced since we are ultimately building a string variable from concatenating character data together to form an executable SQL statement. This example actually mitigates SQL injection due to the explicit declaration of the input parameter as a uniqueidentifier data type. This means

■ **FIGURE 3.15** Output of the New sp_UID2IP Stored Procedure

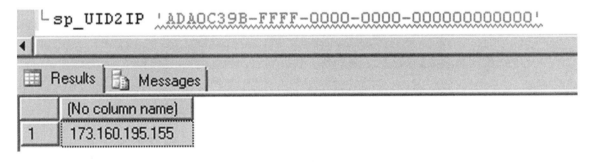

that SQL will validate the parameter format when the variable is passed into the procedure. If we try to pass non-GUID data, such as "Greg is a criminal" instead of ADA0C39B-FFFF-0000-0000-000000000000, then SQL generates the error shown in Figure 3.16.

This may seem obvious, but the procedure would work just fine if we had declared the input variable as nvarchar data instead of unique-identifier data:

```
CREATE PROCEDURE [dbo].[sp_UID2IP]
    @UIDLong uniqueidentifier
AS
BEGIN...
```

This could very well have been:

```
CREATE PROCEDURE [dbo].[sp_UID2IP]
    @UIDLong nvarchar(50)
AS
BEGIN...
```

And the process would have worked exactly the same from a conversion standpoint. However, Figure 3.17 shows what happens if we provide non-GUID data.

This is a very different error, and a much more serious one. You will see that the error occurred when SQL tried to figure out how to execute *Greg*, which shows that we can pass command data into the procedure. And while this particular procedure may obviate any actual SQL injection vulnerabilities by merit of its operational syntax, the fact remains that building strings within a process that are executed by way of the Sp_executesql system procedure can be dangerous. Some development policies explicitly prohibit the use of Sp_executesql in production environments for this very reason. It is actually a common limitation placed on developers in large or tightly controlled development environments.

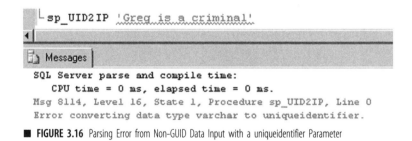

■ **FIGURE 3.16** Parsing Error from Non-GUID Data Input with a uniqueidentifier Parameter

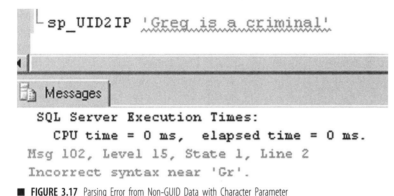

```
└ sp_UID2IP 'Greg is a criminal'
```

Messages

```
SQL Server Execution Times:
   CPU time = 0 ms,  elapsed time = 0 ms.
Msg 102, Level 15, State 1, Line 2
Incorrect syntax near 'Gr'.
```

■ **FIGURE 3.17** Parsing Error from Non-GUID Data with Character Parameter

An Editorial Note

The fact remains that developers use Sp_executesql all the time because the operational environments and functionality requirements they work with dictate that they do so. Developers use the tools they have to perform the functions they are given to design; that is their job. And while we want all developers to know about security risks and threats, we cannot expect them to be risk analysis experts. They are code functionality experts. Development and SDL policies are in place so security and risk analysts can look at the overall risk in allowing a particular development solution to be used in production and arrive at whatever guideline decisions they find appropriate. I agree with this. What I do not agree with is telling developers that they cannot use a particular function (i.e., Sp_executesql) while failing to provide them with functional equivalents that they *can* use.

Allow me to linger on this topic for a moment longer because I think this might help toward developing effective policy as opposed to just policy with this example in mind. Again, while you cannot expect developers to be security and risk analysis experts, you should ensure that they are aware of what problem you are trying to solve when you implement policy restrictions. It is important to have insight into the psychological economy of a developer in this process. If the developer does not explicitly know how SQL injection occurs, then just prohibiting Sp_executesql is not necessarily going to prevent it.

For instance, suppose I have to use a piece of system-generated data as part of a query—in this case, a piece of the GUID that I have to extract and convert to something else. As a SQL developer, it is my job to create T-SQL strings to get things done, so I may want to build a string and use Sp_executesql. However, the security guys tell me I cannot because of some injection issue, but they do not tell me what to do instead. So rather than just building the string, I retrieve the values, build them as I need them, and write them to a temp table. I then write a stored procedure to take parameterized character input to perform my function based on the data in the table. As far as meeting the code requirements are concerned, I have done my job because I have not used Sp_executesql, and I am happy because I did something creative that works well. My developer psychological economies of scale are balanced. However, the exact same SQL injection vector still exists because all an attacker has to do is alter the data in the table rather than the data in the string to accomplish the same attack. The mini-lesson here is that if you are going to limit what developers can and cannot do in code for security policies, make sure there are appropriate alternative solutions because it is in our nature to find a way to do what we want.

Introducing SQL CLR

We shall explore one of those alternative solutions now, and once done we can finally move on to creating the TMG Computer Sets we need to finish up. T-SQL is obviously a very powerful language, but it does have its limits. I believe that the previous data conversion and parsing examples illustrated that. While SQL is all about data management, sometimes T-SQL is not the most efficient way of dealing with highly customized data manipulation functions.

This is where we shall call upon SQL CLR as we have in other chapters. We will explore how we can use SQL CLR in C# code to accomplish the same thing we have done in T-SQL but without having to worry about SQL injection or other procedure- or function-based issues.

I will again reference you to read Chapter 1 in regard to the database configuration requirements necessary to post custom CLR assemblies into a SQL install and continue with the assumption that this has been done.

In my opinion, this is yet another perfect opportunity to familiarize you with the power of CLR, particularly in regard to how it supports your security posture and SDL requirements. Reviewing the fn_SQLString2Long function where we convert a dotted IP to an integer, we see the T-SQL implementation is as shown in Code Sample 3.5.

```
SET ANSI_NULLS ON
GO
SET QUOTED_IDENTIFIER ON
GO
-- ==========================================
-- Author:        Timothy "Thor" Mullen
-- Description:   Convert IP dot notation to integer
-- ==========================================
CREATE FUNCTION [dbo].[fn_SQLString2Long]
(
```

■ **CODE SAMPLE 3.5** fn_SQLString2Long: Reference Code Sample 3.2

```
@ip CHAR(15)
)
RETURNS BIGINT
AS
BEGIN
 DECLARE @rv BIGINT,
 @o1 BIGINT,
 @o2 BIGINT,
 @o3 BIGINT,
 @o4 BIGINT,
 @base BIGINT
 SELECT
 @o1 = CONVERT(BIGINT, PARSENAME(@ip, 4)),
 @o2 = CONVERT(BIGINT, PARSENAME(@ip, 3)),
 @o3 = CONVERT(BIGINT, PARSENAME(@ip, 2)),
 @o4 = CONVERT(BIGINT, PARSENAME(@ip, 1))
 IF (@o1 BETWEEN 0 AND 255)
 AND (@o2 BETWEEN 0 AND 255)
 AND (@o3 BETWEEN 0 AND 255)
 AND (@o4 BETWEEN 0 AND 255)
 BEGIN
 SET @rv = (@o1 * 16777216 ) +
 (@o2 * 65536) +
 (@o3 * 256) +
 (@o4)
 END
 ELSE
 SET @rv = -1
 RETURN @rv
END
```

■ **CODE SAMPLE 3.5—cont'd**

Using C# and CLR, we accomplish the same function with the simple function declaration shown in Code Sample 3.6.

```
[Microsoft.SqlServer.Server.SqlFunction]
public static SqlInt64 fn_String2Long(string IP)
{
SqlInt64 intAddress = BitConverter.ToUInt32(IPAddress.
-- Parse(IP).GetAddressBytes().Reverse().ToArray(), 0);
return intAddress;
}
```

■ **CODE SAMPLE 3.6** fn_String2Long: C# CLR to Convert Dotted IP to Integer (Int32)

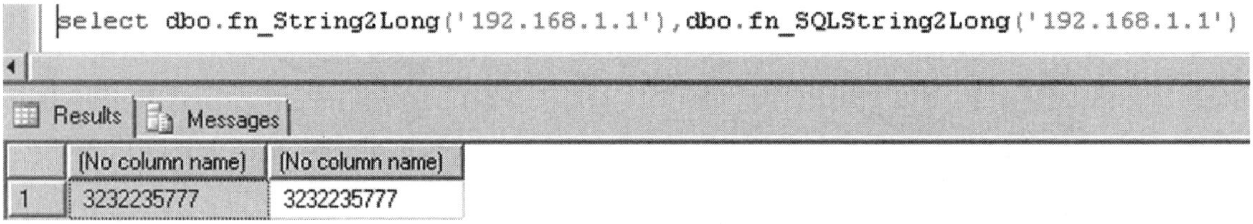

```
select dbo.fn_String2Long('192.168.1.1'),dbo.fn_SQLString2Long('192.168.1.1')
```

	(No column name)	(No column name)
1	3232235777	3232235777

■ **FIGURE 3.18** Comparison of SQL CLR and T-SQL–Based String2Long Functions (note the difference between "String2Long" and "SQLString2Long.")

Simple, eh? When this CLR function is published to our SQL server, it can then be called in the same way any other function is called, as we see when executed side to side, as shown in Figure 3.18.

Solving for the bulky and SQL injection susceptible sp_UID2IP procedure we wrote to convert the IP GUID into a string, we can meet our simplicity, security, and compliance goals with the CLR function definition shown in Code Sample 3.7.

```
[Microsoft.SqlServer.Server.SqlFunction]
public static SqlString fn_UID2String(string UID)
{
string hexValue = UID.Substring(0, 8);
UInt32 intAddress = UInt32.Parse(hexValue, System.
-- Globalization.NumberStyles.HexNumber);

IPAddress oldIP = new IPAddress(intAddress);
byte[] me = oldIP.GetAddressBytes();
Array.Reverse(me);
UInt32 newAddress = BitConverter.ToUInt32(me, 0);
IPAddress newIP = new IPAddress(newAddress);
string IPString = newIP.ToString();
return IPString;
}
```

■ **CODE SAMPLE 3.7** fn_UID2String: C# CLR to Convert TMG GUID to Dotted IP

In fact, we can securely build all of the necessary functions we have, as well as some new ones we will need, in less lines of code than the single function we found on the Internet. Code Sample 3.8 shows the *entire* bit of source code you need to post these CLR functions to your SQL server.

```
using System;
using System.Data;
using System.Data.SqlClient;
using System.Data.SqlTypes;
```

■ **CODE SAMPLE 3.8** Multiple C# CLR Conversion Functions

(continued)

```
using Microsoft.SqlServer.Server;
using System.Net;
using System.Linq;

public partial class UserDefinedFunctions
{
[Microsoft.SqlServer.Server.SqlFunction]
public static SqlInt64 fn_String2Long(string IP)
{
SqlInt64 intAddress = BitConverter.ToUInt32(IPAddress.Parse(IP).
-- GetAddressBytes().Reverse ().ToArray(), 0);
return intAddress;
}


[Microsoft.SqlServer.Server.SqlFunction]
public static SqlInt64 fn_UID2Long(string UID)
{
string hexValue = UID.Substring(0, 8);
UInt32 intAddress = UInt32.Parse(hexValue, System.
-- Globalization.NumberStyles.HexNumber);
return intAddress;
}


[Microsoft.SqlServer.Server.SqlFunction]
public static SqlString fn_UID2String(string UID)
{
string hexValue = UID.Substring(0, 8);
UInt32 intAddress = UInt32.Parse(hexValue, System.
-- Globalization.NumberStyles.HexNumber);

IPAddress oldIP = new IPAddress(intAddress);
byte[] me = oldIP.GetAddressBytes();
Array.Reverse(me);
UInt32 newAddress = BitConverter.ToUInt32(me, 0);
IPAddress newIP = new IPAddress(newAddress);
string IPString = newIP.ToString();
return IPString;
}


[Microsoft.SqlServer.Server.SqlFunction]
public static SqlString fn_Long2String(Int64 intAddress)
{
```

■ **CODE SAMPLE 3.8—cont'd**

```
UInt32 intAddress32 = Convert.ToUInt32(intAddress);
IPAddress oldIP = new IPAddress(intAddress32);
byte[] me = oldIP.GetAddressBytes();
Array.Reverse(me);
UInt32 newAddress = BitConverter.ToUInt32(me, 0);
IPAddress newIP = new IPAddress(newAddress);
string IPString = newIP.ToString();
return IPString;
}


[Microsoft.SqlServer.Server.SqlFunction]
public static SqlString fn_Long2UID(Int64 intAddress)
{
UInt32 intAddress32 = Convert.ToUInt32(intAddress);
string IPString = string.Format("{0,8}", intAddress32.
-- ToString("X8")) + "-FFFF-0000-0000-000000000000";
return IPString;
}
};
```

■ CODE SAMPLE 3.8—cont'd

This collection of functions allows you to convert a dotted IP to an integer, a TMG GUID to an integer or dotted IP, and an integer to a dotted IP or GUID. In combination, you can perform all associated functions.

You should now have all the information and tools you need to report on any aspect of country-by-country traffic patterns. Now we are ready to build the sets in order for you to block or allow any or all traffic to or from anywhere you deem appropriate.

Building ISA Server/TMG Computer Sets

A Computer Set in ISA Server/TMG allows you to build a collection of differently named IP address ranges, individual computers, or subnets (in any combination) into a single object for use in access or publishing rules. This is the perfect object type to use in representing a country as each component range of the set is independent, but they can all be bound together as one object, as shown in Figure 3.19.

Computer Sets are very flexible objects, but they are difficult to work with because you must manually create each named entry one at a time in the UI. With more than 106,000 ranges in our data table, manual entry is not an

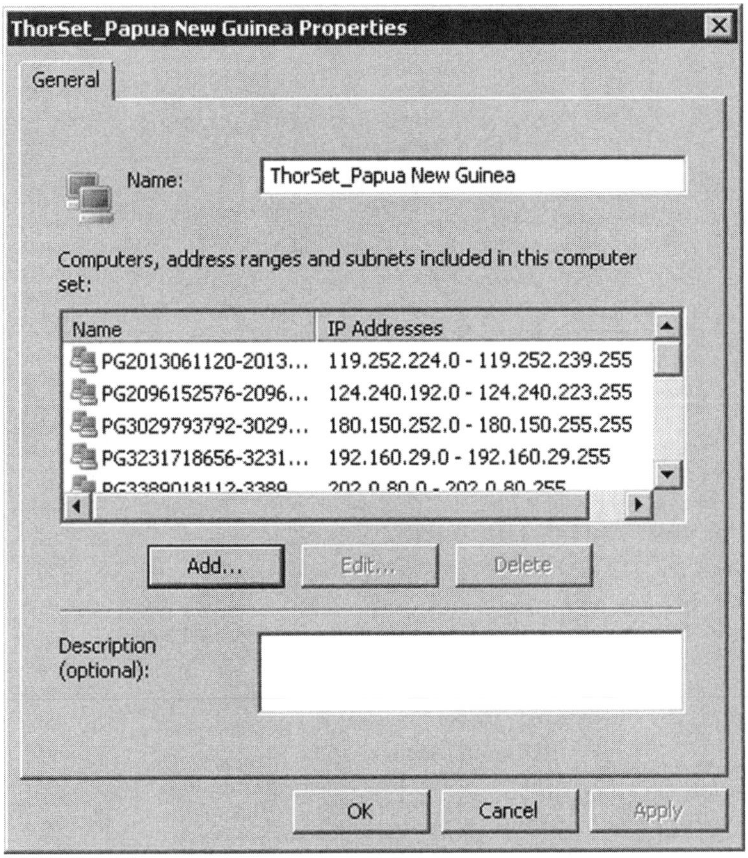

FIGURE 3.19 The TMG User Interface (UI) for a Computer Set (Papua New Guinea in This Example)

option. So we will have to programmatically create each country's Computer Set container and then create each named range within that container.

If we refer to MSDN[6] as a resource for accessing TMG objects from code, we will see Visual Basic for Applications (VBA) and C++ references. Knowing that we will need to access both code objects and data objects, I decided to use Microsoft Access as the interface for building our sets. This does a couple of things for us:

1. It gives us very easy access to the SQL data we already have for the IpToCountry data, and it fully supports VBA code.

---

[6]http://msdn.microsoft.com/en-us/library/dd435764.aspx

2. The only way to make these sets portable is to export them from TMG as XML. We can also do that programmatically, but different versions of ISA Server (2004 and 2006, both Standard and Enterprise) have different XML tags by version and edition. ISA Server 2006 Standard Edition exports can also be imported into TMG, which makes things a bit easier, but to support multiple platforms, you still have to run the generation code from each server install. Doing this in Access is very easy because the VBA code stays the same even though the exported XML format is different.

For instance, here is an XML snippet for Papua New Guinea in ISA Server 2004:

```
<?xml version="1.0" encoding="UTF-8"?>
<fpc4:Root xmlns:fpc4="http://schemas.microsoft.com/isa/
-- config-4" xmlns:dt="urn:schemas-microsoft-com:
-- datatypes"
-- StorageName="FPC" StorageType="0">
    <fpc4:Build dt:dt="string">4.0.2161.50</fpc4:Build>
    <fpc4:Comment dt:dt="string">0</fpc4:Comment>
    <fpc4:Edition dt:dt="int">80</fpc4:Edition>
    <fpc4:ExportItemClassCLSID dt:dt="string">{0B964D61-
-- 5EBE-4837-9AE1-00FEF4ABCB0F}</fpc4:
-- ExportItemClassCLSID>
    <fpc4:ExportItemStorageName dt:dt="string">{20FBE63A-
-- 7146-442E-B695-F5C9E2FE65E5}</fpc4:
-- ExportItemStorageName>
    <fpc4:IsaXmlVersion dt:dt="string">1.0</fpc4:
-- IsaXmlVersion>
    <fpc4:OptionalData dt:dt="int">0</fpc4:OptionalData>
    <fpc4:Upgrade dt:dt="boolean">0</fpc4:Upgrade>
    <fpc4:Arrays StorageName="Arrays" StorageType="0">
        <fpc4:Array StorageName="{BD3510F7-8661-4381-8898-
-- 3B31BE6EAB42}" StorageType="0">
        <fpc4:Components dt:dt="int">-1</fpc4:Components>
        <fpc4:Name dt:dt="string"/>
        <fpc4:RuleElements StorageName="RuleElements"
-- StorageType="0">
        <fpc4:ComputerSets StorageName="ComputerSets"
-- StorageType="0">
        <fpc4:ComputerSet StorageName="{20FBE63A-7146-
-- 442E-B695-F5C9E2FE65E5}" StorageType="1">
        <fpc4:Name dt:dt="string">ThorSet_Papua New
-- Guinea</fpc4:Name>
        <fpc4:AddressRanges StorageName="AddressRanges"
-- StorageType="1">
```

```
      <fpc4:AddressRange StorageName="{A1342783-43AC-
-- 49B3-A96E-8561EE21134F}" StorageType="1">
         <fpc4:IPFrom dt:dt="string">119.252.224.0</
-- fpc4:IPFrom>
         <fpc4:IPTo dt:dt="string">119.252.239.255</
-- fpc4:IPTo>
         <fpc4:Name dt:dt="string">PG2013061120-
-- 2013065215</fpc4:Name>
      </fpc4:AddressRange>
```

And here is the same XML section in ISA Server 2006:

```
<?xml version="1.0" encoding="UTF-8"?>
<fpc4:Root xmlns:fpc4="http://schemas.microsoft.com/isa/
-- config-4" xmlns:dt="urn:schemas-microsoft-com:-
datatypes"
-- StorageName="FPC" StorageType="0">
   <fpc4:Build dt:dt="string">5.0.5720.100</fpc4:Build>
   <fpc4:Comment dt:dt="string">0</fpc4:Comment>
   <fpc4:Edition dt:dt="int">16</fpc4:Edition>
   <fpc4:ExportItemClassCLSID dt:dt="string">{0B964D61-
-- 5EBE-4837-9AE1-00FEF4ABCB0F}</fpc4:
-- ExportItemClassCLSID>
   <fpc4:ExportItemScope dt:dt="int">0</fpc4:
-- ExportItemScope>
   <fpc4:ExportItemStorageName dt:dt="string">{9F5C68F1-
-- 7E90-4A7B-80E1-9390B4757596}</fpc4:
-- ExportItemStorageName>
   <fpc4:IsaXmlVersion dt:dt="string">5.30</fpc4:
-- IsaXmlVersion>
   <fpc4:OptionalData dt:dt="int">0</fpc4:OptionalData>
   <fpc4:Upgrade dt:dt="boolean">0</fpc4:Upgrade>
   <fpc4:Arrays StorageName="Arrays" StorageType="0">
      <fpc4:Array StorageName="{C4B4D104-2560-473D-9740-
-- A8B39B68DBD7}" StorageType="0">
         <fpc4:Components dt:dt="int">-1</fpc4:Components>
         <fpc4:DNSName dt:dt="string"/>
         <fpc4:Name dt:dt="string"/>
         <fpc4:RuleElements StorageName="RuleElements"
-- StorageType="0">
         <fpc4:ComputerSets StorageName="ComputerSets"
-- StorageType="0">
         <fpc4:ComputerSet StorageName="{9F5C68F1-7E90-
-- 4A7B-80E1-9390B4757596}" StorageType="1">
         <fpc4:Name dt:dt="string">ThorSet_Papua New
-- Guinea</fpc4:Name>
```

```
              <fpc4:AddressRanges StorageName="AddressRanges"
-- StorageType="1">
              <fpc4:AddressRange StorageName="{88535F57-00F8-
-- 477F-B7DF-D6DC132EC648}" StorageType="1">
                   <fpc4:IPFrom dt:dt="string">119.252.224.0</
-- fpc4:IPFrom>
                   <fpc4:IPTo dt:dt="string">119.252.239.255</
-- fpc4:IPTo>
                   <fpc4:Name dt:dt="string">PG2013061120-
-- 2013065215</fpc4:Name>
              </fpc4:AddressRange>
```

Being able to easily export each different format style was important to me, so I needed something portable, stand-alone, and that supported data access and VBA. Now that TMG is the standard and ISA Server versions are no longer being developed, I will concentrate on writing up a C# version that is a bit faster and easier. But for now, we will have to use Access (or whatever else you would like) to get the job done quickly.

I will include the skeleton Access file as a resource for the book, but what I have done is created a linked reference in Access to my IpToCountry table in SQL, as well as a form with a couple buttons to which I have attached code, and a status window, as shown in Figure 3.20.

In design mode, I have Code Sample 3.9 built for the **Create Sets (Write that Funky Stuff)** button.

```
This code is written specifically for usability and flexibi-
lity during the TMG object creation process for execution
directly by the user. SQL strings are dynamically created, and
are not intended for accepting input from any external source,
as it provides SQL injection capabilities.

Private Sub CreateSets_Click()
On Error Resume Next
'
' Grab Source IP Country data from SQL and Create TMG sets.
'
' Create the root object.
Dim root ' The FPCLib.FPC root object
Set root = CreateObject("FPC.Root")
```

■ **CODE SAMPLE 3.9** Create Sets VBA Code to Create TMG Computer Set Objects

(continued)

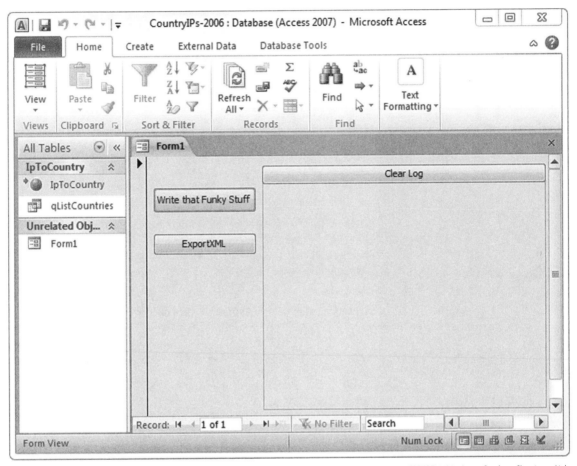

■ **FIGURE 3.20** Access Database Showing a Link to My IpToCountry SQL Table and a Form Example

```
' Declare the other objects needed.
Dim isaArray
Dim ComputerSets
Dim ComputerSet
Dim AddressRanges
Dim AddressRange

Dim rstCountries As Recordset
Dim rstAddresses As Recordset
Dim sCountry As String
Dim sSQL As String
```

■ **CODE SAMPLE 3.9—cont'd**

```
Dim sRangeName As String
Dim sLogText As String

'Connect to array
Set isaArray = root.GetContainingArray()
Set ComputerSets = isaArray.RuleElements.ComputerSets

Log.SetFocus

'Get a distinct list of countries
'If this code somehow makes it to production, use parameterized
-- queries.
sSQL = "SELECT distinct GeoIPCountry.CountryName FROM
-- GeoIPCountry order by CountryName"

'Test sql to only get selected countries
'sSQL = "SELECT distinct GeoIPCountry.CountryName FROM
-- GeoIPCountry where CountryName like 'F*' order by
-- CountryName"


Set rstCountries = CurrentDb.OpenRecordset(sSQL)

Do 'Countries loop
Log.Text = ""
sCountry = rstCountries!CountryName
Log.Text = Log.Text + "Working on " + sCountry + Constants.
-- vbNewLine
Set ComputerSet = ComputerSets.Add("ThorSet_" + sCountry)
sSQL = "Select BegIP,EndIP,BegIPNo,EndIPNo,Country,
-- CountryName from GeoIPCountry where CountryName = '" +
sCountry + "' Order by BegIPNo"


Set rstAddresses = CurrentDb.OpenRecordset(sSQL)
Log.Text = Log.Text + Str(rstAddresses.RecordCount) +
-- "address ranges found" + Constants.vbNewLine
Do 'Addresses Loop
sRangeName = Trim(rstAddresses!Country) +
-- Trim(Str(rstAddresses!BegIpNo)) + "-" +
Trim(Str(rstAddresses!EndIpNo))
Set AddressRanges = ComputerSet.AddressRanges
Set AddressRange = AddressRanges.Add(sRangeName,
-- rstAddresses!BegIP, rstAddresses!EndIP)
rstAddresses.MoveNext

Loop Until rstAddresses.EOF

Log.Text = Log.Text + "... saving"
'ComputerSet.Save
```

■ **CODE SAMPLE 3.9—cont'd**

```
rstCountries.MoveNext

Loop Until rstCountries.EOF

ComputerSets.Save

MsgBox ("Done.")
End Sub
```

■ **CODE SAMPLE 3.9—cont'd**

This code creates the necessary TMG objects, creates a data record set representative of each distinct country, and then creates another record set of each country's IP ranges. It moves through each top country record set creating the set, and moves through each range record for each country until all sets are created. At that point, it tells TMG to save the data via its save method. This will take some time, so be patient.

To export the data, the code shown in Code Sample 3.10 is bound to the **ExportXML** button.

```
Private Sub ExportSets_Click()

'On Error Resume Next

' Create the root object.
Dim root ' The FPCLib.FPC root object
Set root = CreateObject("FPC.Root")

' Declare the other objects needed.
Dim isaArray
Dim ComputerSets
Dim ComputerSet
Dim AddressRanges
Dim AddressRange
Dim sFilename As String
Dim i As Integer


Log.SetFocus
Log.Text = ""
'Connect to array
Set isaArray = root.GetContainingArray()
Set ComputerSets = isaArray.RuleElements.ComputerSets

i = 0
For Each ComputerSet In ComputerSets
i = i + 1
'Set ComputerSet = ComputerSets.Item
```

■ **CODE SAMPLE 3.10** Export Sets VBA Code to Export TMG Computer Set Objects to XML

(continued)

```
sFilename = ComputerSet.Name + ".xml"
Log.Text = Log.Text + "Exporting " + sFilename + "..."
ComputerSet.ExportToFile "C:\temp\" + sFilename, 0
If i = 20 Then Log Text = "": i = 0
Next

End Sub
```

■ **CODE SAMPLE 3.10—cont'd**

This code is much simpler and simply instantiates a Computer Set object, loops through each set present, and then exports it.

With the XML files, you can now select which countries you wish to work with and import them into whatever server you wish to. Once you have the sets, you can create whatever rules you wish to based on these sets. Figure 3.21 shows my SMTP inbound rule, which only allows SMTP from a select number of countries. I find that easier than blocking lots of other countries instead.

And with that, we wrap up this process example.

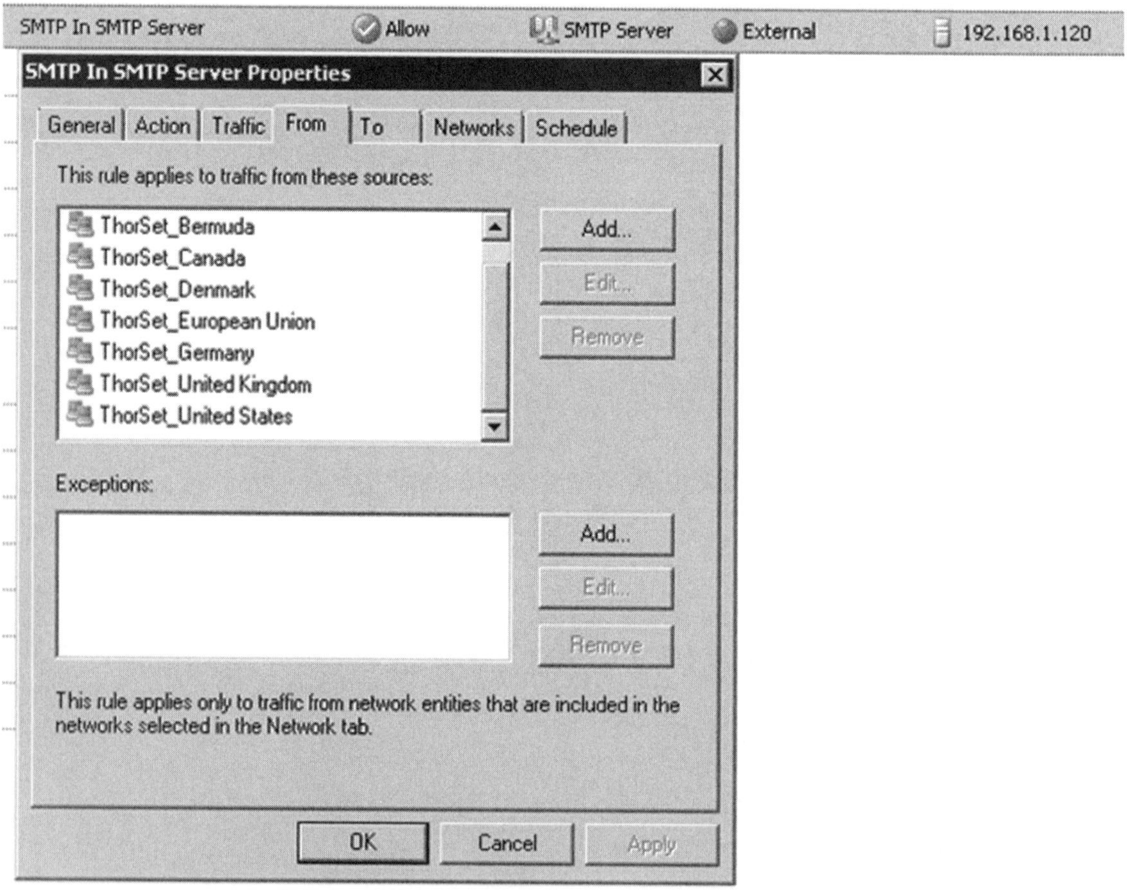

■ **FIGURE 3.21** Sample SMTP Publishing Rule Limiting Sources for SMTP to Specific Countries

■ SUMMARY

In this chapter, we explored the methods of how you can research and analyze traffic from multiple different geolocations, and how to report on that data. We further illustrated different ways to block or allow data based on our wants and needs, learned how to manage our data within SQL server, and discovered how to use TMG programming objects to build Computer Sets to report from. We also introduced SQL CLR to handle some of the heavy lifting of data conversion.

REFERENCES

Mullen, T. M. (2011). Blocking traffic by country on production networks. *Symantec Connect*, April 22, www.symantec.com/connect/articles/blocking-traffic-country-production-networks.

Belarus, (2011). FREE IP to country database (IPV4 and IPV6). In *webnet77 Low cost domain names, domain transfers, web hosting, email accounts, and so much more*, April 22, http://software77.net/geo-ip/.

"Network Calculators," (2011). *Network Calculators,* April 22, http://www.subnetmask .info/.

"Creating the root forefront TMG object [Windows]," (2011). *MSDN | Microsoft Development, Subscriptions, Resources, and More,* April 22. http://msdn.microsoft.com/en-us/library/dd435764.aspx.

Creating an Externally Accessible Authenticated Proxy in a Secure Manner

---

INFORMATION IN THIS CHAPTER:

- Build It and They Will Come

PRODUCTS, TOOLS, AND METHODS:

- TMG
- AD
- Hyper-V
- Alternate Network in TMG
- Web Proxy
- Server Publishing
- Custom Protocol

INTRODUCTION

One of the great things about being in this business is that you get to meet people from around the world, either in person or virtually. I am quite fortunate to have some really cool friends around the globe. A couple of them, Steve and Greg, who are part of a little group we call *The Boyz*, live in Bermuda and Australia, respectively. Of course there are others, and I do not care if you know Steve and Greg's real names. Whether you realize it or not, the Internet is not always global, particularly when it comes to U.S.-based Internet television broadcasts or streaming media content providers: Many broadcasters and Internet video houses simply ban access to their content from locations outside the United States. One may, if so inclined, decide to allow people such as Steve and Greg access to U.S. content, purely for the technical challenges if nothing else. I have no idea what the legal implications are of this, but this is not any different than any other remote access method of virtual private network (VPN), DirectAccess, and so on, other than that it will let you connect from anywhere without having a dependency on other software. The main purpose of this is to illustrate methods of providing alternate access to web content, and ways to secure this type of access.

BUILD IT AND THEY WILL COME

Basically, we want to allow any authenticated user access to our outbound TMG[1] proxy so that all connections appear to come from our U.S.-based server here in the U.S. Hammer of God labs, as opposed to our Bermuda labs run by Steve "Raging Haggis" Moffat. All we want the user to do is configure their browser to use our proxy address and port, and to have to authenticate.

TMG is used as example product many times in this book, but remember, the concepts here are what are most important.

While this sounds easy enough, there are some issues we have to address in order to do this securely. We have got the following considerations: We have to authenticate to the proxy, which has its own associated issues. We then have to figure out how to actually publish external incoming requests to ISA's own internal interface in order to accept the web proxy connection to then route it back out again. And we also might want to consider the ramifications of allowing traffic originating outside our network to comingle with our internal web proxy traffic, meaning we way want to physically separate that traffic. The main goal is to use what we have insofar as the capabilities of ISA to have our solution be secure, and not spend too much time configuring it.

Authentication is going to be our main concern here for a few reasons. We are limited in our authentication mechanisms, and we are limited in our choices for the protocols over which the credentials will travel. So we shall start with the web proxy listener, which is located in the **Web Proxy** tab of the **Internal Properties** in ISA, as shown in Figure 4.1.

This is what you will see when you configure regular internal traffic to use the internal network as a web proxy target. As you can see, there are not many choices to make. We can enable web proxy clients on the network, HTTP or HTTPS, and you can choose a port to listen on. Further, we see that Digest, Integrated, Basic, Secure Sockets Layer (SSL) cert, and Remote Authentication Dial-in User Service (RADIUS) are the available authentication protocols.

---

[1]Other products let you set up simple proxies, but I use TMG because of the level of control you have.

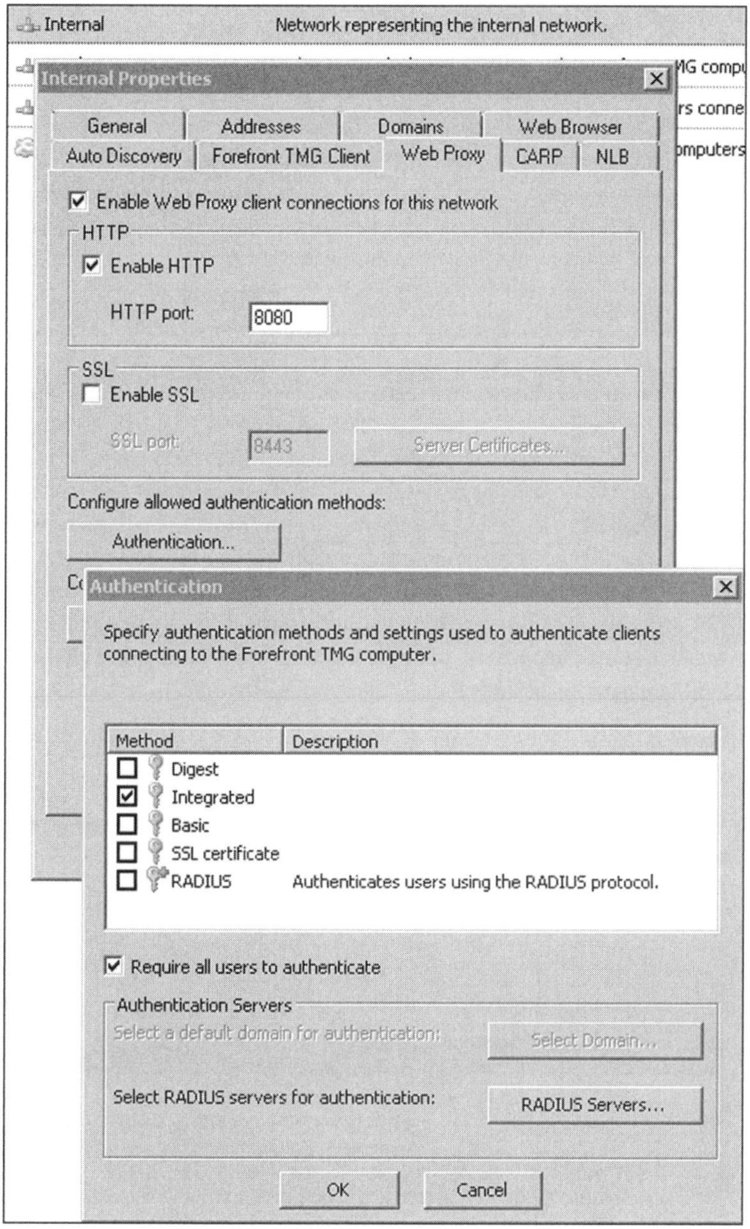

■ **FIGURE 4.1** TMG Authentication Methods

Authentication Challenges

We need to start by authenticating users, otherwise the proxy will allow anonymous connections. We cannot just request authentication either, because all outbound web requests start off as anonymous requests. If we allow anonymous requests at all, they will be anonymous for this reason. Before we talk more about that, we have to settle which protocol we will use to connect to the web proxy listener. You might immediately choose to **Enable SSL** on port 8443 and use that, but unfortunately this will not work. The SSL listener configuration of ISA's web proxy is for chaining only, where you specifically chain from one proxy to another, and requires the traffic as a whole to be encrypted. IE clients *cannot* use this. Remember, our external clients will simply put in a hostname, such as http://proxy.hammerofgod .com and an associated port, such as 8080. Since we will have IE clients (or any Conseil Européen pour la Recherche Nucléaire [CERN]-compliant browser) we must use HTTP to connect. Yes, I know. HTTP is an in-the-clear protocol and when our external clients enter their credentials to authenticate to the web proxy listener, they will be transmitted in their original unencrypted format. We will, therefore, use the default **Enable HTTP** configuration on port 8080, and select only **Integrated** for the authentication. Again, since all proxy requests begin as anonymous, we must select the option to **Require all users to authenticate**, as shown in Figure 4.2.

This will force the web proxy listener to ignore the initial anonymous request from a browser, and send an authentication challenge back.

> **WARNING**
> Requiring outbound proxy traffic to be authenticated may keep certain services from working, as illustrated by the warning triggered by enabling the authentication requirement, as shown in the dialog box in Figure 4.3.

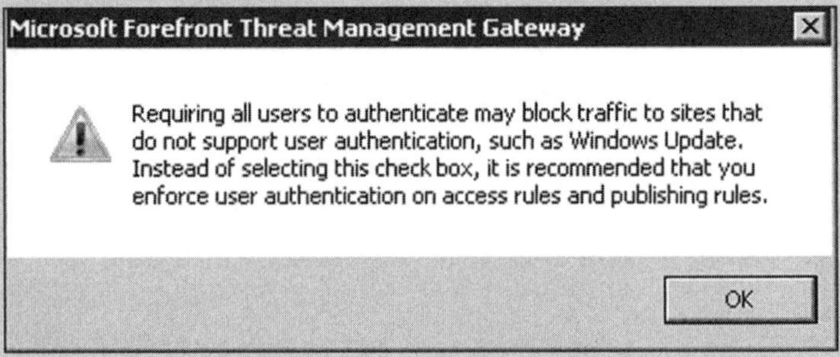

Microsoft Forefront Threat Management Gateway

Requiring all users to authenticate may block traffic to sites that do not support user authentication, such as Windows Update. Instead of selecting this check box, it is recommended that you enforce user authentication on access rules and publishing rules.

OK

■ **FIGURE 4.3** TMG Default Warning about Authenticated Outbound Access

☑ Require all users to authenticate

■ **FIGURE 4.2** TMG Authentication Options

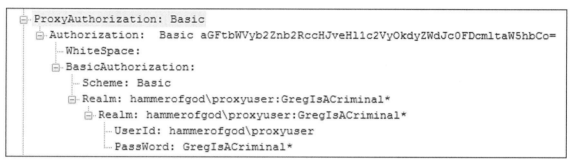

```
ProxyAuthorization: Basic
   Authorization:  Basic aGFtbWVyb2Znb2RccHJveHl1c2VyOkdyZWdJc0FDcmltaW5hbCo=
      WhiteSpace:
   BasicAuthorization:
      Scheme: Basic
      Realm: hammerofgod\proxyuser:GregIsACriminal*
         Realm: hammerofgod\proxyuser:GregIsACriminal*
            UserId: hammerofgod\proxyuser
            PassWord: GregIsACriminal*
```

■ **FIGURE 4.4** Network Packet Capture of an HTTP Basic Authentication Transaction

Most people assume that all authentication over HTTP is insecure because HTTP is not encrypted, but this is not really the case. HTTP is just HTTP. It is the authentication method itself that is or is not secure. Basic Authentication is merely a mechanism by which the username and password is encoded in a base64 string and sent over the wire. This is a trivial encoding method, and it looks like Figure 4.4 in a network capture.

The key string of data we are looking for is the authentication bits, which are:

```
Basic aGFtbWVyb2Znb2RccHJveHl1c2VyOkdyZWdJc0FDcmltaW5hbCo=
```

This simply decodes to say *hammerofgod\proxyuser:GregIsACriminal*.* Clearly, we see that Basic Authentication over HTTP is completely insecure, which is a bad idea given Greg's disposition. But what about integrated authentication protocols such as NTLM or Kerberos? The actual methods used and encryption algorithms leveraged with Integrated Authentication will vary over OS flavors and Registry settings. My internal lab requires NTLMv2 authentication, which you may or may not be able to support, but Figure 4.5 shows a partial network capture from just one part of the authentication negotiation via Integrated Authentication.

The full authorization string of this part of the challenge/response is:

```
Negotiate
YIIGdQYGKwYBBQUCoIIGaTCCBmWgMDAuBgkqhkiC9xIBAgIGCSqGSIb3
EgECAgYKKwYBBAGCNwICHgYKKwYBBAGCNwICCqKCBi8EggYrYIIGJwYJ
```

■ **FIGURE 4.5** Network Packet Capture of an Integrated Windows Authentication

```
ProxyAuthorization: Negotiate
   Authorization:  Negotiate YIIGdQYGKwYBBQUCoIIGaTCCBmWgMDAuBgkqhkiC9xIBAgIGCSqGS
      WhiteSpace:
   NegotiateAuthorization:
      Scheme: Negotiate
```

KoZIhvcSAQICAQBuggYWMIIGEqADAgEFoQMCAQ6iBwMFACAAAACjggSk
YYIEoDCCBJygAwIBBaERGw9IQU1NRVJPRkdPRC5DT02iJjAkoAMCAQKh
HTAbGwRIVFRQGxN1YWcuaGFtbWVyb2Znb2QuY29to4IEWDCCBFSgAwIB
EqEDAgEBooIERgSCBEIeIGORGoa97JM6ef6ms21WrlvjSuYrTlp959E/
KBALgPwjJbSXbT97FUyPWPulPgJBxa7utfShf+Yd3EJna1WnRj/0jtt5
gmADULFOuyFS29kBCzlgdJlPcIQBNylnHmw+LXOpERuHt5DiFpYTLpW7
pjOKP5dP4y2q9LvM+J75kmHIj7PU2T5YPCL2xiF1zWa1FNnOz8Xjr3Ap
sGr9mF1WSi+qGmLZTY9kOje2GuDqUPGPP//j7xErfLNfCWQmFbjKoAC/
bhEE9hNhxNlAqyYIk3FRzFLi8WMu1O32mkXCFBwYnp5Vult3wAO3P7V8
E2yb25jmKXUGVUfghtCY9rDQ5zB47ZrihdrQc29Q/UKKV25vQ9D24iaN
bfvNPXTWYUlfYd28s3J01r+kf15Axn5P8fEi5IBuB9a757Y9aj8nzVqI
Lf4By8iupJEwsb6CpDiKBP6ZbAd8nlKKB7RBH2dw8jBQr9i1zeI/d3RC
WdK+FOOL7TpYqVGmLCSB91R4uhb9DhDHogLFXkIKkDmJLh/uCXimPi38
YFAsYDgf5 cr6E+kzFqEZ+BYOPQCFau8f1glIVWF6IOQZ+JTwGkjvisY
GX+iUcuwq2wOzP9Tcri043lP4B6AvO5xU+2LJ4e3YCJTMVVDgv+27pQ
BioYf380dH7Mjp5mofynX6mgeObo7dqxdRNeCrAVquOCNHiAQ/yBUmI1
znQIuEKbUAOAJmbua9k6oENCwdWOyTed7VZeMRS/M7fF5fxJmh3Z/mN7
Y8GVq6y6R8bdU74Dr4LKjT8p84LowqktS4y0Onk4Uxk3T1ZhtPsf4mbn
hAkquGyOsd9CnovlZKkC5UW4ExRh1dbLb+SmcdMtYNj8f21R8fbHaPsQ
M/6OkK57b+92hFSgu4UTPbOjKpzOAv+xKvPiLb+eknRS2QwrsVnj5+8
uitP521YSv1J+8fZfJJT/7t28ckpXlkYWYpRb2Rb3vojv/JXkTt7s11V
1SyC1aFQFpHojMxbf1zbEORj61N3Xp24TomdcAqNWUQNhWy4YzvvWn8g
EqzlAvtNbjq51t+xgLx5twecrdIjt4VOLj/9o/TSq4HX31wOchO+txCZ
ZmfdpTvtBsPnAI6YdvZJYqUC9ymTnB5oWGhCdzPnXhKW6stlq1Txlxr5W
pt4LiVR/Ow3nIU8oOZhXjPusrakzOTaLJDU3u+7Tf/9r+kHg5wcx7zz
+sAjq3ui3FXe+sFxMSmXx4W/xmCjwP3sCuk3lzLsfJKho/AcOdBHKCveo
5TVs4c8hNWLmIxyCqmOGa99olzMgeO8XRKX2dYxnXLKtoShnCsTE1oyD
5aSeOW152MDegtu3i3Zs3RX231rA6sbSKQzg4JnpplBQrZAXAi30iDXz
y7rhVZ3QB1QqINXbBOTVFB9uT/xvEGltVm6axjCk7QDrLoLsOdUQOm3S
jlccHsjroZgO8bf3LdpIIBUzCCAU+gAwIBEqKCAUYEggFCrtnF5Y7S6z
w3Sqw8SqQQ4sdBJ5CpRvKkqeeOJxmDyp1jD9+7LN8ycb34/4U2B+HvgU
Sh9rnPhJKQLaKOdKm6qRsnrjKStHVpdxivnogdwsw1BgPOvaWTZepM3D
BOry3zIUflN4ZkHizHXZbqsWgcukE7ehOz/0H6r3KKOds19elnuRXENE
ppTiFOqEZxPfpRMmlczG6WE/VFZP6ysbicNyBL+Am4sttDv7o1r9CwMs
4J71CM24LYaBa88s9hjgsLRpHukcoa4wQ1+G1RYmRfDXqixHO4nMwm736
4XkxUBmtGDdApYG6WOI6nXqOfq9AohDFKT7HsyK/fOQ2UoM4xx5hlTIz
DO/EhWXF3NKbZAgtWGjHID2xU6Nt6MXn3o5+1BGSQ5fd4HYEJfOFojyz
AvV9njiyAppgDsqrtTvqyJSPykQ==

Authentication Mechanisms

Though transmitted over HTTP, my NTLMv2 negotiation is a full 128-bit encrypted, base64-encoded challenge and response. Even if your system encoded the password in 64-bit RC4, a long complex password would take far longer to crack before your password expiry policy required a change (hopefully). Now, it is very important to understand that this is not a typical feature of Integrated Authentication. You cannot log on remotely via NTLM in IIS by default for example. TMG specifically negotiates this for us, and that is an important distinction.

Everyone is all abuzz about how rainbow tables can crack an NTLM password in seconds, but that is typically only for seven-, maybe nine-, character lowercase alpha-numeric passwords. I cover passwords and security extensively in Chapter 5, "The Creation and Maintenance of Low-Privileged Service Users," so you will see exactly how difficult it is to brute-force smart passwords. If you can enforce NTLMv2, then the user's domain name is used in the encryption key, which effectively obviates you from rainbow table attacks unless an attacker generates custom rainbow tables for your particular domain, which just is not going to happen because it would be far more efficient to run a brute force attack rather than create a custom rainbow table. Even with NTLM, if you have a 12- or 14-character password with some complexity, NTLM authentication over HTTP will do just fine for our purposes here. More importantly, for this type of connection, it is really the best we can do outside of publishing a RemoteApp of Internet Explorer (covered in Chapter 7, "Securing RDP"), which would have reduced performance and would carry its own set of unique issues. As a restriction of the way the TMG proxy functions, clients must connect to our internal network over HTTP only, so we are limited by what options we have within HTTP authentication mechanisms. So, we have now required Integrated Authentication to our web proxy listener, and Steve and Greg will have to enter their usernames and passwords to the proxy upon connection. It is important to remember that in this case Integrated Authentication does not mean that we need some sort of trust relationship or that a centralized authentication infrastructure be present to provide single sign-on capabilities. Windows Authentication over HTTP functions the same way Basic Authentication does in that you are challenged for username and password at the time of resource access; Integrated Authentication just changes the negotiation protocol. It does not specifically matter if this is based on a local or domain user. It is also important to note that you cannot use Windows Authentication via HTTP on the Internet to authenticate directly to a web server or service. This option only works when connecting to TMG because it is built as an authentication solution. More of this is discussed in Chapter 2, "Internet Information Server (IIS) Authentication and Authorization Models, and Locking Down File Access with Encrypting File System (EFS) and Web Distributed Authoring and Versioning (WebDAV)."

> **NOTE**
> Rainbow tables are precalculated hashes of passwords with a given character base (e.g., a–z, A–Z, 0–9, and 7 characters long) that can be quickly looked up to determine a password.

Publishing the Proxy

We have to get the access to the proxy itself via a TMG publishing rule, but this may be a bit counterintuitive. TMG has a prebuilt protocol for HTTP proxy, but it is only for outbound traffic (for clients to be able to make proxy calls through the firewall when configured). Out of the box, TMG does not know what to do with inbound HTTP 8080 traffic. Even though you might consider the connection to the proxy listener to be outbound from the client to the internal network, when we publish that service it will really be inbound as far as the publishing rule is concerned. Therefore, we must create a custom protocol definition for inbound proxy traffic on port 8080. I have called mine *Inbound Proxy* and it is shown in Figure 4.6.

Notice that I have selected **Web Proxy Filter** in the **Application Filters** as well. This will ensure that the incoming traffic is analyzed and inspected for valid HTTP commands, and it will prevent an attacker from using the open port to send anything other than valid traffic down the pipe. Next we need to create a server publishing rule for our custom Inbound Proxy protocol from the external network to the internal network interface IP address that is listening for web proxy requests. I have simply called my rule *External Proxy*, and yours should look something similar to Figure 4.7.

Figure 4.8 shows the specification of the Inbound Proxy custom protocol during the rule generation. Figure 4.9 shows the assignment of the server that we are publishing to, which is the IP of the internal NIC configured to listen for web proxy traffic as shown earlier in Figure 4.1.

The important thing to note here is that we must change the default setting for requests for the published server from **Requests appear to come from the original client** to **Requests appear to come from the Forefront TMG computer**. This may be counterintuitive, so we shall cover the reasons why this is required.

Traffic Analysis

Normally, when we have a publishing rule, we would want to capture the originating client's actual IP address at the published server (the one on the back end) for logging purposes. Take the typical web publishing rule

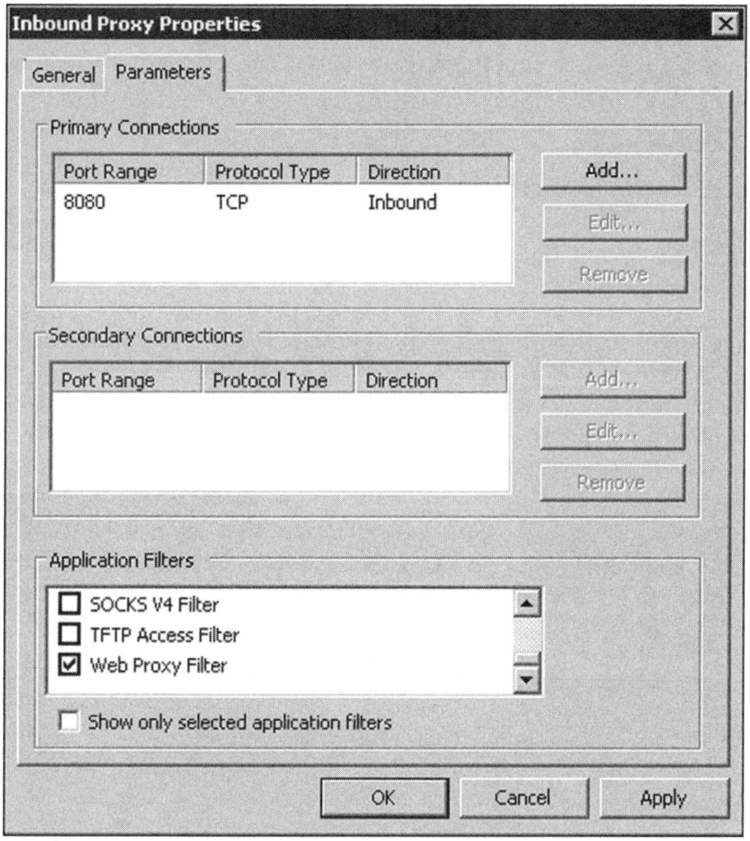

■ **FIGURE 4.6** Inbound Proxy Protocol Web Proxy Filter Assignment

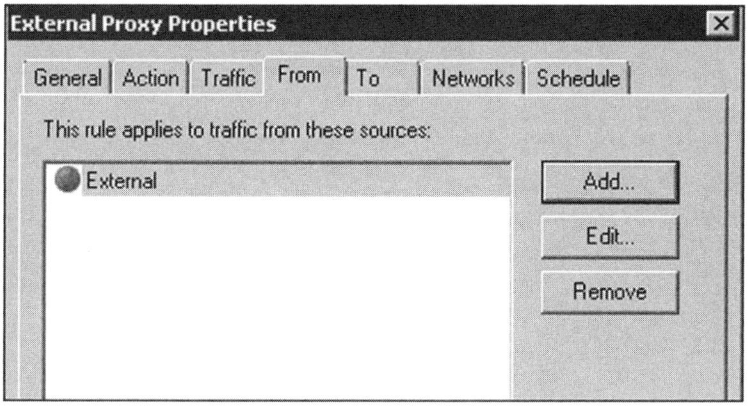

■ **FIGURE 4.7** Rule Set Identifying What Network to Accept Traffic from

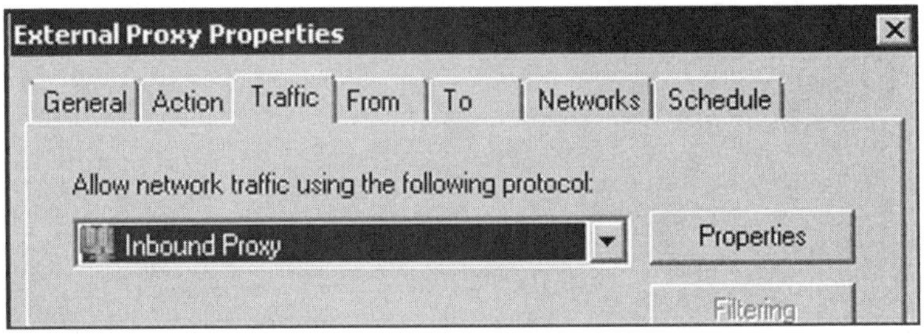

■ **FIGURE 4.8** Assigning the Custom Protocol as the Traffic

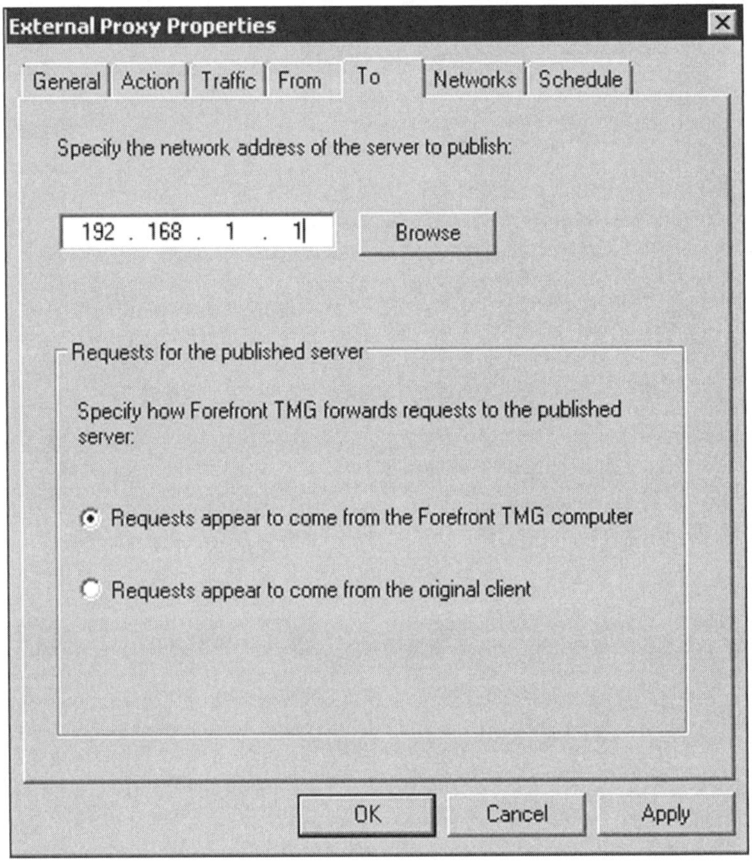

■ **FIGURE 4.9** Specifying the Remote System to Publish to and the Request Appearance Mode

for example. We publish an internal IIS web server to TMG so that external Internet clients will access pages through TMG. If TMG did not make the request look like it came from the original client's IP rather than its own (where the request is really coming from), then all log entries would look like:

```
192.168.1.1, -, 01/20/10, 7:55:20, W3SVC2, SERVER, 192.168.1.10,
4502, 163, 3223, 200, 0, GET, /image.gif, -,
192.168.1.1, -, 01/20/10, 7:55:20, W3SVC2, SERVER, 192.168.1.10,
4502, 163, 3223, 200, 0, GET, /image1.gif, -,
192.168.1.1, -, 01/20/10, 7:55:20, W3SVC2, SERVER, 192.168.1.10,
4502, 163, 3223, 200, 0, GET, /image2.gif, -,
```

where 192.168.1.1 is the TMG server's internal address and 192.168.1.10 is the address of the web server. What you want it to typically look like is:

```
209.158.2.5, -, 01/20/10, 7:55:20, W3SVC2, SERVER, 192.168.1.10,
4502, 163, 3223, 200, 0, GET, /image.gif, -,
209.158.2.5, -, 01/20/10, 7:55:20, W3SVC2, SERVER, 192.168.1.10,
4502, 163, 3223, 200, 0, GET, /image1.gif, -,
209.158.2.5, -, 01/20/10, 7:55:20, W3SVC2, SERVER, 192.168.1.10,
4502, 163, 3223, 200, 0, GET, /image2.gif, -,
```

This allows us to see the actual originating client's IP address. However, in this case, we cannot do that. What we are doing is something a bit different in regard to the normal functions of TMG. An external client will connect to the external interface of TMG, which will then be published directly to the internal interface of TMG (the web proxy listener), at which point the request will then go back out the external TMG interface and access the Internet in the same way an internal proxy client would. Given this, if a request to the published server (TMG itself in this case) looked like it came from the original client, then TMG will not be able to route back to the source IP address from the proxy listener IP address. In other words, the source IP will be destined for the internal web proxy, but since TMG is publishing to itself, it has to look like it came from its external IP address so it can route back out. If this is not the case, the error message shown in Figure 4.10 will illustrate my point.

It will still log the original client request IP to TMG, though it will look internally like its external interface. You need to know this because the source and destination log entries will *not* change once you get this working; however, this is great for us since we can still capture who is using our external proxy connection.

■ **FIGURE 4.10** Publishing Rule Fail

Denied Connection
Log type: Firewall service
Status: A non-SYN packet was dropped because it was sent by a source that does not have an established connection with the Forefront TMG computer.
Rule: None - see Result Code
Source: External (192.168.10.10:49326)
Destination: Local Host (192.168.100.5:8080)
Protocol: HTTP Proxy
⊟ Additional information
  • **Number of bytes sent:** 0 **Number of bytes received:** 0
  • **Processing time:** 0ms **Original Client IP:** 192.168.10.10

Introducing the Alternate Proxy Segment

This brings me to our last point. The preceding examples showed us publishing external requests to our normal internal web proxy listener, but this presents problems as previously mentioned. One, we have to require authentication on the internal network listener which will drive you crazy and keep some applications from working. Second, I just do not like the fact that external clients are accessing my internal network's proxy listener. It makes me nervous, and breaks security in depth.

Instead, what we should do is create our own dedicated TMG network, and use that for the external proxy access. Our true internal network proxy will be protected, we can require authentication without breaking anything, and we will not mix logging data with internal traffic.

I have chosen to actually deploy TMG in a Hyper-V environment which makes it a snap to create a virtual network on the host and then add virtual NIC functionality to our virtual machines.

If you do not leverage virtualized environments, you should take a look at doing so because it really makes configuration options easy, and it can be very well secured. For me, I will just create a private virtual network in Hyper-V and access it as an NIC interface in my virtual machine. Figure 4.11 shows how that looks in Hyper-V Virtual Network Manager.

■ **FIGURE 4.11** Configuring the Virtual Alternate Internal Proxy Segment in Hyper-V

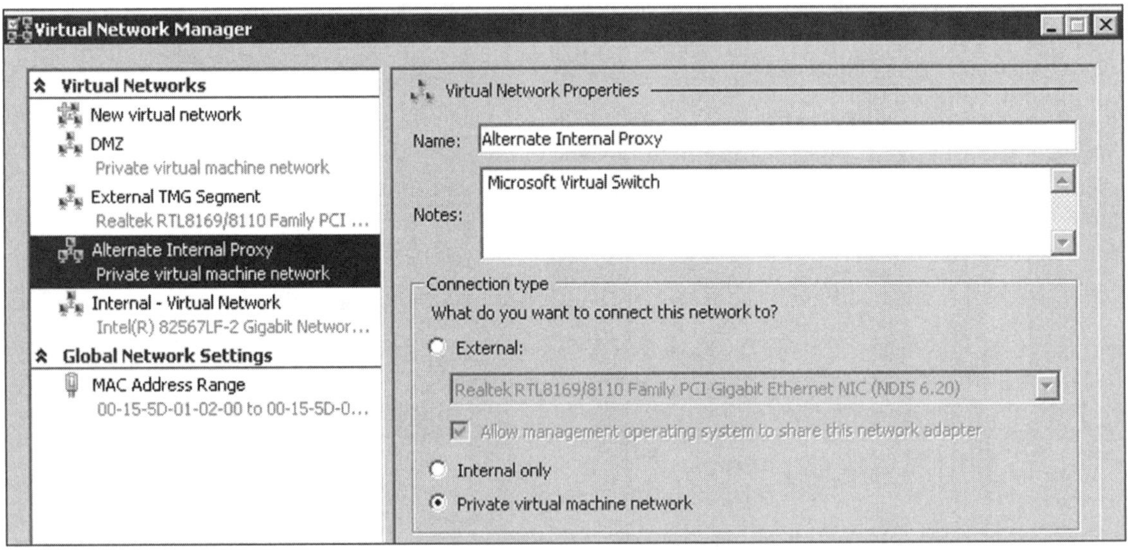

With the virtual network segment created, we just configure a new NIC in our TMG virtual machine as shown in Figure 4.12.

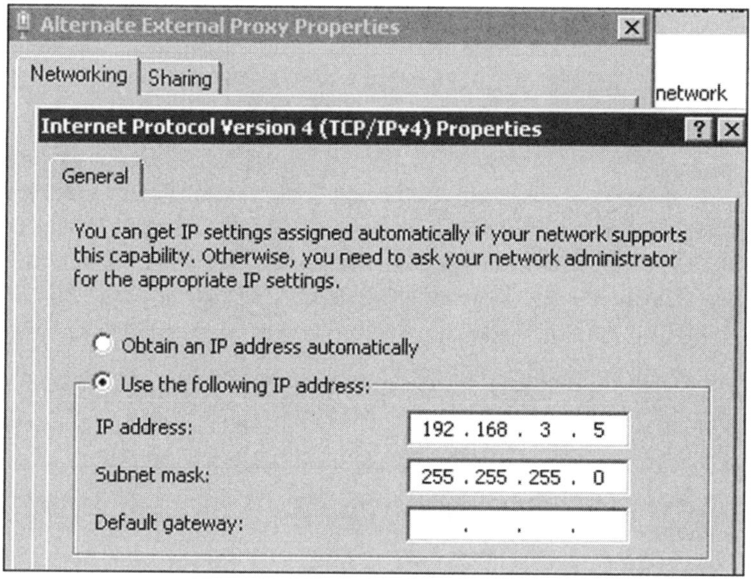

FIGURE 4.12 Configure IP Settings for the Alternate Interface

Now that the NIC is configured, we will create a new network in TMG, as shown in Figure 4.13.

With this network created, we can set our internal web proxy network configuration in TMG to not require authentication at the proxy listener, instead choosing to require authentication on our new 192.168.3.0 network segment web proxy listener. There is a bit more to it than that as you will see shortly, but for now we will move on to other things.

Troubleshooting Connections

In the previous example, we simply published to our existing internal web proxy listener, which worked because TMG already knew about the internal interface and its relationship to the other networks because this is defined by

FIGURE 4.13 Define the TMG Networks

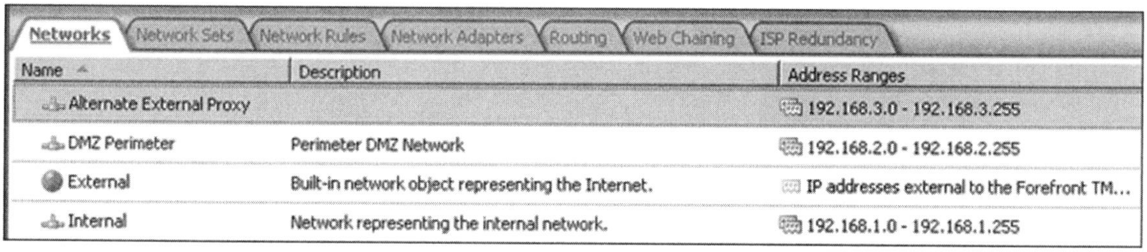

Name ▲	Description	Address Ranges
Alternate External Proxy		192.168.3.0 - 192.168.3.255
DMZ Perimeter	Perimeter DMZ Network	192.168.2.0 - 192.168.2.255
External	Built-in network object representing the Internet.	IP addresses external to the Forefront TM...
Internal	Network representing the internal network.	192.168.1.0 - 192.168.1.255

the TMG network rules configuration. By default, the internal network has a network address translation (NAT) relationship to the external network. All traffic originating from addresses defined in the internal network configuration will use NAT when making outbound calls.

When the alternate external proxy network was created, the existing network rules were not changed. Therefore, TMG would by default, insofar as the context of a publishing rule is concerned, consider the destination of 192.168.3.5 as the local host. For the purposes of illustration, we will leave this alone for now and go about our business of changing the publishing rule to reflect the new proxy configuration, as shown in Figure 4.14.

If we apply this configuration and attempt to connect to port 8080 externally via our client's proxy server configuration, the connection will fail and we will see something like Figure 4.15 in our TMG logs.

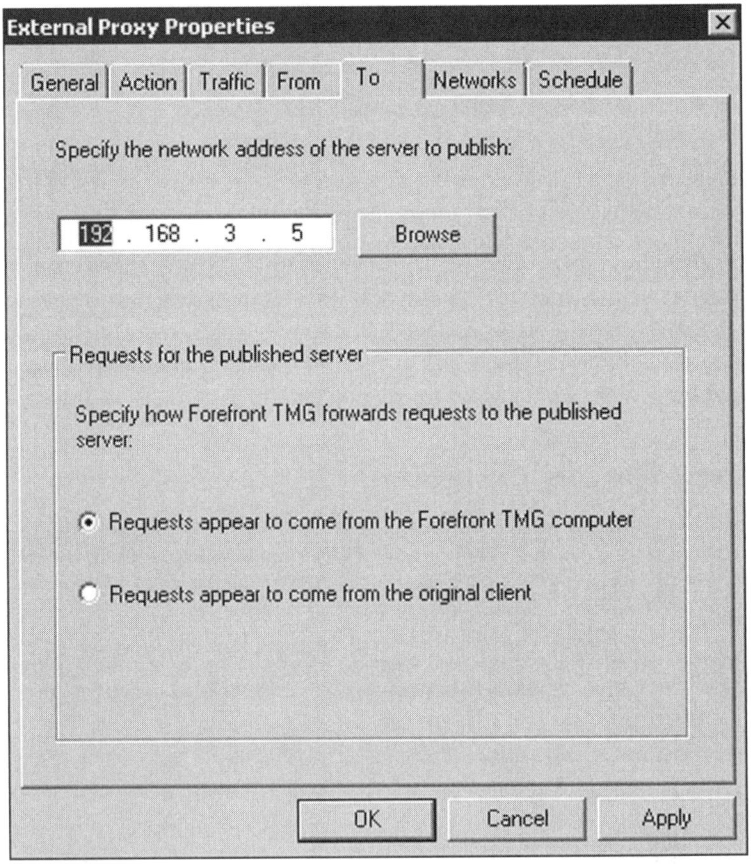

■ **FIGURE 4.14** Publishing to the Alternate Interface Proxy Listener

Action	Rule	Result Code	Source Network	Destination Net...
Denied Connection	Default rule	0xc004000d FWX_E_POLICY_RULES_DENIED	External	Local Host

■ **FIGURE 4.15** Publishing Fail

The key here is the identification of the destination network as *Local Host*. That tells you that something is wrong. When you expect TMG to identify a network as something other than what it identifies on its own, you need to look at your network rules.

As stated previously, we did not define the alternate external proxy in our network relationships, so TMG did not know what we wanted to do with it. While we could create a new relationship via an entirely new network rule, it will be easier to add the alternate external proxy to our existing Internet Access default rule, as demonstrated in Figure 4.16.

This will now work immediately, depending upon the authentication method chosen in the web proxy configuration. If we choose not to require any authentication to the new web proxy network, external requests will immediately succeed as the rules stand now via this simplified sequence of transactions. This presumes that the external client somewhere on the Internet has their browser configured to use port 8080 on my external IP address as their proxy.

The publishing rule requires no authentication, so the publishing transaction to 8080 succeeds.

The connection to the web proxy port on 8080 requires no authentication, so the connection succeeds.

The external client's request for www.bing.com is processed by the proxy, and the connection from TMG to Bing on behalf of the external client succeeds based on the default firewall policy rule of **Allow all HTTP traffic from Forefront TMG to all networks (for CRL downloads)**, which is allowed for all users. The external user may now browse the Internet at will, sourced from the TMG server.

■ **FIGURE 4.16** Configuring Network Relationships

Name	Relation	Source Networks	Destination Networks
Local Host Access	Route	Local Host	All Networks (and Local Host)
VPN Clients to Internal Net...	Route	Quarantined VPN Clients VPN Clients	Internal
Internet Access	NAT	Alternate Proxy Internal Quarantined VPN Clients VPN Clients	External

Troubleshooting Authentication

If I were to change the web proxy authentication configuration to require Basic Authentication, it would also work given the existing access rules. The publishing rule requires no authentication, so the publishing transaction to 8080 succeeds. The connection to the web proxy on port 8080 requires Basic Authentication, so the connection will fail initially since all IE connections are initiated under the context of an anonymous user. When TMG challenges the browser for authentication, the logon box will appear, and when the user successfully authenticates the connection to the proxy succeeds. The external proxy for www.bing.com succeeds and the same default rule as in the previous example applies. However, this time TMG knows who the user is, so any logging of this connection will reflect the user who logged on.

TIP

This works perfectly, however we are stuck with Basic Authentication now, which is insecure. If you are not concerned with insecure authentication mechanisms at this point, your current configuration will meet your needs. But our goal is to leverage a more secure authentication mechanism: NTLM over HTTP. Again, it is not as secure as an encrypted channel overall, but it is more secure than Basic Authentication over HTTP.

Security through Obscurity

Before we dive into how to support Windows Integrated Authentication, we will talk about security through obscurity. Many people opine that security through obscurity is not security at all. In actuality, security through obscurity is perfectly secure as long as whatever gives you the security remains obscure. You may have already guessed at what I am getting at: a custom port configuration. HTTP proxy 8080 is common and easily identified. Changing your proxy listening port is an absolutely valid method of helping to secure the connection. While someone could indeed scan your entire port range to see that you are using, say, 52011 for your proxy instead, they would have to go to the trouble of scanning your entire port range. It is no longer obscured once they find it though, and that layer of security is gone. But it is valid until that point.

To that effect, I will remind you about a very easy way to do this. Rather than publishing 8080 straight out by way of a custom Transmission Control Protocol (TCP) on 8080 to the listener on 8080, we will just create the custom protocol using TCP 52011 instead. In the publishing rule, we shall simply choose the appropriate protocol, select the **Traffic** tab, and click **Ports**, as shown in Figure 4.17.

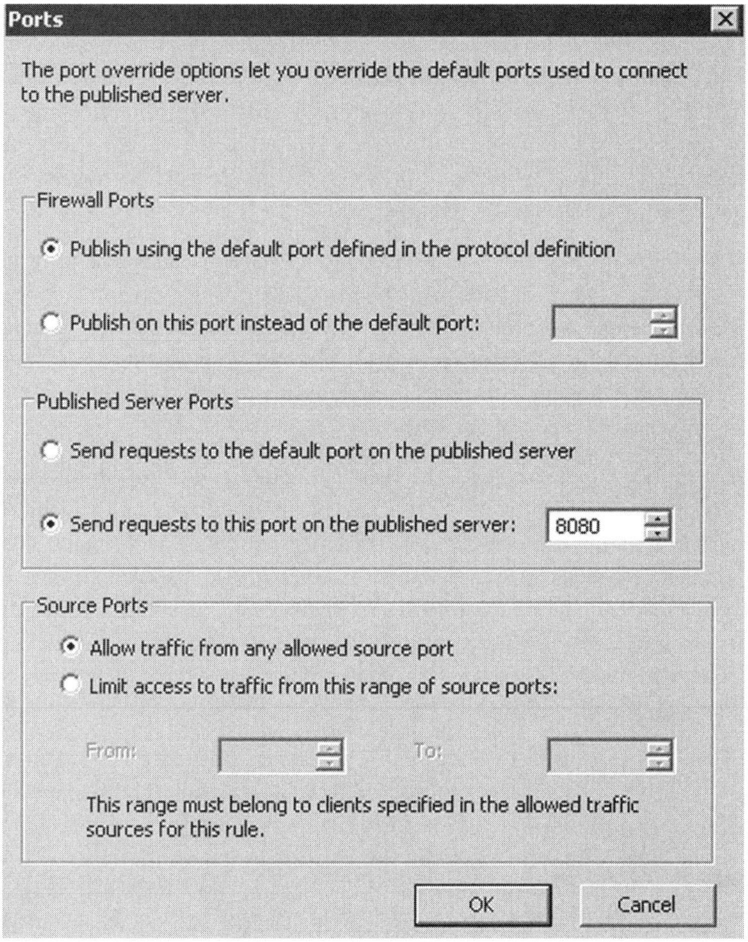

■ FIGURE 4.17 Redirecting Inbound Protocol Definition to a Different Inbound Port

As illustrated, though the new port for the inbound proxy protocol is 52011, we redirect it to 8080 which is the default listening port of the proxy itself. Now the external user can configure their proxy to use port 50211 and you will have that extra layer of security (albeit, through obfuscation) if you so desire.

NTLM and External Connections

You might be wondering why I bothered to carve out Anonymous Authentication and Basic Authentication in the previous examples from NTLM, when we could have just forced Windows Authentication at the web proxy and be challenged for authentication the same way we were with Basic Authentication. In most cases, you would be right to wonder. Typically, the exact same behavior would be exhibited by the browser irrespective of the server-based authentication required: It would attempt an anonymous connection, be challenged for a given type of authentication, and the browser would prompt the user for credentials and provide the server with authentication based on its requirements.

Things work differently with NTLM. On a Windows client, you have to keep in mind that other authentication requirements might exist from group policy inheritance or direct local security policy entries and settings. In other words, you do not always control the client that is connecting up to your system, and there might be restrictions on the use of NTLM or requirements surrounding its use (such as NTLMv2).

For example, suppose one of the people I want to give access to works at a company like Microsoft, which takes internal systems security about as seriously as anyone can. In these cases, group policy will dictate that a client is not allowed to make an external NTLM connection via the web browser unless an extraordinary number of policies and standards are met. Meaning, if you are on such a laptop and try to log on to a remote resource using NTML, the local policy on the client will put the kibosh on that and deny the request.

Here is what happens in that case. The publishing rule requires no authentication, so the publishing transaction to 8080 succeeds. The connection to the web proxy on port 8080 requires Windows Integrated Authentication, so the initial connection will fail anonymously as it did with Basic. When TMG challenges the browser for authentication, the client will simply refuse, and the connection proceeds as if the user was anonymous. The outbound request will fail because the user is anonymous and the web proxy filter (the proxy listener) requires authentication. Your log will then look something like Figure 4.18.

I think this is a valuable example because it is not immediately intuitive that the client might be the one causing the connection issues. The access to the web proxy filter is a reference to the web proxy listener itself, and not the fact that you have got the custom protocol set to use the web proxy filter (in the checkbox under the properties of the custom protocol). Clearing that

■ **FIGURE 4.18** Log Entry for Anonymous Access Attempt Fail

Destination IP	Destination Port	Protocol	HTTP Status Code	Client Username	Action
192.168.3.5	8080	Alternate Pro...			Initiated Connection
192.168.3.5	80	http	12209 Forefront TMG requires authorization to fulfill the request. Access to the Web Proxy filter is denied.	anonymous	Denied Connection
192.168.3.5	8080	Alternate Pro...			Closed Connection

option will not make a difference here because this is a client-based authentication issue and has nothing to do with you. The other good thing about this example is that it really *is* about the client, and not just something we say to them when we do not feel like figuring out why the server is doing what it is doing.

■ SUMMARY

In this chapter, we covered how authentication works in an Internet environment, and how to leverage different methods of authentication to secure an otherwise unsecure connection. We discussed how to set up and configure an alternate proxy segment for external use, and how that segment had to be configured in order for authentication and publishing to function correctly.

Chapter 5

The Creation and Maintenance of Low-Privileged Service Users (with a Focus on SQL)

INFORMATION IN THIS CHAPTER:

- Creating and Configuring Service User Accounts
- Real, Quantifiable Password Strength, and How to Measure It

---

PRODUCTS, TOOLS, AND METHODS:

- AD
- Least Privilege Service Users
- Delegation
- Password Strength
- MS SQL Server
- Visual Studio (C#)

INTRODUCTION

Every process running on your system runs in the context of some account entity, be that an actual user account, a machine account, *LOCAL SYSTEM*, *LOCAL SERVICE*, *NETWORK SERVICE*, or some other built-in or speci-fied security principal. In an ideal environment, a service or process would only have the minimum set of permissions and access required for it to per-form its function. However, it is not feasible from an operational or admin-istrative standpoint to specifically apply an access control list (ACL) to every process to limit and ensure that it operates within a least privilege environment. To achieve a balance between security and usability, a number of varying built-in accounts were created in Windows, each with a certain access level so that one could most closely match a service to an account context of appropriate privilege. That clearly leaves many processes with wiggle room in respect to restricting rights. At the basic level, system services have three accounts to work within: LOCAL SYSTEM, LOCAL SERVICE, and NETWORK SERVICE, as previously mentioned. LOCAL SYSTEM has full access to the system, and can make network connections within the context of the machine account it is running on. On a domain controller, LOCAL SYSTEM has access to all directory services as well. It is important to understand this, because LOCAL SYSTEM services on a domain controller have full access to the domain itself. Some refer to this as the *super-user*, *uber-user*, or *god account*. I strip the adjective references away and simply refer to it as what it is: an account with all rights on a system. Obviously, not all services need this much access, and I would venture a guess that most do not. To accommodate restricted access, LOCAL SERVICE and NETWORK SERVICE entities were created. The LOCAL SERVICE account for all intents and purposes is a built-in user account that has the same rights as a member of the users group. It is also considered an authenticated user. I have seen it reported that local service cannot access the network, but it actually can. It just does so as a null user with no credentials. That amounts to no network access, but I think it is a technical point worth mentioning. The network service account is just like the local service account, except that it accesses the network under the credentials of the machine account it is running on. The following are some examples of services in each context on default server installations:

local system: Server, EFS, Plug and Play, Print Spooler, Netlogon, and Themes

local service: UPnP Device Host, Windows Audio, COM+ Event System, and the Link-Layer Topology Discovery Mapper

network service: NAP Agent, DNS Client, Remote Desktop Services, RPC, Workstation

I find some of these interesting because Plug and Play runs as local system, but UPnP Device Host runs as local service. There was a vulnerability in Plug and Play a while ago that everyone, the FBI included, freaked out over when it was reported that the Plug-and-Play service was vulnerable. Instead, it was the UPnP Device Host that was vulnerable. That makes a huge difference when it comes to exploiting vulnerabilities, and shows how the application of least privilege principles can provide some security in depth. Also, the fact that Themes runs as local system yet the Workstation service runs as network service seems counterintuitive as well. This illustrates why one should not assume that the perceived function equates to assigned rights and that verification is required.

The basis for the different access levels is the protection from unauthorized or malicious use should a vulnerability or procedural error allow control of the service to be taken over. If code exploits a service running as local system, it has access to everything, including user files. If the service was running as local service, the code would have no access to my files at all. Exploitation of network service would allow attacks under the context of my machine, where local service would not expose this potential attack vector.

This clearly illustrates why you should control the context of services. That said, sometimes you simply have no choice. I have actually had participants of the classes I have lead get somewhat upset when I cover this topic. The argument is that software vendors often require local system access to their services (sometimes just because it is easier) and any other context is not supported. If that is the case, then it is what it is. But if you have a choice, you should at least test different options and see what works and what does not. There have been many times where I have asked vendor support to give specific examples of why services have to run as SYSTEM, and the response is usually, "Because it has to," which is normally computer-speak for "I have no idea."

CREATING AND CONFIGURING SERVICE USER ACCOUNTS

We want to extend the concepts of least privilege illustrated in the use of these different service contexts to services that we have control over, and to create user accounts specifically for different services we deploy in order to tightly control what they can and cannot do in this chapter. I have specifically illustrated the use of such an account in this book in the assignment of a service user to web application pools, the context of running SQL Server and the SQL Agent (which we will cover in depth in this chapter), the use of service accounts to retrieve remote log information and access network DCOM components, and others. For me, controlling a specific user is far more manageable and flexible than even local and network service. I sometimes have services use EFS to access sensitive data, and while this can indeed be done with SYSTEM accounts, it is far easier to manage with user accounts. It is also portable with a user where SYSTEM accounts using EFS are not.

I have had some interesting conversations with associates regarding the pros and cons of creating user accounts for services. The basis of the argument is that even if a machine is popped with local system rights, the scope of an attacker's control would be limited to that machine given the network access limits of the local system. I believe there is substance to this argument in theory; however, in practice I have a very high confidence level that if I gain SYSTEM rights on a networked system that I will gain subsequent access to assets downrange. This point is further substantiated when one considers that systemic services would expose similar, if not identical, vulnerabilities as were used to pop the box as SYSTEM in the first place. And remember that popping SYSTEM on a domain controller is game over.

So yes, if a service is running as a domain user, then the attacker will automatically inherit network access. But we know who the user is. We have already created the user in such a way as to limit what they can do. If a SYSTEM process is used to attack the network, there is no immediate way to identify that the attack is taking place. However, if the user account that is running a web application starts trying to log on to your domain controller, you immediately know that something sketchy is going on. With the Management Interface Log Fetcher application provided in Chapter 6, "Remote Security Log Collection in a Least Privilege Environment," automating responses based on service user events is easily accomplished.

AD Structure

Now we will talk about the service user and group structures that we might use, and how we can leverage AD objects to increase the security posture of services deployed in our infrastructure.

When it comes to the organization of your AD structure, there seems to be as many opinions regarding structure and approach as there are people deploying it. It is kind of like the way different people organize their garage or tool shed. Some will have a specific place on the wall for each tool, complete with an outline of the tool marked on the wall, and some will have little labeled boxes of items that are themselves organized into other labeled boxes that make up a large panel of labeled boxes. And, of course, there are people with crap all over the place who could not find a flashlight even if they had it already. AD is like that. I have built examples here based on the structure that the Hammer of God network is built on, and in some cases use actual examples of my production environment. As such, there will be a level of simplicity illustrated that you very well may not be able to attain or even get close to. I have had the opportunity of reviewing some of the biggest AD deployments anywhere, and I can tell you that I do not envy the teams responsible for keeping that house in order. Regardless, the main concepts and techniques shown here are applicable to any AD structure, but you will probably have to adapt methods to suit your environment.

Account Characteristics

The first thing to do is identify what services or application you wish to migrate to a service user context. SQL Server and IIS should be immediate candidates, though in typical environments there is a plethora of services and processes to choose from. But I will go ahead and stick with SQL and IIS. We will not build users to run the WWW Publishing Service, but rather for the applications and sites running in IIS.

Several aspects of service users require them to be treated differently from other accounts. For instance, you probably want to restrict a service user from changing its own password. You most likely do not want service users to automatically have mailboxes created as part of your exchange organizational policy. You also need to consider possible DoS conditions where a service account becomes locked out if too many unsuccessful logon attempts occur. This may even be done on purpose, so it is common for service users to have no lockout threshold specified. Pursuant to that, if accounts cannot be locked out, you had better make sure that your service accounts have very strong passwords. Of course, the question is, "What is strong?" I will delve very deeply into that at the end of this chapter.

Organizational Units

In order to control account attributes like lockout settings, auditing, user rights, and the like in a manner different than you do other user accounts, we need to create an OU for them to live in. In this way, we can create a customized GPO for the particular OU where our service users live their happy little lives. I will also show you a way to create a customized password policy just for the groups you want, as opposed to having a domain-wide policy apply to all users.

I have a full-on development environment running in a virtual environment under Hyper-V, and I really, really like it. On the domain controller of that network, I have created an OU for my service users. After much thought and consideration, I decided to name the OU *ServiceUsers*. I know—it's a gift.

I created all my service users as well as the groups that I wish for the users to be members of in this OU, as demonstrated in Figure 5.1.

The reason I have multiple groups like the ones displayed in Figure 5.1 is so that if I choose to use the same user account for different services, I can carve out the permissions via groups based on the role I want. For instance, I may want to use *Gertrude* as the service user for some web applications as well as the user running or accessing media services on my media servers. I will base access for the web application using the *gWebApps* group and

Active Directory Users and Computers [HyperV.H	Name	Type
⊞ Saved Queries	DotNet User	User
⊟ hammerofgod.com	ExchangeUser	User
⊞ aSpecial Use	Gertrude	User
⊞ Builtin	gExchangeBoxes	Security Group - Global
⊞ Computers	gMedia	Security Group - Global
⊞ Domain Controllers	gRDPApplications	Security Group - Global
⊞ ForeignSecurityPrincipals	gServiceUsers	Security Group - Global
⊞ HammerOfGod	gSQLUsers	Security Group - Global
⊞ HOG-Users	gWebApps	Security Group - Global
⊞ LostAndFound	RDP	User
⊞ Managed Service Accounts	SQLUser	User
⊞ Microsoft Exchange Security Groups	TGP	User
⊞ Program Data		
ServiceUsers		
⊞ System		
⊞ Users		
Microsoft Exchange System Objects		
⊞ NTDS Quotas		

■ **FIGURE 5.1** AD Users and Computers Snap-In Displaying the Service Users OU with Associated User and Group Contents

media access on the *gMedia* group even though they contain the same user. That lets me control access to subsets of resources in one place without automatically giving the user rights that could be used in another place.

The thing to look out for is that the event logs will not have the group that tried to log on in a failure audit; it will have the username, so be careful if you create just one user and distribute it among multiple groups because you might not be able to isolate the source of the logon attempt.

That all may seem a bit confusing at first, but as you begin to work with service users like this it will become clearer.

Group Membership Maintenance

Creating a least privilege user is so easy a caveman could do it. We simply need to disassociate them from their default membership in domain users, which by inheritance makes them members of the local users group on all domain members. Though this is a simple step, it is important because users can log on locally, and they can access domain member computers from the network by default. When the user is created, not only are they in the domain users group by default, but that group is also set as the primary group. The primary group feature exists for use with Mac clients or for Portable Operating System Interface for Unix (POSIX)-compliant applications and I have never had any cause to use it. You cannot just delete membership from a primary group. You have to set another group as primary first, and then you delete the domain users membership. This is why the first thing I do is to create my base gServiceUsers group, so that when I start creating users, I will have a group to assign them to. Now I will take what will be our SQL user, for instance, and keeping true to my creative nomenclature, I will call the SQL user *SQLUser*. When we first create SQLUser, the account looks like Figure 5.2.

We add the gServiceUsers group to make this account a member, set it as the primary group, and then remove the domain users group membership, as shown in Figures 5.3a and 5.3b.

Setting the primary group as illustrated is all that is necessary at this point. The user now has no inherited rights anywhere other than being part of the authenticated users and everyone groups, and is ready to be configured to run SQL Server and the SQL Agent.

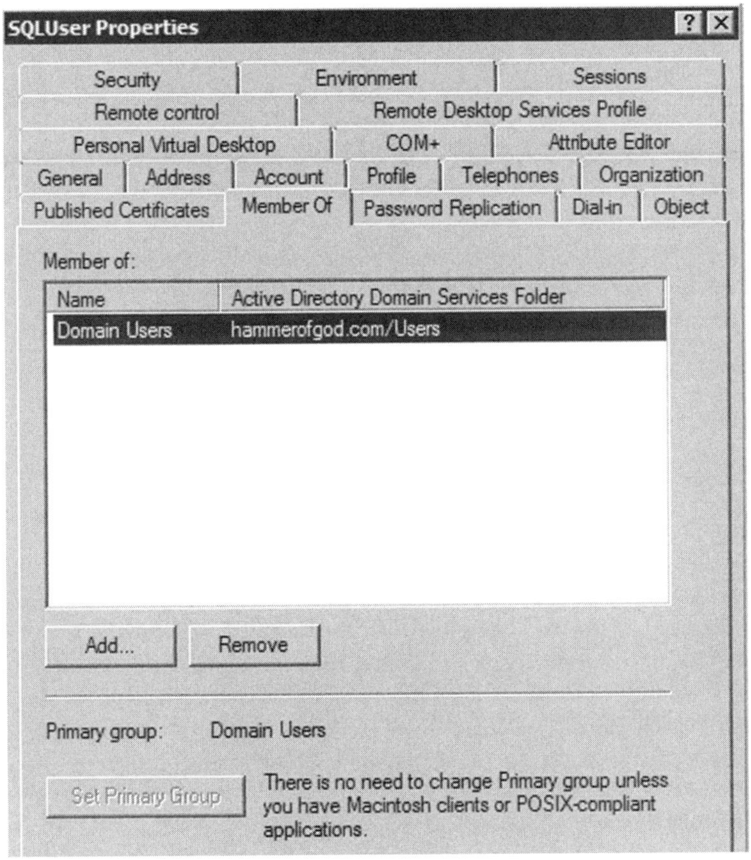

■ **FIGURE 5.2** SQLUser with Default Domain Users Membership, Which Is Also the Primary Group

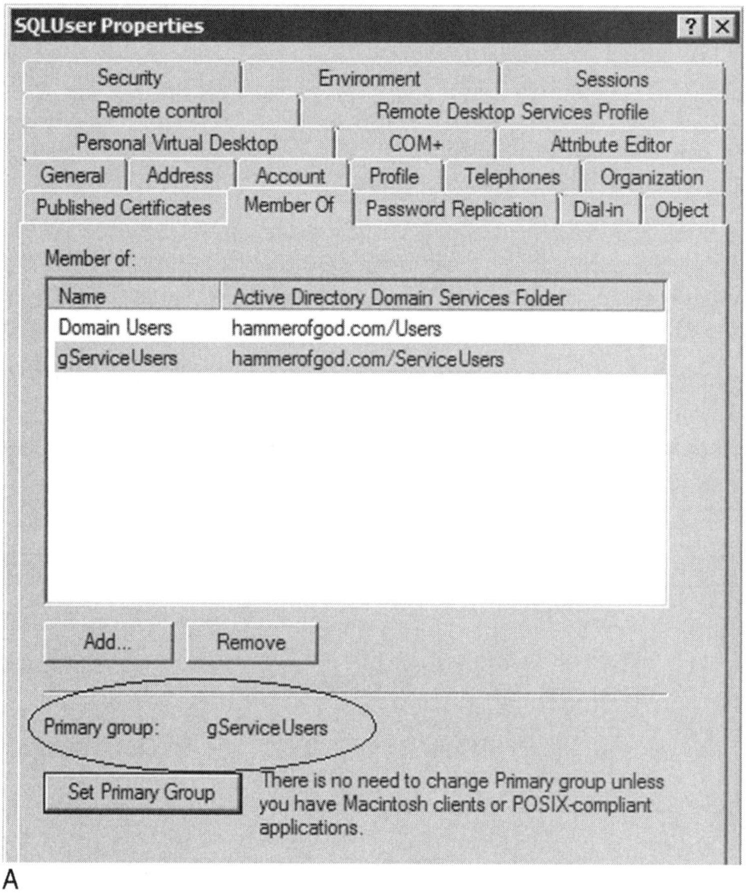

A

■ **FIGURE 5.3A** SQLUser with gServiceUsers Membership Newly Set to Primary

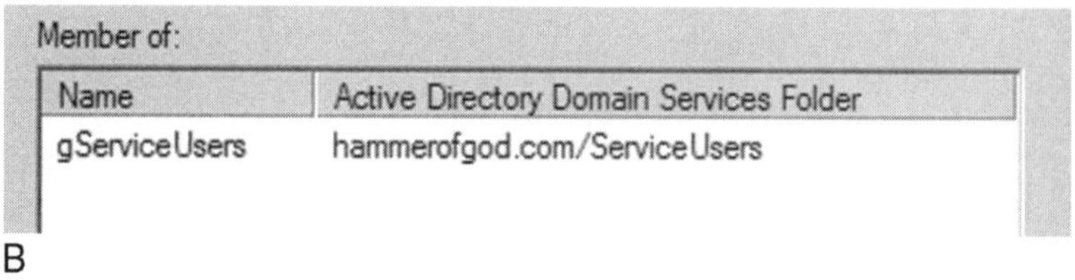

B

■ **FIGURE 5.3B** A Snip Showing the Domain Users Membership Removal

Preparing Your Application (SQL)

As it stands, SQLUser could not be used to run the SQL Server service or the SQL Agent service. If you have SQL already installed and (for the sake of argument) have it running as SYSTEM, if you simply went in and changed the logon user to SQLUser, it would fail. This is because as far as your SQL installation is concerned, SQLUser does not have the proper permissions to run SQL. The easiest way by far to assign SQLUser the rights it needs is to specify it during the installation of SQL Server itself. That way, you let the SQL installation give the account the rights it needs which it will do automatically. More importantly, you know it will be done right. However, this is not a realistic expectation and it is not likely you will read this and decide to install SQL for the first time using a service user. SQL will already be running, and you will want to migrate your existing installation over to a service user. But we should cover the SQL installation side of things anyway, as there are a couple of SQL-specific tweaks I would like to address.

During the installation of SQL, you will have the option of choosing the user/account you want the different SQL services you have selected for install to use when the services start and log on. These services can vary greatly between installations depending on what SQL roles you have decided to install, like the reporting and analysis services. It also depends if the installation of SQL is a component of another application suite, such as SharePoint. Bundled applications exemplify the value of carving out limited users from highly privileged ones because the more services you bundle together for an overall solution, the larger the attack surface area, and the more potential for exploitation. As such, you would think that administrators would take particular care to limit access rights where multiple dependencies exist, but I often see just the opposite. When presented with several services, LOCAL SYSTEM is assigned to all of them just so they will not have to worry about something not working properly. That may work from an engineering perspective, but not from a security one. I have done this kind of work for a very long time, and I cannot tell you how many times people have said they would go back and fix it and did not. I know people have the best intentions at heart, as I have been guilty of doing the exact same thing, but I urge you not to take that approach. If you have time to go back and fix it later, then you have time to do it right to begin with. That does not mean I am not sensitive to the instances where you simply have to give a service escalated permissions. The SQL writer service, for example, runs as local system by default, and you might have some requirement that it stay that way, but I rarely see instances where it really must be run like that. Okay, I shall stop preaching and get back to choosing our service user for the SQL installation. You select the service user you wish to use for the services you wish to

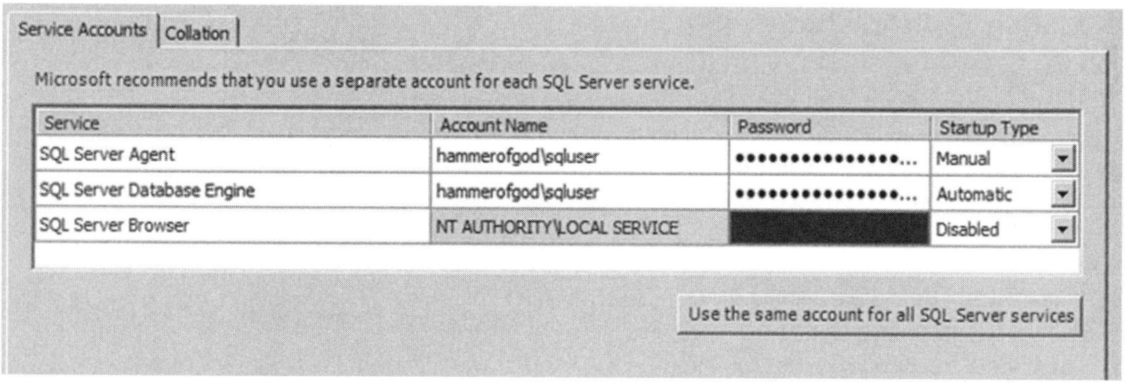

Service Accounts | Collation |

Microsoft recommends that you use a separate account for each SQL Server service.

Service	Account Name	Password	Startup Type
SQL Server Agent	hammerofgod\sqluser	●●●●●●●●●●●●●●●●...	Manual ▾
SQL Server Database Engine	hammerofgod\sqluser	●●●●●●●●●●●●●●●●...	Automatic ▾
SQL Server Browser	NT AUTHORITY\LOCAL SERVICE		Disabled ▾

Use the same account for all SQL Server services

■ **FIGURE 5.4** Security Configuration for Services during SQL Server Installation

enable, and provide the password for those accounts. The SQL installation validates this when you click **Next**, so make sure you have the actual password at this point. If you do not need a service, leave it disabled, as shown in Figure 5.4.

Notice that the default account selection for the *SQL Server Browser* service is set to LOCAL SERVICE, and that it is disabled. I would actually go ahead and set my SQLUser as the account for the SQL browser, but then leave it disabled so that if I ever go back and start that service or some other process enables it and starts it, it is still in the context of my controlled SQLUser. Again, depending on the services you have selected, the account chosen will be given the appropriate rights.

Also note the recommendation from Microsoft that you use a separate account. *My* recommendation is that you use a separate account if you need one, and if you know why you need one. More importantly, ask yourself what access privileges will be granted differently and why. If you create another service user that has the exact same permissions as SQLUser, then what problem does that solve? A different account will not buy you more security just because it is different. Security can be complex, but just because something is complex does not mean it is secure.

TIP

I want to make just a tiny detour while we are discussing SQL Server installation. At one point in the install, you will be asked to choose between Windows Authentication (or Windows Integrated) mode and Mixed Mode Authentication, which combines Windows Integrated Authentication with local SQL Server-based authentication. Windows Authentication mode is the strongest selection because you can inherit security policies directly from the OS, and that is the suggested model. However, during installation I specifically choose Mixed Mode for the sole purpose of being able to set a password for the SQL system administrator (sys admin) account. I do this because if you simply continue with the installation after selecting Windows Authentication, you could easily leave yourself with a blank sys admin password should someone come along behind you and switch modes on you. This happens far too often, particularly in development, where permissions do not work properly or the developer needs to test a specific account and Mixed Mode is used so that they can specify the account during connection. It is a good idea to make sure that you have a very strong password on the sys amdin account first, as illustrated in Figure 5.5, and then change it to Windows Authentication when the installation completes.

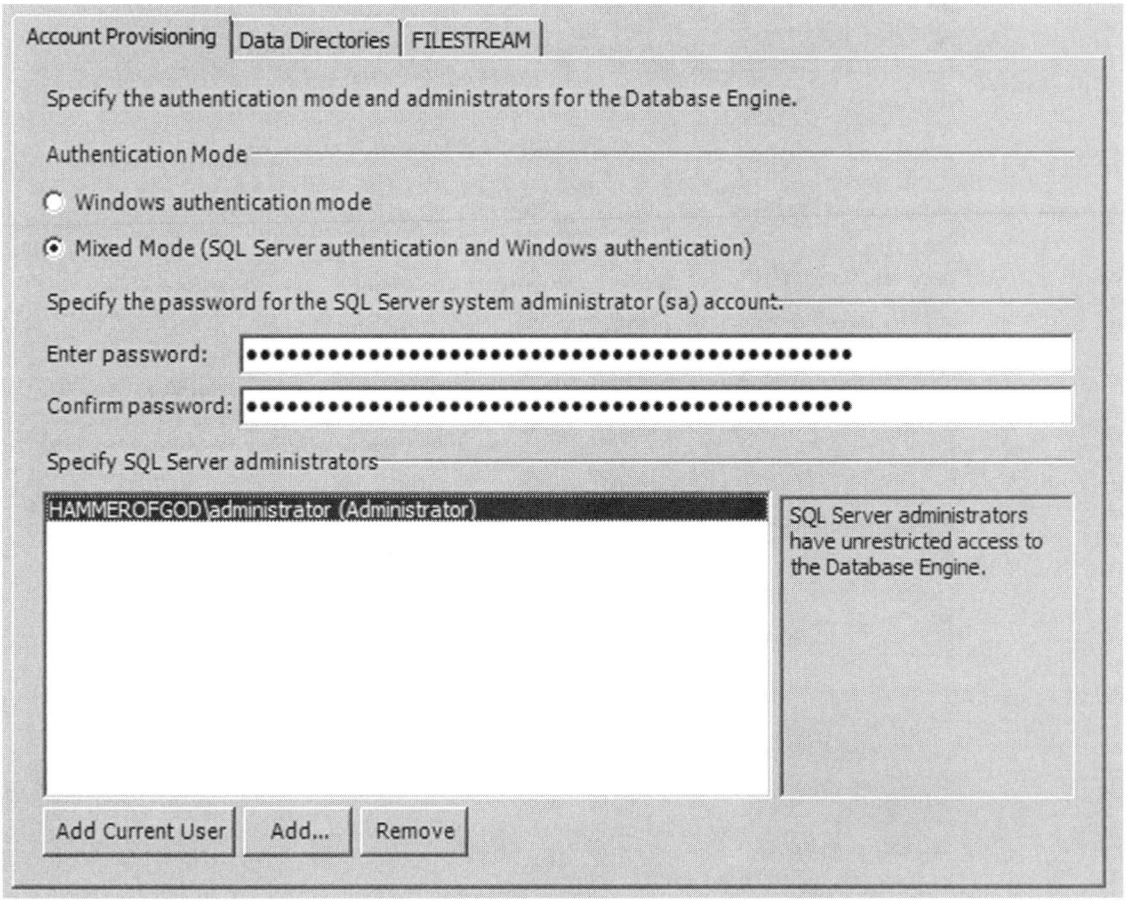

■ **FIGURE 5.5** Explicit Selection of Mixed Mode for the Purposes of Setting a Strong Password on the Sys Admin Account

Specific Permission Requirements

Once you continue on with your installation, you will see a summary of what the procedure is about to do, similar to Figure 5.6.

The changes you make here will not be applied until after the installation is complete, so if you think you can take a shortcut and reinitiate the installation process on top of your existing one to sneak in a shortcut for the account change requirements, do not bother, because it will not work.

SQL is an extremely complex application suite, so specific details will change based on what SQL must do, but in general the user account is altered to have the following rights in general:

- Logon as a service
- Adjust memory quotas for a process

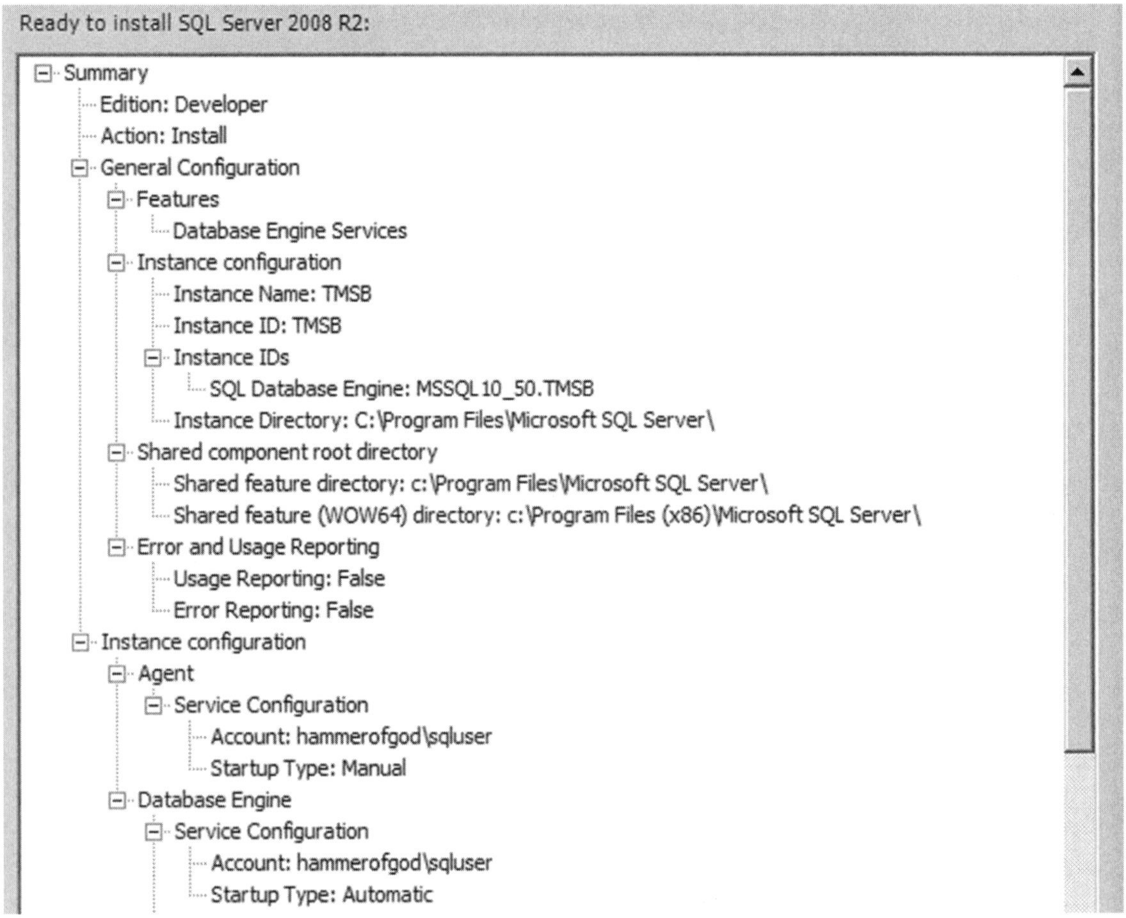
Ready to install SQL Server 2008 R2:
Summary
Edition: Developer
Action: Install
General Configuration
Features
Database Engine Services
Instance configuration
Instance Name: TMSB
Instance ID: TMSB
Instance IDs
SQL Database Engine: MSSQL10_50.TMSB
Instance Directory: C:\Program Files\Microsoft SQL Server\
Shared component root directory
Shared feature directory: c:\Program Files\Microsoft SQL Server\
Shared feature (WOW64) directory: c:\Program Files (x86)\Microsoft SQL Server\
Error and Usage Reporting
Usage Reporting: False
Error Reporting: False
Instance configuration
Agent
Service Configuration
Account: hammerofgod\sqluser
Startup Type: Manual
Database Engine
Service Configuration
Account: hammerofgod\sqluser
Startup Type: Automatic

FIGURE 5.6 Final SQL Installation Summary Including Verification of Service Configuration

- Bypass traverse checking
- Replace a process-level token
- Have the appropriate file-level access permissions

This sounds complicated, but many of these rights will be inherited by the account being a member of the local users group, which SQL does for you during installation. Exceptions to this are the rights to replace a process-level token and to adjust memory quotas for a process, but these are not actually required for what I consider standard SQL operations (starting, running, and managing SQL data).

After going through all that, you very well may find that you can fully support your SQL installation with a user that you grant **Logon as a service** to and make a member of the local users group. If I had just told you that in the beginning you would have missed all the fun. Also keep in mind that you may have ancillary configuration options that require access control changes, such as SSL binding to protocol libraries. If we had SQL running already and our libraries were configured to support SSL connections as specifically detailed in Chapter 7, "Securely Writing Web Proxy Log Data to SQL Server and Programmatically Monitoring Web Traffic Data," then we would have to give the selected service user read permissions to the public key of the configured certificate. If you changed everything except that and then tried to restart the SQL service under the SQLUser account, it would fail to start just for that reason. Note that Microsoft supports this type of least privilege user configuration, and they have a very nicely prepared MSDN article[1] on the subject, which gets into great detail about the specific permissions required of a given operation. I recommend you read it.

Instance Awareness

Many of you may deploy SQL Services with multiple instances of SQL running on the same physical server like many larger organizations do. Microsoft also supports least privilege for instance-aware services, meaning that you can have multiple instances of the SQL Server service running, each with its own specific service user. An example of where this would be valuable is when you have a single physical machine but support several SQL instances as if they were completely separate SQL installations. You would want to carve service and file structure permissions out from each other for separation of roles between servers. That way a breach of Instance1 would not immediately grant an attacker access to the data on Instance2, even though they exist on the same physical system.

---

[1] http://msdn.microsoft.com/en-us/library/ms143504.aspx

Not all SQL services are instance aware, however. You can set different user accounts for multiple instances of the SQL Server, Agent, Reporting, and Full-Text services. While the Analysis Services generally are instance aware as well, the Analysis Services in SharePoint reportedly require a specific named instance, meaning you can only have one per server, though I have not verified this.

Integration Services, the SQL Server Browser, the AD Helper, and the SQL Writer are not instance aware, so you can set users for them as desired, but not different users for different instances. Now that you have an idea of what to look out for and what considerations to keep in mind when creating your service users, I will talk about ways to increase your security outside of the direct and explicit assignment of the users to your services.

Examples of Group Policy Object Configuration Settings

Here are a couple of examples of specific policy settings that we may want to apply to our service users and how to go about it. Although group policy maintenance in itself is an administrative topic and not a security topic, I would like to briefly discuss some group policy structure as it applies to our OU. I will load my Group Policy Management MMC (or just go to **Administrative Tools** on the domain controller or remote administration box you may have). Finding my ServiceUsers OU and displaying the properties, I see the screen shown in Figure 5.7, although I have combined the tabs into one screenshot to save space and redundancy.

The first thing we want to look at is the group policy inheritance, because that will tell us what series of existing GPOs may be applied before a GPO for this OU will. I obviously have no idea what your default domain policy contains, but I know that mine has specific policy lockout, auto-enrollment

■ **FIGURE 5.7** Group Policy Management Showing No GPOs for Service User and Also Showing the Default Domain Policy Being Inherited by the OU

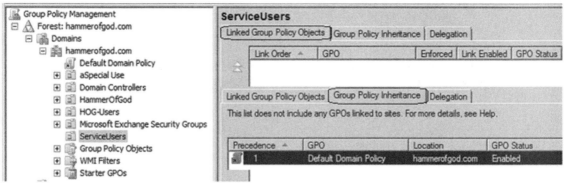

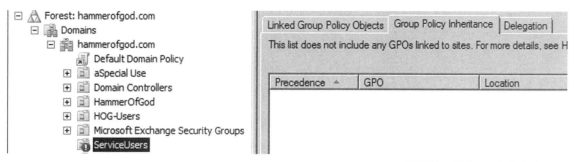

■ **FIGURE 5.8** OU Showing the Block Inheritance Option Is Selected

of certificates, EFS polices, and more. Since I am going to be building GPOs for my service users that live in the ServiceUsers OU, I actually do not want any of these GPOs to be inherited. I need to block the inheritance of the default domain policy by selecting **Block Inheritance** from the properties context menu. Doing so removes the link to the default domain policy and indicates that the OU is blocking inheritance with an irritating little blue circle and white exclamation point (see Figure 5.8). Note that **No Override** takes precedence over **Block Inheritance**, which is contrary to the typical model of deny trumps all.

We will now select **Create a GPO in this domain, and Link it here,** specifying the name of our GPO when prompted.

If you did not see it coming, we named the service users GPO *Service User GPO* in Figure 5.9. Older implementations of group policy actually created the policy under the object where you created it, then you could link to them, but now all GPOs are just created in the domain, and you create links to them wherever you want them. This is actually easier for larger environments because you can create a single GPO but link it to multiple OUs or objects.

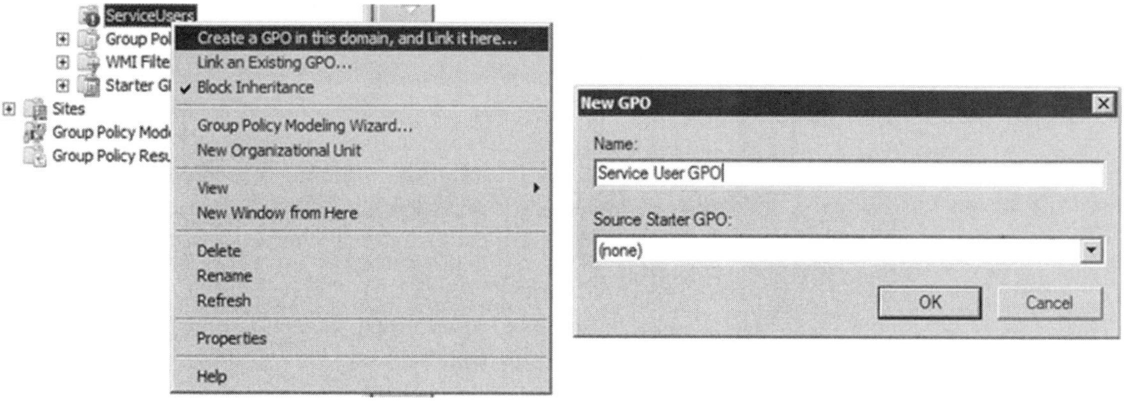

■ **FIGURE 5.9** Creating a GPO Linked to Our ServiceUsers OU Named Service User GPO

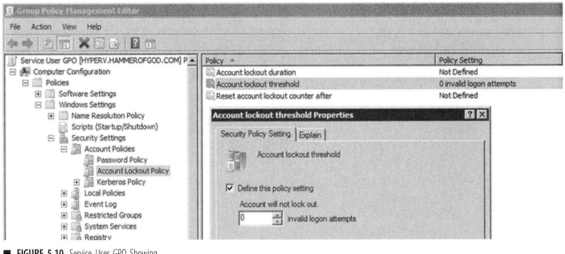

■ **FIGURE 5.10** Service User GPO Showing Computer Configuration\Windows Settings\Security Settings\Account Policies\Account Lockout Policy\ Account Lockout Threshold Policy Being Enabled

I will edit the GPO once it is created, and then I am ready to go in and set the options I want. The first thing I will do is set the account lockout threshold to *0*, meaning that the account will never be locked out, as displayed in Figure 5.10.

Rather than showing screenshot after screenshot of GPO settings, I will just list some interesting ones in Table 5.1. I trust that you will be able to find the information you need to duplicate these as well as be able to read the **Explain** tab for each item.

You may feel any number of other settings are appropriate, but these should get you started.

Customizing Password Complexity

I will let you make your own decision about password complexity based on some work I have been doing in that area, which is included in this chapter. This is an appropriate place to discuss how to enforce your own custom password policy for this group in particular though. You can select **Enforce password complexity** in the GPO for any users you want, but that will, by default, be limited to the system password policy that dictates that the password must:

■ Not contain the user's account name or parts of the user's full name that exceed two consecutive characters
■ Be at least six characters in length

Table 5.1 Sample of Suggested GPO Elements for the ServiceUsers GPO

Section Title	Policy Setting Name	Value	Description
Password Policy	Password must meet complexity requirements	Enabled	Requires that all passwords meet the default defined policy for password complexity.
Password Policy	Minimum password length	Enabled	This will be determined by you based on your research. I put 20.
Account Lockout Policy	Account lockout threshold	0	Accounts will not be locked from invalid logon attempts.
Kerberos Policy	Enforce user logon restrictions	Enabled	KDC validates every session request against user rights.
Audit Policy	Audit account logon events	Failure	Log any logon attempts that fail.
Audit Policy	Audit account management events	Failure	Log any account management that fails.
Audit Policy	Audit privilege use	Failure	Audit failed attempts to exercise a right.
Audit Policy	Audit system events	Failure	Audit failed attempts to shut down the system, change time, muck about with log files, etc.
Restricted Groups	Group to restrict	gServiceUsers	Ensures that only the accounts we define can be members of the gServiceUsers group.

- Contain characters from three of the following four categories:
  - □ English uppercase characters (A through Z)
  - □ English lowercase characters (a through z)
  - □ Base 10 digits (0 through 9)
  - □ Non-alphabetic characters (for example, !, $, #, %)
- Complexity requirements are enforced when passwords are changed or created.

We will want more restrictive password composition than this, so we are going to create our own policy and store it in the *Password Settings Container* within AD. I do this in ADSI Edit, an AD editing tool. From within ADSI Edit, you will drill down past your domain object to the *CN=System* object, and find the *CN=Password Settings Container* object. We will create a new object, selecting **msDS-PasswordSettings** for the class, as shown in Figure 5.11.

This will walk you through a wizard where you can set your customized password policy to meet the requirements for your gServiceUsers group. When you are done with the wizard, you can select **Manage more properties** to explicitly set detailed options for your policy. A little warning first though: This is not an easy-breezy exercise, and the options can get complex. You should make sure you do some thorough research on custom password policies before you jump in and start making your own.

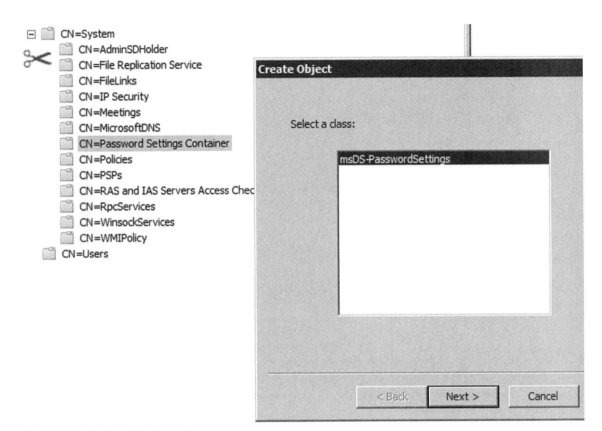

■ **FIGURE 5.11** Creating a Custom Password Policy Object in the Password Settings Container in ADSI Edit (the Scissors Indicate a Section Was Removed to Save Space)

Know Your Network

I would now like to talk about additional GPO settings that can be set on other systems in respect to interaction with service accounts. I am willing to venture that most of us find out about security issues or breaches when we discover something that should *not* be happening. "Hey, is our web page supposed to have a naked girl on it?" or "Hey, our FTP server sure has a bunch of bit torrent movies on it today." It is so obvious of a statement that it seems silly to bring it up, but in order for us to be able to identify when something sketchy is going on, we really have to have a good idea of what normal activity is and when normal starts becoming abnormal. It is in this threshold that things become difficult. Anyone in your organization will know something is wrong if naked pictures start showing up on your website (or if that is the business you are in, when clothed people start showing up), but Joe User probably would not notice at all if some EXE files started showing up on a share somewhere. It is not the presence of files coming and going that should alert people (because that is what the share is for); it is the type, or number, of files that should alert someone. Again, this is a threshold thing. Too many variables exist in trying to determine when something is wrong.

It is like in the movies where the person trying to get away merges into a crowd of people in a parade or a mob of sports enthusiasts moving through the streets. You can be looking right at them, but they look just like any other person walking along, so you cannot know which one is the bad one. What if you did not even know there was a parade in the first place? Then they would *all* look pretty out of place walking down the middle of the street, and you would be in the same position.

This is why I like to clearly define what is normal on my network not only by assigning permissions for what people are supposed to do, but also by denying permissions for what I know they are not supposed to be doing. This is where knowing your network comes in. It is almost anyone's guess as to what the users will be doing on a day-to-day basis, but your server infrastructure is a different story. You should be able to map out your network in such a way so that by merit of its organization and your in-depth knowledge of server roles, you build an early warning system that will alert you to issues by the presence of certain traffic before you have to determine what the traffic itself is. In other words, if you find out when and where a parade is going to be, then it will be easier for you to figure out a way to catch the bad guy among the other people. The larger the network, the more difficult this becomes, but this is basically the concept behind the functional deployment of intrusion detection systems (IDSs). An IDS placed on the network backbone could be completely worthless due to the sheer volume and disparate nature of the data. An IDS would be better used if it were deployed on a more narrowly defined and controlled segment.

If you overlay the template of qualifying, and quantifying, network traffic on top of the structure of your OUs, you can appreciate much of the same benefits. One of the ways we did this was to carve users into service groups and explicitly audit logon events because we know those accounts should never be logging on to other systems unless specifically designed to do so. This, in combination with the Management Interface Log Fetcher application we build in Chapter 6, "Remote Security Log Collection in a Least Privilege Environment," is a good example of how in-depth knowledge of our network combined with an appropriate structure of organization can immediately alert us to potentially malicious activities.

Leveraging Deny Controls

While having this system in place could be considered proactive, the response to traffic events is still reactive. If we see failed attempts of a service user to log on, it means that bad things have already happened at the service where that user lives. It also does not tell us anything about the connection attempts that succeeded. This is where deny logic can play an important role.

Deny access controls always win. You can have a user that is part of a million different groups that all have full control of a resource, and the moment the system encounters a deny rule anywhere in the ACL, it will be shut down. Knowing our network allows us to leverage deny rules where we could not before. When I see deny ACLs used, they are typically attached to a resource. You allow certain people access to a resource, and then deny the rest, so it is a more secure posture. I want to deny access based on the user, in this case the service users, because I know what they should not be doing.

Here is an example. I will create a single GPO with some simple deny rules in it and identify the gServiceUsers group as the deny target. We will then do some testing and see how this affects the user. First, I will create a separate OU for testing, as shown in Figure 5.12. This will be in my production network since I have got more systems to muck about with. Yes, I know. You will see the names of my computers, and I will be viciously hacked and ridiculed, but it is for the best.

I keep all of my production server and workstations in two separate OUs, which are both nested under my *HammerOfGod* OU. In this way, I can have

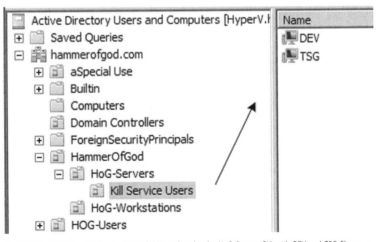

■ **FIGURE 5.12** The Kill Service Users OU Nested under the HoG-Servers OU with DEV and TSG Shown as Computer Objects Stored in the OU Container

one GPO with settings that apply to all child objects, and have other GPOs specific to roles on each of the server and workstation GPOs.

I have created the Kill Service Users GPO under servers for the same purpose, and I tried to make the object name more exciting this time. With the OU created, I will go into group policy management and create a new GPO called *Deny Access GPO*. Again, this is a generic GPO which I may want to link to any number of other OUs in my organization, so it will only contain the deny objects I want and is named appropriately. We will make this one really simple.

The computer referenced in Figure 5.13 will apply to whatever computer object is in the OU to which the GPO is applied. It is quite simple, really. Before I apply this policy, we will do a little test. In Chapter 6, "Remote Security Log Collection in a Least Privilege Environment," I quite rudely point out the security issues with a third-party proposal of how to dump event logs to files for import. This was done with xp_cmdshell, and while I know you would normally never enable xp_cmdshell, nevertheless we will follow suit and try some things. In the following example, I have created a share on each of the two computers in the Kill Service Users OU and everyone has read access.

Testing Settings

From the SQL box, I will issue two xp_cmdshell commands, *Whoami* and *dir \\tsg\movies*, and display the results in Figures 5.14a and 5.14b.

We see that the user was immediately able to view the contents of the movies share. Trying to get a list of our DEV users share, we get the results in Figure 5.15.

■ **FIGURE 5.13** New Deny Access GPO Specifying that the gServiceUsers Group Will Be Denied Access to this Computer from the Network in Security Settings\Local Policies\User Rights Assignment

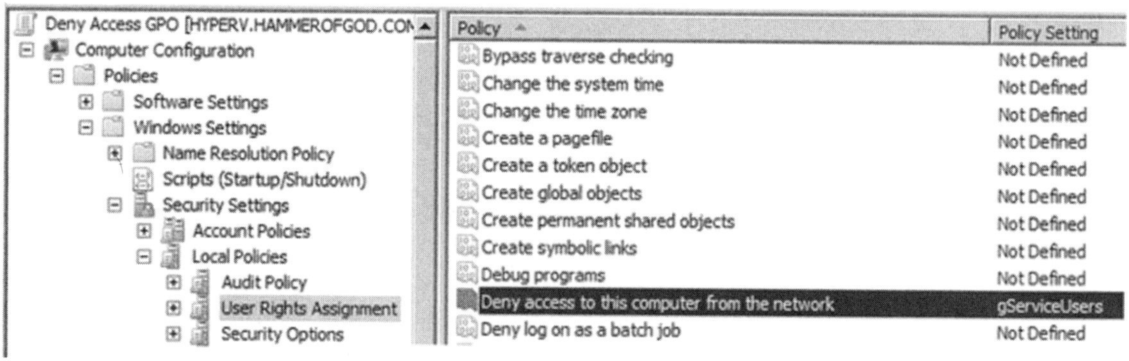

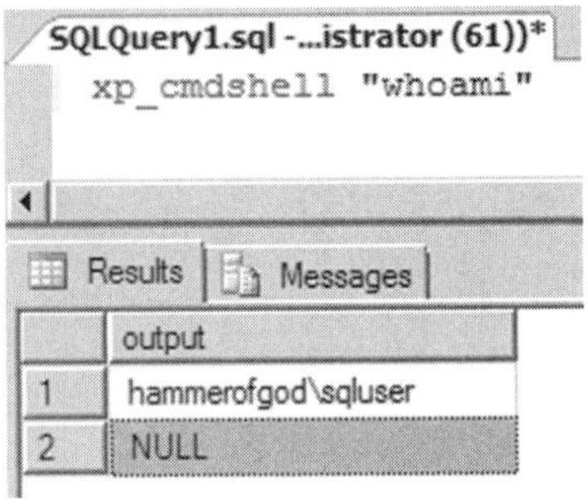

SQLQuery1.sql -...istrator (61))*

```
xp_cmdshell "whoami"
```

◀

▦ Results | ▣ Messages

	output
1	hammerofgod\sqluser
2	NULL

A

■ **FIGURE 5.14A** xp_cmdshell Output Showing the SQL Service Running under SQLUser

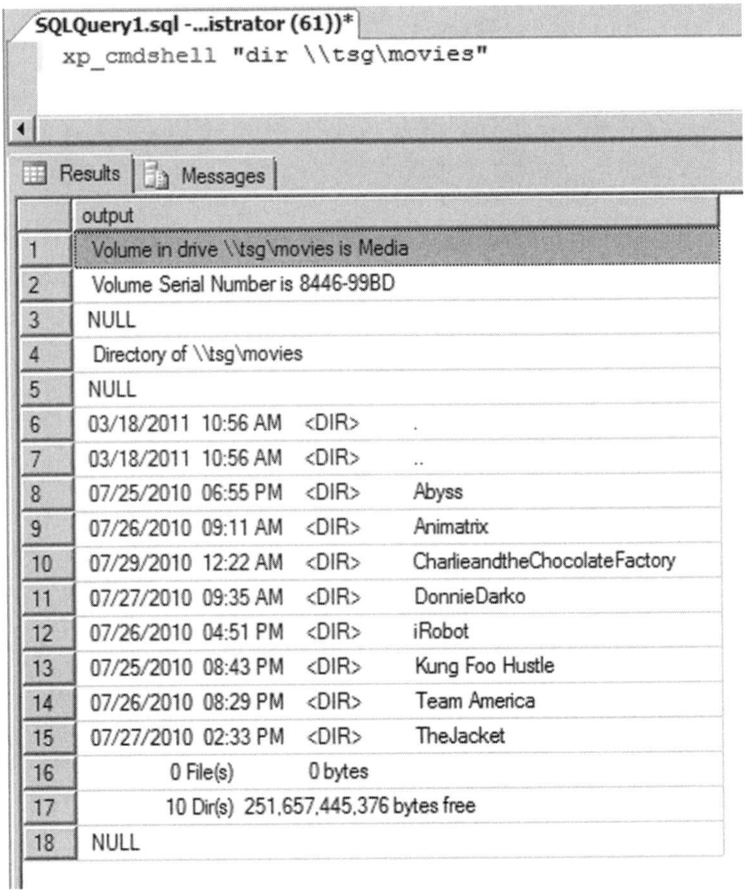

SQLQuery1.sql -...istrator (61))*

```
xp_cmdshell "dir \\tsg\movies"
```

◀

▦ Results | ▣ Messages

	output
1	Volume in drive \\tsg\movies is Media
2	Volume Serial Number is 8446-99BD
3	NULL
4	Directory of \\tsg\movies
5	NULL
6	03/18/2011 10:56 AM <DIR> .
7	03/18/2011 10:56 AM <DIR> ..
8	07/25/2010 06:55 PM <DIR> Abyss
9	07/26/2010 09:11 AM <DIR> Animatrix
10	07/29/2010 12:22 AM <DIR> CharlieandtheChocolateFactory
11	07/27/2010 09:35 AM <DIR> DonnieDarko
12	07/26/2010 04:51 PM <DIR> iRobot
13	07/25/2010 08:43 PM <DIR> Kung Foo Hustle
14	07/26/2010 08:29 PM <DIR> Team America
15	07/27/2010 02:33 PM <DIR> TheJacket
16	0 File(s) 0 bytes
17	10 Dir(s) 251,657,445,376 bytes free
18	NULL

B

■ **FIGURE 5.14B** The Results of a Simple dir \\tsg\movies Command

Now I will apply the GPO to our Kill Service Users OU, update the policy, and attempt access again, as illustrated in Figures 5.16a and 5.16b.

This is a Good Thing. Now that the Deny Access GPO object exists, we can simply link to it from any other group of servers that we wish to block access to. If we have used the SQLUser on a number of different SQL boxes, we can use global groups created for SQL permissions (you may remember seeing a gSQLUsers group a screenshot created for this purpose). We would do that in this case because our WebAppUser created in Chapter 2 needs access to the users' directory.

The single policy illustrated here creates a substantial access control in it-self. Any breach of the SQL Server where an exploit would run in the

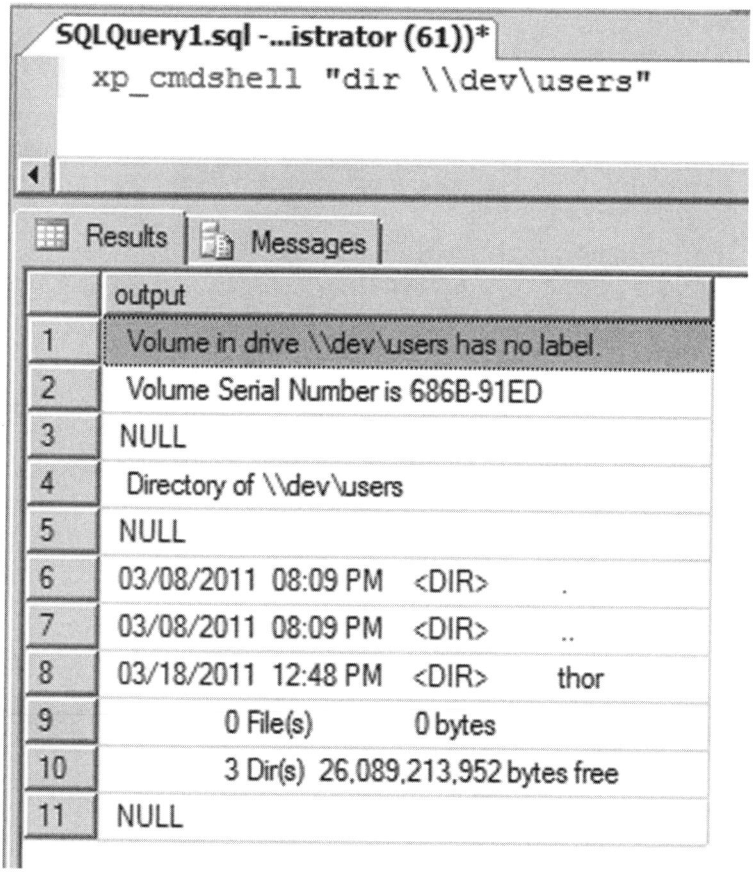

■ FIGURE 5.15 SQLUser Listing Contents to Users Share on the DEV System

context of the SQLUser would automatically be denied access to other network resources. Leap-frog attacks are an attacker's key method of expanding system compromise, and this is a good method of preventing that. Many other rights and actions can be denied explicitly (and not just for service users), so you should review these to see what works best for you.

At this point, we have illustrated how to migrate highly privileged services over to least privilege user context, how to organize service accounts into different management groups for easier administration, and how we can very tightly control where that account can be leveraged in case of a breach or a vulnerability being exploited.

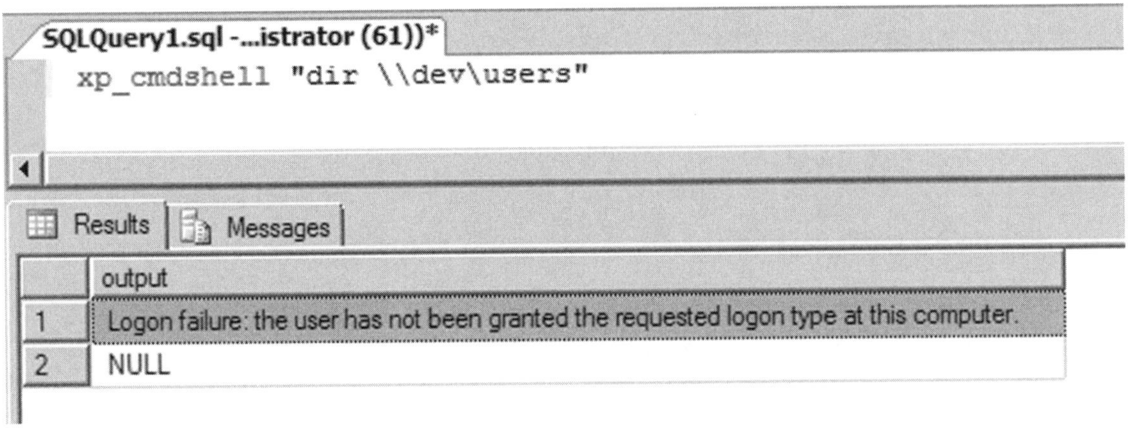
SQLQuery1.sql -...istrator (61))*
xp_cmdshell "dir \\dev\users"
Results
Messages
output
1
Logon failure: the user has not been granted the requested logon type at this computer.
2
NULL

A

■ **FIGURE 5.16A** Results of SQLUser Trying to Access the Shares on DEV

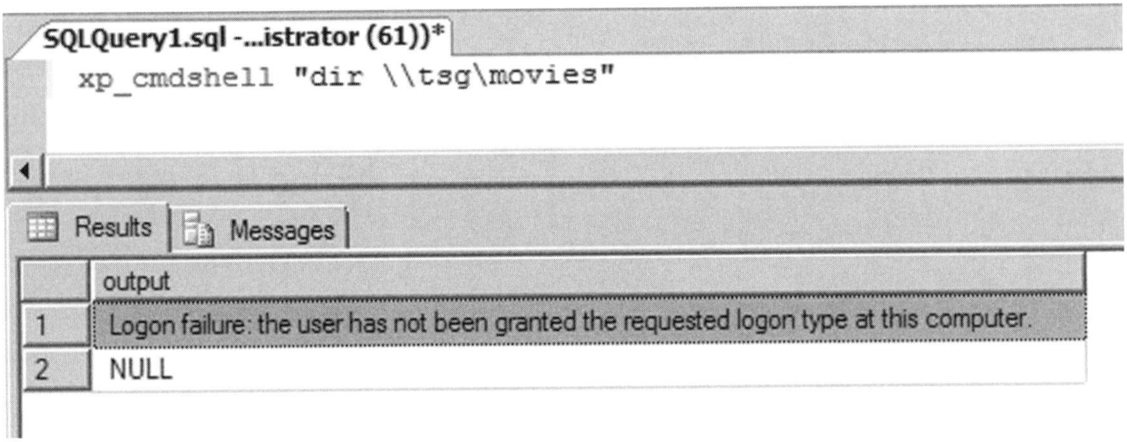
SQLQuery1.sql -...istrator (61))*
xp_cmdshell "dir \\tsg\movies"
Results
Messages
output
1
Logon failure: the user has not been granted the requested logon type at this computer.
2
NULL

B

■ **FIGURE 5.16B** TSG and the Explicit Deny Result

REAL, QUANTIFIABLE PASSWORD STRENGTH, AND HOW TO MEASURE IT

Since our service user accounts cannot be locked out, they are better targets for brute force password attacks. Ideally, all accounts should have strong passwords, but service accounts (and other nonlockable accounts) should have special attention.

Some of you may have seen my dissertation on passwords on my website[2] in which I have outlined a different method of rating passwords than simple

[2]www.hammerofgod.com/passwordcheck.aspx

complexity rules. Given the positive response it has received, I thought it would be a good addition to this chapter. I also figured I would go ahead and give you the source code in case you wanted to write your own password strength checker. Here is how I go about it and how my method works.

Administrators tell users that passwords must be complex (which users hear as difficult), but they do not tell us what actually makes a good password or passphrase strong. The password strength meters I have seen simply make a best effort to grade bad, good, or better or some other ambiguous qualification. But nothing ever actually quantifies a strong passphrase. Assumptions are made based on complexity—the more complex the better. While this is true, we still never get any information as to how complex a password should be, or even why it needs to be that way.

Because of this, I wanted to do something differently. As such, I decided to add a measurable and valuable attribute where I actually calculated how long it would take to crack the keyspace (the total number of all possible keys) of the password you have selected based on the base characters you use. Password strength is all about making them hard or infeasible to crack. The longer and more complex it is, the longer it will take to crack, and just like a safe combination lock, the more numbers you have the better.

To really pick a good password in my opinion, you should assume the best-case scenario for the attacker and the worst-case scenario for you. When an attacker uses brute force on your password, they basically iterate through all possible character combinations: a–z, A–Z, 0–9, the top row characters of !@#$%^&*()-=_+, and then the other printable characters like ~, {, >, and so forth. It is not always like this of course, but it is typically how they go about it. If you enter *abcd* as your password, four lowercase characters, that is, the attacker should not have any knowledge of the structure. They have to assume that it could be anything, which means they have to make a choice on how they will go about attacking your password, and what base characters to include when they do. If an attacker *does* know how your passwords are structured, you could be toast. The more knowledge they have, the more they can reduce the keyspace.

A New Approach

All an attacker has to do is iterate through all possible combinations until they get your password. In this case, begin with *a* and then loop through over and over incrementing one character each time. Maybe I should not say *all* they have to do since that makes it seem trivial. Regardless, the entire keyspace to guess a four-character lowercase password is 475,254. Most of the brute force applications or whitepapers I see on the Internet tell you that using brute force on a four-character lowercase password requires 456,976 (or 26^4) steps, which is incorrect. The iterations would only be 26^4 if you *started out* with four characters as the base. So, starting at *aaaa* instead of starting at *a*. You have to get to *aaaa* first by going through *a*, *aa*, and *aaa*. To properly compute this, you must use 26^4+26^3+26^2+26^1 as your formula. The difference between 475,254 and 456,976 may not seem like much, but there is a 5.6 trillion iteration difference just when you get to 10 characters. So right from the start, systems using that formula are simply wrong. I want to calculate the entire brute force effort required to get there from *a* because that is where an attacker would start.

In order to determine what base of characters to use, I look at the password and try to determine the minimal base keyspace it uses. If you type in *abcd*, then I will only use a–z as the base. Meaning, only lowercase characters from a–z will be used to attempt the crack. If you type *abcd1*, then I will use both a–z and 0 through 9 (increasing the base to 36). If you type *abcD*, then you get a–z and A–Z, or base 52. If you use *abcD1*, you get base 62. A *!* or & character gets you to base 76, and finally a *[* or ~ character gets you to base 95.

Now, I obviously have to make some assumptions here, but there is no other way to do it (that I can figure out). Deriving the base from what an attacker would have to use makes sense to me. Combining that with the known information of what you are typing in makes even more sense. Since I am measuring strength here, I do not want to tilt the scales in my favor. I will give that to the attacker. I assume what an attacker would have to assume if he knew some of what I know (as odd as that may sound). So I group the bases as a–z, A–Z, 0 through 9, ! through =, and then everything else. So if you type *A*, then I have to assume that you probably have lowercase letters in your password, too. A single *A* is then up to 52 possibilities since I counted lowercase characters, too. 0 through 9 is always just added in when used: *a1* is 36 (26+10), and *A1* is 62 (52+10). A single *!* is 76, so *A!* is base 76. A single *[* is 95, so *A[* is base 96. So finally, if you had *Ab44!*, the entire keyspace would be 76^5+76^4+76^3+76^2+76^1 or 2,569,332,380 combinations. For reference, the actual base characters I use are broken out as follows. These base character sets are what correlate to the keyspace:

```
Base 10: 0123456789
Base 26: abcdefghijklmnopqrstuvwxyz
Base 36: abcdefghijklmnopqrstuvwxyz 0123456789
Base 52: abcdefghijklmnopqrstuvwxyz ABCDEFGHIJKLMNOPQRSTUV
-- WXYZ
Base 62: abcdefghijklmnopqrstuvwxyz ABCDEFGHIJKLMNOPQRSTUV
-- WXYZ 0123456789
```

```
Base 76: abcdefghijklmnopqrstuvwxyz ABCDEFGHIJKLMNOPQRSTUV
-- WXYZ 0123456789 !@#$%^&*()-=_+
Base 95: abcdefghijklmnopqrstuvwxyz ABCDEFGHIJKLMNOPQRSTUV
-- WXYZ 0123456789 !@#$%^&*()-=_+ []\"{}|;':,./<>?'~
```

The preceding groupings are just how I chose to organize character sets based on how I have seen different crackers implemented, and how people tend to group top-row special characters together like *T$i*D3*, as opposed to *T$i]D3*. Nothing in the hacker handbook says you should check for any particular special characters in order, other than some that iterate in ASCII order, but I try to group these the way a person would create the password even though it is a computer cracking it. There is no right way, nor is there a rule that hackers do it *this* way. Just know this as you think about how this applies to your password policy. For those paying close attention, I did not forget the A–Z, 0–9 combinations. I just did not find value in all uppercase and digits, because I normally do not see that. I see all lowercase and digits because it is the default. That is not to say passwords will not be all uppercase with digits, but rather that I have chosen to have that set represented by base 62, and that all uppercase and digits are mathematically the same as all lowercase and digits, so it makes sense to use that base if you really want to identify the keyspace for uppercase plus digits.

Now we will take a look at Figure 5.17 (which is from the application I wrote, and is included on the CD) with a view toward password strength.

With the information I have on base character sets, I then take the highest class of cracking (Class F) standardized by the industry, which is one million attempts per second. That is a lot of attempts. Again, I want the worst-case scenario for us so we know how strong our password is. I then calculate the amount of time it would take to crack the keyspace of the password tested and display that. In the previous example where I used *Ab44!*, the entire keyspace would take a whopping 2.56933238 seconds to crack! That should tell you something. It may be considered complex since it has uppercase, lowercase, numbers, and a special character, but 2.5 seconds is not that much. Granted, most ankle-biters with a cracker will only get a few hundred thousand attempts per second, but we have to be sure. And this is where the power of this type of analysis comes in. Do not tell your users to have a strong password (whatever that means), but rather, require that they have a password that can withstand a Class F attack for X amount of time (whatever you decide). That way you have something you can measure, and that is good. So let us look at Figure 5.17 again. I used *aaaaaaNotGood* as the password. That is 13 mixed-case characters. The keyspace to crack that would take over 650,000 *years* to crack at Class F. Seems strong, right? Well, that

■ FIGURE 5.17 Cropped Screenshot of Password Strength Calculator Application

very idea got me thinking. I let the point of view I had of the attacker limit how I was looking at things. Now, 650,000 years is the best-case scenario for us (and the worst for the attacker) because that represents the *entire* keyspace. So this is when I decided to write an algorithm to calculate the iterations required for the *actual password* entered to be reached, not the entire keyspace. The real value comes in when you quantify the actual password, not just the keyspace. The algorithm I wrote worked well, but it was not super fast. I now use a formula my buddy Will Fischer came up with (Thanks, Will!) since it is better than mine. He has actually helped me quite a bit with this, so thanks doubly. Since we know the password, we basically calculate the steps required to hit each individual letter in each column based on an index string I define in memory from *a* onward. That string allows me to easily determine what the character is, a column at a time, for each character in the password. I then compile the column-by-column data into a final iterations value that is then in turn compared to Class F. As such, we see that the 650,000-year keyspace for aaaaaaNotGood is reduced to 12,637.66 years because I chose to begin my passphrase with six lowercase *a*'s. Simply changing the first *a* to an *H* takes the calculation from 12,637.66 years (based on 398,541,262,291,912,000,000 combinations) to 13,297,482,476, 338,200,000,000 iterations, or 421,660.40 years. This is a big difference between an *a* and an *H* and the overall 20,724,145,598,800,400,000,000 iterations for the keyspace at 657,158.35 years. From an actual application standpoint, you should be able to choose your own crack class (sounds like the school I went to). If you build your password strength from the worst case, a Class F at one billion iterations per second, then you really do not have to worry about attacks on slower platforms. However, I can see the value in being able to select your own class.

Part of the reason for this is so that you can see what a real-world attack will look like. Not everyone has the NSA trying to get to their data. Also, I think it is valuable for when you do not get to choose your password strength and want to know how much risk you are at by normal, everyday attackers. For instance, take a look at the screenshot in Figure 5.18 from a Cisco product.

In this product, you had to create an administrative user, but note the message saying, "Your password must be less than 8 characters and cannot contain spaces or special characters." Thanks, guys. In these cases, I am forced to use a crappy password. Selecting the worst case for the attacker, a Class A attack at 10,000 per second (which your printer could probably do in its spare time), you get a max of 61 hours to crack the keyspace of a base62 (a–z, A–Z, 0–9) password. Something like *AaZzaa99* cracks in 26 hours. When you consider this, the value of a user-defined cracking class makes more sense.

This also could give you insight into how secure certain other restricted and default passwords are. For instance, let us just do a quick search for a mailing list memberships reminder. This query will provide all sorts of links to archived e-mails where the administrators of mailing lists did not think about how their reminder notices to users, which contain the full username and password, are archived to lists and thus indexed via your favorite search

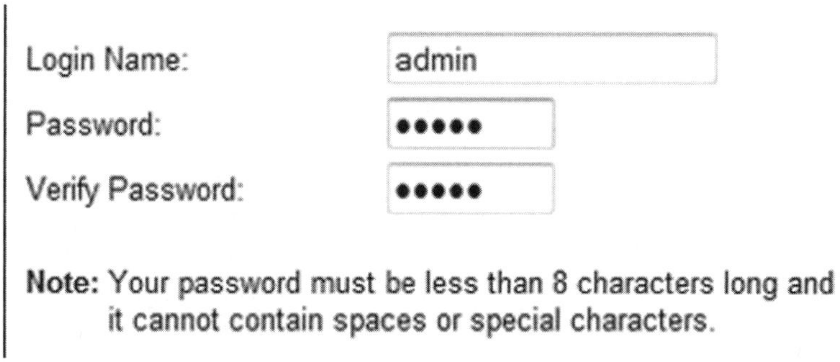

Login Name:	admin
Password:	•••••
Verify Password:	•••••

Note: Your password must be less than 8 characters long and it cannot contain spaces or special characters.

■ **FIGURE 5.18** UI Where Password Length and Complexity Is Explicitly Limited by the Developer

engine. While we will not need to crack these as they are already cleartext, you can see how most are simple lowercase eight-character random passwords. You can brute-force the entire keyspace for that, using the slowest class there is, in only 217 seconds, or roughly the time it takes to listen to AC/DC's "Have a Drink on Me."

Dictionary Attacks and Other Attack Methodologies

The first thing the l33t hacker types will say is, "What if I start with *Z* and go backward, tough guy?" Well then, do that. If it is something you are legitimately concerned about, the formula would work the same way if you counted the letter position backward. Or just start everything with *M*. Of course, an attacker might then decide to start in the middle on the off chance that you did, and so on and so forth. It is an argument of diminishing returns.

I think the same sort of logic applies to dictionary attacks. Will and I call this the "bananadog syndrome." You can have a dictionary of 10,000 words, and use it to attack people who are so unconcerned with security that they use *banana* or *dog* as their password. Suppose you double up on the words and combine them all together (resulting in one hundred million dictionary words), so that even if they were very clever and used bananadog, the attacker would still get it in milliseconds. The bananadog keyspace would only take about 94.11 minutes to crack. In that time, the attacker would get any possible combination of 5,646,683,826,134 lowercase and up to nine-character passwords. Any of them. The bananadog attack will always be limited to one hundred million total possible passwords, and will miss things like *bannaadig*. Attackers want your password, so they will make sure they get it. As such, I am not worried about bananadog. And if you are the bananadog type, I doubt you would be reading this anyway.

Will's point, and it is a good one, is that if I as an attacker can spend a couple of milliseconds getting x passwords up front from a dictionary attack, why not do so? And I agree. The logical extension of that is to build some sort of sanity check into the password strength checker to weed out bananadogs. And I may do this. The difference is the level of assumption one must make, meaning the actual application of dictionary attack logic is very subjective, but the assumptions made around ordering brute force attacks (in regard to a–z, A–Z, 0–9, and so on) are fairly established by current implementations. Do I concatenate words to score BananaDog? Do I do it three times to score DogBananaDog? What about BananaDog1? Or B4n4n4D0g? I find the application of dictionary attack logic too random. It certainly can be done, but I do not know how applicable it would be to build into a tool. As such, I am

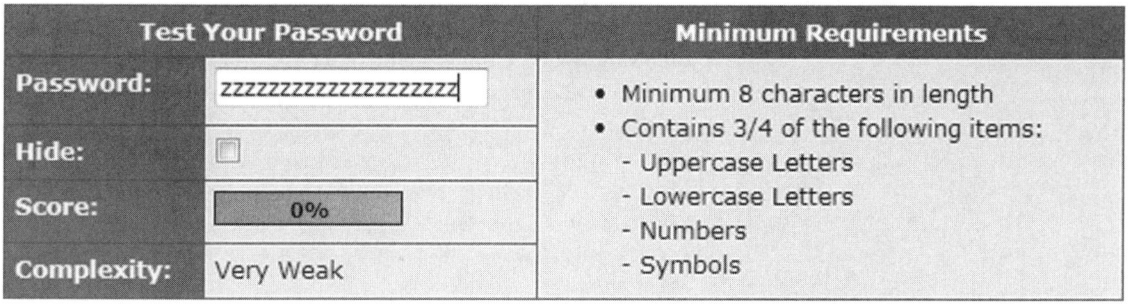

Test Your Password		Minimum Requirements
Password:	zzzzzzzzzzzzzzzzzzzz	• Minimum 8 characters in length
Hide:	☐	• Contains 3/4 of the following items:
Score:	0%	- Uppercase Letters
		- Lowercase Letters
		- Numbers
Complexity:	Very Weak	- Symbols

■ **FIGURE 5.19** Password Strength Meter Showing Twenty z's as a 0 Percent Score and Very Weak

putting that on the back burner. If anyone has any suggestions on this, feel free to contact me at thor@hammerofgod.com. I will do what I can to reply.

I think this approach is far more valuable than other measures of strength. Figure 5.19 gives an example from an undisclosed website.

This system rates the strength based on a set of rules with minimum requirements. Apparently twenty z's all in a row is a very weak password, but if you do the math, you will find that there are 20,725,274,851,017,800,000,000,000,000 iterations required to crack that keyspace. This is a time investment of 657,194,154,332.12 years. In Figure 5.20, we have a very different password.

Again, the assumption is that since $Aa!1\_$ is more complex than twenty z's, it is a stronger password, but look at the math. This password has only 2,569,332,380 iterations in its keyspace, which would require a time investment of 2.56933238 seconds. This is why I have always stood by my tried and true position that you should use a passphrase, and not a password. I can easily remember the password *hey hey mamma see the way you move*, but each time I typed $Aa!1\_$ I had to look up at it to make sure I had it right. So now you have a quantifiable measure by which to base your complexity. How many years are you okay with?

■ **FIGURE 5.20** Password Strength Meter Showing Five Characters with Uppercase, Lowercase, Digits, and Symbols as a 50 Percent Score and Noted as Good

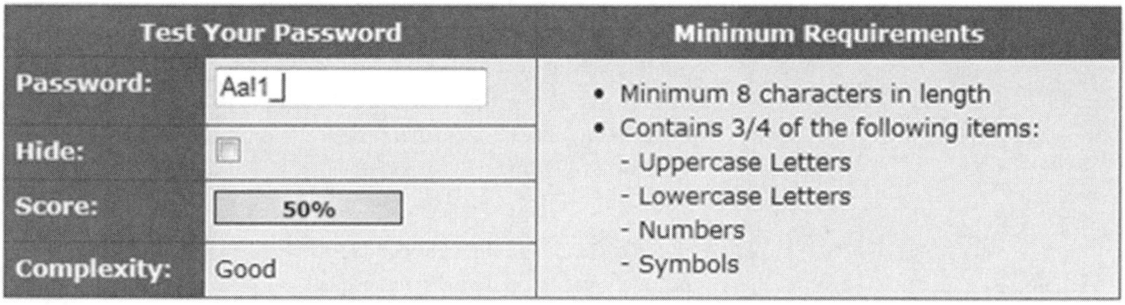

Test Your Password		Minimum Requirements
Password:	Aa!1	• Minimum 8 characters in length
Hide:	☐	• Contains 3/4 of the following items:
Score:	50%	- Uppercase Letters
		- Lowercase Letters
		- Numbers
Complexity:	Good	- Symbols

Show Me the Code!

The following is the C# source code for the password checker. It is also on the included DVD.

```csharp
using System;
using System.Collections.Generic;
using System.ComponentModel;
using System.Data;
using System.Drawing;
using System.Linq;
using System.Text;
using System.Text.RegularExpressions;
using System.Windows.Forms;

namespace PasswordChecker
{
  public partial class frmPassword : Form
  {

  // Assumptions:
  // lower is only lower
  // upper is only upper
  // numbers are only numbers
  // Bangs assumes upper and lower and numbers
  // Spec assumes upper lower numbers and Bang
  public static int iLength;

  public static double uCombinations;
  public static double uPerSecond;
  public static string sPassword;
  public static int iBase = 0;
  public static int iaz = 0;
  public static int iAZ = 0;
  public static int iNum = 0;
  public static int iBang = 0;
  public static int iSpec = 0;
  public static string brute = "abcdefghijklmnopqrstuvwxyz" +
  "ABCDEFGHIJKLMNOPQRSTUVWXYZ" +
  "0123456789!@#$%^&*()-=+" +
  "[]\""+"{}|;':" +",./<>?'~";

  public static double dSeconds;
  public static double dMinutes;
  public static double dHours;
```

```csharp
public static double dDays;
public static double dYears;

public frmPassword()
{
InitializeComponent();
uPerSecond = 1000000000;
uCombinations = 0;
txtPerSecond.Text = "1,000,000,000";
txtPassword.Focus();
}

private void frmPassword_Load(object sender, EventArgs e)
{
}

private void txtPassword_TextChanged(object sender,
EventArgs e)
{
GetBase();
}


public void GetBase()
{
sPassword = txtPassword.Text;
iLength = txtPassword.TextLength;
iaz = 0; iAZ = 0; iNum = 0; iBang = 0; iSpec = 0;
dSeconds = 0; dHours = 0; dDays = 0; dYears = 0;
uCombinations = 0;

MatchCollection az = Regex.Matches(sPassword, @"[a-z]");
MatchCollection AZ = Regex.Matches(sPassword, @"[A-Z]");
MatchCollection Num = Regex.Matches(sPassword, @"[0-9]");
MatchCollection Bang = Regex.Matches(sPassword, @"[!@#$%
-- ^&*\(\)\-_=+]");
MatchCollection Spec = Regex.Matches(sPassword, @"[\[\]
-- \{\}\;\:\'\,\.\<\>\/\|\\\'\~\?\ ]\"""");

if (az.Count > 0) {iaz = 26;}
if (AZ.Count > 0) { iAZ = 26; }
if (Num.Count > 0) { iNum = 10; }

if (Bang.Count > 0)
{
iBang = (26 + 26 + 10 + 14);
iaz = 0;
```

```
iAZ = 0;
iNum = 0;
}

if (Spec.Count > 0)
{
iSpec = (26 + 26 + 10 + 14 + 20);
iBang = 0;
iaz = 0;
iAZ = 0;
iNum = 0;
}

iBase = iaz + iAZ + iNum + iBang + iSpec;
txtBase.Text = "Dervies " + Convert.ToString(iBase) + "
-- of 96";
txtLength.Text = Convert.ToString(sPassword.Length);

for (int i = 1; i <= sPassword.Length; i++)
{
uCombinations = uCombinations + System.Math.Pow(iBase, i);
}

txtCombinations.Text = Convert.ToString(uCombinations);

dSeconds = uCombinations / uPerSecond;
dMinutes = dSeconds / 60;
dHours = dSeconds / 60;
dDays = dHours / 24;
dYears = dDays / 365;

txtMinutes.Text = string.Format("{0:n}", dMinutes);
txtHours.Text = string.Format("{0:n}", dHours);
txtDays.Text = string.Format("{0:n}", dDays);
txtYears.Text = string.Format("{0:n}", dYears);
}


}
}
```

■ SUMMARY

This chapter outlined the many ways one can limit the authority of a service user account, and how to configure such an account to perform its required function with minimal privileges. We discussed how to manage and administer this account in AD with group policy, and we discussed a new method of measuring your password strength in a way that gives you tangible results. Finally, we ended with code that will allow you to customize your own application to check password strength.

REFERENCES

Installations, and named instances. (2001). Setting up Windows service accounts. In *MSDN | Microsoft Development, Subscriptions, Resources, and More.* N.p., n.d., April 22. http://msdn.microsoft.com/en-us/library/ms143504.aspx.

"Hammer of God," (2011). *Hammer of God.* N.p., n.d., April 22. www.hammerofgod .com/passwordcheck.aspx, accessed April 22, 2011.

Remote Security Log Collection in a Least Privilege Environment

---

INFORMATION IN THIS CHAPTER:

- Log Fetcher Architecture
- Accessing WMI
- Show Me the Code!

PRODUCTS, TOOLS, AND METHODS

- AD
- MS SQL Server
- Distributed Component Object Model (DCOM)
- Windows Management Instrumentation (WMI)
- Event Logs
- Service Users
- Visual Studio (C#)

INTRODUCTION

Okay, time to be honest. Certain aspects of our jobs are simply not sexy. In an industry where the presentation of security vulnerabilities has actually become a competitive sport, it is easy to lose sight of this. Security has moved from a practice, a discipline if you will, into a business model. The thought seems to be that if someone can illustrate some amazingly l337 hacking technique, they must be complete experts at normal security and you should hire them to secure your assets. In real life, it seldom works that way. Sure, using infrared imaging on a keypad to create thermograms from residual finger-heat in order to discern the codes entered is cool. Combining 27 different vulnerabilities together in order to own a machine is cool, as is freezing live memory sticks for transport and forensic analysis. I can turn a canned air duster upside down and freeze a housefly in its tracks, and that is cool too (particularly watching as the frost develops all over it and then simultaneously starts to "steam"), but doing so does not mean I know anything at all about entomology.

We have to be careful not to let industry jazz hands distract us from the basics of security, no matter how boring they may be. When companies suffer a breach, the most common cause by far is some simple misconfiguration or poor security practice. Even IT security companies get hacked, and it is almost always because of some basic issue and not the use of a gauss meter to bypass Faraday cages to get remote screen scrapes from magnetic resonance.

Building a Secure Log Repository Process

One basic security practice that I often see overlooked is the analysis of log files. Put more simply: People do not read their logs because poring over a log sucks. I would rather get a tetanus shot in the ear than go through security logs. All manner of entries exist that I really do not have an interest in, and the event log interface does not provide the user experience or data retrieval methods I want. I want to know about failed logon attempts and object access, and while I personally do not need success audits for services or interfaces,* I very well may want success audits for when a member was added to a group, like EventID 4732. Depending on the group, it could possibly indicate something sketchy going on. Very large companies do indeed automate log management with products like Microsoft Operations Manager, and that is fantastic, but the fact remains that many organizations cannot afford the manpower, equipment, and financial cost to implement such a system.

I want to illustrate a method by which you can automate log collection in a secure way using what you already have, or what you can get for free (such as SQL Express) in this chapter. When administrators create a home-grown solution, it has to be given a codename because it is in our guild charter. I started out with *Thor's Cheap Horker*, but that just sounds wrong. So, I would like to introduce my new project, *Managed Interface Log Fetcher*.

As with all stories told in this book, not only does this provide a useful and fully functional process, but it also represents security measures one can apply to any number of features. As you read through, I again encourage you to think about how this can apply to other areas of your infrastructure.

---

*As described in Chapter 5, Creation and Maintenance of Low Privileged Service Users.

LOG FETCHER ARCHITECTURE

Designing a log collection feature is by no means a new idea. Examples of how to do this abound on the Internet. However, the ones that I have seen promote what I consider to be very risky and insecure methods of operating. I am not discounting the logging and event features built into Windows that help with this process in any way. Many powerful features in Windows Server allow for event triggers based on log data, filtering, custom views, and subscriptions to other logs. But, while there is a lot one can do with the default installation of Windows, I want to do more, and I want it to be highly secure.

Conceptually, the process is easy. We want to gather event log records of interest and store them in a SQL database for more robust searching and reporting capabilities, as well as to perform triggers based on any number of events. For instance, we could certainly have the security event log set to fire off an e-mail when there is a failed logon, but x number of events would result in x number of triggers. With SQL, we could base triggers on aggregate. If we saw, say, a service account fail logon, we would indeed want an immediate notification because they should all be automated. But for group actions, we may want to only be notified if there are more than 10 of event 4732 per hour, or whatever our desired threshold is. The point is that we can do all manner of things in SQL that we cannot do in the event viewer. A tremendous benefit is that we can perform any number of analyses of log data without actually having to be working directly on the server logs themselves, and we can easily add and remove users from read access to the data, create audit reports, and the list goes on.

Retrieving Log Data: The Good, the Bad, and the Really Ugly

Technically, you can retrieve log data in a couple of ways, and a number of examples can of course be found on the Internet. However, many of the popular solutions (as defined by top query returns) have serious security issues. A common theme is for the administrator to log on to the server in question, and export the log to an EVT file, and then use Log Parser in a SQL job. I have also seen instructions on how to have SQL drop to a command shell and execute the *DumpEvt* tool to grab the events out of the local logs, write them to a file, and then import that file into SQL. It was good to see references to the *manage auditing and security logs* user rights assignment option in place of administrative access, which I will discuss, but even that has some issues as well.

Even though these methods work, they just do not meet the level of security I believe is appropriate for use in a production environment. And note that

I am not picking on any specific blog posts you may find. I just want to point out the common security mistakes that are made, even by professionals. Here are my issues with these methods, in no particular order.

- An automated process should never be run in the context of an administrator unless it is required for execution. This goes for the installation of the SQL Server service as well. Unless there is some identifiable requirement for SQL Server to be installed under the context of LocalSystem or an administrative user, it should be deployed as a low-privileged service user as discussed in Chapter 5, aptly entitled "The Creation and Maintenance of Low-Privileged Service Users."
- Anytime you see a reference to xp_cmdshell in any SQL solution, it should send up a red flag. I am not saying that there are never any reasons to deploy it, but you should be intimately familiar with the associated security issues of doing so. The enabling of xp_cmdshell is by way of a server configuration setting. If it is enabled on the server, then any process with permissions on the server can execute it, and that is a huge entry point for attacks. Processes presented like some of the aforementioned tell me a few things. With no mention of permissions or delegation, that means the process is running as administrator (obviously, otherwise they would have detailed the process). If the logs being retrieved from DumpEvt (or another similar tool) are from a remote computer, it means that a domain account is used since LocalSystem cannot make network calls. Further, depending on the tools, it means remote administration pipes are exposed such as \PIPE\EVENTLOG and that data is probably being sent in the clear. An example of DumpEvt logs-in-transit are illustrated in Figure 6.1.

Do not quote me on this as I am no expert in payment card industry auditing, but I am pretty sure that remote log data collection must be (or should be) encrypted in transit by matter of policy. Something simple like this could manifest itself in somewhat serious audit results, or as we say in the business, put you in deep doo-doo.

I guess the worst thing about these types of solutions is that for the purposes of auditing security you will end up making OS command–based calls from highly privileged accounts to remote computers using elevated domain credentials to get log data that is sent over the wire in cleartext. It is one of those "when you put it *that* way" moments you should avoid!

I will illustrate a method by which you can use a low-privileged service user that has minimal read rights to individual event logs in a way that can provide remote access to servers without remote administration ports being enabled, and where the log data is encrypted in transit. Remote component

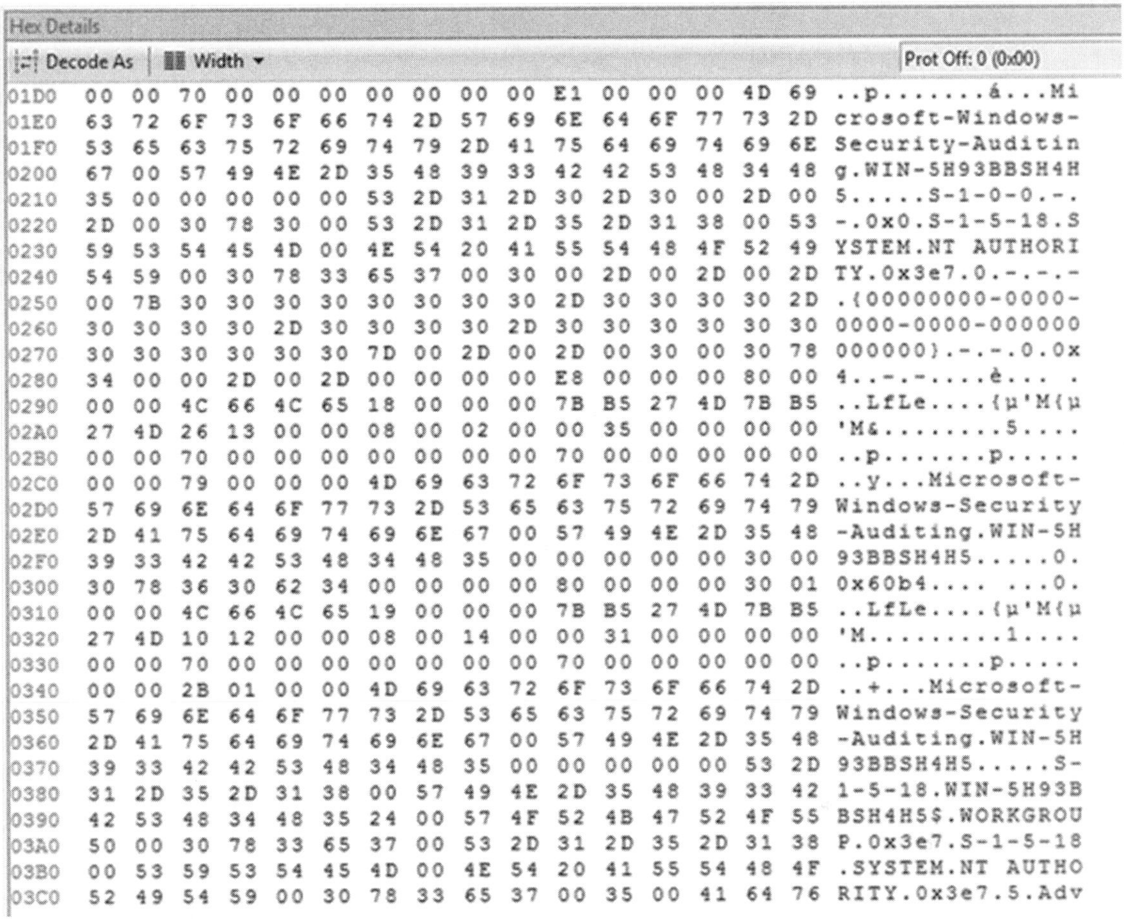

■ **FIGURE 6.1** Remote Event Log Data Being Sent in the Clear

object model (COM) connections will be strictly controlled, as will access to the instrumentation objects that will retrieve the data. This data will be selectively retrieved from the logs based on any criteria we wish, and will be posted into a SQL database where access permissions can be granted at a granular level. This will all be done without invoking any command-level processes or accessing any file-system objects. And it will be surprisingly easy to do. Well, easy because I have done all the work for you up front! The workflow is illustrated in Figure 6.2.

We will end up with a process where a SQL job, run in the context of a low-privileged service user, will call a CLR assembly function we will write that instantiates a WMI object over DCOM. This WMI object will connect up to the event log provider over an encrypted channel in the context

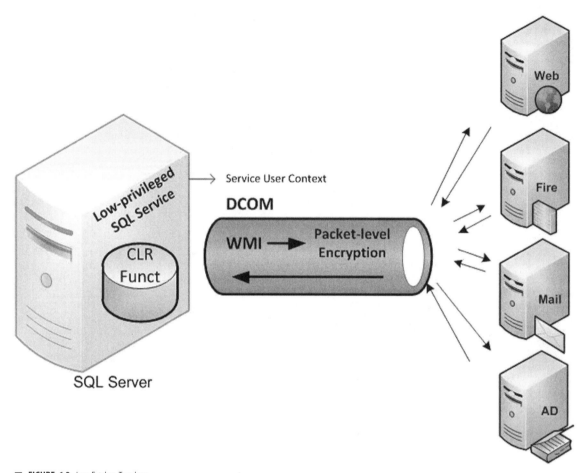

of our service user, and it will directly access the event log data using permissions granted explicitly to individual event logs by assigning access controls with SDDL. The log data will then be directly posted into a SQL table after parsing out some of the message data for more details. The WMI connection consists of SQL-like query structures, and we will request the data with *SELECT * FROM Win32_NTLogEvent WHERE EventType = 5* just like T-SQL. This is one of the other reasons we will be using WMI to access the logs as opposed to something like the C# EventLog class because we can easily filter the returned results to only give us what we want. More on this in the WMI section later in this chapter.

It sounds far more complicated than it really is. You can have this up and running in your environment in no time; however, I am going to stop along the way and dive deeply into each segment so as to provide you with the most information in case you choose to deploy other solutions using some of the same features.

Preparing the SQL Server

We need to first prepare our SQL server installation properly. In this example, it will be the same user created and configured as per Chapter 5, "The Creation and Maintenance of Low-Privileged Service Users." For a quick review, this user only exists as a member of the gServiceUsers group (with other service users) and explicitly does not belong to any other domain group because it was removed from the default of domain users after gServiceUsers was set as the primary group. When the user was specified for use during the installation of SQL Server, it was added to the local users group on the server, and was explicitly assigned to log on as a service. Its membership in the local users group gives it implicit assignment of the following user rights: access this computer from the network, allow to log on locally, and increase a process working set. That is all. The next steps of this process example will assume that SQL was installed consistently with the instructions in Chapter 5 about low-privileged service users.

Connecting to Remote Servers

Next I will talk about how we are going to connect to remote servers, and how we will query the WMI provider on that system to give us the event record information we want. We will initiate the connection itself via the DCOM interface, and request access to the WMI component services. When that is granted, we will simply issue WMI queries to the instrumentation interface we want, and get the data back.

DCOM is a common interface for requests to supported component services. The request comes in via regular Remote Procedure Call (RPC) for DCOM which is available by default. We are using standard RPC, so we will not need any firewall rules opened up to support it. This is in contrast to some other tools, including the built-in Event Viewer MMC which requires remote administration firewall rules to be in place when you use **Connect to other computer**. Not only does DCOM figure out what service we are looking for and establish that connection, but it also enforces access controls set on the different components. You need access to the component through DCOM to reach the component and have your request passed through. In this case, our WMI component needs authentication as well to enumerate the interface. And if that were not enough, from an OS standpoint, we need permissions to use DCOM in general via the *Distributed COM Users* group. Think of it as different layers of security that you have to pass through. You have got to be a member of the DCOM users group to access DCOM, you have to have permission to call the particular COM object through DCOM, and then the COM object itself may also require permission. This is actually a good model because it provides the best granularity. You may want some users to have access to DCOM, then WMI through DCOM, but then drill down and give different users access to particular WMI subroots, or namespaces. Note that this permission structure has nothing to do with the permissions required to actually access the logs, because that is a different segment.

When this is worked out, we will be able to issue WMI queries, so we shall now start doling out permissions.

Adding the group as illustrated in Figure 6.3 is easy enough. Find the local Distributed COM Users group on the target server(s) and add the global gServiceUsers group to the local group. This can also be done via group policy. Our SQL service user will now be able to use DCOM on the server.

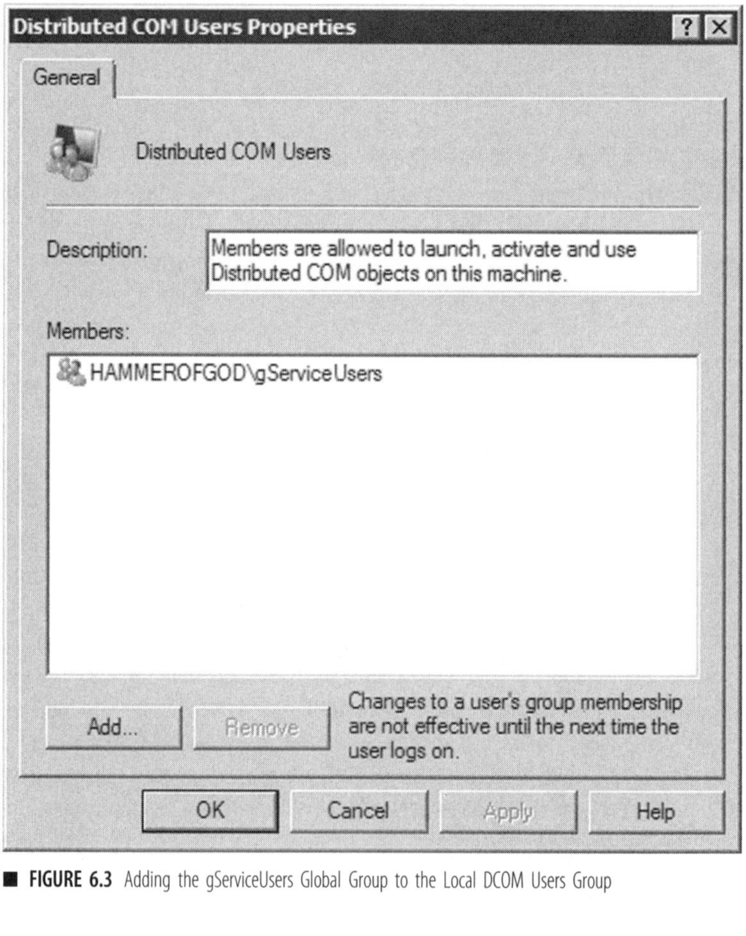

FIGURE 6.3 Adding the gServiceUsers Global Group to the Local DCOM Users Group

DCOM Components and Permissions

The next step is to actually give permissions to the DCOM component we want, which is done via the *DCOMCNFG* utility. Launching it allows us to expand the DCOM configuration folder and to scroll down to the WMI folder, as illustrated in Figure 6.4.

To expose the permissions for DCOM to allow you to hit the WMI component, go to **Properties | Security**. As you see, DCOM security settings are a

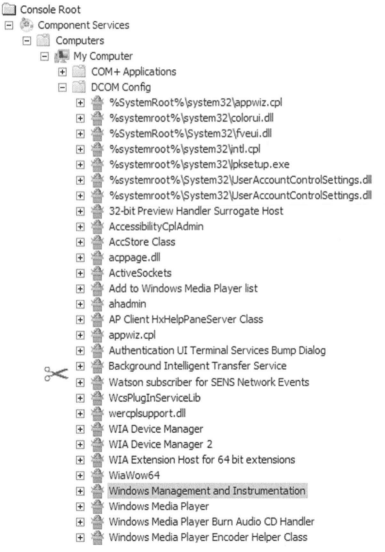

■ **FIGURE 6.4** DCOMCNFG Utility Showing the WMI Folder Selected (Scissors Indicate Omitted Content)

bit different in that there are different classes of access, and each has its own permissions setting. These classes are divided into Launch and Activation, Access, and Configuration. Within the Launch and Activation and Access classes are scope options for local and remote sources. Local is when a user attempts to perform an action while interactively logged on to the COM server, and remote is over the network from a different client.

WMI Configuration

Launch and Activation means that an entity can start a COM server if it is not already started (launch) or create objects in a COM server that is already running (activate). Access permissions allow the entity to use the component or object once it is running or created.

Configuration lets you view or set DCOM configuration options for the component.

It may not make immediate sense, but these permissions are not dependent upon each other. One user may be able to launch, but not use, a component. So it would be like a user launching an application even though that user cannot log in to the application and use it after it is started.

The same goes for access. A user may have local and remote access to a component, but they cannot launch the server or create objects. And it is the same for configuration, too. An entity can have any combination of these permissions.

> **NOTE**
> You may notice in Figure 6.5 that the default permission set for Launch and Activation and Configuration is **Customize**. It seems like a cyclic redundancy, and I am not really sure why it is like that; it just is.

The scope for Launch and Activate is local launch, remote launch, local activation, and remote activation. The default permissions are all permissions for the local administrators group, which contains the domain administrators group. Authenticated users have local launch, local activation, and remote activation. Our service user will belong to the authenticated users context, so these default permissions are fine for us. Noticing the absence of remote launch, you may be tempted to add the gServiceUsers group with full access in case the WMI DCOM component is not started, but I do not do that, as evidenced by Figure 6.6. The server is started by default (note this is the DCOM server, not the physical server), and while I do not know what circumstances would exist under which the server would stop, it would mean something, so I would not give our user permissions to just launch it again. I would rather err on the side of caution.

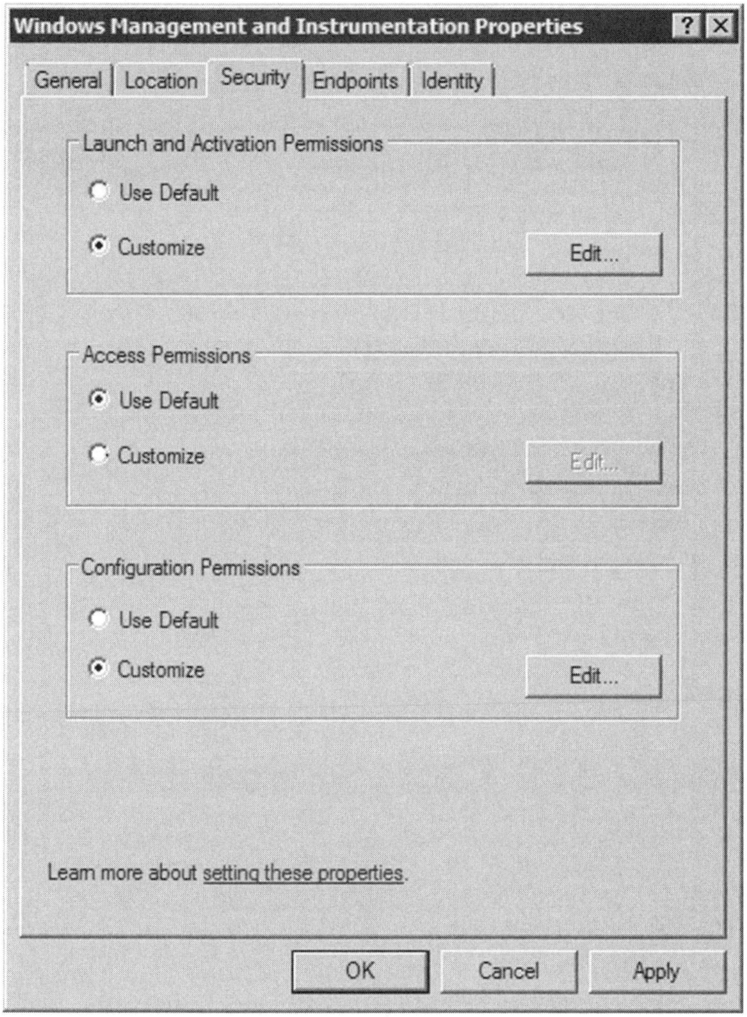

■ FIGURE 6.5 Default DCOM Access Permission Structure for the WMI Component

Skipping to Configuration Figure 6.7, we see the default custom permissions give SYSTEM and local administrators full control and the local users (which contains the Domain Users group) read access to configuration options. Special permissions are inherited from the root for all assigned users and they are actually set to nothing. In other words, a permissions container for each user is created with special permissions even though no permissions are set. This lets you drill down into a user to assign advanced special permissions to set values or enumerate subkeys and the like if necessary.

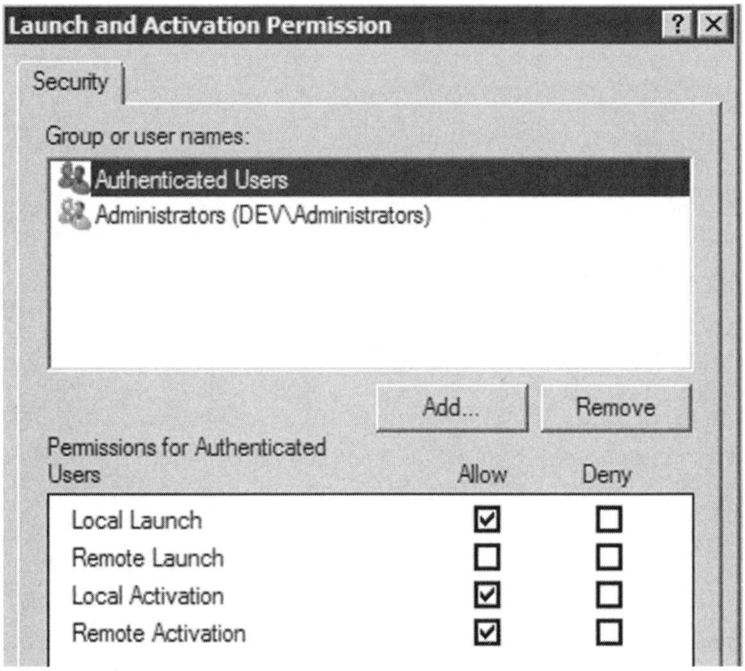

■ **FIGURE 6.6** Default Launch and Activation Permissions for Authenticated Users

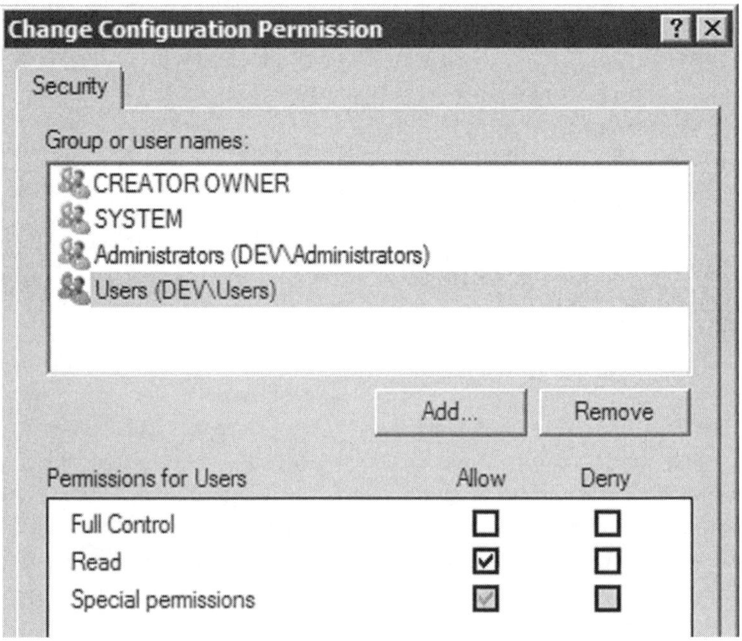

■ **FIGURE 6.7** Default Configuration Permissions for Local Users Group

The access permissions class is the only one set to *Default* for the actual default setting (as opposed to *Customize*) and allows self and local administrators local and remote access, and SYSTEM local access. SYSTEM could only have local access anyway, but I like that Microsoft drilled so deeply into the configuration to explicitly set local access only. That shows a great attention to detail.

It is here we need to change the permissions by selecting **Customize**, and adding our gServiceUsers group, giving them remote access to the COM object as shown in Figure 6.8. If you are setting permissions on the SQL Server, or any physical server where the service user is being used, and you want it to pull logs from itself, then you would also set local access.

Remember that these permissions only apply once a user has been given overall access to DCOM by membership in the Distributed COM Users group. Place a mental bookmark here as I will return to this permission scope when we talk more about actual log permissions in the customizing Windows log permissions section of this chapter.

WMI Permissions

To finish up the necessary permissions to required objects we need to set permissions on the WMI instrumentation hives. I use that term since the WMI namespace folders are similar in structure to the system Registry. We can get to the WMI management plug-in by running WMIMGMT.msc.

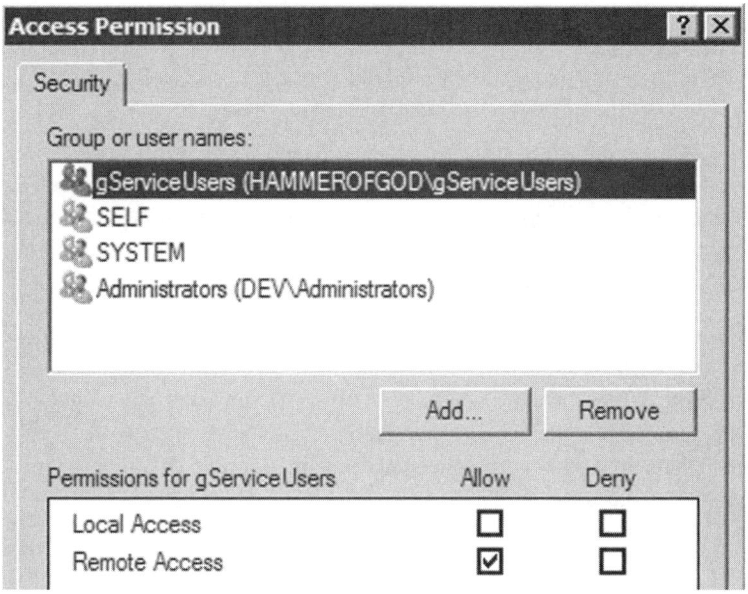

■ **FIGURE 6.8** Customized Permissions for the gServiceUsers Group for Remote Access to the COM Object

As is the case with DCOM components, you can control access to different WMI namespaces. This again allows more granular access control. We are interested in the *Win32_NTLogEvent* object which lives in the second version of the Common Information Model (CIMV2), as shown in Figure 6.9.

To set security, you have to click **Security**, then **Properties**, and then select the **Security** tab like you normally do. I do not know the reason for this UI change.

The programmatic interface to WMI in general supports all manner of functions, including reading properties, reading security controls, writing values, and even executing different methods of a component (like SQL directives, launching subprocesses to connect to other systems, formatting drives, and so on).

By default, authenticated users, LOCAL SERVICE, and NETWORK SER-VICE can Execute Methods, Provider Write, and have the Enable Account flag set. Local administrators have full permissions, which are Execute Methods, Full Write, Partial Write, Provider Write, Enable Account, Remote Enable, Read Security, and Edit Security. Special permissions do not expose any other controls, which becomes evident when you look at the graphical UI (GUI) dialog where no special permissions are selected or checked.

Since our gServiceUsers group would be represented in the authenticated users group, the default permissions would serve if the WMI namespace was being accessed locally because of the inherited **Enable Account** flag being set. Since that will not suffice in our environment, we will add our gServiceUsers group to this list, and grant them **Remote Enable** as well. This is all that is necessary for us to read the event logs. It is this set of permissions that dictates what actions can be taken via WMI queries from a client. Again, this is not where the permissions for the event log itself are; this is just controlling access to any given namespace and subnamespace via the instrumentation interface. This is why we only need the accounts we are using to have **Enable Account** and **Remote Enable** set. We could set permissions at the root, but we know we only need namespaces within CIMV2, so we will only set those as shown in Figure 6.10.

Remember that there are subnamespaces that we need as well, but by default this setting will only apply to the current namespace, so setting these permissions is not enough. You have to go to **Advanced Settings** and edit the permission entry for the gServiceUsers group, and change the **Apply to** option from **This namespace only** to **This namespace and subnamespaces** as illustrated in Figure 6.11.

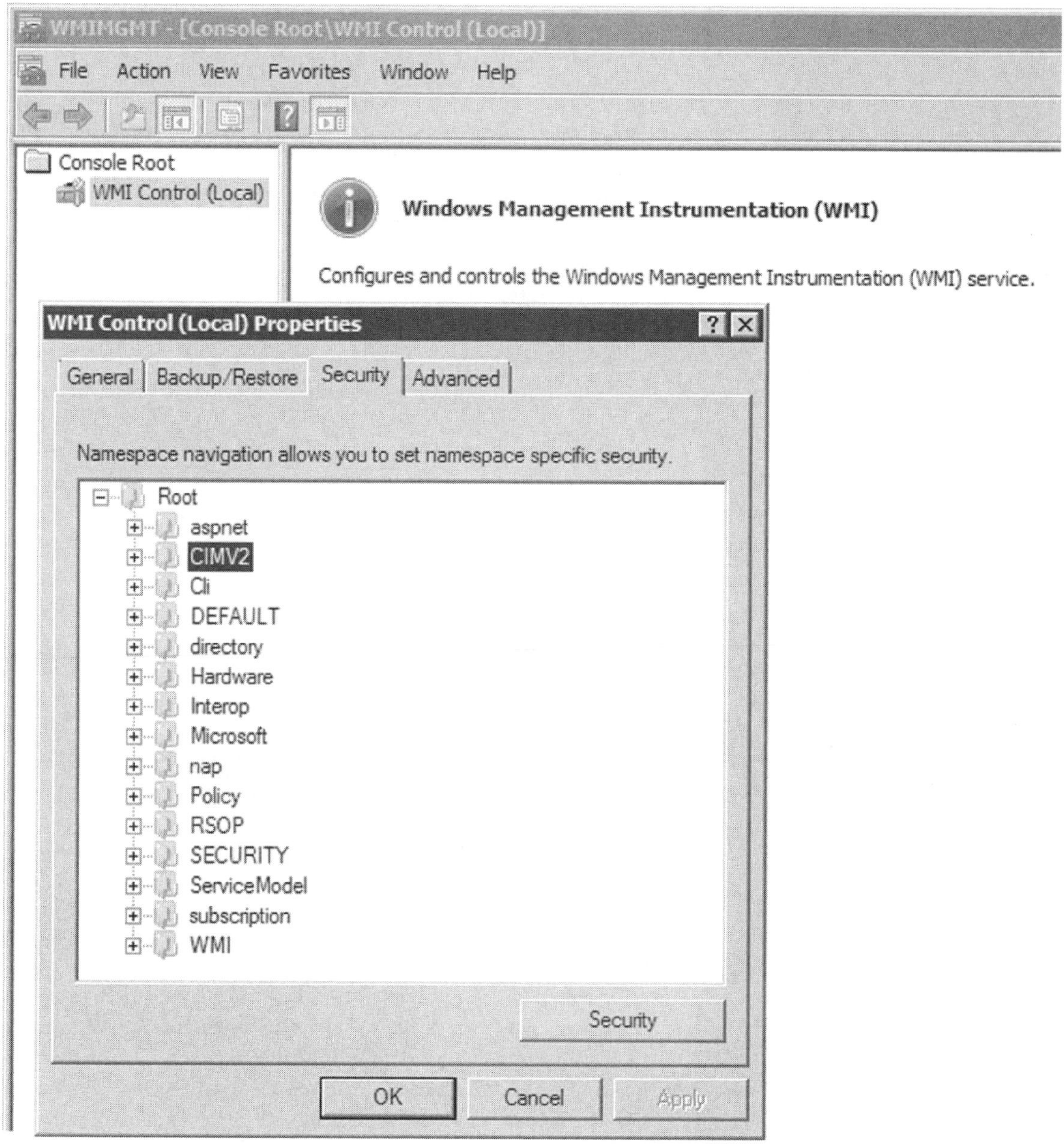

■ **FIGURE 6.9** WMI Management Console
Expanded to the CIMV2 Namespace

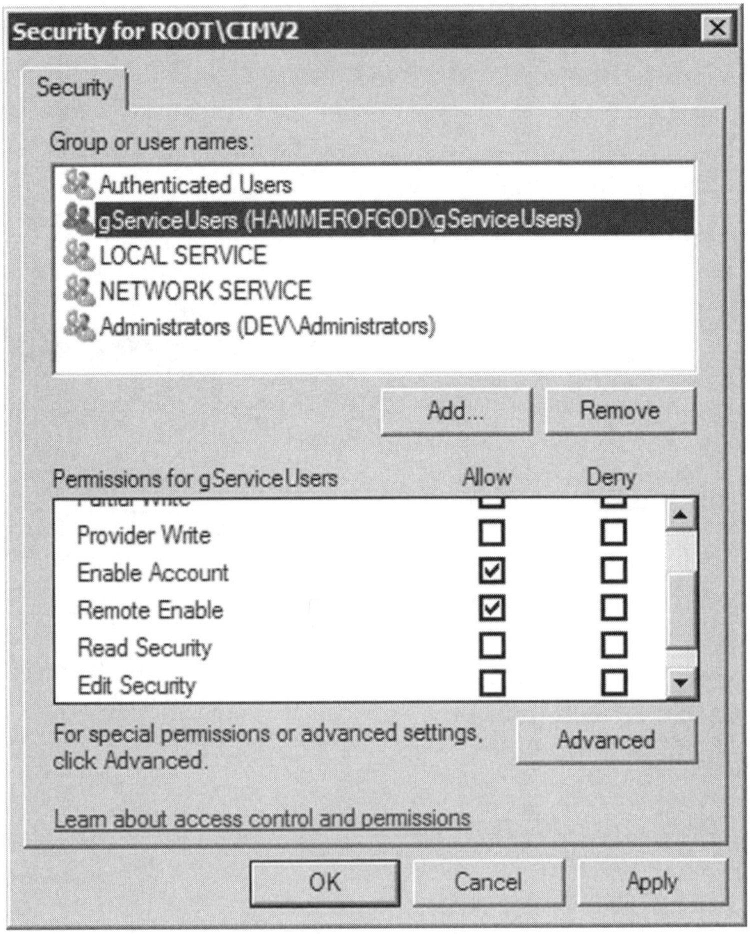

■ **FIGURE 6.10** WMI root\CIMV2 Permissions for gServiceUsers Including Remote Enable

There we go. Again, it may seem like a lot to do, but it is pretty easy to set up once you get it down. Keep that mental bookmark for customizing log permissions in mind again since it applies here as well. We are now ready to address the permissions required to work directly with the log files. But before we start that process, we will review Figure 6.12, which shows the overall permissions structure, so we have it pictured properly in our minds.

I thought it would be a good idea to summarize before we get into the log permissions, as things can get a bit thick once we start getting deep into how the event log permissions work.

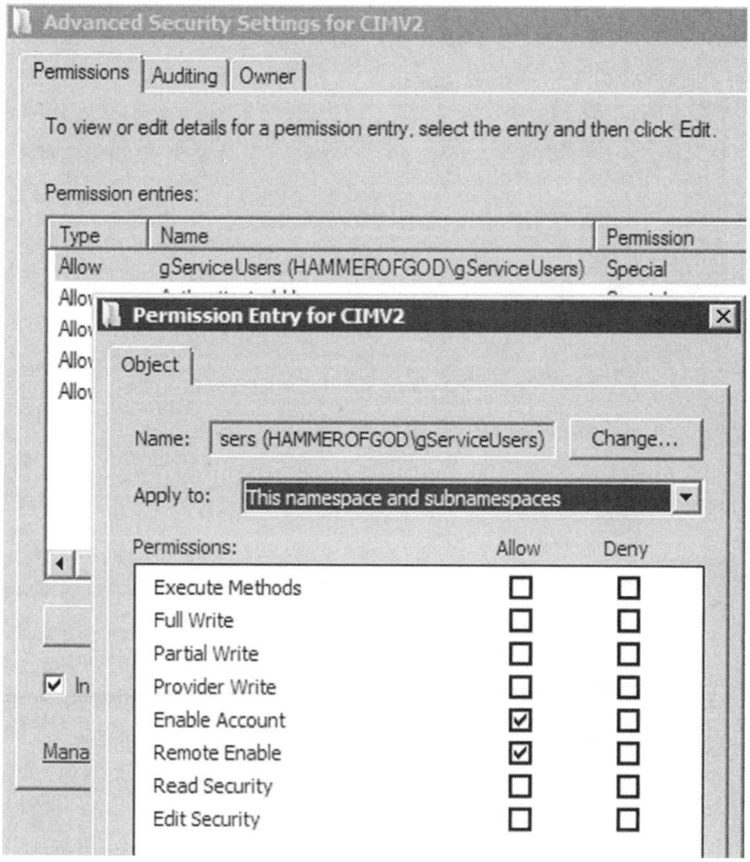

■ **FIGURE 6.11** Advanced Permissions of CIMV2 Namespace Applied to Both the Namespace and the Subnamespaces

Log File Access and Permissions

From a general security standpoint, your event logs, the security log in particular, are interacted with as very sensitive data sources. While the application log and system log can contain confidential information regarding any number of tracked events produced by any number of applications or subsystems, the security log contains very detailed information about logon events, protocol data, granular security privileges for various processes, authentication methods, comprehensive users and computers/domain data, and basically a wealth of important information regarding your overall system security health. As such, the default permissions for the logs are very tight.

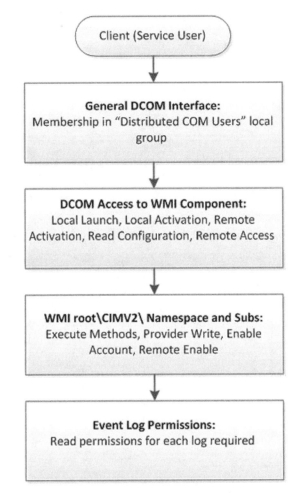

■ **FIGURE 6.12** Permissions Tier for Overall Log Fetcher Remote Access Process

The default log file access controls are based on built-in and well-known security identifiers (SIDs). Actually, all permissions are based on this structure; however, you cannot pull up the security settings for the logs and view them in a friendly UI the way you can other permissions. This is an important distinction. The default permissions for the application log are:

- SYSTEM: Full Control
- Built-in Administrator and Server Operators: Read, Write, and Clear
- Interactive Users, users set to Logon as a Service, and Batch Users (S-1-5-3), LOCAL SERVICE (S-1-5-33): Read and Write
- Event Log Readers (S-1-5-32-573): Read

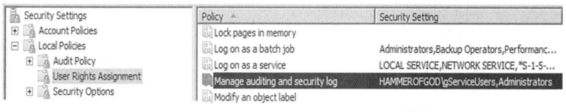

■ **FIGURE 6.13** Assigning the User Rights Security Setting to Manage Auditing and Security Log

The last SID representing *Event Log Readers* is a new built-in local group introduced in Windows Server 2008 that allows you to manage group membership for users you wish to have read-only access to a log. Before this, the only way to grant other users the ability to view logs was to assign them the **Manage Audit** and **Security Log** user right. User rights are not based on security group membership. Instead, they are assigned rights based on the policy management plug-in found in **Local Security Settings | Local Policies | User Rights Assignment**. Of course, this could also be assigned by group policy, but Figure 6.13 shows where users would be assigned this right.

The main concern with granting this right to users is that it gives them blanket permissions for all log files with rights to read, write, and clear. Anytime I have had to give auditors this type of permission, or even when I have had to have it myself as an auditor, it always made me feel a bit sketchy. When giving auditors access to logs for security review, and the access you have to give them is **Read**, **Write**, and **Clear**, it does not exactly generate warm fuzzies regarding the integrity of the logs in the first place. Before actual auditing can take place, you sometimes have to give them information about who has had that type of access before and it can get messy.

Default Permissions and Remote Administration

The event log readers local group is a very valuable configuration option for scenarios like this where you must grant someone permission to view logs. They can only read, and cannot write or clear anything. Note though that the Event Log Readers group gives read access to all logs, and you can use the group to limit access. While we are on the subject of limited read access to the logs, know that you do not have to go through all the steps we must here to give someone this access. If you wanted a user to have temporary access to read logs, you could simply make them a member of this group (they have to log on again for the changes to be reflected) and you could enable remote administration for a short time, which would allow

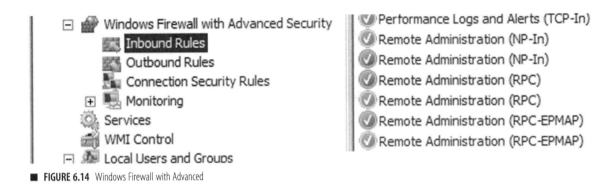

■ **FIGURE 6.14** Windows Firewall with Advanced Security Inbound Rules for Remote Administration

them to use the event viewer snap-in to connect up to the remote computer. Though deprecated, you can quickly use NETSH.exe to enable and disable remote administration with the command: *netsh firewall set service remoteadmin enable or disable*. This has the effect of turning on remote administration as seen in the Windows Advanced Firewall configuration for inbound connection rules, as shown in Figure 6.14.

> **NOTE**
> Windows Server 2008 and Windows 7 have prebuilt Windows Advanced Firewall rule sets to specifically support Remote Event Log Management should you wish to limit other Remote Administration services.

Again, this is not required for our solution since we are using regular old RPC, as Figure 6.15 illustrates. Our process will succeed even when the firewall is in this state.

Moving on, the default permissions for the system log are:

- SYSTEM: Full Control
- Built-in Administrator: read, write, and clear
- Backup Operators, users set to logon as a service: read and write
- Server Operators: read and clear
- LOCAL SERVICE (S-1-5-33): write
- Authenticated Users, Batch Users (S-1-5-3), Event Log Readers (S-1-5-32-573): read

■ **FIGURE 6.15** Windows Firewall with Advanced Security with Remote Administration Turned Completely Off

Remote Administration (NP-In)	Remote Administration	All	No	Allow	No
Remote Administration (RPC)	Remote Administration	All	No	Allow	No
Remote Administration (RPC-EPMAP)	Remote Administration	All	No	Allow	No

And finally, the default permissions for the security log are:

- SYSTEM: read and clear with Discretionary Access Controls (DACs) of READ_Control, WRITE_DAC, WRITE_Owner, and Delete
- Built-in Administrator: read and clear (no DACs)
- Event Log Readers (S-1-5-32-573): read

As you can see, the security log is quite restrictive, considering that no user other than the SYSTEM context is granted any write rights at all. Given this strictly controlled permission set, you can see why the Event Log Readers group is so valuable, and why administrators would use the *manage auditing and security log* user rights assignment even though it did not exactly represent the most secure of postures.

Customizing Windows Log Permissions

Remember the mental bookmark I talked about with the gServiceUsers group with DCOM and WMI permissions? Well, we can make the administration of those permissions a bit easier if your server version supports the Event Log Readers group, and if you do not mind the fact that this group allows members to read all event logs.

We would have to add the gServiceUsers global group to the Event Log Readers local group to give our service users read access, so we may as well leverage that one bit of membership to make DCOM and WMI permissions a bit easier. Once the Event Log Readers group contains gServiceUsers, you can use it to set permissions for DCOM and WMI as well. It is really up to you, but I like keeping things as organized as possible, so if I use Event Log Readers for log access permissions, then I also use Event Log Readers for the DCOM and WMI permissions, which I show in Figure 6.16.

Getting back to the actual event log permissions, there is still a way to leverage the least privilege of read-only for event logs if you do not have 2008, or if you do not want to grant a user read access to all logs via Event Log Readers. This would be an absolutely valid concern if you have altered the log permissions or if the default permissions do not meet with your approval.

Security Descriptor Definition Language

The key to directly setting custom event log permissions is in the SDDL. SDDL is a bit cryptic when you first look at it, but it is basically a string of data that represents a collection of security controls for an object. For instance, here is the SDDL representation for the security log:

```
O:BAG:SYD:(A;;0x5;;;BA)(A;;0xf0005;;;SY)(A;;0x1;;;S-1-
5-32-573)
```

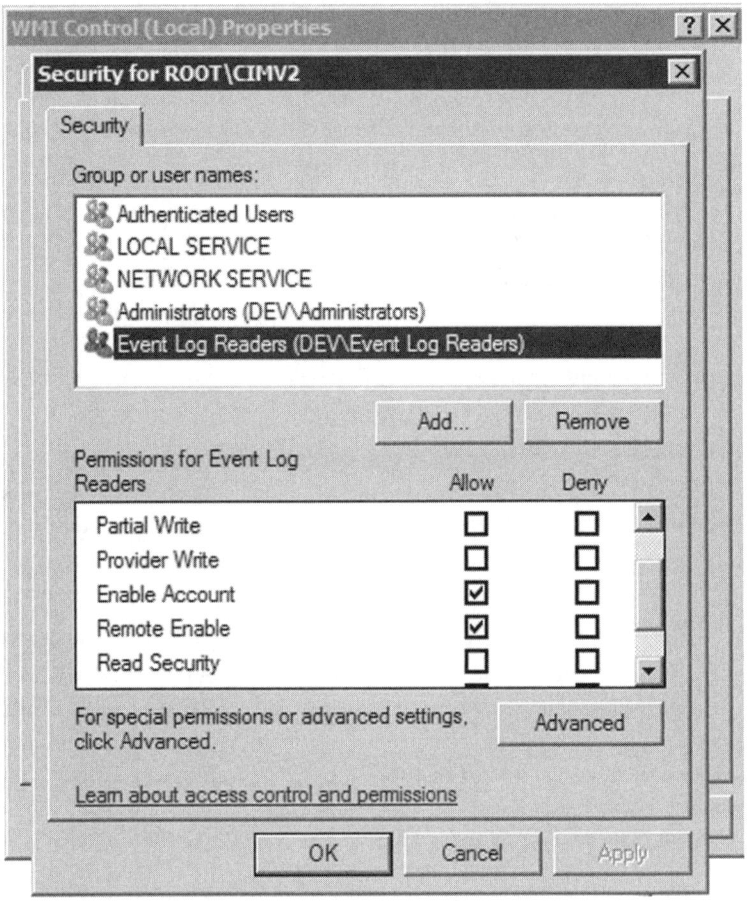

■ **FIGURE 6.16** Organizational Option of Using the Event Log Readers Built-In Group Instead of gServiceUsers When gServiceUsers Is a Member of the Event Log Readers Group

SDDL is a complex subject, and applies to many objects, so I will try to keep this on point and limit the scope of our SDDL discussion to prevent boring you. An SDDL-formatted ACL has four parts to it: an Owner:SID pair, a Group:SID pair, DACL:SID groupings, and system access control lists (SACLs). It is important to understand the SDDL format in respect to altering log file permissions, as it requires a Registry entry, and you want to make sure you get it right.

A discretionary access control list (DACL) identifies what users or trustees are allowed or denied access, and what type of access is being controlled. You set auditing options on an object with an SACL. This is how the system knows when you want to audit success, failure, or whatever else on any particular object. DACLs and SACLs are what make up an overall ACL. The preceding security log SDDL ACL actually does not contain any SACLs.

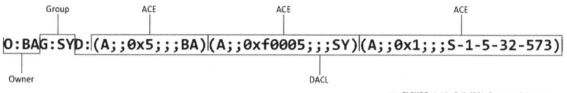

The first part of the SDDL contains the owner and group data:

> *O:BA*G:SYD: – This tells us the Owner is BA, or the built-in administrator account.
>
> O:BA*G:SY*D: – This tells us the Group is SY, or LOCAL SYSTEM.
>
> O:BAG:SY*D:* – This tells us that the DACL list begins. Each *access control entry* in the DACL is called an *ACE*.

Figure 6.17 offers a reference to match up BA, SY, and other constants to their respective entities. This component diagram illustrates the SDDL structure as a whole.

Here is what the first ACE in the DACL string tells us:

> (*A*;;0x5;;;BA) – The "*A*" tells us to allow the action; deny would have a "*D*" instead.
>
> (A;;*0x5*;;;BA) – The "*0x5*" tells us the actual rights we are allowing based on a simple sum of three categories: 1 = read, 2 = write, and 4 = clear. If the access is read, it gets a 1. If it is write, it gets a 2. So if it is read and write, it gets a 3 (1 + 2). If it is clear and write, it gets a 6 (2 + 4), and so on. So the preceding 0x5 tells us that we are allowing read and clear permissions (1 + 4). The third element is the user or trustee.
>
> (A;;0x5;;;*BA*) – The "BA" tells us that the user is the built-in administrator. So an entire SDDL entry for a log consisting of O:BAG:SYD: (A;;0x5;;;BA) gives the built-in administrator read and clear permissions, and specifies that BA is the owner and SY is the group.

The second user is a bit different since the xf000 permissions dictate the DACs we spoke of earlier (READ_Control, WRITE_DAC, WRITE_Owner, and Delete).

> (*A*;;0xf0005;;;SY) – The "A" means "Allow."
>
> (A;;*0xf0005*;;;SY) – The 0xf0005 designates the overall ACE.
>
> (A;;*0xf000*5;;;SY) – The 0xf000 designates special permissions for the ACE.
>
> (A;;0xf000*5*;;;SY) – The "5" means READ and CLEAR (1 + 4 = 5).
>
> (A;;0xf0005;;;*SY*) – The "SY" means the user is the LOCAL SYSTEM account.
>
> (*A*;;0x1;;;S-1-5-32-573) – The "A" means "Allow."
>
> (A;;*0x1*;;;S-1-5-32-573) – The "0x1" means READ.

(A;;0x1;;;*S-1-5-32-573*) – The "S-1-5-32-573" is the SID for the Event Log Readers group. The Event Log Readers group, no matter what system it is on, is always referenced to as S-1-5-32-573. This is what is meant by well-known SID. The user identity field can be either the SID of the user or group you wish to represent, or one of many preset string codes. Figure 6.18 lists some common string constants that you can use instead of the well-known SID.[1]

These will come in handy if you decide to dive deeper into SDDL. You may also want a reference[2] to the actual well-known SIDs, since the SDDLs of the logs reference them as well (such as S-1-5-32-573 for the Event Log Readers group). A number of ways exist to actually get the ACL information from an object, mostly in code. For example, calls like *GetExplicitEntriesFromACL* or *GetAuditedPermissionsFromACL* allow you to do so. But that does not help us with the event logs. However, a tool on 2008 makes that easy for us, though 2003 still requires manual assignment of SDDL ACLs to the logs via a Registry entry that I will show you in a moment. It is better for us to start out with the 2008 tool called *WEVTUTIL* (presumably for Windows Event Log Utility), because it better illustrates the usage of SDDLs. A full reference for WEVTUTIL is available on TechNet,[3] but I will show you the basics. First, we need to get a list of all logs. This is done with a simple *el* flag telling WEVTUTIL to enumerate logs. I suspect that there are far more than you may have thought (depending on what services you have loaded, of course), so it is worth listing them in Figure 6.19 for effect if nothing else. The full code listing is available in Appendix A.

I know that is a lot of paper used, and I have probably contributed to global warming (other than that sun thing), but I like seeing it all sprawled out like that.

We want to view the available information for the security log, which includes the SDDL ACL. This is done by passing *gl*, orget-log, and the log name to WEVTUTIL. Note that you must explicitly run your command interpreter as administrator to view the security log ACL shown in Figure 6.20; you cannot just log on as an administrator and run it.

The SDDL is in the *channelAccess:* field (as previously illustrated). See the application and system logs in Figures 6.21 and Figure 6.22 as well.

---

[1]More available from http://msdn.microsoft.com/en-us/library/aa379602.aspx.

[2]http://support.microsoft.com/kb/243330

[3]http://technet.microsoft.com/en-us/library/cc732848(WS.10).aspx

"AN"	SDDL_ANONYMOUS
"AU"	SDDL_AUTHENTICATED_USERS
"BA"	SDDL_BUILTIN_ADMINISTRATORS
"BG"	SDDL_BUILTIN_GUESTS
"BO"	SDDL_BACKUP_OPERATORS
"BU"	SDDL_BUILTIN_USERS
"CA"	SDDL_CERT_SERV_ADMINISTRATORS
"CO"	SDDL_CREATOR_OWNER
"DA"	SDDL_DOMAIN_ADMINISTRATORS
"DC"	SDDL_DOMAIN_COMPUTERS
"DD"	SDDL_DOMAIN_DOMAIN_CONTROLLERS
"DG"	SDDL_DOMAIN_GUESTS
"DU"	SDDL_DOMAIN_USERS
"EA"	SDDL_ENTERPRISE_ADMINS
"ED"	SDDL_ENTERPRISE_DOMAIN_CONTROLLERS
"IU"	SDDL_INTERACTIVE_USERS
"LA"	SDDL_LOCAL_ADMIN
"LG"	SDDL_LOCAL_GUEST
"LS"	SDDL_LOCAL_SERVICE
"NS"	SDDL_NETWORK_SERVICE
"NU"	SDDL_NETWORK
"RD"	SDDL_REMOTE_DESKTOP
"SO"	SDDL_SERVER_OPERATORS
"SU"	SDDL_SERVICE
"SY"	SDDL_LOCAL_SYSTEM
"WD"	SDDL_EVERYONE

■ **FIGURE 6.18** List of Common String Constants and Corresponding Security Entities

```
Analytic
Application
DirectShowFilterGraph
DirectShowPluginControl
EndpointMapper
ForwardedEvents
HardwareEvents
Internet Explorer
Key Management Service
Microsoft-IE/Diagnostic
Microsoft-IEFRAME/Diagnostic
Microsoft-IIS-Configuration/Administrative
Microsoft-IIS-Configuration/Analytic
Microsoft-IIS-Configuration/Debug
Microsoft-IIS-Configuration/Operational
Microsoft-PerfTrack-IEFRAME/Diagnostic
Microsoft-PerfTrack-MSHTML/Diagnostic
Microsoft-Windows-ADSI/Debug
Microsoft-Windows-API-Tracing/Operational
Microsoft-Windows-ATAPort/General
Microsoft-Windows-ATAPort/SATA-LPM
Microsoft-Windows-ActionQueue/Analytic
Microsoft-Windows-AppID/Operational
Microsoft-Windows-AppLocker/EXE and DLL
Microsoft-Windows-AppLocker/MSI and Script
Microsoft-Windows-Application Server-Applications/Admin
Microsoft-Windows-Application Server-Applications/Analytic
Microsoft-Windows-Application Server-Applications/Debug
Microsoft-Windows-Application Server-Applications/Operational
Microsoft-Windows-Application Server-Applications/Perf
Microsoft-Windows-Application-Experience/Problem-Steps-Recorder
Microsoft-Windows-Application-Experience/Program-Compatibility-Assistant
Microsoft-Windows-Application-Experience/Program-Compatibility-Troubleshooter
Microsoft-Windows-Application-Experience/Program-Inventory
Microsoft-Windows-Application-Experience/Program-Inventory/Debug
Microsoft-Windows-Application-Experience/Program-Telemetry
Microsoft-Windows-Audio/CaptureMonitor
Microsoft-Windows-Audio/Operational
Microsoft-Windows-Audio/Performance
Microsoft-Windows-Audit/Analytic
Microsoft-Windows-Authentication User Interface/Operational
```

■ **FIGURE 6.19** Full List of Server 2008 Logs via the WEVTUTIL Tool

(continued)

```
Microsoft-Windows-Bits-Client/Analytic
Microsoft-Windows-Bits-Client/Operational
Microsoft-Windows-CAPI2/Operational
Microsoft-Windows-CDROM/Operational
Microsoft-Windows-COM/Analytic
Microsoft-Windows-COMRuntime/Tracing
Microsoft-Windows-Calculator/Debug
Microsoft-Windows-Calculator/Diagnostic
Microsoft-Windows-CertPoleEng/Operational
Microsoft-Windows-CertificateServicesClient-CredentialRoaming/Operational
Microsoft-Windows-ClearTypeTextTuner/Diagnostic
Microsoft-Windows-CmiSetup/Analytic
Microsoft-Windows-CodeIntegrity/Operational
Microsoft-Windows-CodeIntegrity/Verbose
Microsoft-Windows-ComDlg32/Analytic
Microsoft-Windows-ComDlg32/Debug
Microsoft-Windows-CorruptedFileRecovery-Client/Operational
Microsoft-Windows-CorruptedFileRecovery-Server/Operational
Microsoft-Windows-CredUI/Diagnostic
Microsoft-Windows-Crypto-RNG/Analytic
Microsoft-Windows-DCLocator/Debug
Microsoft-Windows-DNS-Client/Operational
Microsoft-Windows-DUI/Diagnostic
Microsoft-Windows-DUSER/Diagnostic
Microsoft-Windows-DXP/Analytic
Microsoft-Windows-DateTimeControlPanel/Analytic
Microsoft-Windows-DateTimeControlPanel/Debug
Microsoft-Windows-DateTimeControlPanel/Operational
Microsoft-Windows-Deplorch/Analytic
Microsoft-Windows-DeviceSync/Analytic
Microsoft-Windows-DeviceSync/Operational
Microsoft-Windows-DeviceUx/Informational
Microsoft-Windows-DeviceUx/Performance
Microsoft-Windows-Dhcp-Client/Admin
Microsoft-Windows-Dhcp-Client/Operational
Microsoft-Windows-DhcpNap/Admin
Microsoft-Windows-DhcpNap/Operational
Microsoft-Windows-Dhcpv6-Client/Admin
Microsoft-Windows-Dhcpv6-Client/Operational
Microsoft-Windows-DiagCpl/Debug
Microsoft-Windows-Diagnosis-DPS/Analytic
Microsoft-Windows-Diagnosis-DPS/Debug
```

■ **FIGURE 6.19—cont'd**

```
Microsoft-Windows-Diagnosis-DPS/Operational
Microsoft-Windows-Diagnosis-MSDE/Debug
Microsoft-Windows-Diagnosis-PCW/Analytic
Microsoft-Windows-Diagnosis-PCW/Debug
Microsoft-Windows-Diagnosis-PCW/Operational
Microsoft-Windows-Diagnosis-PLA/Debug
Microsoft-Windows-Diagnosis-PLA/Operational
Microsoft-Windows-Diagnosis-Perfhost/Analytic
Microsoft-Windows-Diagnosis-Scripted/Admin
Microsoft-Windows-Diagnosis-Scripted/Analytic
Microsoft-Windows-Diagnosis-Scripted/Debug
Microsoft-Windows-Diagnosis-Scripted/Operational
Microsoft-Windows-Diagnosis-ScriptedDiagnosticsProvider/Debug
Microsoft-Windows-Diagnosis-ScriptedDiagnosticsProvider/Operational
Microsoft-Windows-Diagnosis-TaskManager/Debug
Microsoft-Windows-Diagnosis-WDC/Analytic
Microsoft-Windows-Diagnosis-WDI/Debug
Microsoft-Windows-Diagnostics-Networking/Debug
Microsoft-Windows-Diagnostics-Networking/Operational
Microsoft-Windows-DirectShow-KernelSupport/Performance
Microsoft-Windows-DirectSound/Debug
Microsoft-Windows-DirectWrite-FontCache/Tracing
Microsoft-Windows-Disk/Operational
Microsoft-Windows-DisplaySwitch/Diagnostic
Microsoft-Windows-Documents/Performance
Microsoft-Windows-DriverFrameworks-UserMode/Operational
Microsoft-Windows-DxgKrnl/Diagnostic
Microsoft-Windows-DxgKrnl/Performance
Microsoft-Windows-DxpTaskSyncProvider/Analytic
Microsoft-Windows-EFS/Debug
Microsoft-Windows-EapHost/Analytic
Microsoft-Windows-EapHost/Debug
Microsoft-Windows-EapHost/Operational
Microsoft-Windows-EaseOfAccess/Diagnostic
Microsoft-Windows-EnrollmentPolicyWebService/Admin
Microsoft-Windows-EnrollmentWebService/Admin
Microsoft-Windows-EventCollector/Debug
Microsoft-Windows-EventCollector/Operational
Microsoft-Windows-EventLog-WMIProvider/Debug
Microsoft-Windows-EventLog/Analytic
Microsoft-Windows-EventLog/Debug
Microsoft-Windows-FMS/Analytic
```

■ FIGURE 6.19—cont'd

```
Microsoft-Windows-FMS/Debug
Microsoft-Windows-FMS/Operational
Microsoft-Windows-FailoverClustering-Client/Diagnostic
Microsoft-Windows-Feedback-Service-TriggerProvider
Microsoft-Windows-FileInfoMinifilter/Operational
Microsoft-Windows-Firewall-CPL/Diagnostic
Microsoft-Windows-Folder Redirection/Operational
Microsoft-Windows-Forwarding/Debug
Microsoft-Windows-Forwarding/Operational
Microsoft-Windows-GroupPolicy/Operational
Microsoft-Windows-HAL/Debug
Microsoft-Windows-HealthCenter/Debug
Microsoft-Windows-HealthCenter/Performance
Microsoft-Windows-HealthCenterCPL/Performance
Microsoft-Windows-Help/Operational
Microsoft-Windows-HomeGroup Control Panel Performance/Diagnostic
Microsoft-Windows-HomeGroup Control Panel/Operational
Microsoft-Windows-HttpService/Trace
Microsoft-Windows-IKE/Operational
Microsoft-Windows-IKEDBG/Debug
Microsoft-Windows-IPBusEnum/Tracing
Microsoft-Windows-IPSEC-SRV/Diagnostic
Microsoft-Windows-International-RegionalOptionsControlPanel/Operational
Microsoft-Windows-International/Operational
Microsoft-Windows-Iphlpsvc/Debug
Microsoft-Windows-Iphlpsvc/Operational
Microsoft-Windows-Iphlpsvc/Trace
Microsoft-Windows-Kernel-Acpi/Diagnostic
Microsoft-Windows-Kernel-Boot/Analytic
Microsoft-Windows-Kernel-BootDiagnostics/Diagnostic
Microsoft-Windows-Kernel-Disk/Analytic
Microsoft-Windows-Kernel-EventTracing/Admin
Microsoft-Windows-Kernel-EventTracing/Analytic
Microsoft-Windows-Kernel-File/Analytic
Microsoft-Windows-Kernel-Memory/Analytic
Microsoft-Windows-Kernel-Network/Analytic
Microsoft-Windows-Kernel-PnP/Diagnostic
Microsoft-Windows-Kernel-Power/Diagnostic
Microsoft-Windows-Kernel-Power/Thermal-Diagnostic
Microsoft-Windows-Kernel-Power/Thermal-Operational
Microsoft-Windows-Kernel-Prefetch/Diagnostic
Microsoft-Windows-Kernel-Process/Analytic
```

■ **FIGURE 6.19—cont'd**

```
Microsoft-Windows-Kernel-Processor-Power/Diagnostic
Microsoft-Windows-Kernel-Registry/Analytic
Microsoft-Windows-Kernel-StoreMgr/Analytic
Microsoft-Windows-Kernel-StoreMgr/Operational
Microsoft-Windows-Kernel-WDI/Analytic
Microsoft-Windows-Kernel-WDI/Debug
Microsoft-Windows-Kernel-WDI/Operational
Microsoft-Windows-Kernel-WHEA/Errors
Microsoft-Windows-Kernel-WHEA/Operational
Microsoft-Windows-Known Folders API Service
Microsoft-Windows-L2NA/Diagnostic
Microsoft-Windows-LDAP-Client/Debug
Microsoft-Windows-LUA-ConsentUI/Diagnostic
Microsoft-Windows-LanguagePackSetup/Analytic
Microsoft-Windows-LanguagePackSetup/Debug
Microsoft-Windows-LanguagePackSetup/Operational
Microsoft-Windows-MPS-CLNT/Diagnostic
Microsoft-Windows-MPS-DRV/Diagnostic
Microsoft-Windows-MPS-SRV/Diagnostic
Microsoft-Windows-MSPaint/Admin
Microsoft-Windows-MSPaint/Debug
Microsoft-Windows-MSPaint/Diagnostic
Microsoft-Windows-MUI/Admin
Microsoft-Windows-MUI/Analytic
Microsoft-Windows-MUI/Debug
Microsoft-Windows-MUI/Operational
Microsoft-Windows-MemoryDiagnostics-Results/Debug
Microsoft-Windows-NCSI/Analytic
Microsoft-Windows-NCSI/Operational
Microsoft-Windows-NDF-HelperClassDiscovery/Debug
Microsoft-Windows-NDIS-PacketCapture/Diagnostic
Microsoft-Windows-NDIS/Diagnostic
Microsoft-Windows-NDIS/Operational
Microsoft-Windows-NTLM/Operational
Microsoft-Windows-Narrator/Diagnostic
Microsoft-Windows-NetShell/Performance
Microsoft-Windows-Network-and-Sharing-Center/Diagnostic
Microsoft-Windows-NetworkAccessProtection/Operational
Microsoft-Windows-NetworkAccessProtection/WHC
Microsoft-Windows-NetworkLocationWizard/Operational
Microsoft-Windows-NetworkProfile/Diagnostic
Microsoft-Windows-NetworkProfile/Operational
```

■ **FIGURE 6.19—cont'd**

```
Microsoft-Windows-Networking-Correlation/Diagnostic
Microsoft-Windows-NlaSvc/Diagnostic
Microsoft-Windows-NlaSvc/Operational
Microsoft-Windows-OLEACC/Debug
Microsoft-Windows-OLEACC/Diagnostic
Microsoft-Windows-OOBE-Machine/Diagnostic
Microsoft-Windows-OneX/Diagnostic
Microsoft-Windows-OobeLdr/Analytic
Microsoft-Windows-PCI/Diagnostic
Microsoft-Windows-PortableDeviceSyncProvider/Analytic
Microsoft-Windows-PowerCfg/Diagnostic
Microsoft-Windows-PowerCpl/Diagnostic
Microsoft-Windows-PowerEfficiencyDiagnostics/Diagnostic
Microsoft-Windows-PowerShell/Analytic
Microsoft-Windows-PowerShell/Operational
Microsoft-Windows-PrimaryNetworkIcon/Performance
Microsoft-Windows-PrintService/Admin
Microsoft-Windows-PrintService/Debug
Microsoft-Windows-PrintService/Operational
Microsoft-Windows-QoS-Pacer/Diagnostic
Microsoft-Windows-RPC-Proxy/Debug
Microsoft-Windows-RPC/Debug
Microsoft-Windows-RPC/EEInfo
Microsoft-Windows-ReliabilityAnalysisComponent/Operational
Microsoft-Windows-RemoteApp and Desktop Connections/Admin
Microsoft-Windows-Remotefs-UTProvider/Diagnostic
Microsoft-Windows-Resource-Exhaustion-Detector/Operational
Microsoft-Windows-ResourcePublication/Tracing
Microsoft-Windows-RestartManager/Operational
Microsoft-Windows-Security-Audit-Configuration-Client/Diagnostic
Microsoft-Windows-Security-Audit-Configuration-Client/Operational
Microsoft-Windows-Security-Configuration-Wizard/Diagnostic
Microsoft-Windows-Security-Configuration-Wizard/Operational
Microsoft-Windows-Security-SPP/Perf
Microsoft-Windows-Sens/Debug
Microsoft-Windows-ServerManager/Analytic
Microsoft-Windows-ServerManager/Operational
Microsoft-Windows-ServiceReportingApi/Debug
Microsoft-Windows-Services-Svchost/Diagnostic
Microsoft-Windows-Services/Diagnostic
Microsoft-Windows-Setup/Analytic
Microsoft-Windows-SetupCl/Analytic
```

■ **FIGURE 6.19—cont'd**

```
Microsoft-Windows-SetupQueue/Analytic
Microsoft-Windows-SetupUGC/Analytic
Microsoft-Windows-Shell-AuthUI-BootAnim/Diagnostic
Microsoft-Windows-Shell-AuthUI-Common/Diagnostic
Microsoft-Windows-Shell-AuthUI-CredUI/Diagnostic
Microsoft-Windows-Shell-AuthUI-Logon/Diagnostic
Microsoft-Windows-Shell-AuthUI-PasswordProvider/Diagnostic
Microsoft-Windows-Shell-AuthUI-Shutdown/Diagnostic
Microsoft-Windows-Shell-Core/Diagnostic
Microsoft-Windows-Shell-DefaultPrograms/Diagnostic
Microsoft-Windows-Shell-Shwebsvc
Microsoft-Windows-Shell-ZipFolder/Diagnostic
Microsoft-Windows-Shsvcs/Diagnostic
Microsoft-Windows-StorDiag/Operational
Microsoft-Windows-StorPort/Operational
Microsoft-Windows-Subsys-Csr/Operational
Microsoft-Windows-Subsys-SMSS/Operational
Microsoft-Windows-Sysprep/Analytic
Microsoft-Windows-TCPIP/Diagnostic
Microsoft-Windows-TSF-msctf/Debug
Microsoft-Windows-TSF-msctf/Diagnostic
Microsoft-Windows-TSF-msutb/Debug
Microsoft-Windows-TSF-msutb/Diagnostic
Microsoft-Windows-TZUtil/Operational
Microsoft-Windows-TaskScheduler/Debug
Microsoft-Windows-TaskScheduler/Diagnostic
Microsoft-Windows-TaskScheduler/Operational
Microsoft-Windows-TaskbarCPL/Diagnostic
Microsoft-Windows-TerminalServices-ClientUSBDevices/Admin
Microsoft-Windows-TerminalServices-ClientUSBDevices/Analytic
Microsoft-Windows-TerminalServices-ClientUSBDevices/Debug
Microsoft-Windows-TerminalServices-ClientUSBDevices/Operational
Microsoft-Windows-TerminalServices-LocalSessionManager/Admin
Microsoft-Windows-TerminalServices-LocalSessionManager/Analytic
Microsoft-Windows-TerminalServices-LocalSessionManager/Debug
Microsoft-Windows-TerminalServices-LocalSessionManager/Operational
Microsoft-Windows-TerminalServices-PnPDevices/Admin
Microsoft-Windows-TerminalServices-PnPDevices/Analytic
Microsoft-Windows-TerminalServices-PnPDevices/Debug
Microsoft-Windows-TerminalServices-PnPDevices/Operational
Microsoft-Windows-TerminalServices-RDPClient/Analytic
Microsoft-Windows-TerminalServices-RDPClient/Debug
```

■ **FIGURE 6.19—cont'd**

```
Microsoft-Windows-TerminalServices-RDPClient/Operational
Microsoft-Windows-TerminalServices-RdpSoundDriver/Capture
Microsoft-Windows-TerminalServices-RdpSoundDriver/Playback
Microsoft-Windows-TerminalServices-RemoteConnectionManager/Admin
Microsoft-Windows-TerminalServices-RemoteConnectionManager/Analytic
Microsoft-Windows-TerminalServices-RemoteConnectionManager/Debug
Microsoft-Windows-TerminalServices-RemoteConnectionManager/Operational
Microsoft-Windows-ThemeCPL/Diagnostic
Microsoft-Windows-ThemeUI/Diagnostic
Microsoft-Windows-TunnelDriver
Microsoft-Windows-UAC-FileVirtualization/Operational
Microsoft-Windows-UAC/Operational
Microsoft-Windows-UIAnimation/Diagnostic
Microsoft-Windows-UIAutomationCore/Debug
Microsoft-Windows-UIAutomationCore/Diagnostic
Microsoft-Windows-UIAutomationCore/Perf
Microsoft-Windows-UIRibbon/Diagnostic
Microsoft-Windows-USB-USBHUB/Diagnostic
Microsoft-Windows-USB-USBPORT/Diagnostic
Microsoft-Windows-User Control Panel Performance/Diagnostic
Microsoft-Windows-User Profile Service/Diagnostic
Microsoft-Windows-User Profile Service/Operational
Microsoft-Windows-User-Loader/Analytic
Microsoft-Windows-UserModePowerService/Diagnostic
Microsoft-Windows-UserPnp/DeviceMetadata/Debug
Microsoft-Windows-UserPnp/DeviceNotifications
Microsoft-Windows-UserPnp/Performance
Microsoft-Windows-UserPnp/SchedulerOperations
Microsoft-Windows-UxTheme/Diagnostic
Microsoft-Windows-VAN/Diagnostic
Microsoft-Windows-VDRVROOT/Operational
Microsoft-Windows-VHDMP/Operational
Microsoft-Windows-VolumeControl/Performance
Microsoft-Windows-VolumeSnapshot-Driver/Operational
Microsoft-Windows-WABSyncProvider/Analytic
Microsoft-Windows-WER-Diag/Operational
Microsoft-Windows-WFP/Analytic
Microsoft-Windows-WFP/Operational
Microsoft-Windows-WMI-Activity/Trace
Microsoft-Windows-WUSA/Debug
Microsoft-Windows-WWAN-NDISUIO-EVENTS/Diagnostic
Microsoft-Windows-WebIO-NDF/Diagnostic
```

■ **FIGURE 6.19—cont'd**

```
Microsoft-Windows-WebIO/Diagnostic
Microsoft-Windows-WebServices/Tracing
Microsoft-Windows-Win32k/Concurrency
Microsoft-Windows-Win32k/Power
Microsoft-Windows-Win32k/Render
Microsoft-Windows-Win32k/Tracing
Microsoft-Windows-Win32k/UIPI
Microsoft-Windows-WinHTTP-NDF/Diagnostic
Microsoft-Windows-WinHttp/Diagnostic
Microsoft-Windows-WinINet/Analytic
Microsoft-Windows-WinRM/Analytic
Microsoft-Windows-WinRM/Debug
Microsoft-Windows-WinRM/Operational
Microsoft-Windows-Windeploy/Analytic
Microsoft-Windows-Windows Firewall With Advanced Security/ConnectionSecurity
Microsoft-Windows-Windows Firewall With Advanced Security/ConnectionSecurityVerbose
Microsoft-Windows-Windows Firewall With Advanced Security/Firewall
Microsoft-Windows-Windows Firewall With Advanced Security/FirewallVerbose
Microsoft-Windows-WindowsColorSystem/Debug
Microsoft-Windows-WindowsColorSystem/Operational
Microsoft-Windows-WindowsUpdateClient/Operational
Microsoft-Windows-Wininit/Diagnostic
Microsoft-Windows-Winlogon/Diagnostic
Microsoft-Windows-Winlogon/Operational
Microsoft-Windows-Winsock-AFD/Operational
Microsoft-Windows-Winsock-WS2HELP/Operational
Microsoft-Windows-Winsrv/Analytic
Microsoft-Windows-Wired-AutoConfig/Diagnostic
Microsoft-Windows-Wired-AutoConfig/Operational
Microsoft-Windows-Wordpad/Admin
Microsoft-Windows-Wordpad/Debug
Microsoft-Windows-Wordpad/Diagnostic
Microsoft-Windows-ntshrui
Microsoft-Windows-osk/Diagnostic
Microsoft-Windows-stobject/Diagnostic
Security
Setup
System
TabletPC_InputPanel_Channel
Windows PowerShell
microsoft-windows-RemoteDesktopServices-RemoteDesktopSessionManager/Admin
```

■ **FIGURE 6.19—cont'd**

```
C:\>dsquery computer -samid dev$
["CN=DEV,CN=Computers,DC=hammerofgod,DC=com"]
```

■ **FIGURE 6.20** Information Dump of Security Log via the WEVTUTIL Tool

```
C:\>dsget computer -sid "CN=DEV,CN=Computers,DC=hammerofgod,DC=com"
[sid S-1-5-21-4091052028-1783736372-2863742994-3673
dsget succeeded]
```

■ **FIGURE 6.21** Information Dump of the Application Log via the WEVTUTIL Tool

```
C:\ >dsquery group -name gServiceUsers|dsget group -sid
[sid S-1-5-21-4091052028-1783736372-2863742994-1111
dsget succeeded]
```

■ **FIGURE 6.22** Information Dump of the System Log via the WEVTUTIL Tool

Custom Log File Permissions

Armed with the information presented in Figures 6.21 and 6.22, we may now move forward with the assignment of custom ACEs to the event log DACLs in order to assign read permissions to our gServiceUsers group. Again, this requires a Registry entry, and now that you have the SDDL syntax down, you can move forward with creating the entries needed to assign your groups (or users) read permissions. Assuming we are going to grant read access to the security log only, we need to append an ACE to the existing SDDL ACL for the group. We know now that the format of the ACE will be *A;;0x1;;;SID of Group*, but we do not know the SID. There are many ways to look this up, but I will show you an easy one that you can use for other things as well if you are running 2008. Included with the Server 2008 AD Domain Services role is a utility called *DSQUERY* (Directory Services Query) that works with another tool called *DSGET* (Get Directory Services Entry). For example, we could use DSQUERY to get the SAMID for a particular computer, and use that SAMID with DSGET to get the computer SID. We will do this with our DEV box used in the book (results enclosed in brackets; the *[]* are not part of the output):

```
C:\>dsquery computer -samid dev$ ["CN=DEV,CN=Computers,
DC=hammerofgod,DC=com"]
C:\>dsget computer -sid "CN=DEV,CN=Computers,DC=hammerof-
god,DC=com"
[sid S-1-5-21-4091052028-1783736372-2863742994-3673
dsget succeeded]
```

We get the full computer SAMID for DEV with DSQUERY and with that we get the SID from DSGET. This is how we will get the SID for our gServiceUsers group, but this time we will make it easier by piping the results of DSQUERY into DSGET:

```
C:\ >dsquery group -name gServiceUsers|dsget group -sid
[sid S-1-5-21-4091052028-1783736372-2863742994-1111
dsget succeeded]
```

Once we have the SID we want, we just plug it into the full SDDL ACE like so:

```
O:BAG:SYD:(A;;0xf0005;;;SY)(A;;0x5;;;BA)(A;;0x1;;;S-1-5-
32-573)(A;;0x1;;;S-1-5-21-4091052028-1783736372-
2863742994-1111)
```

We will now use the *set log* flag of WEVTUTIL to change the ACL for our security log, specifying the new channel access value with the */ca:* flag. After setting this, we will pull the information again to see if it worked. See Figure 6.23 for the results.

Ta-da! Our permissions are set. WEVTUTIL sets the permissions and sets the Registry setting I talked about earlier. If you do not have Server 2008, then you have to create this Registry entry manually. You can set it manually in Server 2008 as well, but the tool validates syntax and ensures everything

```
C:\>wevtutil sl security /ca:O:BAG:SYD:(A;;0xf0005;;;SY)(A;;0x5;
;;BA)(A;;0x1;;;S-1-5-32-573)(A;;0x1;;;S-1-5-21-4091052028-1783736372-2863742994-1111)

C:\>wevtutil gl security
name: security
enabled: true
type: Admin
owningPublisher:
isolation: Custom
channelAccess: O:BAG:SYD:(A;;0xf0005;;;SY)(A;;0x5;;;BA)(A;;0x1;;;S-1-5-32-573)(A
;;0x1;;;S-1-5-21-4091052028-1783736372-2863742994-1111)
logging:
  logFileName: %SystemRoot%\System32\Winevt\Logs\security.evtx
  retention: false
  autoBackup: false
  maxSize: 134217728
publishing:
```

■ **FIGURE 6.23** Setting New ACL with SDDL via WEVTUTIL and Checking Results

is applied properly. For those of you thinking ahead, you may be wondering what to do in cases where you need to give read access to logs on a domain controller (DC). You cannot just add groups to the local Event Log Readers group because one does not exist. DCs do not have local groups. That is not to say that you cannot add it anyway. Just because it does not exist on the DC does not mean we cannot go ahead and assign group members to Event Log Readers through the built-in OU in the AD Users and Groups plug-in. But personally, I like directly setting Registry entries on my DCs. It is easier to audit and verify. Anyway, back to the Registry, Figure 6.24 shows the resulting Registry entry value called *CustomSD* that is created.

Figure 6.25 shows the corresponding *Edit String* dialog box.

The CustomSD string value is added to the HKEY_LOCAL_MACHINE\SYSTEM\CurrentControlSet\services\eventlog\Security key, as it would be for corresponding application and system logs. You would add the CustomSD value to each respective key for manual entry directly into the Registry.

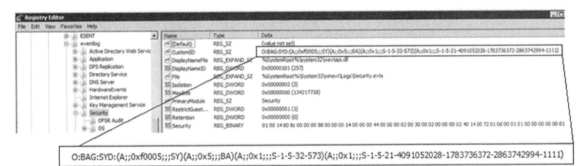

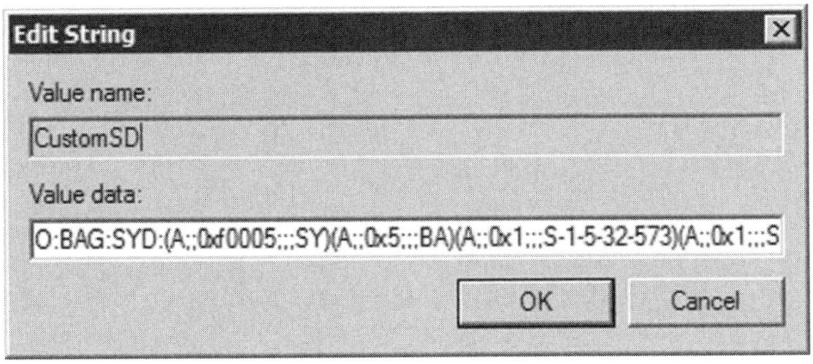

O:BAG:SYD:(A;;0xf0005;;;SY)(A;;0x5;;;BA)(A;;0x1;;;S-1-5-32-573)(A;;0x1;;;S-1-5-21-4091052028-1783736372-2863742994-1111)

■ **FIGURE 6.24** Registry View of the Security Log Hive Showing an Exploded View of the CustomSD String Value Data

Edit String
Value name:
CustomSD
Value data:
O:BAG:SYD:(A;;0xf0005;;;SY)(A;;0x5;;;BA)(A;;0x1;;;S-1-5-32-573)(A;;0x1;;;S
OK
Cancel

■ **FIGURE 6.25** Edit String Dialog Box for CustomSD with SDDL Value Data

Our segment on permissions is now complete, and we can move on to the next steps of covering WMI objects, data formatting, and queries. It is best to get permissions completed first so that you know you will not run into problems during this phase, or if you do, you will know they are not based on permissions.

ACCESSING WMI

WMI is actually quite flexible and easy to work with. Object creation is simple and straightforward and even scriptphobic users can catch on quickly. One of the key benefits of WMI is that the syntax for key functionality is consistent across development platforms. Once your objects are created, the application interface for WMI is the same whether you are using simple WSCRIPT/CSCRIPT batch files or C# applications. In fact, we are going to do both in this chapter. If you have got your test environment ready to go, then hopefully you will be pulling log data within a couple of minutes with the simple VBS file script illustrated in Figure 6.26. Be sure to note the *strComputer* variable that you will need to change to suit your testing environment.

```
strComputer = "dev.hammerofgod.com"
Set objWMIService = GetObject("winmgmts:\\" & strComputer & "\root\CIMV2")
Set colItems = objWMIService.ExecQuery( _
"SELECT * FROM Win32_NTLogEvent WHERE EventType = 5 and Logfile = 'Security'",,48)
For Each objItem in colItems
        Wscript.Echo "************"
        Wscript.Echo "Win32_NTLogEvent object"
        Wscript.Echo "************"
        Wscript.Echo "EventIdentifier: " & objItem.EventIdentifier
        WScript.Echo "CategoryString: " & objItem.CategoryString
        WScript.Echo "EventType: " & objItem.EventType
        WScript.Echo "LogFile: " & objItem.LogFile
        WScript.Echo "Message: " & objItem.Message
        WScript.Echo "RecordNumber: " & objItem.RecordNumber
        WScript.Echo "SourceName: " & objItem.SourceName
        WScript.Echo "TimeGenerated: " & objItem.TimeGenerated
        WScript.Echo "Type: " & objItem.Type
        WScript.Echo "User: " & objItem.User
        WScript.Echo ""
Next
```

■ **FIGURE 6.26** WMI Example Script to Retrieve Failure Audit Record Type from the DEV's Security Log

Building WMI Components

At its most basic level, that is what we need to pull data from the logs. In a nutshell, we set a variable for the name of the remote computer (the local computer would be represented by a.), and we instantiate a WMI object by calling the *winmgmts* service on the remote computer (which, by the way, is running in the SVHOST process) and requesting the \root\CIMV2 namespace. If all of our permissions are working properly, the object will be created on the client, and will query the winmgmts service, asking for all the fields it has from the Win32_NTLogEvent object for the security log where the log Event Type = 5 (audit failure). This is represented by the query *SELECT * FROM Win32_ NTLogEvent WHERE EventType = 5 and Logfile = ' 'Security'*. A set of all the records (log file entries) that match our criteria will be built by the remote system and shipped over to our object. We then create an object to represent each log file entry, *objItems*, and fill that item with all the record's columns (fields) from the *colItems* property. Then we loop through each item of each log record returned, printing out each field in the object.

I have saved this as a text file named *eventlog.vbs*, and execute it via the *CSCRIPT* console script host tool (CSCRIPT outputs to the console; WSCRIPT outputs in Window dialogs, which is a lot for every echo in this script). This is executed by issuing a *cscript eventlog.vbs* at your command prompt (of an authorized user). This is the returned text, edited to show only one record returned. Note the top three lines in Figure 6.27 indicate the WMI object name came from the code, not the returned object data.

So we are getting the data we need. However, let us take a look at Figure 6.28, which shows a network capture during the log fetch.

Encrypting the DCOM WMI Connection

We need to ensure that the data is encrypted. This can be done in two ways. We can go back to our DCOM configuration for WMI and specify encryption directly on the object, as Figure 6.29 illustrates.

Setting an authentication level here will require all WMI component calls to use the selected policy. We may not want to opt for configuring this here as it will limit options for other WMI objects we might need in the future. I prefer to set authentication/encryption settings on a per-call basis because it gives me more flexibility. Setting authentication and encryption options is quite easy: You basically tag the *authenticationLevel* property when you create the WMI object. This would change:

```
Set objWMIService = GetObject("winmgmts:\\" & strComputer
& "\root\CIMV2")
```

to

```
C:\temp\>cscript eventlog.vbs
Microsoft (R) Windows Script Host Version 5.8
Copyright (C) Microsoft Corporation. All rights reserved.
--------------------------------------------------------
Win32_NTLogEvent instance
--------------------------------------------------------
EventIdentifier: 4625
 CategoryString: Logon
 EventType: 5
 LogFile: Security
 Message: An account failed to log on.


Subject:
        Security ID:              S-1-5-18
        Account Name:             WIN-5H93BBSH4H5$
        Account Domain:           WORKGROUP
        Logon ID:                 0x3e7

Logon Type:                       2

Account For Which Logon Failed:
        Security ID:              S-1-0-0
        Account Name:             Administrator
        Account Domain:           WIN-5H93BBSH4H5

Failure Information:
        Failure Reason:           The specified account's password has expired.
        Status:                   0xc0000224
        Sub Status:               0x0

Process Information:
        Caller Process ID:        0x1b4
        Caller Process Name:      C:\Windows\System32\winlogon.exe

Network Information:
        Workstation Name:         WIN-5H93BBSH4H5
        Source Network Address:   127.0.0.1
        Source Port:              0

Detailed Authentication Information:
        Logon Process:            User32
        Authentication Package:   Negotiate
```

■ **FIGURE 6.27** WMI eventlog.vbs Returned Data from the DEV Security Log

(continued)

```
Transited Services:          -
Package Name (NTLM only):    -
Key Length:                  0
```

This event is generated when a logon request fails. It is generated on the computer where access was attempted.

The Subject fields indicate the account on the local system which requested the logon. This is most commonly a service such as the Server service, or a local process such as Winlogon.exe or Services. exe.

The Logon Type field indicates the kind of logon that was requested. The most common types are 2 (interactive) and 3 (network).

The Process Information fields indicate which account and process on the system requested the logon.

The Network Information fields indicate where a remote logon request originated.

Workstation name is not always available and may be left blank in some cases.

The authentication information fields provide detailed information about this specific logon request.

        -- Transited services indicate which intermediate services have participated in this logon request.

        -- Package name indicates which sub-protocol was used among the NTLM protocols.

        -- Key length indicates the length of the generated session key. This will be 0 if no session key was requested.
RecordNumber: 99
SourceName: Microsoft-Windows-Security-Auditing
TimeGenerated: 20110108005358.028960-000
Type: Audit Failure
User:
```

■ **FIGURE 6.27—cont'd**

```
Set objWMIService = GetObject("winmgmts:
{authenticationLevel=pktPrivacy}!\\" & strComputer " "\root
\CIMV2")
```

After adding the authenticationLevel, we see in Figure 6.30 that our network capture confirms encrypted data on the wire.

The following is a quick rundown of the various authenticationLevel options you have:

■ Default: Specifies that the default DCOM option will be used.
■ None: Explicitly sets encryption to none, regardless of other settings.
```

```
Hex Details
┌┴┐ Decode As   ▓▓ Width ▾                                                    Prot Off: 2 (0x02)
0260  35 2D 32 31 2D 34 30 39 31 30 35 32 30 32 38 2D  5-21-4091052028-
0270  31 37 38 33 37 33 36 33 37 32 2D 32 38 36 33 37  1783736372-28637
0280  34 32 39 39 34 2D 33 36 34 31 0D 0A 09 41 63 63  42994-3641...Acc
0290  6F 75 6E 74 20 4E 61 6D 65 3A 09 09 74 68 6F 72  ount Name:..soft
02A0  0D 0A 09 41 63 63 6F 75 6E 74 20 44 6F 6D 61 69  ...Account Domai
02B0  6E 3A 09 09 48 41 4D 4D 45 52 4F 46 47 4F 44 0D  n:..HAMMEROFGOD.
02C0  0A 09 4C 6F 67 6F 6E 20 49 44 3A 09 09 30 78 35  ..Logon ID:..0x5
02D0  30 61 34 39 0D 0A 0D 0A 43 72 79 70 74 6F 67 72  0a49....Cryptogr
02E0  61 70 68 69 63 20 50 61 72 61 6D 65 74 65 72 73  aphic Parameters
02F0  3A 0D 0A 09 50 72 6F 76 69 64 65 72 20 4E 61 6D  :...Provider Nam
0300  65 3A 09 4D 69 63 72 6F 73 6F 66 74 20 53 6F 66  e:.Microsoft Sof
0310  74 77 61 72 65 20 4B 65 79 20 53 74 6F 72 61 67  tware Key Storag
0320  65 20 50 72 6F 76 69 64 65 72 0D 0A 09 41 6C 67  e Provider...Alg
0330  6F 72 69 74 68 6D 20 4E 61 6D 65 3A 09 52 53 41  orithm Name:.RSA
0340  0D 0A 09 4B 65 79 20 4E 61 6D 65 3A 09 6C 65 2D  ...Key Name:.le-
0350  48 6F 47 43 6F 64 65 53 69 67 6E 69 6E 67 56 32  HoGCodeSigningV2
0360  2D 66 38 35 31 61 62 66 35 2D 30 37 38 37 2D 34  -f851abf5-0787-4
0370  34 61 64 2D 39 34 66 65 2D 30 33 61 66 32 64 39  4ad-94fe-03af2d9
0380  32 31 35 34 30 0D 0A 09 4B 65 79 20 54 79 70 65  21540...Key Type
0390  3A 09 55 73 65 72 20 6B 65 79 2E 0D 0A 0D 0A 41  :.User key.....A
03A0  64 64 69 74 69 6F 6E 61 6C 20 49 6E 66 6F 72 6D  dditional Inform
03B0  61 74 69 6F 6E 3A 0D 0A 09 4F 70 65 72 61 74 69  ation:...Operati
03C0  6F 6E 3A 09 49 6D 70 6F 72 74 20 6F 66 20 70 65  on:.Import of pe
03D0  72 73 69 73 74 65 6E 74 20 63 72 79 70 74 6F 67  rsistent cryptog
03E0  72 61 70 68 69 63 20 6B 65 79 2E 0D 0A 09 52 65  raphic key....Re
03F0  74 75 72 6E 20 43 6F 64 65 3A 09 30 78 38 30 30  turn Code:.0x800
0400  39 30 30 32 39 00 00 4F 74 68 65 72 20 53 79 73  90029..Other Sys
0410  74 65 6D 20 45 76 65 6E 74 73 00 0A 00 00 00 BC  tem Events.....╝
0420  02 00 00 EC 02 00 00 F2 02 00 00 FF 02 00 00 08  ...ì...ò...ÿ....
0430  03 00 00 31 03 00 00 36 03 00 00 70 03 00 00 78  ...1...6...p...x
0440  03 00 00 80 03 00 00 00 53 2D 31 2D 35 2D 32 31  ........S-1-5-21
0450  2D 34 30 39 31 30 35 32 30 32 38 2D 31 37 38 33  -4091052028-1783
```

■ **FIGURE 6.28** Network Capture of WMI Log
Record Fetch Showing Unencrypted Data

■ Connect: Requires authentication only when the connection is made.
■ Call: Requires authentication each time a call is made; only the headers are signed, and nothing else is signed or encrypted.
■ Packet: Every packet header is signed, and only the headers; nothing else is signed or encrypted.
■ Packet Integrity: The entire packet is signed (not just the header). Integrity is guaranteed, but nothing is encrypted.
■ Packet Privacy: All data packets are signed and encrypted.

The C# implementation of authenticationLevel is far more elegant, and I prefer it. You will see an example shortly in Figure 6.29.

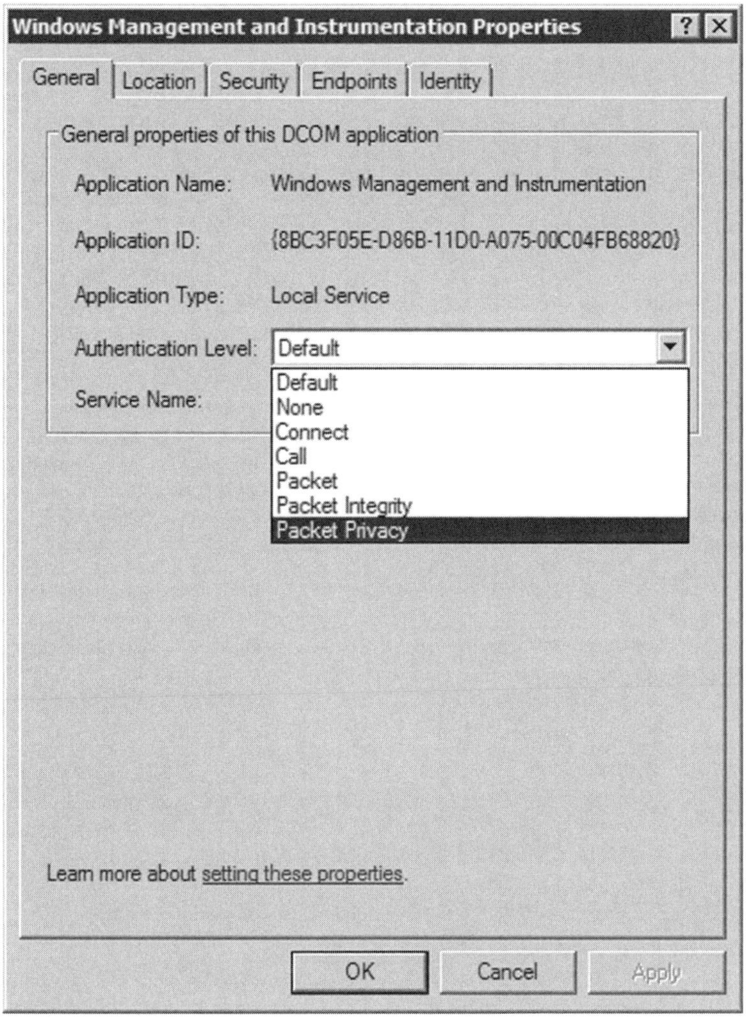

■ **FIGURE 6.29** DCOM WMI Component Properties with Packet Privacy Being Selected for the Authentication Level

Other WMI Examples

You can do any number of other things with WMI, and I am going to give you another example of performing nested WMI queries before we get back to the job at hand and get the preceding blob of text into a structured database. Many WMI objects are subsets of other WMI objects. A good example of this would be network adapters, which have their own set of data, and then the protocols bound to each adapter, which then have their own set of records. For instance, each adapter has an index, and that index is referenced in the adapter configuration objects. You have to first get the adapter, get

Hex Details

	Decode As	Width ▾													Prot Off: 0 (0x00)

```
0260  60 23 AD DC BC 65 53 E7 47 22 9D C8 BA 36 E2 73   `#-Ü4eSçG" È°6ás
0270  FD B1 AA AE 98 4E 13 68 A4 76 16 BE 06 96 FE 92   ý±ª® N.h¤v.¾. þ
0280  62 BA C7 7D A1 ED 77 48 4F A6 90 AC C4 96 25 2B   bº}¡íwHO¦ ¬Ä %+
0290  E9 17 56 BF 5E E8 BD 7B 9A DD DB 4C 3F DB 7B 73   é.V¿^è¾{ ÝÛL?Û{s
02A0  83 8C 27 0A 54 AA 07 32 63 4A 6B CD 86 E0 A4 37   '.Tª.2cJkÍ à¤7
02B0  3D BB 62 F1 5E 6F 83 23 4F 88 BC A0 89 DB 31 BC   =»bñ^o #O 4  Û14
02C0  DC 0E 12 2B C7 57 8F 81 8F D6 79 AB AC 39 08 0D   Ü..+ÇW    Öy«¬9..
02D0  F6 0B 7E 06 AE CF 88 DB B3 67 D1 4E 48 28 A9 07   ö.~.®Ï Û³gÑNH(©.
02E0  16 5B 45 1D 39 A3 E1 2E FF 43 6C F0 8C 4D 2E 7A   .[E.9£á.ÿClð M.z
02F0  3D 03 3D 3E 1B 81 90 4C E5 8F BB E6 53 59 BE 64   =.=>.  Lå »æSY¾d
0300  2A FA 5C BF 66 94 94 5A 95 E7 2D 15 2F DA 0A 5C   *ú\¿f   Z ç-./Ú.\
0310  15 24 78 B2 98 F1 93 8F 77 1E 30 45 96 E8 56 46   .$xª ñ   w.0E èVF
0320  8E 79 6D 78 5D 70 2B 84 B4 2E F1 B3 8D 22 77 88   ymx]p+ '.ñª "w
0330  C1 1B 2C 53 EA 2A B9 47 BF 51 00 1F 6B 83 85 49   Á.,Sê*¹G¿Q..k  I
0340  6E 7F AA 62 97 88 94 F7 B4 56 0D 92 EC 65 76 3D   nª*b   ÷'V. ìev=
0350  39 1B 29 33 C0 6B F8 51 30 09 C6 D2 69 B7 61 F2   9.)3AkøQO.Æòi·aò
0360  9D DB 6C 98 6B 14 86 1F 11 B7 A3 8C C2 51 49 B3   Ûl k. ...£ ÅQI³
0370  0E 1A 59 09 3A AD 58 7B 4D B7 3D 3E B1 D7 80 04   ..Y.:-X{M·=>±× .
0380  2D 9B AA A0 2B FE 41 32 04 A2 AF E9 77 18 43 38   - ª +þA2.¢‾éw.C8
0390  CC D6 14 DD 8E 44 16 B8 35 3A 04 34 F5 AE 60 F9   ÌÖ.Ý D.,5:.4õ®`ù
03A0  86 3D 0B B3 6F E5 AA 5F 4C 22 5A 09 EC 2E 7D 62   =.³oåª_L"Z.ì.}b
03B0  BD F3 6C 58 74 FB 62 27 CF FF 5B C8 64 9D F6 6A   ½ólXtûb'Ïÿ[Èd öj
03C0  2A 77 62 85 93 7C 77 33 A7 D4 45 81 E0 FA 55 77   *wb |w3§ÔE àúUw
03D0  5B 8C 96 2A 0F 13 3F 7D A4 CA 09 6C 2E 47 B4 3C   [ *..?}¤Ê.l.G'<
03E0  C6 15 E5 69 B1 D9 08 81 AA B1 79 5A 5C EE 40 39   Æ.åi±Ù. ª±yZ\î@9
03F0  FF 9F 0B A0 DA 13 33 2B 5B FD 4B 23 74 43 FA E1   ÿ . Ú.3+[ýK#tCúá
0400  D4 67 EF 78 B7 ED E5 98 90 2E 8A 51 6E 0D 72 9F   Ôgïx·íå   . Qn.r
0410  30 CC AD 67 BC A1 E6 2C 22 68 AE 4D 2E B1 93 02   0Ì-g¼¡æ,"h®M.± .
0420  8A F2 28 AD 9C FC 14 41 05 F7 B3 C5 2C 2C AC DC   ò(- ü.A.÷³Å,,¬Ü
0430  1D B4 BC 8B FE 76 78 64 D5 6B A2 02 2F 87 8D 9E   .'4 þvxdÕk¢./
0440  47 9A A8 D0 AC 26 EF 65 9B D6 1D 36 2E DF 26 F2   G ¨Ð¬¼e Ö.6.ß&ò
0450  04 6B BE AB F9 16 3C A9 C1 EA BF BE 0F 9A D3 63   .k¾«ù.<©Áê¿¾. Óc
```

■ **FIGURE 6.30** Network Capture of WMI Log Record Fetch Showing Encrypted Data by Setting the authenticationLevel Property

its index, and then use that index to get all the protocol information bound to the adapter. This means you have to loop through each adapter, but each time you loop through the adapter, you do a sub-loop through all the configuration parameters. We then might want to branch and do another sub-loop to get all the route information. You can get remote configuration information from a box, but it is not as easy to get each individual adapter's IP address (as opposed to all the IPs on the system) and the corresponding routes on each adapter. This kind of data is very helpful in, say, finding all the boxes on your network that are dual homed (meaning they can hit two separate network segments, which is typically a bad thing). To illustrate this, I have written a little C# console application for you that does just that, illustrated in Figure 6.31. Normally, you have to be the administrator to get this information, but with this app, you can give read permissions

```
using System;
using System.Collections.Generic;
using System.Linq;
using System.Text;
using System.Management;
using System.Management.Instrumentation;

namespace NICoMatic
{
    class Program
    {
        static void Main(string[] args)
        {
            Console.WriteLine("Thor's NIC o' Matic Adapter Enumerator");
            Console.WriteLine("Yet another Gift with Purchase from Thor's Microsoft
Security Bible");
            Console.WriteLine("Usage:");
            Console.WriteLine("");
            Console.WriteLine("NICoMatic [computername - defaults to local]");
            Console.WriteLine("");

            get_remotenet(args.Length == 0 ? "." : Convert.ToString(args[0]));

            //get_remotenet(Convert.ToString(args[0]));
        }
        static void get_remotenet(string box)
        {
            string RemoteComputer = "\\\\" + box + "\\root\\CIMV2";
            string AdaptersSQL = "SELECT * FROM Win32_NetworkAdapter WHERE AdapterTypeID = 0";
            string RouteSQL = "SELECT * FROM Win32_IP4RouteTable";
            string ThisAdapterSQL;
            try
            {
                Console.Write(string.Format("Network information for {0}\n\n", box.
ToUpper()));
                ManagementObjectSearcher Adapters = new ManagementObjectSearcher(Remo-
teComputer, AdaptersSQL);
                foreach (ManagementObject Adapter in Adapters.Get())
                {
                    Console.Write(string.Format("Name: {0}", Adapter["Name"]));
                    Console.Write(string.Format(" :Index: {0} ", Adapter["Index"]));
                    Console.Write(string.Format(" :Type: {0}\n", Convert.ToString
(Adapter["AdapterType"])));
                    ThisAdapterSQL = "SELECT * FROM Win32_NetworkAdapterConfiguration
WHERE Index=" + Adapter["Index"];
                    ManagementObjectSearcher thisAdapter = new ManagementObjectSearcher
(RemoteComputer, ThisAdapterSQL);
```

■ **FIGURE 6.31** NICoMatic C# Code Example of WMI Nested Queries

(continued)

```csharp
                foreach (ManagementObject adapterObj in thisAdapter.Get())
                {
                    if (adapterObj["IPAddress"] != null)
                    {
                        String[] arrIPAddress = (String[])(adapterObj["IPAddress"]);
                        foreach (String arrValue in arrIPAddress)
                        {
                            Console.Write(string.Format("-IPAddress: {0}\n",
arrValue));
                        }
                    }
                    if (adapterObj["DefaultIPGateway"] != null)
                    {
                        String[] arrDefaultIPGateway = (String[])(adapterObj
["DefaultIPGateway"]);
                        foreach (String arrValue in arrDefaultIPGateway)
                        {
                            Console.Write(string.Format("-DefaultIPGateway: {0}
\n", arrValue));
                        }
                    }

                }

            }
                ManagementObjectSearcher Routes = new ManagementObjectSearcher
(RemoteComputer, RouteSQL);
                foreach (ManagementObject Route in Routes.Get())
                {
                    Console.Write(string.Format("Route: {0} ", Route
["Description"]));
                    Console.Write(string.Format("Gateway: {0} ", Route["NextHop"]));
                    Console.Write(string.Format("Metric: {0} \n", Route
["Metric1"]));
                }
            }
            catch (ManagementException ex)
            {
                Console.Write(ex.Message);
            }
            Console.Write("—end—");
        }
    }
}
```

■ **FIGURE 6.31—cont'd**

```
Thor's NIC-o'-Matic Adapter Enumerator
Yet another Gift with Purchase from Thor's Microsoft Security Bible!
Usage:

NICoMatic [computername - defaults to local]

Network information for .

Name: NVIDIA nForce Networking Controller :Index: 7 :Type: Ethernet 802.3
Name: Broadcom NetXtreme Gigabit Ethernet :Index: 10 :Type: Ethernet 802.3
—IPAddress: 192.168.12.15
Name: Intel(R) PRO/1000 GT Desktop Adapter :Index: 13 :Type: Ethernet 802.3
—IPAddress: 121.133.232.55
—IPAddress: 121.133.232.54
—IPAddress: 121.133.232.53
—DefaultIPGateway: 121.133.232.58
Name: Virtual Machine Network Services Driver :Index: 16 :Type: Ethernet 802.3
Name: Virtual Machine Network Services Driver :Index: 17 :Type: Ethernet 802.3
Route: 0.0.0.0 - 0.0.0.0 - 121.133.232.58 Gateway: 121.133.232.58 Metric: 276
Route: 127.0.0.0 - 255.0.0.0 - 0.0.0.0 Gateway: 0.0.0.0 Metric: 306
Route: 127.0.0.1 - 255.255.255.255 - 0.0.0.0 Gateway: 0.0.0.0 Metric: 306
Route: 127.255.255.255 - 255.255.255.255 - 0.0.0.0 Gateway: 0.0.0.0 Metric: 306
Route: 121.133.0.0 - 255.255.0.0 - 0.0.0.0 Gateway: 0.0.0.0 Metric: 276
Route: 121.133.232.53 - 255.255.255.255 - 0.0.0.0 Gateway: 0.0.0.0 Metric: 276
Route: 121.133.232.54 - 255.255.255.255 - 0.0.0.0 Gateway: 0.0.0.0 Metric: 276
Route: 121.133.232.55 - 255.255.255.255 - 0.0.0.0 Gateway: 0.0.0.0 Metric: 276
Route: 121.133.255.255 - 255.255.255.255 - 0.0.0.0 Gateway: 0.0.0.0 Metric: 276
Route: 192.168.12.0 - 255.255.255.0 - 0.0.0.0 Gateway: 0.0.0.0 Metric: 266
Route: 192.168.12.15 - 255.255.255.255 - 0.0.0.0 Gateway: 0.0.0.0 Metric: 266
Route: 192.168.12.255 - 255.255.255.255 - 0.0.0.0 Gateway: 0.0.0.0 Metric: 266
Route: 224.0.0.0 - 240.0.0.0 - 0.0.0.0 Gateway: 0.0.0.0 Metric: 306
Route: 224.0.0.0 - 240.0.0.0 - 0.0.0.0 Gateway: 0.0.0.0 Metric: 276
Route: 224.0.0.0 - 240.0.0.0 - 0.0.0.0 Gateway: 0.0.0.0 Metric: 266
Route: 255.255.255.255 - 255.255.255.255 - 0.0.0.0 Gateway: 0.0.0.0 Metric: 306
Route: 255.255.255.255 - 255.255.255.255 - 0.0.0.0 Gateway: 0.0.0.0 Metric: 276
Route: 255.255.255.255 - 255.255.255.255 - 0.0.0.0 Gateway: 0.0.0.0 Metric: 266
---end---
```

■ **FIGURE 6.32** Output from NICoMatic WMI Enumerator Example

to whatever users you want in the same way we have already done. This data is not encrypted in transit.

There you go. Not only do you get a possibly useful tool out of this, but it should help you better understand WMI.

SHOW ME THE CODE!

In both our real event log parser and the example NICoMatic app, we are just dumping text to the console, which is not very valuable. Using the same structure I did with the NICoMatic C# application, I have written another C# app to retrieve the event log information, parse it out, and then post each record into a database. The parsing part is important because there is some valuable information in the logs that is not broken down into fields. Rather, it is delivered in the Message text-blob field. Consider the following snippet from the security log entry output in our test script:

```
Subject:
               Security ID:                S-1-5-18
               Account Name:               WIN-5H93BBSH4H5$
               Account Domain:             WORKGROUP
               Logon ID:                   0x3e7

Logon Type: 2

               Account For Which Logon Failed:
               Security ID:                S-1-0-0
               Account Name:               Administrator
               Account Domain:             WIN-5H93BBSH4H5
```

Though the subject of this message text displays the Account Name as the WIN-5H93BBSH4H5$ computer, the real data we want is displayed in the *Account For Which Logon Failed* section. However, there is no field output we can get that data from. To best suit a production environment, I went ahead and wrote a parsing routine to extract the security ID, account name, and account domain data into individual fields for posting into the database.

SQL Data Structure

Speaking of the database, we need a table to post the data into. Figure 6.33 shows a simple table structure I have created to accommodate our data.

Figure 6.34 shows the same structure represented by the T-SQL build of the table.

Posting Data into SQL

Now we need a way of posting data into the table. I have written the following stored procedure for this, which takes the appropriate input parameters and inserts them in the corresponding SQL fields. In Figure 6.34, you may

SQL.TMSB - dbo.EventLogs		
Column Name	Data Type	Allow Nulls
LogID	bigint	☐
ServerName	nvarchar(50)	☑
LogFile	nvarchar(50)	☑
EventID	int	☑
CategoryString	nvarchar(100)	☑
EventType	smallint	☑
Message	text	☑
RecordNumber	bigint	☑
SourceName	nvarchar(100)	☑
TimeGeneratedString	nvarchar(50)	☑
TimeGenerated	datetime	☑
Type	nvarchar(50)	☑
Username	nvarchar(50)	☑
Shiny1	nvarchar(50)	☑
Shiny2	nvarchar(50)	☑
Shiny3	nvarchar(50)	☑
		☐

■ **FIGURE 6.33** The EventLogs SQL Table Structure in Design View

have noticed a unique index that I created on the *TimeGeneratedString* field. I will explain the reason for this after we go over the posting procedures. Note also the *Shiny* fields Figure 6.35, which are where I will post the account ID, account name, and domain name we get from parsing the message string. Since there may be other fields we want in other logs, I did not want to set a column name.

The reason that the unique index was created was to ensure that duplicate log entries could not be stored in the database. The *timegenerated* field from the logs is a *YYYYMMDDHHMMSS.ms* notation. No two entries from the same log can have the exact same timegenerated field. I am pretty confident they cannot anyway. But just in case I happen upon that one-in-a-gajillion chance of getting two entries from different servers with

```
CREATE TABLE [dbo].[EventLogs](
      [LogID] [bigint] IDENTITY(1,1) NOT NULL,
      [ServerName] [nvarchar](50) NULL,
      [LogFile] [nvarchar](50) NULL,
      [EventID] [int] NULL,
      [CategoryString] [nvarchar](100) NULL,
      [EventType] [smallint] NULL,
      [Message] [text] NULL,
      [RecordNumber] [bigint] NULL,
      [SourceName] [nvarchar](100) NULL,
      [TimeGeneratedString] [nvarchar](50) NULL,
      [TimeGenerated] [datetime] NULL,
      [Type] [nvarchar](50) NULL,
      [Username] [nvarchar](50) NULL,
      [Shiny1] [nvarchar](50) NULL,
      [Shiny2] [nvarchar](50) NULL,
      [Shiny3] [nvarchar](50) NULL
) ON [PRIMARY] TEXTIMAGE_ON [PRIMARY]

CREATE UNIQUE NONCLUSTERED INDEX [UniqueTimestamp] ON [dbo].[EventLogs]
(
      [TimeGeneratedString] ASC
)
WITH (PAD_INDEX = OFF, STATISTICS_NORECOMPUTE = OFF, SORT_IN_TEMPDB = OFF,
IGNORE_DUP_KEY = OFF, DROP_EXISTING = OFF, ONLINE = OFF, ALLOW_ROW_LOCKS = ON,
ALLOW_PAGE_LOCKS = ON) ON [PRIMARY]
GO
```

■ **FIGURE 6.34** The EventLogs SQL Table Structure in T-SQL Including Unique Index

the exact same fraction of a second, I will take the timegenerated string from the logs, which looks like 20110108005358.028960-000, and prepend it with the computer name, as in DEV-20110108005358.028960-000. This way, I can be reasonably sure I will never have duplicate entries. Thus, if I post the logs from a system that overlaps dates or something, the unique key restriction will keep duplicate records from being posted. It is a referential integrity thing. See Figure 6.36 for a screenshot of the client-side app I wrote, after which we will check out the code (see Figure 6.37). The SQL CLR version is forthcoming.

```
- - ================================================
- - Author: Timothy Thor Mullen
- - Create date: 03/10/11
- - Description: Post Event Log Data
- - ================================================
ALTER PROCEDURE [dbo].[sp_PostEventRecord]

@ServerName nvarchar(50),
@LogFile nvarchar(50),
@EventID int,
@CategoryString nvarchar(50),
@EventType smallint,
@Message text,
@RecordNumber int,
@SourceName nvarchar(50),
@TimeGeneratedString nvarchar(50),
@TimeGenerated datetime,
@Type nvarchar(50),
@Username nvarchar(50),
@Shiny1 nvarchar(50),
@Shiny2 nvarchar(50),
@Shiny3 nvarchar(50)

AS
BEGIN
      INSERT INTO EventLogs
      (ServerName,LogFile,EventID,CategoryString,EventType,Message,RecordNumber,
SourceName,
      TimeGeneratedString,TimeGenerated,Type,Username,Shiny1,Shiny2,Shiny3)
      values
      (@ServerName,@LogFile,@EventID,@CategoryString,@EventType,@Message,@RecordNumber,
@SourceName,

@TimeGeneratedString,@TimeGenerated,@Type,@Username,@Shiny1,@Shiny2,@Shiny3)
END
```

■ **FIGURE 6.35** sp_PostEventRecord SQL Stored Procedure Taking Input Parameters and Posting into the EventLogs Table

Log Fetcher Application

Code Summary

This code will build the connection to your selected server, retrieve the log data based on date, parse out relevant logon data, and post it all into a SQL database for you to do with as you wish.

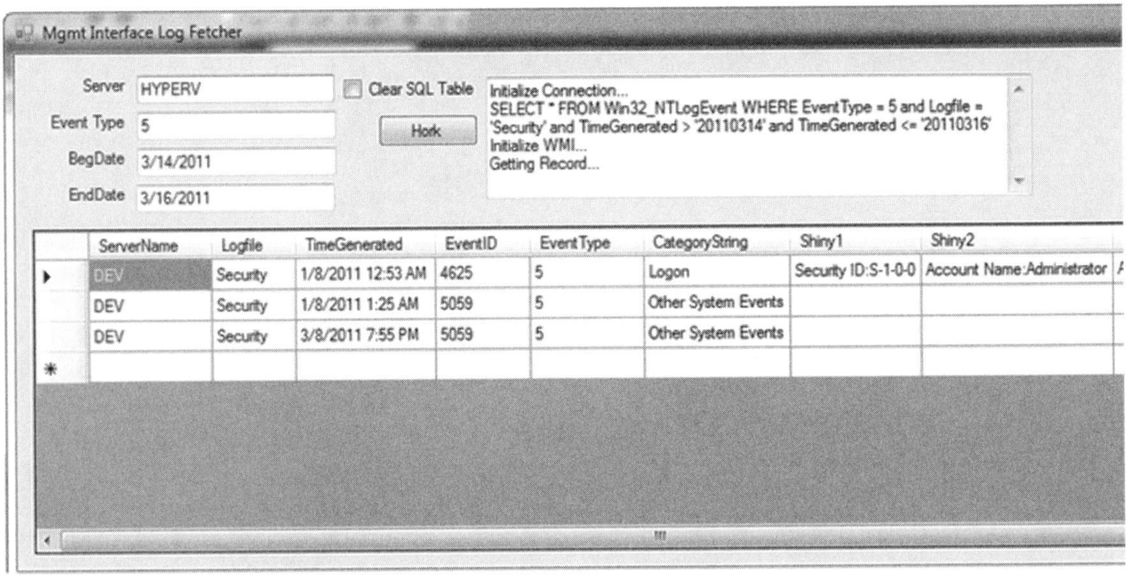

■ **FIGURE 6.36** Screenshot of the Management
Interface Log Fetcher Application

```csharp
using System;
using System.Collections.Generic;
using System.ComponentModel;
using System.Data;
using System.Drawing;
using System.Diagnostics;
using System.Linq;
using System.Text;
using System.Windows.Forms;
using System.Management;
using System.Globalization;
using System.Management.Instrumentation;
using System.Security.Principal;
using System.Data.SqlClient;

namespace EventHorker
{
    public partial class frmHork : Form
    {
```

■ **FIGURE 6.37** C# Code for Management Information Log Fetcher Application

(continued)

```csharp
public frmHork()
{
    InitializeComponent();
}
private void cmdHork_Click(object sender, EventArgs e)
{
    //Call the post function when user clicks Hork.
    PostEventData();
}

private void PostEventData()
{
    //Create and set variables for use in function
    string strConnection = "Data Source=sql.hammerofgod.com;Initial Catalog=TMSB;
Trusted_Connection=yes;";
    string strRemoteComputer = txtRemoteComputer.Text.ToString().Trim();
    string strWMIRemoteComputer = "\\\\" + strRemoteComputer + "\\root\\CIMV2";
    string strUseLogFile = "'Security'";
    string strEventType = txtEventType.Text.ToString();
    DateTime dtBegDate = Convert.ToDateTime(txtBegDate.Text);
    DateTime dtEndDate = Convert.ToDateTime(txtEndDate.Text);
    DateTimeFormatInfo wmiDate = new DateTimeFormatInfo();
    wmiDate.ShortDatePattern = @"yyyyMMdd";
    string strWMIQuery = "SELECT * FROM Win32_NTLogEvent WHERE EventType = " + strE-
ventType + " and Logfile = " + strUseLogFile;
    strWMIQuery += " and TimeGenerated > '" + dtBegDate.ToString("d", wmiDate) +"'
and TimeGenerated <= '" + dtEndDate.ToString("d",wmiDate)+ "'";
    string strLogFile; string strEventID;
    string strCategoryString; string strMessage;
    string strSourceName; string strTimeGenerated;
    string strType; string strUserName;
    int iEventType; int iRecordNumber;
    DateTime dtTimeGenerated;

    //Variables for Message parsing
    int pos1; int pos2; int pos3;
    string strShiny1; string strShiny2; string strShiny3;

    txtResults.AppendText("Initialize Connection...\n");
    txtResults.AppendText(strWMIQuery + "\n");

    //Set up using clause for creation of SQL connection and command structure
using (SqlConnection conn = new SqlConnection(strConnection))
```

■ FIGURE 6.37—cont'd

```
            {
                if (chkClearTable.Checked)
                {
                    //clear the log and clean up the objects
                    txtResults.AppendText("Clear current logs...\n");
                    SqlCommand clear = new SqlCommand("dbo.sp_ClearLog", conn);
                    clear.CommandType = CommandType.StoredProcedure;
                    clear.Connection.Open();
                    clear.ExecuteNonQuery();
                    clear.Connection.Close();
                    clear.Dispose();
                }
                //Command object parameters.
                SqlCommand command = new SqlCommand("dbo.sp_PostEventRecord", conn);
                command.CommandType = CommandType.StoredProcedure;
                command.Parameters.Add("@ServerName", SqlDbType.NVarChar, 50);
                command.Parameters.Add("@LogFile", SqlDbType.NVarChar, 50);
                command.Parameters.Add("@EventID", SqlDbType.Int);
                command.Parameters.Add("@CategoryString", SqlDbType.NVarChar, 50);
                command.Parameters.Add("@EventType", SqlDbType.SmallInt);
                command.Parameters.Add("@Message", SqlDbType.Text);
                command.Parameters.Add("@RecordNumber", SqlDbType.Int);
                command.Parameters.Add("@SourceName", SqlDbType.NVarChar, 50);
                command.Parameters.Add("@TimeGeneratedString", SqlDbType.NVarChar, 50);
                command.Parameters.Add("@TimeGenerated", SqlDbType.DateTime);
                command.Parameters.Add("@Type", SqlDbType.NVarChar, 50);
                command.Parameters.Add("@UserName", SqlDbType.NVarChar, 50);
                command.Parameters.Add("@Shiny1", SqlDbType.NVarChar, 50);
                command.Parameters.Add("@Shiny2", SqlDbType.NVarChar, 50);
                command.Parameters.Add("@Shiny3", SqlDbType.NVarChar, 50);

                command.Connection.Open();

                txtResults.AppendText("Initialize WMI...\n");

                // Built a ConnectionOptions object so I can set the authentication level to
        Packet Privacy.
                // Set those options in the scope, and then the scope in the object query searcher.
                ConnectionOptions wmioptions = new ConnectionOptions();
                wmioptions.Authentication = AuthenticationLevel.PacketPrivacy;
                ManagementScope wmiscope = new ManagementScope(strWMIRemoteComputer,
        wmioptions);
                ObjectQuery wmiquery = new ObjectQuery(strWMIQuery);
```

■ **FIGURE 6.37—cont'd**

```
            try
            {
                wmiscope.Connect();
            }
            catch (Exception ex)
            {
                string exMessage = "Exception: If access denied, ensure user can read logs, access
DCOM,\nand read the proper WMI sub-root.\n";
                MessageBox.Show(exMessage + "\n" + ex.Message);
            }
            using (ManagementObjectSearcher logrecords = new ManagementObjectSearcher(wmi-
scope, wmiquery))
            {
                txtResults.AppendText("Getting Record...\n");
                // if (logrecords.Container != null)
                {
                    foreach (ManagementObject record in logrecords.Get())
                    {
                        try
                        {
                            //Assign variables values from the returned Management Object.
                            //Check to see if they are null values before trying to do anything.
                            strShiny1 = string.Empty; strShiny2 = string.Empty; strShiny3 =
string.Empty;
                            txtResults.AppendText("Posting Record:" + record["RecordNum-
ber"].ToString() + "\n");
                            command.Parameters["@ServerName"].Value = strRemoteComputer;
                            strLogFile = (record["LogFile"] == null ? "" : record["LogFile"].
ToString());
                            command.Parameters["@LogFile"].Value = strLogFile;
                            strEventID = (record["EventIdentifier"] == null ? "" : record
["EventIdentifier"].ToString());
                            command.Parameters["@EventID"].Value = strEventID;
                            strCategoryString = (record["CategoryString"] == null ? "" : record
["CategoryString"].ToString());
                            command.Parameters["@CategoryString"].Value =
strCategoryString;
                            iEventType = Convert.ToInt32(record["EventType"]);
                            command.Parameters["@EventType"].Value = record["EventType"];
                            strMessage = (record["Message"] == null ? "" : record["Message"].
ToString());
                            command.Parameters["@Message"].Value = strMessage;
                            iRecordNumber = Convert.ToInt32(record["RecordNumber"]);
```

■ FIGURE 6.37—cont'd

```
                        command.Parameters["@RecordNumber"].Value = iRecordNumber;
                        strSourceName = (record["SourceName"] == null ? "" : record["Sour-
ceName"].ToString());
                        command.Parameters["@SourceName"].Value = strSourceName;
                        strTimeGenerated = (record["TimeGenerated"] == null ? "" : record
["TimeGenerated"].ToString());
                        dtTimeGenerated = ConvertTime(strTimeGenerated);
                        command.Parameters["@TimeGeneratedString"].Value = strRemote-
Computer + "-" + strTimeGenerated;
                        command.Parameters["@TimeGenerated"].Value = dtTimeGenerated;
                        strType = (record["Type"] == null ? "" : record["Type"].ToString
());
                        command.Parameters["@Type"].Value = strType;
                        strUserName = (record["User"] == null ? "" : record["User"].
ToString());
                        command.Parameters["@UserName"].Value = strUserName;
                        //Content of the Message string is important, but it's just big text
blob when it comes over.
                        //Let's parse that guy out and get the shiny bits we can use.
                        pos1 = 0; pos2 = 0; pos3 = 0;
                        try
                        {
                            if ((pos1 = strMessage.IndexOf("Account For Which Logon
Failed:")) > 0)
                            {
                                string strShinyBits;
                                pos2 = strMessage.IndexOf("Failure Information:");
                                strShinyBits = strMessage.Substring(pos1, pos2 - pos1);
                                pos1 = strShinyBits.IndexOf("Security ID:");
                                pos2 = strShinyBits.IndexOf("Account Name:");
                                pos3 = strShinyBits.IndexOf("Account Domain:");
                                strShiny1 = strShinyBits.Substring(pos1, pos2 - pos1);
                                strShiny2 = strShinyBits.Substring(pos2, pos3 - pos2);
                                strShiny3 = strShinyBits.Substring(pos3, strShinyBits.
Length - pos3);
                            }
                        }
                        catch (Exception)
                        {
                            //bail if something goes wrong with the text parsing.
                            strShiny1 = string.Empty; strShiny2 = string.Empty; strShiny3
= string.Empty;
                        }
```

■ **FIGURE 6.37—cont'd**

```
                    command.Parameters["@Shiny1"].Value = strShiny1;
                    command.Parameters["@Shiny2"].Value = strShiny2;
                    command.Parameters["@Shiny3"].Value = strShiny3;

                    command.ExecuteNonQuery();
                }
                catch (SqlException ex)
                {
                    if (ex.Number == 2601)
                    {
                        //Exception handler for unique key violations.
                        //Using the Remote Server name and full timestamp string we can
guarantee
                        //a unique key.
                        txtResults.AppendText("Record Exists-Skipping...\n");
                    }
                }
            }
        }
        // else
        // {
        // txtResults.AppendText("No records returned from query.\n");
        // }

          //Clean up command and connection objects.
          RefreshGrid();
          txtResults.AppendText("Done.\n");
          command.Connection.Close();
          command.Dispose();
          conn.Dispose();
        }
    }
}
private DateTime ConvertTime(string raw)
{
    // The TimeGenerated value is just a string, so I have to parse the string and
    // build a date string to explicity cast to a datetime type.
    // YYYYMMDDHHMMSS
    return Convert.ToDateTime(raw.Substring(4, 2) + "/" + raw.Substring(6, 2) +
        "/" + raw.Substring(0, 4).ToString() + " " + raw.Substring(8, 2) +
        ":" + raw.Substring(10, 2) + ":" + raw.Substring(12, 2));
}
```

■ FIGURE 6.37—cont'd

```
        private void frmHork_Load(object sender, EventArgs e)
        {
            txtBegDate.Text = DateTime.Now.AddDays(-1).ToShortDateString();
            txtEndDate.Text = DateTime.Now.AddDays(1).ToShortDateString();
            RefreshGrid();
        }
        private void RefreshGrid()
        {
            //refresh the contents of the datagrid after posting.
            sp_GetEventLogTableAdapter.Fill(tMSBDataSet.sp_GetEventLog);
            dataGridView1.Refresh();
        }
    }
}
```

■ **FIGURE 6.37—cont'd**

This application could be easily modified to allow for CmdExec execution in order to automate log collection from any number of servers using the low-privileged user, in this case gServiceUsers, to which the proper permissions were assigned. A more direct method of execution would be to port this code to SQL CLR and simply run the code in the context of the SQL Server service user. In fact, the next step for me when this book is completed is to do just that, and to provide the entire application on the Hammer of God website for your downloading pleasure. Not only will I provide SQL CLR, but an extended version of this application will also be available and better suited for an automated environment leveraging CmdExec.

Note that if you decide to run this via a scheduled CmdExec, you should follow the instructions outlined in Chapter 1, "Securely Writing Web Proxy Log Data to Structured Query Language (SQL) Server and Programmatically Monitoring Web Traffic Data in Order to Automatically Inject Allow/Deny Rules into Threat Management Gateway (TMG)," which covers this exact method of SQL Server execution of external code. Of course, writing your own SQL CLR or using the CLR code I will provide would be the safest method of doing this.

■ SUMMARY

We covered a lot of ground in this chapter. We identified the need for a secure method of accessing archived security (and other) event log data, and outlined the security issues inherent in the typical approaches to the solution. We then designed our own solution based on the use of low-privileged service user accounts, where those accounts were given minimal permissions to access the DCOM interface to create encrypted WMI connections to retrieve the log file data, which we further customized to assign granular log-file permissions using SDDL. Finally, other WMI code examples were provided, as well as a fully functioning Log Fetcher application for your own use.

Securing RDP

INFORMATION IN THIS CHAPTER:

- General RDP Attacks and Mitigation
- RDP Solutions Overview
- Direct Access of Multiple RDP Hosts
- RDG/TSG
- RDP Host Security
- RDWeb and RemoteApp
- Workstation Host Considerations
- Limiting Access with Source Port Access Rules
- Show Me the Code

INTRODUCTION

Long ago when Microsoft released their implementation of the RDP in the way of providing Terminal Services, I thought it was the best thing since sliced bread. Actually, that is not true, because to me sliced bread is really not that big a deal, but it *was* the greatest thing since whatever I used to think the greatest thing was. During the development and deployment of Terminal Services throughout recent years, the terminology has changed a bit. The protocol itself used for a remote desktop connection is called *RDP* and providing a user access to a system via RDP was originally called *Terminal Services*.

Terminal Services came in two flavors: as a remote administration service called *TSAdmin*, and as an overall service offering for multiple users called *TSAppMode*. People started to more commonly use the term *remote desktop* instead of *Terminal Server* just in time for the Terminal Services Gateway (TSG) service to come out, which allows a terminate-and-distribute-type access to RDP hosts via a gateway. Then, RDP became a verb, and not just a noun. So you would RDP into TS via TSG, but that could be either to the TSAdmin or the TSAppMode hosts. Then, TSG was renamed to

Remote Desktop Gateway (RDG), but was put underneath an overall service offering called *Remote Desktop Services* (RDS), which also contained the new Remote App Manager. This was also in time for TSAdmin to start being referred to as just *remote desktop* or *RDP*, and TSAppMode to be called just *Terminal Services* under RDS. So TSG and RDG were the same thing, and RDP and TS were the same thing, except when you meant TS as in TSAppMode under RDS, which was now just Terminal Services rather than TS to mean normal RDPing into a box with the Remote Desktop service running. This is not to be mixed up with actual Remote Desktop Services (capital *S*) since those are two different things. This nomenclature change was made in order to avoid any confusion. I will leave the level of success attained in that change as an exercise for the reader.

I will try to make things simpler by referring to both the process of connecting to a remote host as RDP and the Remote Desktop Protocol itself as RDP. It will be a noun and a verb, as in "I will RDP into that computer," or "I will encrypt RDP with a certificate." We will either RDP to a host directly, or RDP to a host via a gateway service, which I still call *TSG* because there are too many acronyms that start with RD. So when you see TSG or RDG/RD Gateway, they are the same thing.

Operationally, being able to fully interact with a remote system via the UI is a fantastic feature. It is tremendously valuable for any number of situations, from remote administration of assets to the provisioning of overall Terminal Services to the support of multiple simultaneous RDP sessions for users. It is, for all intents and purposes, the extension of a system's console and input devices to a remote system. This is important from a security perspective because you should consider the operation of the remote user to be the same as a user sitting in front of the computer and logged on interactively to the console. This is true from a technical logon perspective as well. When a user logs on to a host via RDP, that logon is considered local or interactive. It is not considered over the network. This has particular relevance when you consider lockout policies based on logon event type. Administrators, for example, cannot be locked out of a system for exceeding an invalid logon attempt threshold when logging on via the console. They can, however, be locked out for logon attempts to resources over the network. This policy is inherited by RDP as well. The immediate concern is the ability to brute-force the administrator account via RDP since it cannot be locked out. Well, that is not exactly true. Locking out the built-in administrator account is something you can indeed do, but there are many dependencies on how this is done, and what type of logon activity it is supported under. For instance, in Server 2008, you can lock out the administrator account on a domain, but it immediately unlocks if you log on at a domain controller.

Regardless, my point is that local logons of the administrator account do not lock out by default, and when it comes to RDP logons, they are considered local. In fact, the actual logon event in the Security Log used for RDP logons used to be Logon Type 2, which is an interactive logon before Logon Type 10 (remote interactive) started being used instead. If someone is trying to use brute force on your administrator account while at the console, you can see them doing it and shoot them. However, if the same types of interactive-by-extension rules apply for RDP clients, then remote brute force attempts become a bigger threat.

GENERAL RDP ATTACKS AND MITIGATION

It was for this reason that attempts at building a RDP brute force tool were made, but given the way RDP works, it became a task far easier to say than do. TSGrinder (a name created by Erik Birkholz) was the only tool to come out that actually worked, and as far as I know is still the only tool in the world that performs brute force attacks against RDP hosts in a way that works. TSGrinder basically pulled up a list of passwords to use against the host, a dictionary file if you will, but you could put whatever you wanted in the list. It would make three attempts at a logon, iterating through the list each time, and then close the connection and fire it back up starting where it left off. This was significant because at the time, RDP logon failures would only be logged after five invalid attempts. Closing after three attempts basically created an environment where attacks against the administrator could continue relentlessly, albeit slowly, connection after connection without ever being logged. And since the connection was encrypted each time, and the attempts would be made within the encrypted RDP session, it was immune to IDS as well. I am not sure how much you have worked with RDP, but in a server environment, two RDP sessions and one console session are supported simultaneously by default. RDP sessions operate within their own session on the server, so it is not like in Vista or Windows 7 where the screen locks when someone else connects to the host via RDP. And since each session is distinct, there are no tell-tale signs of remote compromise, like the mouse moving around on its own. This was always a concern when PCAnywhere hosts were popped and remote access was being exercised. So I am told, anyway.

With all this in mind, you can see how a remote administrator compromise of a server via RDP can be devastating. The domain administrator could be working on the server all day, every day, while a remote attacker could be logged on as well, safe and sound in their own process space. If the administrator ever looked at the RDP service manager, he would just see a disconnected administrator session, which would be perfectly normal. Having unrestricted, virtually undetectable remote administrative access to any number of RDP servers around the world would be a very powerful platform for hackers to launch attacks, or do whatever else they wanted. Again, so I am told.

This is why securing Terminal Services is of particular importance, and why there seems to be a significant stigma to the deployment of RDP on the Internet. It is understandable when scenarios like the one I laid out are considered, particularly when presented in that light, but RDP can be substantially secured with relatively simple methods. You can take some basic measures to immediately increase the security posture of Terminal Services that are really easy, and I will describe some of them for you here.

Renaming the Administrator and Using Strong Passwords

The first thing you can do is rename the administrator account. Yes, I said that. When some folks started talking about renaming the administrator account as a secure measure, lots of people stood up and protested since it would be trivial to retrieve the administrator name by finding the organization SID by way of a well-known group (like Guests), and then take that SID, append a *500* to it, and do an SID-to-Name lookup to get the real account name. In general, I tended to agree with that, back when one could easily enumerate user information with null or anonymous credentials, because it really did not provide much benefit. You cannot do those kinds of things these days, so it makes sense to take advantage of the capability. But RDP has a particular value because people cannot get that kind of remote enumeration data from the Internet, and if they do not know the name of the administrator account, they cannot try to use brute force on it. The second and best defense against attacks is to have a strong passphrase. As you saw in Chapter 5, "The Creation and Maintenance of Low-Privileged Service Users," you can have significantly strong passwords that are very easy to remember and are, for all practical purposes, immune to brute force, dictionary, or rainbow table attacks.

If your administrator password is *is you is or is you ain't my baby?*, then you do not have to worry about brute force attacks. So the first two steps you can take toward securing RDP are changing the administrator name and using a strong password, which are, like I said, quite basic.

RDP Service Ports

Another popular measure is for you to change the default listening port for RDP services from 3389 to something else. This one I would like to talk more about. Changing your RDP listening port is a quintessential example of security through obscurity. I talk about this in Chapter 4, "Creating an Externally Accessible Authenticated Proxy in a Secure Manner," but it is worth repeating here. As far as I am concerned, security through obscurity is a perfectly valid control in depth as long as what is being obscured stays that way. It should not be the only method one chooses to secure something of course, but it can be a valuable part of an overall collection of controls. Specifically, changing your RDP port immediately takes you out of the worm pool because automated processes will not find you, nor will script-kiddie scans. So there is already intrinsic value presented in that form. Supporting alternate ports is also quite easy and helps as well. You simply specify the port after the hostname when you connect, such as *rdp.domain .com:13389.*

The counterargument is that hiding your service port is worthless since all anyone has to do is scan your entire port range and attempt to connect to find Terminal Services. To that, I say, "Meh." The more work you make someone do, the more interested they are in going elsewhere. Another part of the argument for the no-value position is that if anyone is targeting you specifically, changing the port will not help. Well, it will not hurt, and if you are specifically targeted, then 3389 is hosed anyway.

The best argument I have against the port scan claims is actual empirical evidence. Back when I started a seven-month traffic collection research project, I put a VM up directly on the Internet with RDP services deployed on it. I had occasion to use it externally a few times, but all other times were internal, and I know where I was when I was external. Of the 10 billion connections logged in that project, I kept about 15 million of them on hand that were scrubbed of known external access and/or internal access. Of that subset of 15 million connections, there were only nine connections to my hidden port, and they were all from the same place. In fact, I have the logs, and since the box is no longer there, I do not mind showing you. See Figure 7.1.

What is even better is that only one of those hit the actual IP of the server. To be fair, my TMG firewall drops port scans it detects, so I must assume that other scan attempts were made but dropped before they reached 51224. But intrusion detection is part of my network inspection system that is built into TMG, which is another security-in-depth feature that gets counted along with the rest of them. So people can argue for whichever one they wish, but in my opinion (based on seeing the results of actual traffic), I am totally

```
SQLQuery1.sql - s...OFGOD\thor (54))*
```

```
SELECT COUNT(LogID) AS Records FROM xFirewallLog

SELECT LogID, LogTime, SourceIPString, SourceCountry,SourcePort,
DestinationPort FROM xFirewallLog
WHERE DestinationPort = 51224
```

Results | Messages

	(No column name)
1	15275963

	LogID	LogTime	SourceIPString	SourceCountry	SourcePort	DestinationPort
1	181984	2010-07-22 01:27:19.813	76.168.112.95	United States	39951	51224
2	246571	2010-07-22 01:57:56.750	76.168.112.95	United States	45889	51224
3	324883	2010-07-22 01:27:19.970	76.168.112.95	United States	39952	51224
4	326132	2010-07-22 01:27:19.733	76.168.112.95	United States	39952	51224
5	452383	2010-07-22 01:27:19.973	76.168.112.95	United States	39951	51224
6	1136296	2010-07-22 01:14:50.420	76.168.112.95	United States	62595	51224
7	1136364	2010-07-22 01:14:50.243	76.168.112.95	United States	62594	51224
8	1168384	2010-07-22 01:57:56.837	76.168.112.95	United States	45890	51224
9	1168649	2010-07-22 01:57:56.677	76.168.112.95	United States	45890	51224

■ FIGURE 7.1 Firewall Logs Showing Connections to Port 51224 Where RDP Was Moved

fine with recommending that you change your RDP port if that works for you. There is a wealth of information on how to do this available now,[1] but you simply change the [HKEY_LOCAL_MACHINE\SYSTEM\CurrentControlSet\Control\Terminal Server\WinStations\RDP-Tcp] Registry key *PortNumber* to the value you want and restart RDS. Make sure you enter the port in decimal, or the hex equivalent of what you want, because the value is stored in hex.

Before moving on, we will discuss some potential issues with changing the listening port for RDP. The most important is support for outbound TCP in environments where outbound access is controlled. Port 3389 will most likely be allowed in egress-filtered networks, but random outbound ports

---

[1]www.petri.co.il/change_terminal_server_listening_port.htm

will not. I have worked within several networks where this is the case, so it is something to be aware of. There is also the issue of remembering different port assignments where you have distributed RDP services among different listening ports. Expecting clients to remember this may be unreasonable, and publishing the information may be counterproductive. And of course there is the administrative overhead of creating more inbound TCP port availability at the border firewall, as well as local configurations. Along with that comes the security concern about the general inbound access surface area, because the more paths in, the higher your exposure.

Network Level Authentication (NLA)

The last of the quickly configured security options that can make a big difference is to require Network Level Authentication (NLA) at the host. Previous versions of Terminal Services authenticated the user by first building a full RDP session, and having the user log on via the actual logon GUI of the host. This allowed attacking users to see things like the domain the system was a member of, or the actual hostname of the server, but it is also why TSGrinder's speed was suboptimal. A new session had to be created and torn down every time a cycle of three logon attempts occurred.

NLA is actually a mechanism by which the client authenticates itself to the RDP service before the actual RDP connection is established. This allows the user's logon to be validated first, then immediately passed through to the host so that the user never sees the host logon screen. As of the writing of this book, only the Microsoft RDP client version 6.5 and later supports NLA, so it is an excellent method of controlling which clients can even establish a connection. This will also take you out of the pool of brute force targets for TSGrinder since it does not support NLA, nor will it ever support NLA. I did not mention it before, but TSGrinder is my tool, and since I am not going to write in any support for NLA, I can make the previous statement with full confidence that it is accurate. Actually, at this time I have no plans to further develop TSGrinder because the points I wanted to make about RDP security have been made, and also because Microsoft did such an excellent job of further implementing RDP that there is no reason for me to continue to support it.

RDP SOLUTIONS OVERVIEW

That concludes the basic methods. What I want to concentrate on now are methods that will give you production-level security controls around remote desktop provisioning. We will do this in a few different areas of interest. First, we will dig into the RDG, then we will move into the remote desktop web interface, explore remote RDP application deployment (rather than the entire desktop), and finally end up with a special tool I wrote just for the readers of this book that provides what I think are some interesting security options for RDP clients.

RDP Use Cases

A perfect example of use cases where RDP-based administration is an appropriate solution is the management of your demilitarized zone (DMZ). Time after time I have seen DMZ topologies deployed where the assets are members of the internal network domain. The argument I have heard is that domain members are easier to manage, and as such, it is better to have domain members in the DMZ than not, with the logic being that if it is not easy to manage, it will not be managed, and thus you will have vulnerable machines in the DMZ. I disagree with this point of view. This topic has actually been the subject of some rather heated discussions I have had in various forums, and the stopgap for logic seems to always dig in at the argument that it is better because it can be managed. As far as I am concerned, deploying domain members in a DMZ creates more risk than it mitigates. The problem DMZs solve is to provide a logically and physically segmented topology in a least privilege environment to provide defense in depth. DMZs, like the physical characteristics of the area for which the name is coined, exist to separate trust boundaries; that is their purpose. If you populate the DMZ with domain members, then you have extended the trust boundary to the DMZ and defeated the purpose. You no longer have a DMZ; you just have a Z. Domain members require a venerable suite of protocols in order to function properly, which requires that significant communication paths be opened between the DMZ and the internal network. Not only does this allow for direct attacks against key systems via the authentication infrastructure, but if a DMZ asset is compromised, the attacker owns an asset where valid, internal credentials can be collected to access internal assets. Successful exploitation of DMZ systems should never yield credentials that can be used to access internal assets. If your DMZ is populated to the degree that a domain environment is necessary to ease administration, then they should be in their own separate domain/forest. Remote administration via RDP really makes DMZ management a snap. Since RDP requires authentication at connection, leveraging a different set of credentials becomes quite easy. Another strong control that can be leveraged is the use of one-way firewall rules. RDP connections can be allowed to the DMZ from the internal network, but not the other way around. This prevents a persistently open port from being used by an attacker as a path to the internal network should the DMZ be compromised.

I find that one simple question can provide quite a bit of evidence as to which direction you should go, and that is, "What would happen today if an attacker got administrative access to systems in my DMZ?" If they have credentials for the internal network, and a persistent path to get there, you might want to consider a new design.

DIRECT ACCESS OF MULTIPLE RDP HOSTS

The following are examples of how I like to approach the management of a substantial number of RDP hosts. They are applicable to any access model you wish, be it internal to DMZ, or external to DMZ, or even external to internal.

When you start managing multiple RDP hosts that need access from a single or limited source of resources, it does not take very long for administration to become complex. I have seen several different methods used to accommodate growing numbers of hosts who need access in environments with limited access points, and have even used some of these myself when needed. You have got the method using a single IP and multiple ports, as shown in Figure 7.2, where all hosts are accessed via one IP address, but are configured with different listening ports. There is also the multiple IPs and a single port method, as shown in Figure 7.3, where you have enough external IPs to have each machine on its own (I do not see much of that though). And, of course, there is the good ole double-hop method (as shown in Figure 7.4), where you RDP into one box externally, and then use that box to RDP into other boxes.

The first two methods become hard to manage quickly because you have to remember what is where, and that gets messy. The double-hop or jump-box method is actually not all that bad and is used by some larger companies

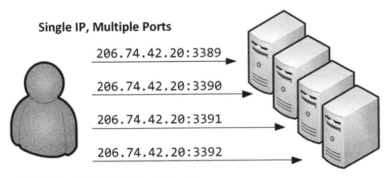

Single IP, Multiple Ports

206.74.42.20:3389

206.74.42.20:3390

206.74.42.20:3391

206.74.42.20:3392

■ **FIGURE 7.2** Single IP, Multiple Ports RDP Host Access

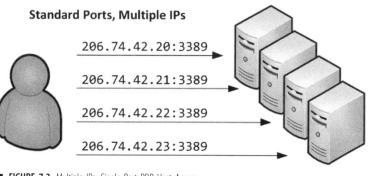

Standard Ports, Multiple IPs

206.74.42.20:3389

206.74.42.21:3389

206.74.42.22:3389

206.74.42.23:3389

■ **FIGURE 7.3** Multiple IPs, Single Port RDP Host Access

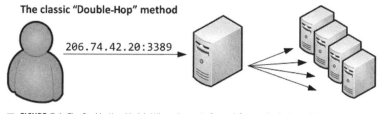

The classic "Double-Hop" method

206.74.42.20:3389

■ **FIGURE 7.4** The Double-Hop Model, Where Access Is Sourced from a Single Jump Point

more than you might think. The problem there is the limit of concurrent connections, and you typically only give administrators access to that box, and of course there is a performance issue of pushing RDP down to another box that is pushing RDP down. I remember being about four hosts deep once, and I needed to get back to the first host, but I did not want to window back out. So, I RDPed back into the first one from the fourth one hoping to grab the second session, but it booted me out of my first session, which of course was the one I was using to get the fourth one to RDP back into the first.

RDG/TSG

RDG (or TSG) is a fantastic solution to this problem. RDG acts as a gateway server, taking RDP requests from clients, and routing them to the appropriate RDP hosts that it serves. However, unlike direct RDP, as used in Figures 7.2 through 7.4, the clients of the RDG server connect over HTTPS on the standard port of 443. The way RDP clients connect to the gateway is via the **Advanced Configuration** tab in the version 6.5 RDP client and later.

With the gateway set as referenced in Figure 7.5, the host you specified in the main connect-to dialog will be used to direct control to the host after you authenticate to the gateway.

■ **FIGURE 7.5** RD Gateway Configuration Dialog from a 6.5 RDP Client

Once this connection is made, RDG will authenticate the user based on different policies (which we will discuss), and if the user is authorized to do so, it will initiate an RDP connection to the back-end RDP host on behalf of the original RDP client. This communications model persists throughout the entire session. The client talks to the RDG over HTTPS, the RDG talks to the back-end host over RDP, and back and forth they go.

The actual protocol structure is a bit more complicated than that, but it is a good place to start. What is really going on is that the client talks to the RDG using the RPC. The RPC requests from the client to the RDG are formatted within HTTP, and are serviced by the RPC over the HTTP proxy service, which is loaded on the RDG when you install RDS. This HTTP stream between the client and RDG is over SSL for security.

The RPC over HTTP proxy takes the request and passes it along to the RPC endpoint within the RDG server on 3388. At this point, we have RPC over HTTP in an SSL tunnel. The client, via RPC, asks the RDG server to create a Terminal Services proxy tunnel so it can start talking to the gateway service. If the client has permission to do this, the RDG authorizes the request, at which point the client makes more RPC calls in the form of health calls to the Network Access Protection (NAP) policies and other validating information about which user he is and what operational state he is in. Now that the RDG has all this information, the client then requests an actual Terminal Services proxy channel to be created to the endpoint host on its behalf. More policies are compared, this time to see if the client has the permission to talk to that particular server, and if it does, RDP send-and-receive pipes are set up between the client and host, and the session begins. So in a way it is RDP through RPC over HTTP within an SSL tunnel.

This offers a number of important security wins. The initial connection is over HTTPS, which means our client can be anywhere for the most part and establish a connection. It is not just any traffic over 443, it is actual HTTP traffic over SSL, so it works through outbound proxies and application-level protocol filters. It can also be published from the Internet (or reverse-proxied or port-forwarded) along with your other HTTPS rules or protocol listeners.

This uses two levels of authentication: first when a tunnel request is generated by the user and second when the channel is created to the host. This means that we individually set permissions on what accounts are allowed to connect to the RDG server itself, and to what back-end servers one has the permissions to connect to. Note that this is not based on the actual authentication to the host since that only happens after both the tunnel and channel are authorized and created. This further allows you to give permissions to the RDG that are actually different than the credentials used to connect up to the host. Even though most of the implementations I have seen use the same account for both connections, there are a number of models you can use based on your needs.

I will walk through a typical RDG setup and configuration, which will include the user and system NAP polices, and then I will move on to what I consider one of the more substantial security controls in RDG, which is the enhanced certificate and authentication features available. Certificate-based authentication in Terminal Services overall has been (and continues to be) commonly misunderstood in its implementation, which has led to some misconceptions about its operation, resulting in a false sense of security. Configuring the gateway is fairly straightforward, but I will quickly cover it and then move on to the important subject of certificate authentication models.

RDG Certificates

Ensure that you have the RDS role installed, along with the RDG, Remote Desktop Web Access, and Remote Desktop Session Host role services.

The first thing to configure in the RDG Manager is the certificate that you want to use to support the primary RDG connection. This certificate needs to match the hostname you will use to connect to the gateway service externally.

Note that if I were to use the certificate specified in Figure 7.6, the *rds .hammerofgod.com* host would have to be reachable by name from the client either by DNS or a hosts file. It is important to understand that the certificate specified here has nothing to do with the certificate you use on the actual RDG host computer when configuring *its* RDP host settings. This certificate is used strictly for the gateway service.

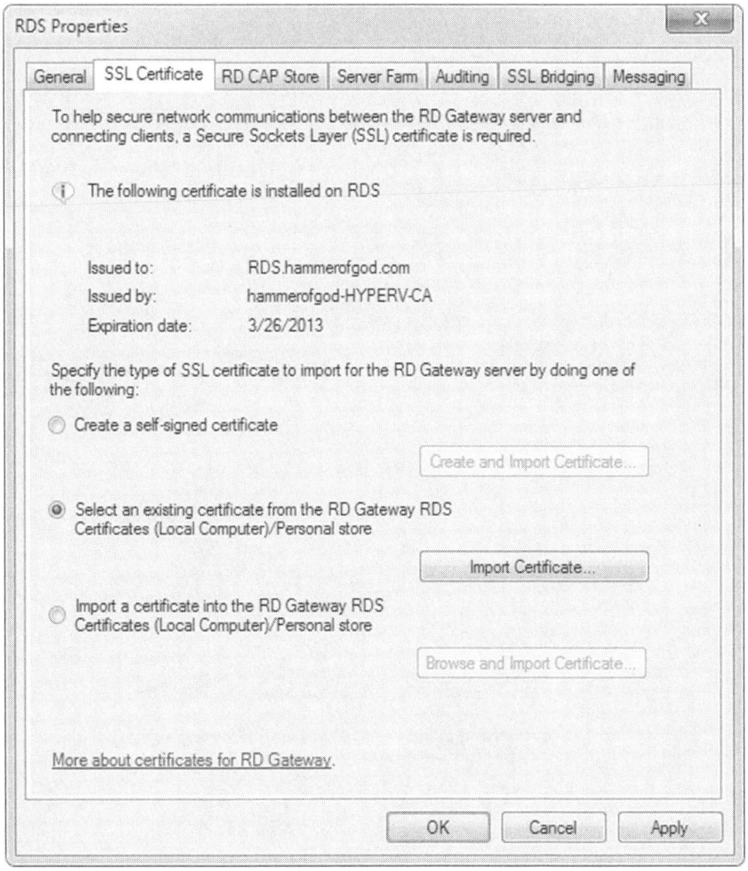

■ **FIGURE 7.6** RD Gateway Certificate Configuration

Once that is done, you need to configure both your Connection Authorization Policy (CAP) and your Resource Authorization Policy (RAP). The CAP controls the tunnel, and the RAP controls the channel, so the CAP specifies what groups of users or groups of client computers can make a connection to the RDG server. This does not control any access to resources at all; the RAP does that. This simply specifies who can use the resources of the gateway. The CAP also defines what client devices can be redirected to the host RDP session, and the timeout values.

Similarly, the RAP shown in Figure 7.7 lets you specify what groups of systems can be connected via the gateway. In Figure 7.8, I am specifying that any host can be contacted.

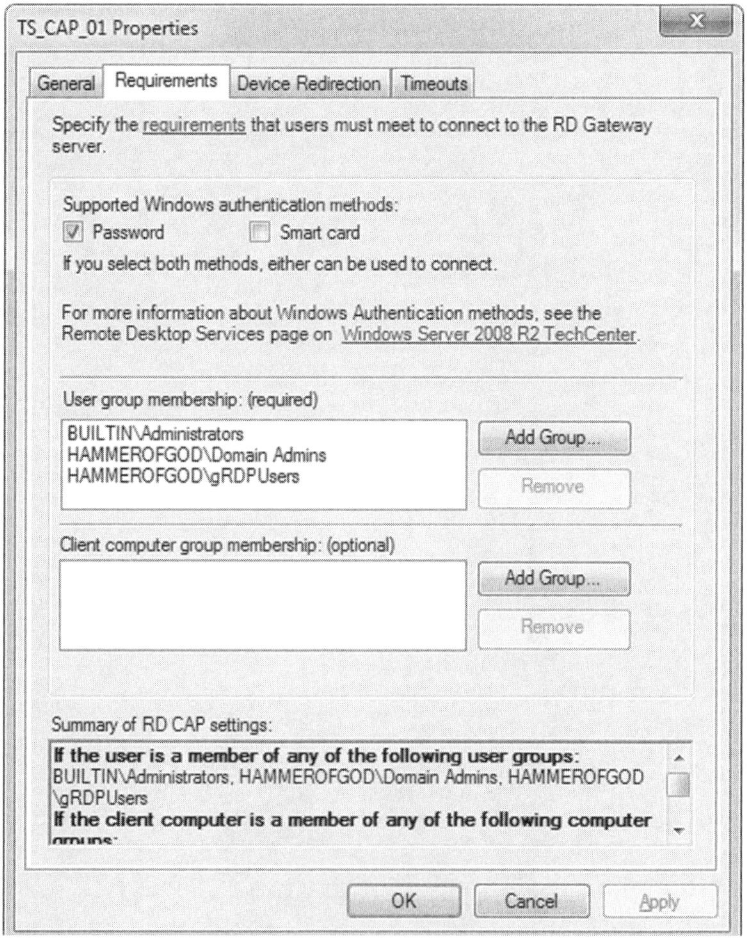

■ **FIGURE 7.7** Connection Authorization Policies Specifying Which Users Can Use the Gateway

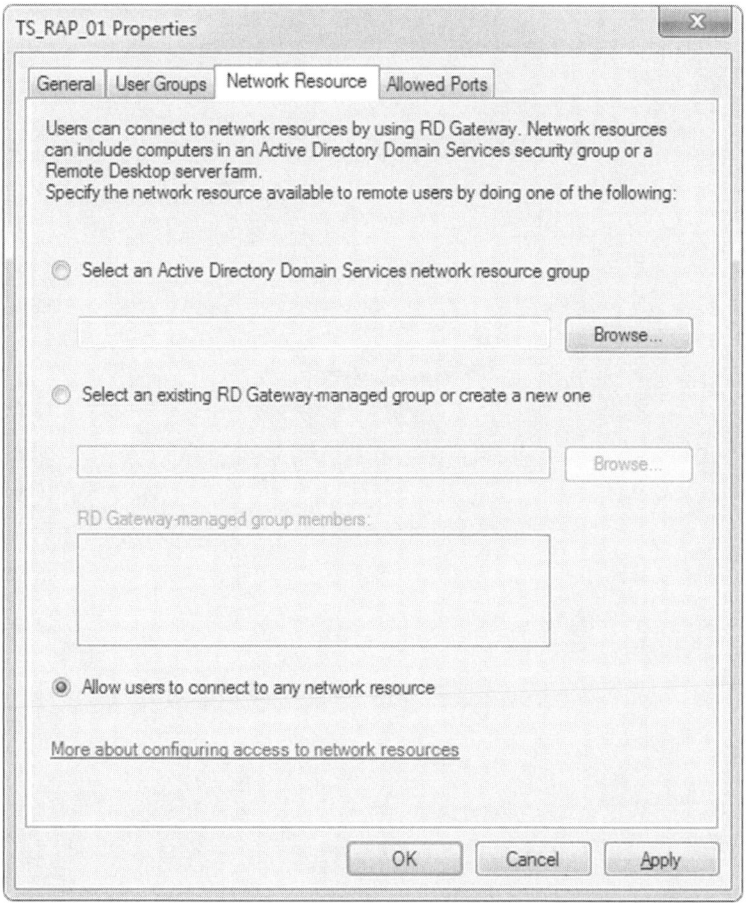

■ FIGURE 7.8 Resource Authorization Policy Specifying That Authorized Users Can Connect to Any Network Resource

This is all you need do in order to begin using the RDG. With your RDP client pointed to your gateway, you simply refer to the name of the internal resource you wish to connect to and fire away. Like I said, this is pretty basic and your typical configuration routine should look like Figure 7.9.

RDP HOST SECURITY

Now we will talk about the different security provisioning that can be applied to both server and client. Though RDG makes the connection to the endpoint RDP host for us, that host still retains any specific RDP session configuration parameters it has. In other words, just because you have a gateway service

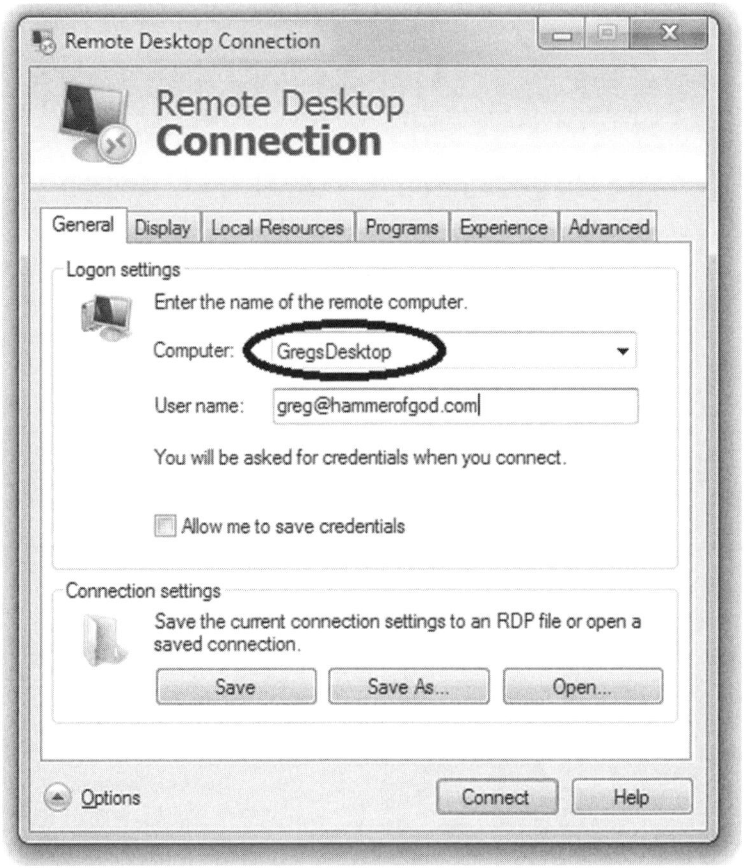

■ **FIGURE 7.9** RDP Clients Specifying the Internal Hostname to Connect via the Gateway

authorizing connections and resources does not mean security stops there; you still need to ensure that your hosts are configured securely.

It was not that long ago that export restrictions prevented certain types of encryption from being shipped outside of U.S. borders. This meant that clients could have varying degrees of support for strong encryption. The version of RDP client they had also restricted certain encryption specifications. As such, the default setting for an RDP host was to negotiate security with the client and use the best method of encryption the client could support. High 128-bit encryption was supported, but the client could limit the connection to 56-bit, or even 40-bit, encryption if you were really unlucky. Also feared were man-in-the-middle attacks, where someone could be sitting between you and the real RDP host you wanted to get to and intercepting everything sent between.

In order to combat weak encryption and identity attacks, we have the capability of setting minimum security requirements on a host-by-host basis. This includes the minimum level of encryption, the type of security layer protocol used, and decisions on whether the client should employ NLA. Support for server certificates was also introduced, and individual hosts could be configured to limit who could connect and use RDP host facilities. If the client was unable to meet any of the security requirements, the client could not connect. These options are set in the RDP Session Host connection configuration.

In this case, SSL encryption is required with the maximum key the server certificate supports (128-bit). Figure 7.10 shows options for configurations

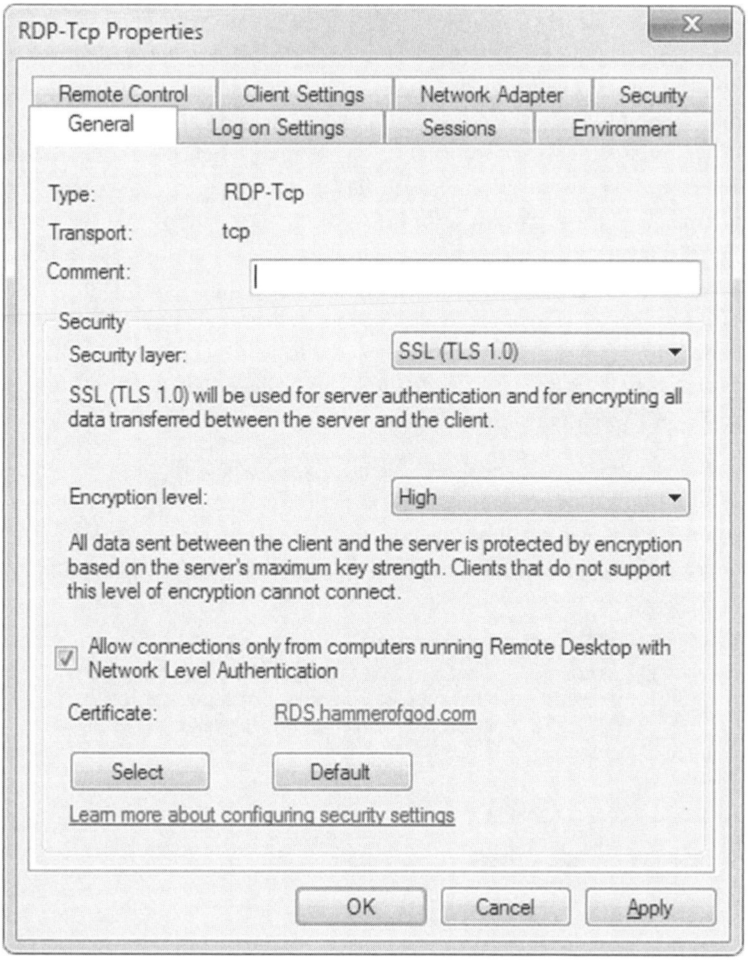

■ FIGURE 7.10 General Security Settings for an RDP Session Connection Object

that allow us to prevent man-in-the-middle attacks and to ensure that all data is being encrypted to the maximum capacity. This is also where a lot of fallacies emerged regarding how certificates were used and what controls could be put in place.

I started to see articles where, for some reason, people got it into their heads that setting a self-signed or private certificate from their own CA could prevent clients from connecting unless they had the issuing CA certificate installed and trusted. I think the client setting in Figure 7.11 had something to do with it.

I guess people noticed that if the client did not trust the issuing certificate authority for the certificate specified in the RDP host settings, it would not connect. One security expert described the process as, "upon connection, the client presents the server with its certificate, and if it is not trusted by the server, then the client cannot connect." This is, of course, doo-doo. While there certainly are instances where a client can present a certificate to a server, and that server can check to see if it was signed by a certificate authority it knows about, the server has no ability to enforce whether or not the client trusts its own certificate. Asking the client if it trusts a certificate is not a server-based security measure; it is a client-based one. If the server required me as the client to trust its cert to connect, I could just tell it I trust it whether I did or not. It is all up to the client. In Figure 7.11, the only reason the client did not connect is because he was told not to if he did not trust the server. But the user could just as easily have changed it to **Connect and don't warn me** and connected away.

The reason for certificate-based authentication on the server is so the client knows that the server is who it says it is, not for the server to restrict who can connect to it. An administrator can certainly configure a workstation to never connect on authentication failures via group policy (which enforces

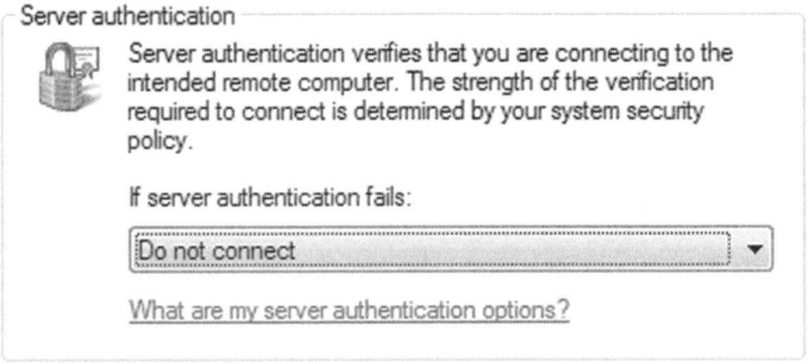

Server authentication

Server authentication verifies that you are connecting to the intended remote computer. The strength of the verification required to connect is determined by your system security policy.

If server authentication fails:

Do not connect

What are my server authentication options?

■ **FIGURE 7.11** RDP Client Authentication Failure Setting of Do Not Connect

Server authentication

Server authentication verifies that you are connecting to the intended remote computer. The strength of the verification required to connect is determined by your system security policy.

If server authentication fails:

Connect and don't warn me ▼

What are my server authentication options?

■ **FIGURE 7.12** Client Setting to Connect Regardless of Server Authentication Failure

the selection made in Figure 7.12), and this is a perfectly good way to prevent your users from connecting to rogue servers, but it will not stop attackers since you have no control over their clients. This is really too bad, because preventing who can connect up to your RDP hosts in the first place is an excellent way to secure your installations. The good news is that there are ways to get very close to this type of control, but unfortunately not all the way. I suppose the easiest way to restrict connections to your RDG is by requiring smartcard logons, which RDG supports. Many of us cannot stipulate that requirement very efficiently without great cost and a fair amount of user complaints though.

RDWEB AND REMOTEAPP

So let us get as close as we can with what we already have. At this point, I am going to introduce RDWeb and RemoteApp. Not only can we get strong controls over connections via these two technologies, but we can increase our overall security posture by deploying only the applications needed for remote users, as opposed to giving them a fully enabled desktop.

RDWeb

RDWeb is a web-based interface where users log in and are presented with a list of preconfigured remote desktop or remote application connections. It is accessed via standard HTTPS, and can be password protected just like any other website. Doing this would be slightly redundant though, because the RDWeb interface requires authentication via a forms-based logon, shown in Figure 7.13.

However, if a different set of credentials is used to access the page than to log on, it is a good way of utilizing two-factor authentication. I do not

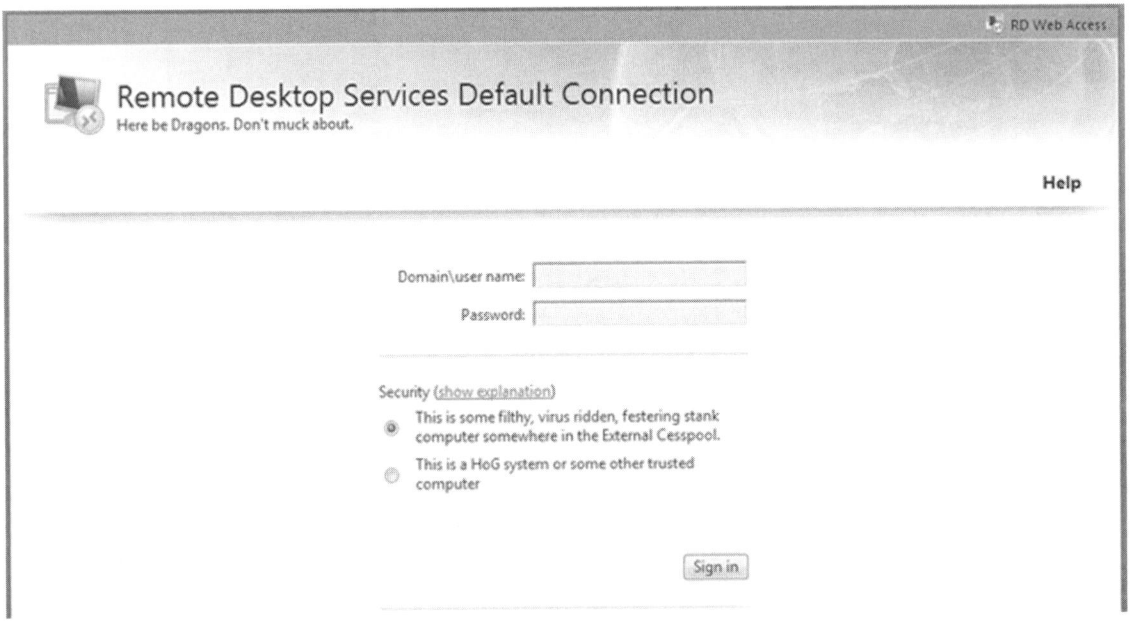

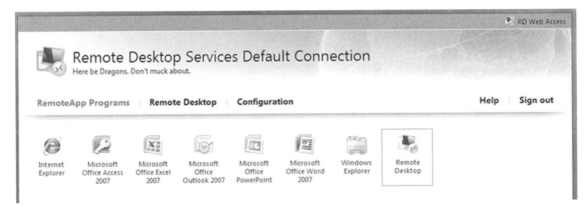

■ **FIGURE 7.13** Remote Desktop Web (Albeit Modified) Forms-Based Logon Screen

necessarily expect users to remember the operational requirements for this, but for administrative interfaces, it is certainly a good option.

In my case, I have got the Office suite, IE, Windows Explorer, and a full remote desktop in my connection collection.

The connection objects displayed in Figure 7.14 are basically RDP files that contain the connection information required to access the remote

■ **FIGURE 7.14** Sample Collection of Remote Applications and Desktop Connections via RDWeb

application. In this case, my RD Session host has the necessary applications installed on it to support remote application delivery—thus, as many users can log on and use these applications as my hardware configuration and licensing agreements will allow.

RemoteApp

I will go into more detail about the remote app configuration, but Figure 7.15 shows the connection objects that populate the web interface.

I have seen the process of launching remote applications from the web interface described incorrectly on several occasions, so I think it is a good idea to outline the connection model. What *does not* happen is some sort of web-proxy connection that is made through the RDWeb system to the back-end system serving up the remote application in an RDP session. RDWeb simply creates remote RDP configuration objects based on the RemoteApp programs list and downloads to the client when selected. The client then parses out the connection object, and connects based on the configuration options set for the remote application. The client initiates a connection to the host specified via a separate connection. Understand that if the client knew all of the connection options contained within the object, they could initiate the connections themselves without the aid of the remote RDP file. That is an important point. It looks like the diagram in Figure 7.16.

The connection object is downloaded from the /RDWeb/ web directory, and the RDP client is launched, pointing to the RDG box (which is via the /RPC/ directory).

The remote desktop tab on the main RDWeb page works the same way. I actually do not find it valuable, because the hostname you enter there must

■ **FIGURE 7.15** A RemoteApp Programs List

RemoteApp Programs			
Name	Path	RD Web Acc...	Arguments
Internet Explorer	C:\Program Files (x86)\Intern...	Yes	Disabled
Microsoft Office Access 2007	C:\Program Files (x86)\Micros...	Yes	Disabled
Microsoft Office Excel 2007	C:\Program Files (x86)\Micros...	Yes	Disabled
Microsoft Office Outlook 2007	C:\Program Files (x86)\Micros...	Yes	Disabled
Microsoft Office PowerPoint 2...	C:\Program Files (x86)\Micros...	Yes	Disabled
Microsoft Office Word 2007	C:\Program Files (x86)\Micros...	Yes	Disabled
Windows Explorer	C:\Windows\explorer.exe	Yes	Disabled

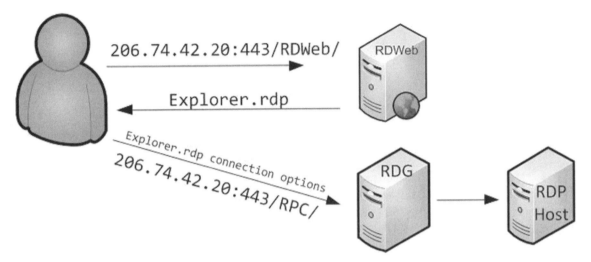

206.74.42.20:443/RDWeb/

RDWeb

Explorer.rdp

Explorer.rdp connection options
206.74.42.20:443/RPC/

RDG

RDP
Host

■ **FIGURE 7.16** Connection Diagram of a Client Connecting to RDWeb, Retrieving Connection Information, and Then Making a Connection to the Host via RD Gateway

be directly reachable by your client. In other words, it does not provide any RDG functionality; it is only a shortcut to access a RDP host. This would be helpful in an internal access environment, but not much good externally.

Regarding the remote app connection structure, the value in this design is twofold. For one, the UI to the remote application is about as easy as it can be: Log in, click application, done. Secondly, since all the information needed to connect to the back-end server (including application information) is contained within the remote RDP file, there is no way for an attacker to gain this information otherwise. They would have to first gain access to the RDWeb site, and then connect to the back-end host via the gateway. Additionally, your users cannot muck about with the connection object to change your connection parameters. Whatever you set in the configuration is what is used. For instance, I have got my applications restricted to options similar to Figure 7.17.

This shows that the back-end host the user will connect to is *backend .hammerofgod.com*, and that the user will connect to that back-end via the *remote.hammerofgod.com* RDG. Additionally, these connection objects will be digitally signed by my *rds.hammerofgod.com* server, and the parameters of that connection will use the RDP settings configured. One of those custom RDP settings allows us to specify the authentication failure behavior.

The default authentication level is *i:2* which indicates that the client will be warned when authorization issues, such as certificate trust chains, are encountered. Changing this value to *1*, as indicated in Figure 7.18, forces the connection to terminate if errors are encountered. The default value allows the client to continue, which is illustrated in Figure 7.19.

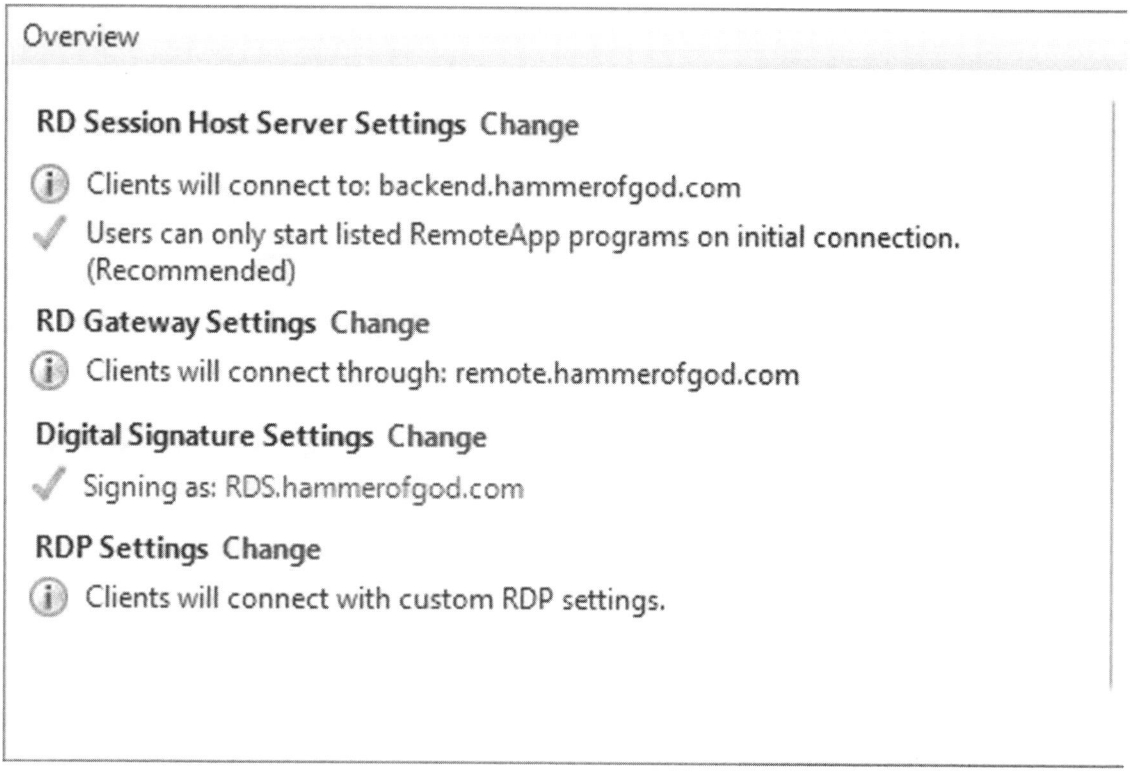

Overview

RD Session Host Server Settings Change

ⓘ Clients will connect to: backend.hammerofgod.com

✓ Users can only start listed RemoteApp programs on initial connection. (Recommended)

RD Gateway Settings Change

ⓘ Clients will connect through: remote.hammerofgod.com

Digital Signature Settings Change

✓ Signing as: RDS.hammerofgod.com

RDP Settings Change

ⓘ Clients will connect with custom RDP settings.

■ **FIGURE 7.17** RemoteApp General Connection Restrictions

Changing the authentication level prevents this behavior, as Figure 7.20 shows.

In this way, you can specify a signing certificate, or a back-end RDP server certificate, only be used where clients that trust the CA are allowed to continue. An attacker simply installing the certificate from the server and trusting it is not enough. In order for the certificate chain to be validated, the actual CA certificate must be installed and trusted by the client system. If one deploys their own certificate authorities (or can control the client's trust), this is an effective way to prevent unauthorized connections to RDP resources.

But again, if you refer to the Figure 7.16 model, you see that it is still the client that initiates the remote connection. An attacker could still initiate this connection with his own RDP settings that you cannot enforce. The upshot here is that the only way the information regarding connections can be discovered is by somehow getting to the RDWeb page in the first place.

Can a user divulge this information to an attacker? Sure they can. They could also just give the attacker their credentials, or just give the attacker

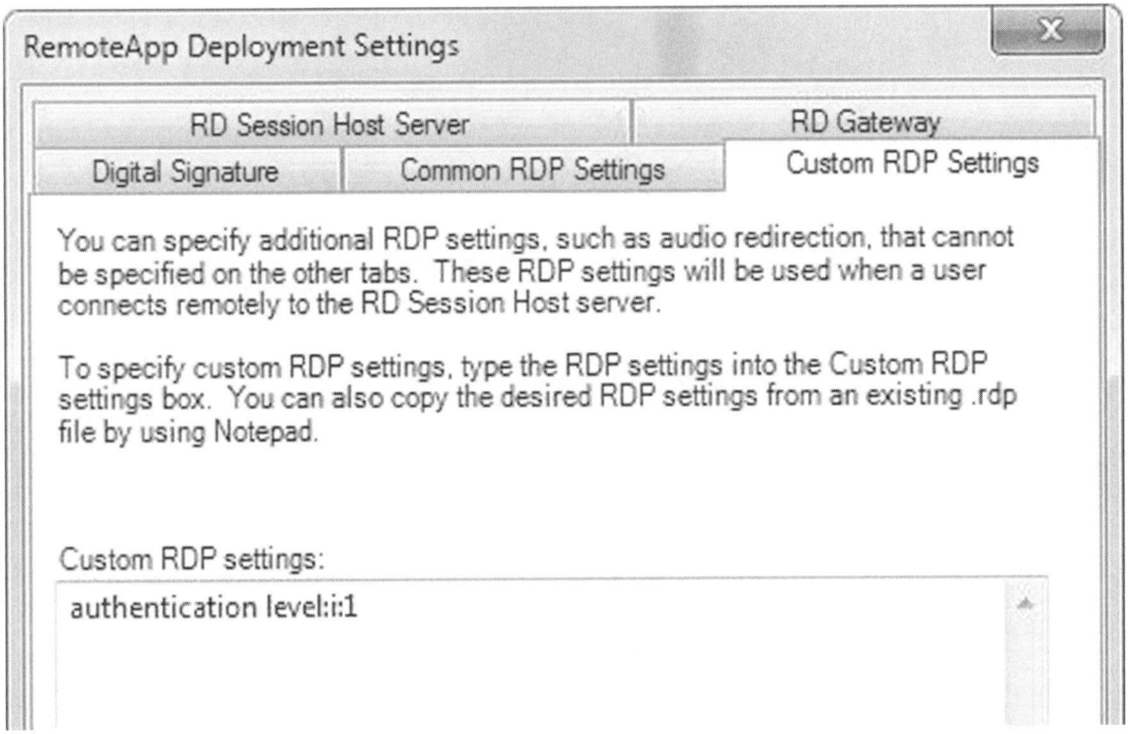

RemoteApp Deployment Settings

RD Session Host Server		RD Gateway
Digital Signature	Common RDP Settings	Custom RDP Settings

You can specify additional RDP settings, such as audio redirection, that cannot be specified on the other tabs. These RDP settings will be used when a user connects remotely to the RD Session Host server.

To specify custom RDP settings, type the RDP settings into the Custom RDP settings box. You can also copy the desired RDP settings from an existing .rdp file by using Notepad.

Custom RDP settings:

authentication level:i:1

■ **FIGURE 7.18** Custom RDP Setting of Authentication Level of i:1 Specified in the RemoteApp Deployment Settings

Certificate errors

The following errors were encountered while validating the remote computer's certificate:

⚠ A revocation check could not be performed for the certificate.

⚠ The certificate or associated chain is invalid (Code: 0x10000).

Do you want to connect despite these certificate errors?

View certificate...   Yes   No

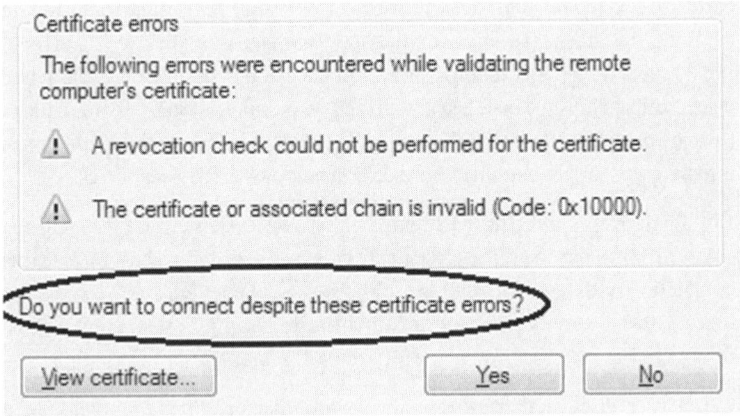

■ **FIGURE 7.19** Default Authentication Level Allowing the Client to Continue in Spite of Certificate Errors

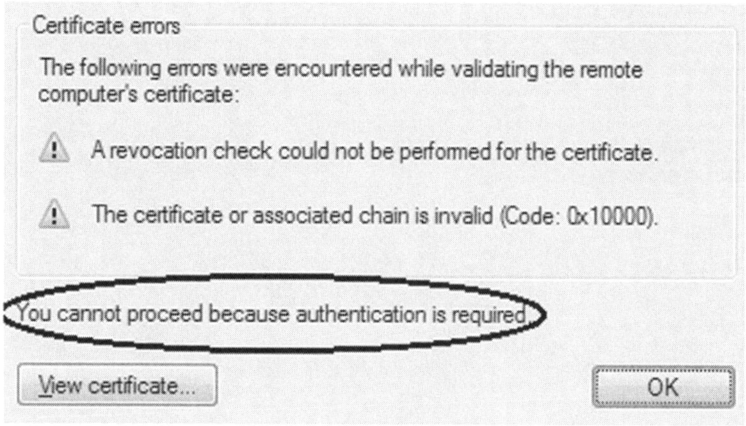

```
Certificate errors

The following errors were encountered while validating the remote
computer's certificate:

⚠   A revocation check could not be performed for the certificate.

⚠   The certificate or associated chain is invalid (Code: 0x10000).

You cannot proceed because authentication is required

[View certificate...]                              [ OK ]
```

■ **FIGURE 7.20** Authentication Level of 1, Preventing User from Continuing

the data they would look for once they got in. You cannot solve people-
based trust issues with technology, but you can perform due diligence
in deploying least privilege access with security in depth as we have
done here.

Deploying Signed RDP Files

Another way of providing users with connection information without having
to publish a separate RDWeb instance is to create actual signed RDP files
and distribute them to users as individual files. Upon execution of these
files, they will initiate a connection just like they would if they loaded it
from the RDWeb site.

From the same explorer remote app specification, I can create either a single
RDP file or an actual installation EXE file.

The options selected in Figure 7.21 actually create a standard RDP text file,
but the file is signed. It looks like this:

```
redirectclipboard:i:1
redirectposdevices:i:0
redirectprinters:i:1
redirectcomports:i:1
redirectsmartcards:i:1
devicestoredirect:s:*
drivestoredirect:s:*
redirectdrives:i:1
session bpp:i:32
```

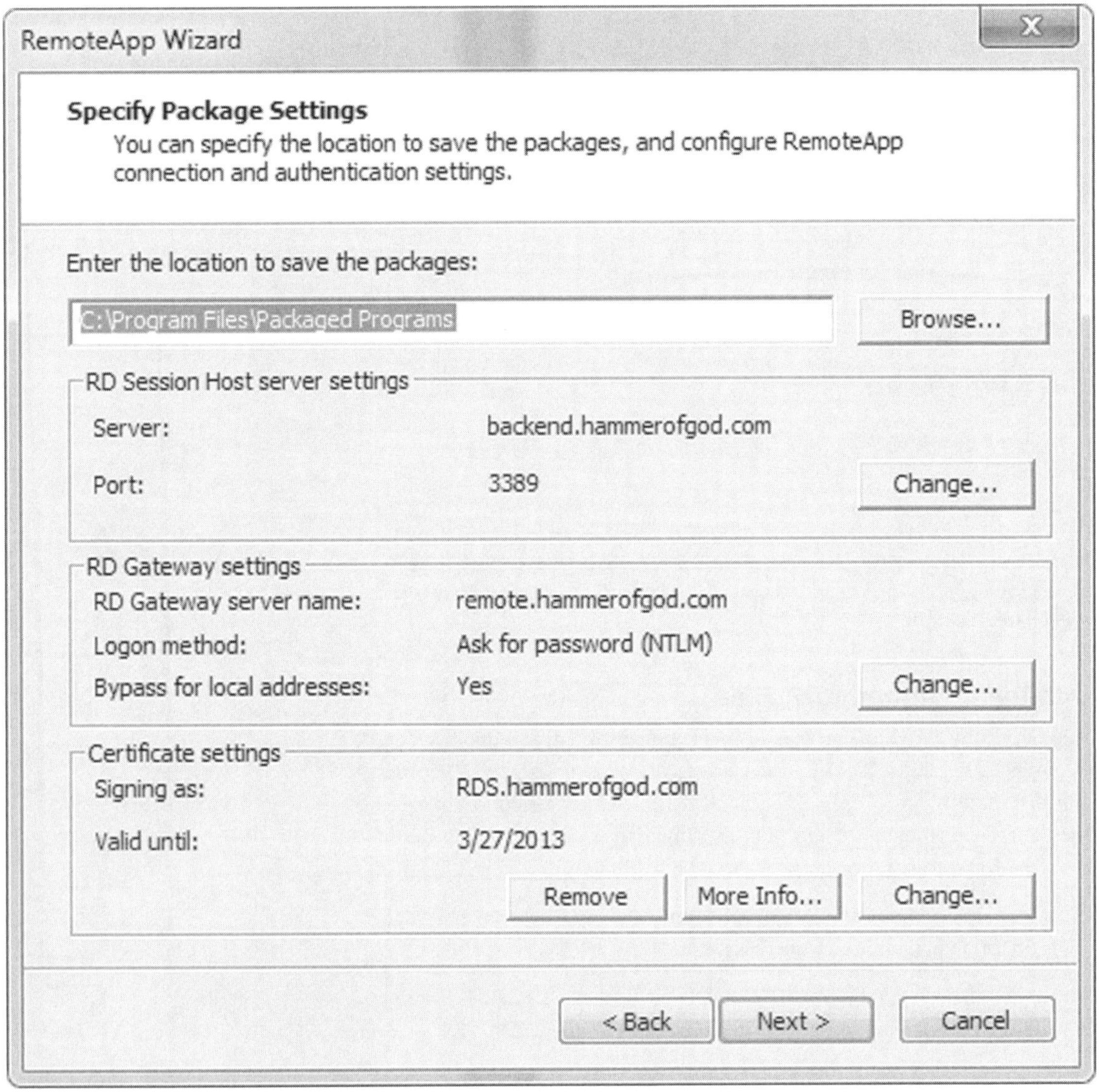

RemoteApp Wizard

Specify Package Settings

You can specify the location to save the packages, and configure RemoteApp connection and authentication settings.

Enter the location to save the packages:

C:\Program Files\Packaged Programs

Browse...

RD Session Host server settings

Server:	backend.hammerofgod.com	
Port:	3389	Change...

RD Gateway settings

RD Gateway server name:	remote.hammerofgod.com	
Logon method:	Ask for password (NTLM)	
Bypass for local addresses:	Yes	Change...

Certificate settings

Signing as:	RDS.hammerofgod.com	
Valid until:	3/27/2013	

Remove   More Info...   Change...

< Back   Next >   Cancel

■ **FIGURE 7.21** RemoteApp Wizard to Create a
Signed RDP File for Distribution

```
prompt for credentials on client:i:1
span monitors:i:1
use multimon:i:1
remoteapplicationmode:i:1
server port:i:3389
allow font smoothing:i:1
promptcredentialonce:i:1
```

```
authentication level:i:1
gatewayusagemethod:i:2
gatewayprofileusagemethod:i:1
gatewaycredentialssource:i:0
full address:s:backend.hammerofgod.com
alternate shell:s:||explorer
remoteapplicationprogram:s:||explorer
gatewayhostname:s:remote.hammerofgod.com
remoteapplicationname:s:Windows Explorer
remoteapplicationcmdline:s:
alternate full address:s:backend.hammerofgod.com
signscope:s:Full Address,Alternate Full Address,Server
Port,GatewayHostname,GatewayUsageMethod,GatewayProfileUsage
Method,Gate wayCredentialsSource,PromptCredentialOnce,Alter
nate Shell,RemoteApplicationProgram,RemoteApplicationMode,
RemoteApplicationName,RemoteApplicationCmdLine,Authentica
tion Level,RedirectDrives,RedirectPrinters,RedirectCOMPorts,
RedirectSmartCards,RedirectPOSDevices,RedirectClipboard,
DevicesToRedirect,DrivesToRedirect
```

```
signature:s:AQABAAEAAADeCgAAMIIK2gYJKoZIhvcNAQcCoIIKyzCC
CscCAQExCzAJBgUrDgMC GgUAMAsGCSqGSIb3DQEHAaCCCRswggOXMIIC
f6ADAgECAhB4/oR+SiTimEgjxMrT UPHdMAOGCSqGSIb3DQEBBQUAMFIx
EzARBgoJkiaJk/IsZAEZFgNjb2OxGzAZBgoJ kiaJk/IsZAEZFgtoYW1t
ZXJvZmdvZDEeMBwGA1UEAxMVaGFtbWVyb2Znb2QtSF1Q RVJWLUNBMB4X
DTA5MTIxNTIxMjcwNloXDTE0MTIxNTIxMzcwNFowUjETMBEGCGgmS JomT
8ixkARkWA2NvbTEbMBkGCgmSJomT8ixkARkWC2hhbW1lcm9mZ29kMR4w
HAYD VQQDExVoYW1tZXJvZmdvZC1IWVBFU1YtQ0EwggEiMAOGCSqGSIb3
DQEBAQUAA4IB DwAwggEKAoIBAQCwtgeT2X2ulH9Bdd/cukNgbEer3a1V
wsp1p5MEgtK9H3TFUczD blttykH4xoYng7Fzxth9u8k/9SVzAxiH13V5
jeeSZ4juelpG9tAzkfSnkqv+r4fV 63Qciyw7QGF2P6AYgDol/UWJdVTP
BKHSPLw+qH9vGIrfSd+cMd+kJbNB6O2BtKZg AN2rPW22Bu+8wnPPmON3+
MPHvZq/4WwmMKOuCRxaqnwCbn9AzmRCPqxOlWtWLaMC F8LhXcYVQ6W7B
11NcSO/EpM55P+69VnDLSGXu4kWO+RobvACWHnDhne3rzhEvZ6GTfq9Y
tzK6QSmWjSBNjxohcL1XFDISdXD7d1XAgMBAAGjaTBnMBMGCSsGAQQBgjcUA
gQGHgQAQwBBMA4GA1UdDwEB/wQEAwIBhjAPBgNVHRMBAf8EBTADAQH/MBO
GA1Ud DgQWBBQCLJO4hsgKkadpvgEYP6Goa5YBcTAQBgkrBgEEAYI3F
QEEAwIBADANBgkqhki G9wOBAQUFAAOCAQEAH5qvuxVWOc8tM+Gjbkby
TTmSB6Efob1yz9KWuCcKKoKemnhOjH1eUOCBhHyyAUU9D7DCx9lfIBI9
nsN1BVEc/vG9OobMRcYI4PhcsMyBTV56 Q9eWYsEsRLdiVW21XJqJOhcG
wXG+JRk2JmxjaczVGAzszOWFQHIPFpe4MnlOiRuFQ71FQdH669orOR4nThO
FHKT3XbB7nPVPwjzYW1LwfOtieiKwrGTKbNqciSYb/kTRqszojKfli7G
1m+HFzMvudExiQutjs7qW18I6i9rX7KhMUmiucPXJsntMxRRfilghJo2
cS8lxoNDL2ii1r+UK/4Xf802hI679ActpWRaTwjCCBXwwggRkoAMCAQI
CCjSrOPQAAAAAAGEwDQYJKoZIhvcNAQEFBQAwUjETMBEGCGgmSJomT8ixkAR
kWA2NvbTEbMBkGCgmSJomT8ixkARkWC2hhbW1lcm9mZ29kMR4wHAYDVQQDE
xVoYW1tZXJvZmdvZC1IWVBFU1YtQ0EwHhcNMTEwMzI3MDMzMzIOWhcNMTMw
```

```
MzI3MDMOMzIOWjAAMIIB IjANBgkqhkiG9wOBAQEFAAOCAQ8AMIIBCgKCAQ
EA5IayGVcx58mGp3OvtWGWMj5R 8s7ECUFJZwW9QCf1djrJ1g+hzV28su
EkwQMC6za1AcrKhASPTANtDwKK9+f8QOFb 02kpFZwU6gzMU2Or2X3meGP
nupHqCmv09eBC1mSQngFkehKqo9Wc1AMx5rIVw8mH dOXaqaOk94/ZIoI
5iPX YHNW1nbFxEK4jUjGrWbkLeAYmbs1rfsa2rTM5gLjIst1F EB5I1YZ
+op+whnUo X2pLRfFdQrya46SJAY6tp3J25a1+S15Xez50PXMgUO5aC52
AJ yr8LSUL6bYTp83x9/TcZdagDpmWoxyrTHJph1/o3oHr5T+yCFYcTj
HY7oLX1QID AQABo4ICpDCCAqAwPAYJKwYBBAGCNxUHBC8wLQY1KwYBB
AGCNxUIh6aScoP36A3thyaO7muEx7Z7gS+BhNI2g4bAZwIBZAIBAzAdBg
NVHSUEFjAUBggrBgEFBQcDAQYI KwYBBQUHAwIwDgYDVROPAQH/BAQDAg
WgMCcGCSsGAQQBgjcVCgQaMBgwCgYIKwYB BQUHAwEwCgYIKwYBBQUHAw
IwHQ YDVROOBBYEFC/S7TqWILMuIdsED1XLJ2pCyFho MB8GA1UdIwQYMB
aAFAI snTiGyAqRp2m+ARg/oahr1gFxMIHWBgNVHR8Egc4wgcswgcggc
WggcKG gb9sZGFwOi8vL0NOPWhhbW11cm9mZ29kLUhZZUEVSVi1DQSxDTj1
IeXB1c1YsQ049QORQLENOPVB1YmxpYyUyUyMEt1eSUyMFN1cnZpY2VzLENOP
VN1cnZpY2VzLENOPUNvbmZpZ3VyYXRpb24sREM9aGFtbWVyb2Znb2QsREM
9Y29tP2N1cnRp Zm1jYXR1UmV2b2NhdGlvbkxpc3Q/YmFzZZT9vYmp1Y3RD
bGFzcz1jUkxEaXN0cm1i dXRpb25Qb21udDCBywYIKwYBBQUHAQEEgb4wg
bswgbgGCCsGAQUFBzAChoGrbGRh cDovLy9DTj1oYW1tZXJvZmdvZC1IW
VBFU1YtQOEsQO49QU1BLENOPVB1YmxpYyUy MEt1eSUyMFN1cnZpY2VzL
ENOPVN1cnZpY2VzLENOPUNvbmZpZ3VyYXRpb24sREM9 aGFtbWVyb2Znb
2QsREM9Y29tP2N1BQ2VydG1maWNhdGU/YmFzZT9vYmp1Y3RDbGFzcz1jZ
XJOaWZpY2F0 aW9uQXV0aG9yaXR5MCEGA1UdEQEB/wQXMBWCE1JEUy5oY
W1tZXJvZmdvZ C 5jb20wDQYJKoZIhvcNAQEFBQADggEBACG3Du3tPmVwV
ts2zQa8Eu61L0 ho6gSXAAi1xkDa2pLbT/GfoxOtwvcoWYPGSJbGMGg3y
cZfiNPtkgzofFkPjINTIJOs19g6tB1217guYi1nbdAPxfbbC3mgetGBe
xI3gKGt3bJyx8VF hIfHBOrnKhPW IXE7bJo/qLd1mIe433WmqG85cipkoL5
wS3cSObYP11XrjQ/QOBn7dw9DVR5OW8qq pdU/B5KjFxV16mqkAqSyvPJObf
5Xn/tmLaiWetKLDg kbdzRhRdSItsqKLg737Fkv uTUao5PteQsQ4m2hmH/Ev
EzvO5HFtuxOp8LTOgbSZahf6jmHZEZOiRb9mCeypikx ggGHMIIBgwIBA
TBgMFIxEzARBgoJkiaJ k/IsZAEZFgNjb20xGzAZBgoJkiaJk/IsZAEZF
gtoYW1tZXJvZmdvZDEeMBwGA1UEAxMVaGFtbWVyb2Znb2QtSF1QRVJWLU
NB AgoOqzjOAAAAAABhMAkGBSsOAwIaBQAwDQYJKoZIhvcNAQEBBQAEgg
EAP3QrO/kn 6Qx1V3x5YQOkqF59P LM1AK84UCISzcANbv9vvXoGPLHVgU
YRJXViMVFsY1qOFLAn K791Ut38u65j 41c3Bj5FBXKPSqQ7eS1iuThnR66u
mMd4aVNzajJJz2AP7mSHe8pfQO5JxTNo/GQWD34Odrd7XTi+vjs2Fh3OKC
2423CC1jyPLu2fGbgIawguEFFNHnhePcpOFOx2oVMCT3V80W191scRBPe
1NF52B21dCBoYzW+5sjUzeNfDA/uSkiP J59QJ k/cN/q391nt/ZLbfjy
25g62ZLE58uj8sOT8E+ LMQQiIuxh12K7i +M3U9mHtoGQYLrmYCKtAe+
q64CQ==
```

The user can certainly change this—for example, to reflect an authentication level of i:2 instead of i:1—but altering the file prevents the file from being parsed, and so you get the results in the dialog box shown in Figure 7.22.

While I would like to report this to be a method to cinch up your connection, I really cannot. If the user has the presence of mind and inclination, they can remove the *signscope:s*: and *signature:s:* lines from the file, save it, and the

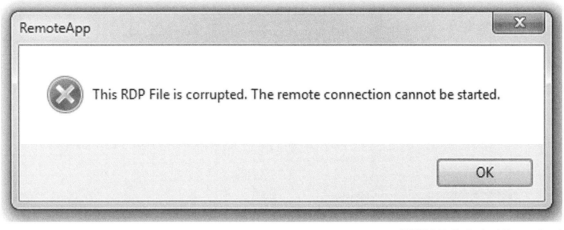

■ **FIGURE 7.22** The Results of Altering a Signed RDP File in Any Way

signature requirement goes bye-bye. But again, the user can see exactly what the connection parameters are and can create a new one if they choose, and you cannot combat trust issues with technology. If you choose to limit distribution to the RDWeb interface, you could also require client certificates to connect, but requiring certificate trust on the RDP files would accomplish the same thing.

RemoteApp and Desktop Connections (WebFeed)

Here is one last feature that makes deployment of RDP files even easier for the user, and while this is not really a security feature, I still think it is kind of cool. We use the RemoteApp Web Feed to automatically populate a start menu folder with the RDP files representing the remote applications you have specified. Part of the RDWeb structure includes an ASPX file for use with Windows 7 and 2008 to specify RemoteApp and Desktop Connections in the control panel. Pointing the configuration to https://remote.domain.com/rdweb/feed/webfeed.aspx results in the population of your start menu with the application specified. It also includes an update feature so that any changes to your applications are automatically reflected on your client.

Figure 7.23b is a view of the resulting populated menu.

This type of configuration offers some very functional and secure maintenance and access models. If we consider the DMZ example introduced at the beginning of the chapter, consider how easy it would be for particular sets of files in the DMZ to be updated in a least privilege environment. An

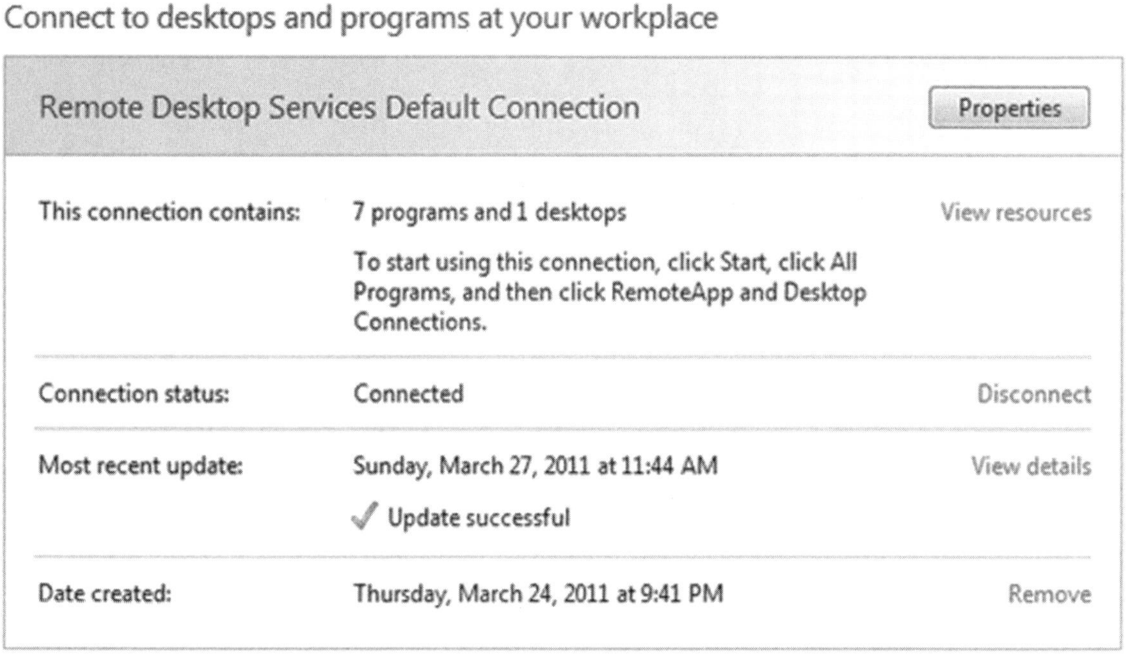

Connect to desktops and programs at your workplace

Remote Desktop Services Default Connection   [Properties]

This connection contains:	7 programs and 1 desktops	View resources
	To start using this connection, click Start, click All Programs, and then click RemoteApp and Desktop Connections.	
Connection status:	Connected	Disconnect
Most recent update:	Sunday, March 27, 2011 at 11:44 AM	View details
	✓ Update successful	
Date created:	Thursday, March 24, 2011 at 9:41 PM	Remove

A

■ **FIGURE 7.23A** The RemoteApp and Desktop Connections Control Panel Applet to Automatically Populate the Client with Start Menu Application Items

administrator could simply open a remote explorer app side by side with their local explorer and copy files directly to the DMZ through RDP nicely, as shown in Figure 7.24.

WORKSTATION HOST CONSIDERATIONS

Another configuration issue with certificates that you need to be aware of if you want users to be able to connect up to their own desktops is that the workstation implementation of Remote Desktop (as in Windows 7 or Vista) uses a self-signed personal certificate to secure the RDP connection. This is all well and good, except for when you try to connect to it from a client that does not trust it. If you have disabled connections with authorization failures, as you should, then you could find yourself in a pickle since you would have to export each individual self-signed certificate to whatever client is going to connect. You cannot simply trust the issuing certificate authority on the client because there is not one. The host signed it itself. Manually configuring this on each client would be a huge administrative burden.

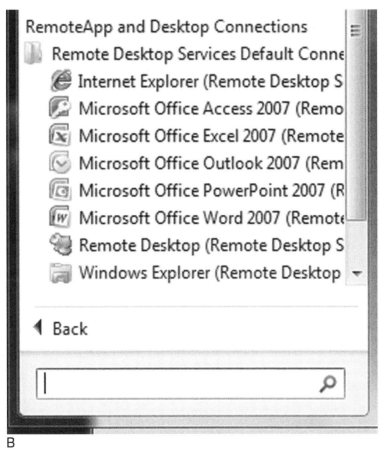

B

■ **FIGURE 7.23B** The Start Menu Populated by the RemoteApp and Desktop Connections Control Panel Applet

In order for the workstation to secure RDP, it creates this self-signed certificate in the remote desktop certificate store. This is the cert it uses, and you cannot change it via a Session Host Configuration app since one is not provided.

This can be frustrating because if you are like me, you have already got an Enterprise Root Certificate Authority in your domain and it is enrolling both users and computers with corresponding certificates. These certificates would be perfectly valid if we could just select them, and clients could be configured to trust them by installing the issuing authority's certificate. Now, the hacker in you might think to look to the Registry for a solution, and you would indeed find the value SSLCertificateSHA1Hash in the

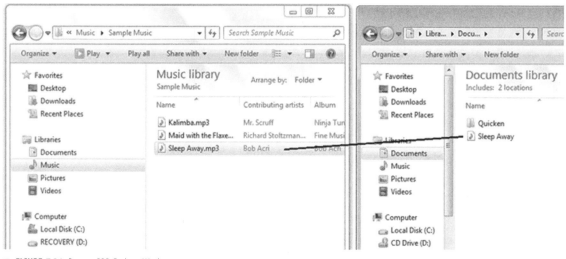

■ FIGURE 7.24 Remote RDP Explorer Windows from the Server Positioned Side by Side with a Local Explorer Window on the Client, Illustrating a Simple Copy-and-Paste Operation

[HKEY_LOCAL_MACHINE\ SYSTEM\ CurrentControlSet\ Control\ Terminal Server\WinStations\RDP-Tcp] hive. The value data would be the SHA1 hash of the self-signed certificate that was created, something like:

```
"SSLCertificateSHA1Hash"=hex:d1,44,0a,06,0d,2b,
d2,0c,00,76,63,10,3b,e7,1d,6e, ab,8f,50,c0.
```

Logic would dictate that all you need to do is copy down the hash of the certificate you want to use and replace the *SSLCertificateSHA1Hash* value with it, and you can, but alas, it does not work. Even if you delete the self-signed certificate and specify the new hash, it just creates the self-signed certificate again. Yes, I tried—it is a real bummer.

Fortunately, there is something we can do, though it is not exactly intuitive. Group policy comes to the rescue again, this time in the form of an option called *Server Authentication Certificate Templates*. This policy option is found in the [Computer Configuration \ Administrative Templates \ Windows Components \ Remote Desktop Services \ Remote Desktop Session Host \ Security] hive of the group policy object editor. This GPO allows us to tell the workstation what certificate to use for RDP security, based on the template that issues the certificate. Fortunately, the certificates from the default machine template used to distribute domain member machine certificates are valid for RDP security.

The machine certificate issued by the CA actually specifies the template it was created from, as shown in Figure 7.26.

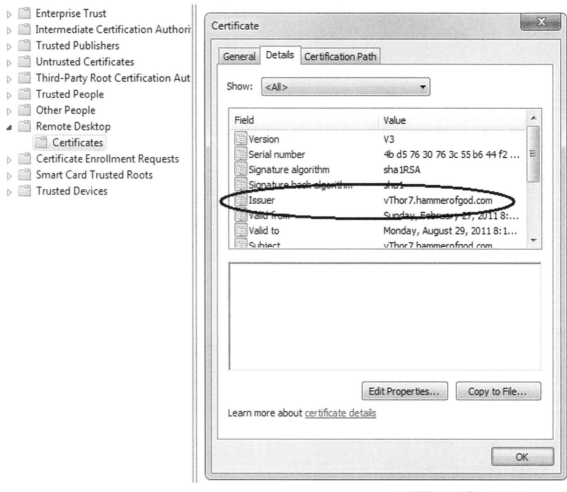

While you may notice this certificate has the same hostname subject, it was created by my CA and displays *Certificate Template Name : Machine* in the certificate details. If we now look to the GPO, we can see that if we enable it, there is a place to enter the template name that we wish to use for the server (workstation in this case) RDP certificate.

The setting that Figure 7.27 highlights is somewhat limiting since you can only specify one template, but you at least have the option of using it, and, more importantly, maintaining your security posture of requiring your clients to trust the CA before connecting.

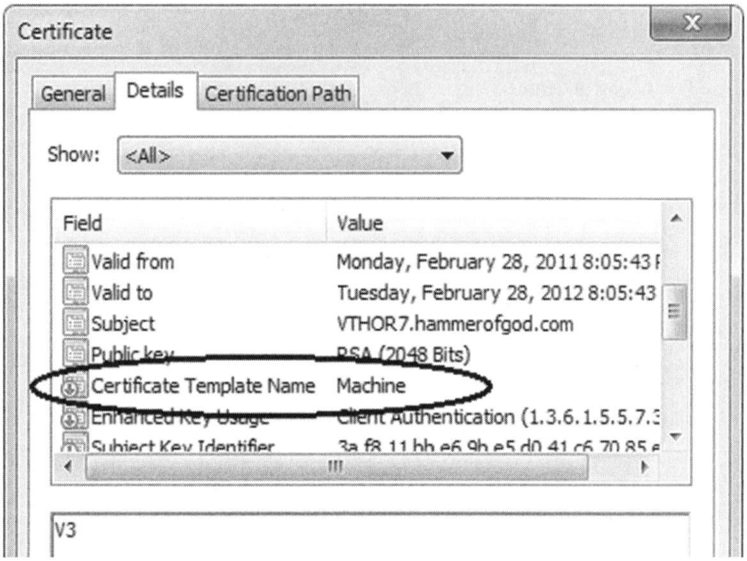

■ **FIGURE 7.26** Default Machine Certificate from the Machine Certificate Template

■ **FIGURE 7.27** Server Authentication Certificate
Template Group Policy Object Specifying to Use
Certificates Created from the Machine Template for
the RDP SSL Server Certificate

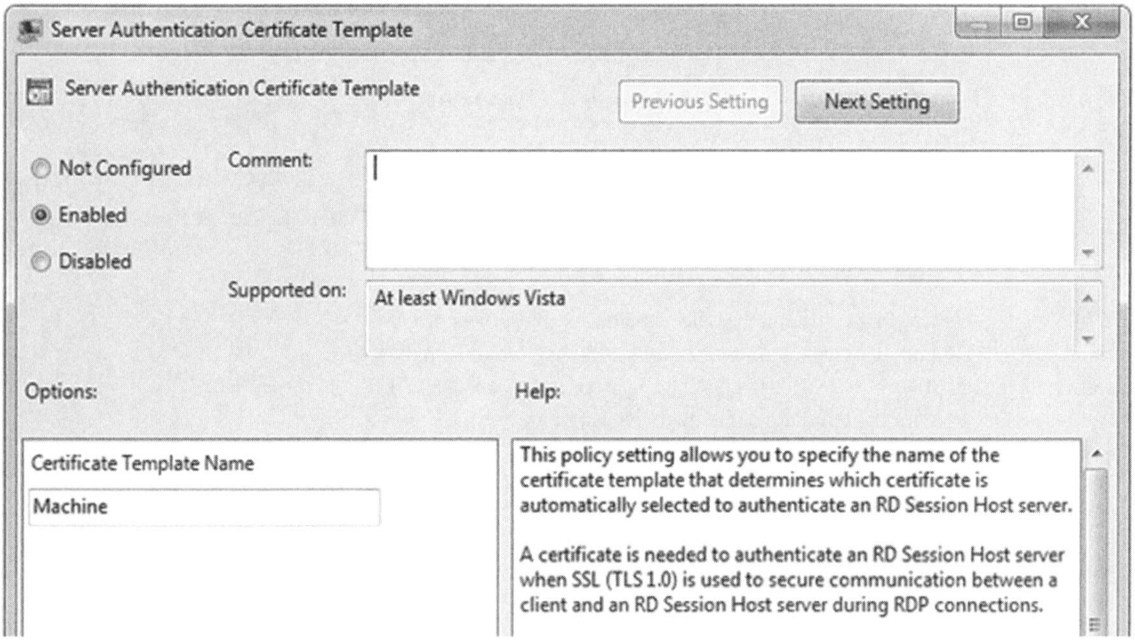

So, that should give you a good place to start as you carve out your security model for RDP. Even with these powerful connection access controls available, I still see people who are scared to death of providing RDP services to the Internet. Yes, RDP can give you a full desktop, but when you think about it, it is really not that different than any other remote access method. I have seen security professionals recommend against RDP publishing, suggesting instead that the client VPN to the network first. This is something I just do not understand. Someone can use brute force on your VPN the same way they can an RDP connection. In fact, attacking the VPN is far easier from a service availability standpoint, and access to the VPN typically gives me full access to the internal network immediately. Regardless, there is a built-in stigma associated RDP deployment, and I think we should halt this trend of discrimination against RDP just because it is different. So let us see if we can do something about that.

LIMITING ACCESS WITH SOURCE PORT ACCESS RULES

I now want to discuss a method of securing access to RDP services that I (and others) have talked about before, but have never actually seen used in any reasonably efficient way. It is the process of creating access control rules based on the source port of the client attempting to make the connection. I have seen implementations of port knocking where seemingly closed ports are sent special sequences of data in order to "unlock" a listening port. SYN packet (or other data) sequences are used like a TCP key to open listening ports. This is an interesting idea, but it is not all that easy to implement in what I would call a normal environment.

Rather than using a port knocking method, I think a perfectly reasonable and (somewhat) easily deployed control can be implemented by basing firewall rules not only on the destination port that the client is connecting to, but the source port that the client is connecting from. As you probably already know, when you establish a normal TCP connection, the client server attempts a connection to the host on a specific port—port 80 (HTTP), for instance. Your client connects to port 80 on the host after a local port is pseudo-randomly chosen by your IP stack. The host will accept this connection, look at what your source port was, and then send response data back to you on the source port you sent it form.

Since these connections are made from random ports typically between 1024 and 65535, firewall rules are configured to allow connections to local ports from any source port. It certainly does not have to be this way. We have discussed how changing the listening port on an RDP host can be used to obfuscate RDP services. And like I have said before, I think this is a perfectly good method of deploying RDP. Yes, an attacker could do a full port scan to see that you have x ports open and then attempt RDP connections to each one (as RDP does not present a banner). The point is that attackers still have to work to do that, and it is an expensive operation for them, meaning they have to spend more time and exert more effort to accomplish this. Lower hanging fruit is much more attractive. However, it is still a possibility, and having administrators go through the motions of changing RDP host ports and maintaining which systems are on which ports is a bit of a pain.

Let us leave our RDP listening port at its default of 3389, but create firewall rules that will only allow this connection to be established if the RDP client's source port is within a particular range. This way, we can ensure that our RDP host port will not even show up as open unless the calling client not only knows that it has to iterate through source ports, but also what source ports it has to iterate through. This is simply something that attackers do not, and will not, do unless they somehow know that they have to. Even if they do figure out the range of source ports you limit into a specific port, they still have to log on and so forth when it comes to RDP. In my opinion, source-port access rules are a perfectly valid access control method and help provide security in depth. It certainly helps when you consider how freaked-out some people get when considering having RDP services available from the Internet. This has also proven invaluable for on-the-road scenarios where you can use IP address filtering, but still want extra control over the connection.

So, how do we get started with this? The obvious issue we have to address first is nailing up a certain source port when we make a call from our RDP client. Microsoft RDP clients do not allow you any control over the source port chosen when an RDP connection is established. I am sure that if someone wanted to they could alter source code of some Linux distribution to customize the open-source RDP client, but in our environment that will not work because we require NLA to establish the connection. We have to use the Microsoft client. So I thought to myself, *Self, you should write some sort of RDP client with a built-in TCP redirecting, source-port nailing proxy connectoid for the book. People would love that, and it would be super cool.* So I did, and have included this on the companion DVD. Always keep in mind that you can theoretically leverage this for any client you want to and this is just an example of doing it with RDP.

ThoRDProxy Client (A New HoG Tool)

I would like to introduce the *ThoRDProxy* client, only available with this book. Here is how it works: Since the behavior of the RDP client cannot be changed, I decided to write a redirecting TCP proxy where I could intercept the outbound RDP client's TCP connection and direct it to the destination server on a new socket where I could muck about with the source address. This was not too hard after I did a bit of research and figured out how to generate push-and-pull socket network streams and spawn separate threads so that I could do background processes.

What I saw as problematic was having the RDP client connect to the proxy, and the proxy connect up to the actual host the RDP client needs to talk to. I could not create two separate connections since I had to make sure NLA would work and I did not want the process to be complicated. While creative security controls are cool and fun, if they are not easy to use and understand, no one will use them. If no one uses them, then they really are not security controls. This meant that instantiating a stand-alone proxy where I had connection parameters set that could take over from the RDP client was out. It would be too difficult for you guys to set it up just for an RDP connection. Ultimately, the model I decided to go with was a single application, within which I could launch both the proxy and the RDP client and control the connection aspects of both. The architecture looks something like Figure 7.28.

The application contains two main components: the RDP ActiveX redistributable control and the TCP proxy. The tool grabs the first local IPv4 address it finds on load-up and uses that for the proxy to listen on. You put in the hostname of the RDP host you want to connect to, and initiate the proxy, and it sits and listens for a connection on 3389. Unfortunately, the client-side implementation of the control does not allow you to set the destination port, which kind of stinks because you cannot have an RDP host listening on your client on the first IP address. But that is not a big deal. Once the proxy is initialized and listening, you initialize the RDP control, which will automatically connect to the IP address bound

ThoRDP Application

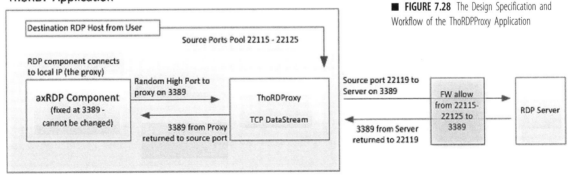

■ **FIGURE 7.28** The Design Specification and Workflow of the ThoRDPProxy Application

by the proxy on 3389. Once a connection is received, the proxy will create a TCP socket for the server connection (from the proxy) and one for the proxy return traffic (since it acts like a client). When the server socket is built, an IP endpoint configuration is bound to the server socket where the source address is selected from a range of source ports previously defined. The connection is then made by the proxy to the RDP host with the source port nailed up, which will match the same range you will have configured on your firewall. We could specify a single port, but I like to have a range of about 10 or so to give me some room.

When the proxy connects to the server, it then takes the return traffic stream and pushes it back to the RDP control, which thinks it has connected to the RDP host. Network data streams are then piped back and forth through the proxy creating a virtual connection between the RDP client and the RDP host. I thought it would be interesting to watch traffic go between the RDP client and server, so I created a console window spawned from the proxy and basically dumped TCP data to the console so you can see what is going on. After going through all that trouble, I realized how dumb I was to do that since the data between the client and server is obviously encrypted and all you see is gobbledygook. But it is attractive gobbledygook, and it is kind of fun to watch when you move the mouse around and see the client telling the server to move the mouse around. And actually, it is valuable to see how the RDP session is encrypted. For instance, if you open Notepad in your session, and repeatedly type *n* over and over, you will see that on each send of the data it is encrypted differently, which I think is cool. The key (or the initialization vector) is obviously being changed each time. It is the small things that are the most entertaining. Figure 7.29 is a shot of the application with the proxy waiting.

Now we will initiate the RDP connection, as shown in Figure 7.30.

Notice that the RDP client thinks it is connecting to the local IP of the machine; however, the connection is made to the host designated in

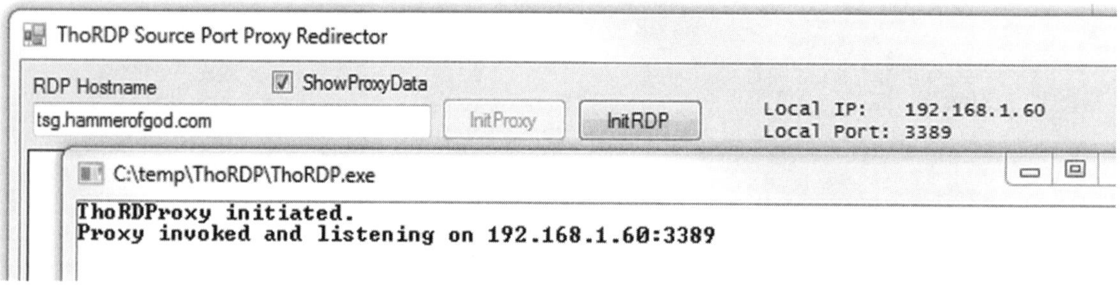

■ **FIGURE 7.29** ThorRDProxy Invoked and Listening

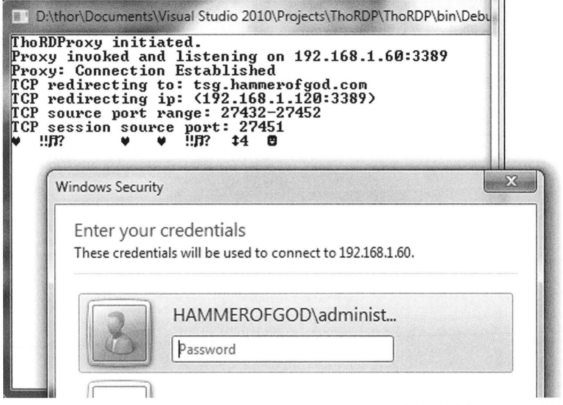

```
D:\thor\Documents\Visual Studio 2010\Projects\ThoRDP\ThoRDP\bin\Debu
ThoRDProxy initiated.
Proxy invoked and listening on 192.168.1.60:3389
Proxy: Connection Established
TCP redirecting to: tsg.hammerofgod.com
TCP redirecting ip: (192.168.1.120:3389)
TCP source port range: 27432-27452
TCP session source port: 27451
```

Windows Security

Enter your credentials

These credentials will be used to connect to 192.168.1.60.

HAMMEROFGOD\administ...

Password

■ **FIGURE 7.30** ThoRDProxy Showing the Nailed Source Port with Connection Request

the RDP Hostname field. Note also that the source port being used is 27451, which will make it through the corresponding firewall rule. We will authenticate to the server, and get the results shown in Figure 7.31.

Ta-da! We now have our RDP session inside the ThoRDP application, and with this we can securely connect to our RDP server on 3389 from anywhere we choose to while anyone else who tries to connect will not even hit the server. Well, there is an x in 64,511 (65,535 – 1024) chance that any random attempt to connect to your server will actually connect from an allowed port, where x is the number of ports you have in your source port range. I am good with that.

SHOW ME THE CODE!

```
using System;
using System.Net;
using System.Net.Sockets;
```

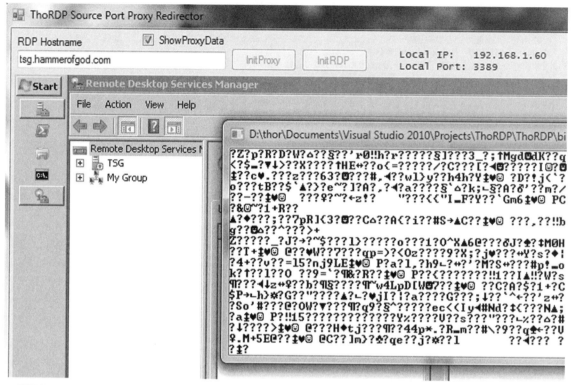

■ **FIGURE 7.31** The ThoRDPProxy Application
Connected to the Host, with the RDP Sniffer Enabled

```
using System.Threading;
using System.Collections.Generic;
using System.ComponentModel;
using System.Data;
using System.Drawing;
using System.Linq;
using System.Text;
using System.Windows.Forms;
using System.ServiceProcess;

namespace ThoRDP
{

  public partial class cRDP : Form
  {
```

```
public cRDP()
{
InitializeComponent();
//I found out the hard way that this doesn't work with embedded
ax control.
//That really suxxOrz. Now I have to disable RDP on client or
change port.
//See if you can do a binary edit on the control to hack it up.
//axRDP.AdvancedSettings2.RDPPort = 3389;

GetIPv4();
int iPort = gVar.gPort;
lIP.Text = "Local IP: " + gVar.gLocalIP.ToString();
lPort.Text = "Local Port: " + Convert.ToString(iPort);

axRDP.AdvancedSettings7.EnableCredSspSupport = true;
axRDP.Server = gVar.gLocalIP.ToString();
}

private void cmdInitProxy_Click(object sender, EventArgs e)
{
// cmdInitProxy.Enabled = false;
cmdRDP.Enabled = true;
ThreadPool.QueueUserWorkItem(new WaitCallback
--(ThreadProxy), "foo");
}

private void ThreadProxy(object foo)
{
gVar.gDestHost = txtDestHost.Text.ToString();
new Proxy().Show();
}

private void cmdRDP_Click(object sender, EventArgs e)
{
cmdRDP.Enabled = false;
axRDP.Connect();
}

private void GetIPv4()
{
string strTemp;
//parse out local IPs and get the first IPv4
//entry for local host TCP listener.
IPHostEntry myIps = new IPHostEntry();
```

```
myIps = Dns.GetHostEntry(Dns.GetHostName());
foreach (IPAddress ip in myIps.AddressList)
{
strTemp = ip.AddressFamily.ToString();
if (strTemp == "InterNetwork")
{
byte[] me = ip.GetAddressBytes();
UInt32 ipInt = BitConverter.ToUInt32(me, 0);
IPAddress ipIP = new IPAddress(ipInt);
gVar.gLocalIP = new IPAddress(ipInt);
break;
}
}
}

private void chkShowProxyData_CheckedChanged(object
--sender, EventArgs e)
{
if (chkShowProxyData.Checked)
gVar.gShowProxyData = true;
else
gVar.gShowProxyData = false;
}
public static void StartService(bool start)
{
string strService = "TermService";
int iTimeout = 10000;
ServiceController service = new ServiceController
--(strService);
try
{
TimeSpan timeout = TimeSpan.FromMilliseconds(iTimeout);
--if (start) service.Start(); else service.Stop();
service.WaitForStatus(ServiceControllerStatus.Running,
--timeout);
MessageBox.Show(service.Status.ToString(), "Service Status");
}
catch (Exception ex)
{
MessageBox.Show("The service is already " + service.Status.
--ToString().ToLower() + " or " + ex.Message, "FYI");
}
}
```

```csharp
    private void Proxy_FormClosing(object sender,
    --FormClosingEventArgs e)
    {
    var result = MessageBox.Show("Would you like to start the
    --TermService on exit?", "Start service?", MessageBoxButtons.
    --YesNo, MessageBoxIcon.Question);
    if (result == DialogResult.Yes) StartService(true);
    }

    private void cRDP_FormClosing(object sender,
    --FormClosingEventArgs e)
    {

    var result = MessageBox.Show("Would you like to start the
    --TermService on exit?", "Start service?", MessageBoxButtons.
    --YesNo, MessageBoxIcon.Question);
    if (result == DialogResult.Yes) StartService(true);
    }
    }
}

    using System;
    using System.Net;
    using System.Net.Sockets;
    using System.Threading;
    using System.Collections.Generic;
    using System.ComponentModel;
    using System.Data;
    using System.Drawing;
    using System.Linq;
    using System.Text;
    using System.Windows.Forms;
    using System.IO;
    using System.Runtime.InteropServices;
    using Microsoft.Win32.SafeHandles;
    using System.ServiceProcess;

    namespace ThoRDP
    {
       public partial class Proxy : Form
       {
       //Carve out the proxy class from my main form in case I want to
       get fancy.
```

```
//For now, just allocate console with interop and write output
to that guy.
[System.Runtime.InteropServices.DllImportAttribute
--("kernel32.dll", EntryPoint = "GetStdHandle")]
public static extern System.IntPtr GetStdHandle(Int32
--nStdHandle);
/// Return Type: BOOL->int
[System.Runtime.InteropServices.DllImportAttribute
--("kernel32.dll", EntryPoint = "AllocConsole")]
[return: System.Runtime.InteropServices.MarshalAsAttribute
--(System.Runtime.InteropServices.UnmanagedType.Bool)]
public static extern bool AllocConsole();

public Proxy()
{
InitializeComponent();
AllocConsole();
InitProxy();

}

public void InitProxy()
{
Console.WriteLine("ThoRDProxy initiated.");
TCPeacePipe myPipe = new TCPeacePipe(gVar.gDestHost, gVar.gPort);
}

public class TCPeacePipe
{
public TCPeacePipe(string sDestHost, int iDestPort)
{
Random random = new Random();
int iSourcePort = random.Next(gVar.gBegSource, gVar.
--gEndSource);
int iLocalPort = 3389; //TCP Listener Port
DoOver:
try
{
TcpListener Listener = new TcpListener(gVar.gLocalIP,
--iLocalPort);
Listener.Start();
Console.WriteLine("Proxy invoked and listening on " + gVar.
--gLocalIP.ToString() + ":" + iLocalPort.ToString());
```

```
int iLoop = 0;
while (true)
{
iLoop++;
TcpClient ClientSock = Listener.AcceptTcpClient();
NetworkStream ClientStream = ClientSock.GetStream();
IPAddress ipServer = Dns.GetHostEntry(sDestHost).
--AddressList[0];
IPAddress ipClient = gVar.gLocalIP;

IPEndPoint localEndPoint = new IPEndPoint(ipClient,
--iSourcePort);
IPEndPoint remoteEndPoint = new IPEndPoint(ipServer,
--iDestPort);
Console.WriteLine("Proxy: Connection Established");
Console.WriteLine("TCP redirecting to: " + sDestHost);
Console.WriteLine("TCP redirecting ip: (" + ipServer.
--ToString() + ":" + iDestPort.ToString() + ")");
Console.WriteLine("TCP source port range: " + gVar.
--gBegSource.ToString() + "-" + gVar.gEndSource.ToString());
Console.WriteLine("TCP session source port: " + iSourcePort.
--ToString());
TcpClient ServerSock = new TcpClient();

ServerSock.Client.Bind(new IPEndPoint(ipClient,iSourcePort));
ServerSock.Connect(ipServer,iDestPort);

NetworkStream ServerStream = ServerSock.GetStream();

TCPassPipe RDPClient = new TCPassPipe("RDPUniqueThread" +
--iLoop)
{
PushStream = ClientStream,
PullStream = ServerStream,
PullSock = ServerSock
};
TCPassPipe ThisClient = new TCPassPipe("MyUniqueThread" +
--iLoop)
{
PushStream = ServerStream,
PullStream = ClientStream,
PullSock = ClientSock
};
}
}
```

```
catch (SocketException ex)
{
if (ex.ErrorCode.ToString() == "10048")
{
var result = MessageBox.Show("Looks like RDP is already
--running, or port is otherwise in use. Do you want to stop the
--service?", "Stop service?", MessageBoxButtons.YesNo,
--MessageBoxIcon.Question);
if (result == DialogResult.Yes) StartService(false);

--goto DoOver;

}
else
MessageBox.Show(ex.ToString(),"TCP Error");

}

}
}
public class TCPassPipe
{
public TcpClient PullSock;
public NetworkStream PushStream;
public NetworkStream PullStream;
Thread ThisThread;
public TCPassPipe(string Name)
{
ThisThread = new Thread(new ThreadStart(StartThread));
ThisThread.Name = Name;
ThisThread.Start();
}

public void StartThread()
{
Byte[] me = new byte[99999];
try
{
while (true)
{
if (PullSock.Available > 0)
{
int iRead = PullStream.Read(me, 0, PullSock.Available);
PushStream.Write(me, 0, iRead);
```

```
if (gVar.gShowProxyData) Console.Write(ASCIIEncoding.
--ASCII.GetString(me, 0, iRead).ToString());
}
Thread.Sleep(13);

}
}
catch (SocketException ex)
{
MessageBox.Show("Error: " + ex.Message, "Error");
}
}
}
public static void StartService(bool start)
{
string strService = "TermService";
int iTimeout = 10000;
ServiceController service = new ServiceController
--(strService);
try
{
TimeSpan timeout = TimeSpan.FromMilliseconds(iTimeout);
if (start) service.Start(); else service.Stop();
service.WaitForStatus(ServiceControllerStatus.Running,
--timeout);
MessageBox.Show(service.Status.ToString(), "Service Status");

}
catch (Exception ex)
{
MessageBox.Show("The service is already " + service.Status.
--ToString().ToLower() + " or " + ex.Message, "FYI");
}
}

private void Proxy_FormClosing(object sender,
--FormClosingEventArgs e)
{

}

}
}
```

I need to clean up some things in the code, such as error recovery and resuming after errors, and there will be updates available on the Hammer of God website, but feel free to change the code as you see fit. I have also added the feature to enter custom starting and ending source ports, which is already updated on the companion DVD.

■ SUMMARY

We covered significant ground in this chapter. We did a deep dive into authentication and authorization of RDP, and discussed ways of publishing RDP directly from the Internet and via Remote Desktop Gateway. Leveraging and configuring certificates was discussed, as were methods of customizing host certificate selection via group policy. Deployment of RemoteApps was discussed as well, via both RDWeb and signed RDP files. And finally, we wrapped up with the introduction of a one-of-a-kind RDP client tool that allows you to further lock down your RDP hosts via source port firewall rules.

List of Acronyms

ACE	Access Control Entry
ACL	Access Control List
AES	Advanced Encryption Standard
ASCII	American Standard Code for Information Interchange
CA	Certificate Authority
CAP	Connection Authorization Policy
CERN	Conseil Européen pour la Recherche Nucléaire (The European Lab for Nuclear Research)
CIFS	Common Internet File System
CLR	Common Language Runtime
COM	Component Object Model
DAC	Discretionary Access Control
DACL	Discretionary Access Control List
DC	Domain Controller
DCOM	Distributed Component Object Model
DMZ	Demilitarized Zone
DoS	Denial of Service
DSN	Database Source Name
EFS	Encrypting File System
GPG	Gnu Privacy Guard
GPO	Group Policy Object
GUID	Global Unique Identifier
HTTP	Hyper Text Transfer Protocol
HTTPS	Hyper Text Transfer Protocol Secure
IDS	Intrusion Detection System
IE	Internet Explorer
IP	Internet Protocol
ISA Server	Internet Security and Acceleration Server
LDAP	Lightweight Directory Access Protocol
MMC	Microsoft Management Console
MSDN	Microsoft Developer Network
NAP	Network Access Protection
NAT	Network Address Translation
NIC	Network Interface Controller
NLA	Network Level Authentication

NTLM	NT LAN Manager
NSA	National Security Association
OU	Organizational Unit
POSIX	Portable Operating System Interface for Unix
PKI	Public Key Infrastructure
RADIUS	Remote Authentication Dial-in User Service
RAP	Resource Authorization Policy
RDG	Remote Desktop Gateway
RDP	Remote Desktop Protocol
RDS	Remote Desktop Services
RPC	Remote Procedure Call
RSA	Rivest, Shamir, and Adleman Algorithm
SACL	System Access Control List
SCM	SQL Configuration Manager
SDDL	Security Descriptor Definition Language
SDK	Software Development Kit
SDL	Software Development Lifecycle
SID	Security Identifier
SMB	Server Message Block
SMTP	Simple Mail Transfer Protocol
SSL	Secure Sockets Layer
SQL	Structured Query Language
TCP	Transmission Control Protocol
TMG	Threat Management Gateway
TSG	Terminal Services Gateway
T-SQL	Transact-SQL
UI	User Interface
URI	Uniform Resource Identifier
VBA	Visual Basic for Applications
VPN	Virtual Private Network
WebDAV	Web Distributed Authoring and Versioning
WMI	Windows Management Instrumentation

Full List of Server 2008 Logs via the WEVTUTIL Tool

```
C:\Windows\system32>wevtutil el
Analytic
Application
DirectShowFilterGraph
DirectShowPluginControl
EndpointMapper
ForwardedEvents
HardwareEvents
Internet Explorer
Key Management Service
Microsoft-IE/Diagnostic
Microsoft-IEFRAME/Diagnostic
Microsoft-IIS-Configuration/Administrative
Microsoft-IIS-Configuration/Analytic
Microsoft-IIS-Configuration/Debug
Microsoft-IIS-Configuration/Operational
Microsoft-PerfTrack-IEFRAME/Diagnostic
Microsoft-PerfTrack-MSHTML/Diagnostic
Microsoft-Windows-ADSI/Debug
Microsoft-Windows-API-Tracing/Operational
Microsoft-Windows-ATAPort/General
Microsoft-Windows-ATAPort/SATA-LPM
Microsoft-Windows-ActionQueue/Analytic
Microsoft-Windows-AppID/Operational
Microsoft-Windows-AppLocker/EXE and DLL
Microsoft-Windows-AppLocker/MSI and Script
Microsoft-Windows-Application Server-Applications/Admin
Microsoft-Windows-Application Server-Applications/
Analytic
Microsoft-Windows-Application Server-Applications/Debug
Microsoft-Windows-Application Server-Applications/
Operational
Microsoft-Windows-Application Server-Applications/Perf
```

```
Microsoft-Windows-Application-Experience/Problem-Steps-
Recorder
Microsoft-Windows-Application-Experience/Program-
Compatibility-Assistant
Microsoft-Windows-Application-Experience/Program-
Compatibility-Troubleshooter
Microsoft-Windows-Application-Experience/Program-
Inventory
Microsoft-Windows-Application-Experience/Program-
Inventory/Debug
Microsoft-Windows-Application-Experience/Program-
Telemetry
Microsoft-Windows-Audio/CaptureMonitor
Microsoft-Windows-Audio/Operational
Microsoft-Windows-Audio/Performance
Microsoft-Windows-Audit/Analytic
Microsoft-Windows-Authentication User Interface/
Operational
Microsoft-Windows-Bits-Client/Analytic
Microsoft-Windows-Bits-Client/Operational
Microsoft-Windows-CAPI2/Operational
Microsoft-Windows-CDROM/Operational
Microsoft-Windows-COM/Analytic
Microsoft-Windows-COMRuntime/Tracing
Microsoft-Windows-Calculator/Debug
Microsoft-Windows-Calculator/Diagnostic
Microsoft-Windows-CertPoleEng/Operational
Microsoft-Windows-CertificateServicesClient-
CredentialRoaming/Operational
Microsoft-Windows-ClearTypeTextTuner/Diagnostic
Microsoft-Windows-CmiSetup/Analytic
Microsoft-Windows-CodeIntegrity/Operational
Microsoft-Windows-CodeIntegrity/Verbose
Microsoft-Windows-ComDlg32/Analytic
Microsoft-Windows-ComDlg32/Debug
Microsoft-Windows-CorruptedFileRecovery-Client/
Operational
Microsoft-Windows-CorruptedFileRecovery-Server/
Operational
Microsoft-Windows-CredUI/Diagnostic
Microsoft-Windows-Crypto-RNG/Analytic
Microsoft-Windows-DCLocator/Debug
Microsoft-Windows-DNS-Client/Operational
Microsoft-Windows-DUI/Diagnostic
Microsoft-Windows-DUSER/Diagnostic
Microsoft-Windows-DXP/Analytic
Microsoft-Windows-DateTimeControlPanel/Analytic
```

```
Microsoft-Windows-DateTimeControlPanel/Debug
Microsoft-Windows-DateTimeControlPanel/Operational
Microsoft-Windows-Deplorch/Analytic
Microsoft-Windows-DeviceSync/Analytic
Microsoft-Windows-DeviceSync/Operational
Microsoft-Windows-DeviceUx/Informational
Microsoft-Windows-DeviceUx/Performance
Microsoft-Windows-Dhcp-Client/Admin
Microsoft-Windows-Dhcp-Client/Operational
Microsoft-Windows-DhcpNap/Admin
Microsoft-Windows-DhcpNap/Operational
Microsoft-Windows-Dhcpv6-Client/Admin
Microsoft-Windows-Dhcpv6-Client/Operational
Microsoft-Windows-DiagCpl/Debug
Microsoft-Windows-Diagnosis-DPS/Analytic
Microsoft-Windows-Diagnosis-DPS/Debug
Microsoft-Windows-Diagnosis-DPS/Operational
Microsoft-Windows-Diagnosis-MSDE/Debug
Microsoft-Windows-Diagnosis-PCW/Analytic
Microsoft-Windows-Diagnosis-PCW/Debug
Microsoft-Windows-Diagnosis-PCW/Operational
Microsoft-Windows-Diagnosis-PLA/Debug
Microsoft-Windows-Diagnosis-PLA/Operational
Microsoft-Windows-Diagnosis-Perfhost/Analytic
Microsoft-Windows-Diagnosis-Scripted/Admin
Microsoft-Windows-Diagnosis-Scripted/Analytic
Microsoft-Windows-Diagnosis-Scripted/Debug
Microsoft-Windows-Diagnosis-Scripted/Operational
Microsoft-Windows-Diagnosis-ScriptedDiagnosticsProvider/
Debug
Microsoft-Windows-Diagnosis-ScriptedDiagnosticsProvider/
Operational
Microsoft-Windows-Diagnosis-TaskManager/Debug
Microsoft-Windows-Diagnosis-WDC/Analytic
Microsoft-Windows-Diagnosis-WDI/Debug
Microsoft-Windows-Diagnostics-Networking/Debug
Microsoft-Windows-Diagnostics-Networking/Operational
Microsoft-Windows-DirectShow-KernelSupport/Performance
Microsoft-Windows-DirectSound/Debug
Microsoft-Windows-DirectWrite-FontCache/Tracing
Microsoft-Windows-Disk/Operational
Microsoft-Windows-DisplaySwitch/Diagnostic
Microsoft-Windows-Documents/Performance
Microsoft-Windows-DriverFrameworks-UserMode/Operational
Microsoft-Windows-DxgKrnl/Diagnostic
Microsoft-Windows-DxgKrnl/Performance
Microsoft-Windows-DxpTaskSyncProvider/Analytic
```

```
Microsoft-Windows-EFS/Debug
Microsoft-Windows-EapHost/Analytic
Microsoft-Windows-EapHost/Debug
Microsoft-Windows-EapHost/Operational
Microsoft-Windows-EaseOfAccess/Diagnostic
Microsoft-Windows-EnrollmentPolicyWebService/Admin
Microsoft-Windows-EnrollmentWebService/Admin
Microsoft-Windows-EventCollector/Debug
Microsoft-Windows-EventCollector/Operational
Microsoft-Windows-EventLog-WMIProvider/Debug
Microsoft-Windows-EventLog/Analytic
Microsoft-Windows-EventLog/Debug
Microsoft-Windows-FMS/Analytic
Microsoft-Windows-FMS/Debug
Microsoft-Windows-FMS/Operational
Microsoft-Windows-FailoverClustering-Client/Diagnostic
Microsoft-Windows-Feedback-Service-TriggerProvider
Microsoft-Windows-FileInfoMinifilter/Operational
Microsoft-Windows-Firewall-CPL/Diagnostic
Microsoft-Windows-Folder Redirection/Operational
Microsoft-Windows-Forwarding/Debug
Microsoft-Windows-Forwarding/Operational
Microsoft-Windows-GroupPolicy/Operational
Microsoft-Windows-HAL/Debug
Microsoft-Windows-HealthCenter/Debug
Microsoft-Windows-HealthCenter/Performance
Microsoft-Windows-HealthCenterCPL/Performance
Microsoft-Windows-Help/Operational
Microsoft-Windows-HomeGroup Control Panel Performance/
Diagnostic
Microsoft-Windows-HomeGroup Control Panel/Operational
Microsoft-Windows-HttpService/Trace
Microsoft-Windows-IKE/Operational
Microsoft-Windows-IKEDBG/Debug
Microsoft-Windows-IPBusEnum/Tracing
Microsoft-Windows-IPSEC-SRV/Diagnostic
Microsoft-Windows-International-
RegionalOptionsControlPanel/Operational
Microsoft-Windows-International/Operational
Microsoft-Windows-Iphlpsvc/Debug
Microsoft-Windows-Iphlpsvc/Operational
Microsoft-Windows-Iphlpsvc/Trace
Microsoft-Windows-Kernel-Acpi/Diagnostic
Microsoft-Windows-Kernel-Boot/Analytic
Microsoft-Windows-Kernel-BootDiagnostics/Diagnostic
Microsoft-Windows-Kernel-Disk/Analytic
Microsoft-Windows-Kernel-EventTracing/Admin
```

```
Microsoft-Windows-Kernel-EventTracing/Analytic
Microsoft-Windows-Kernel-File/Analytic
Microsoft-Windows-Kernel-Memory/Analytic
Microsoft-Windows-Kernel-Network/Analytic
Microsoft-Windows-Kernel-PnP/Diagnostic
Microsoft-Windows-Kernel-Power/Diagnostic
Microsoft-Windows-Kernel-Power/Thermal-Diagnostic
Microsoft-Windows-Kernel-Power/Thermal-Operational
Microsoft-Windows-Kernel-Prefetch/Diagnostic
Microsoft-Windows-Kernel-Process/Analytic
Microsoft-Windows-Kernel-Processor-Power/Diagnostic
Microsoft-Windows-Kernel-Registry/Analytic
Microsoft-Windows-Kernel-StoreMgr/Analytic
Microsoft-Windows-Kernel-StoreMgr/Operational
Microsoft-Windows-Kernel-WDI/Analytic
Microsoft-Windows-Kernel-WDI/Debug
Microsoft-Windows-Kernel-WDI/Operational
Microsoft-Windows-Kernel-WHEA/Errors
Microsoft-Windows-Kernel-WHEA/Operational
Microsoft-Windows-Known Folders API Service
Microsoft-Windows-L2NA/Diagnostic
Microsoft-Windows-LDAP-Client/Debug
Microsoft-Windows-LUA-ConsentUI/Diagnostic
Microsoft-Windows-LanguagePackSetup/Analytic
Microsoft-Windows-LanguagePackSetup/Debug
Microsoft-Windows-LanguagePackSetup/Operational
Microsoft-Windows-MPS-CLNT/Diagnostic
Microsoft-Windows-MPS-DRV/Diagnostic
Microsoft-Windows-MPS-SRV/Diagnostic
Microsoft-Windows-MSPaint/Admin
Microsoft-Windows-MSPaint/Debug
Microsoft-Windows-MSPaint/Diagnostic
Microsoft-Windows-MUI/Admin
Microsoft-Windows-MUI/Analytic
Microsoft-Windows-MUI/Debug
Microsoft-Windows-MUI/Operational
Microsoft-Windows-MemoryDiagnostics-Results/Debug
Microsoft-Windows-NCSI/Analytic
Microsoft-Windows-NCSI/Operational
Microsoft-Windows-NDF-HelperClassDiscovery/Debug
Microsoft-Windows-NDIS-PacketCapture/Diagnostic
Microsoft-Windows-NDIS/Diagnostic
Microsoft-Windows-NDIS/Operational
Microsoft-Windows-NTLM/Operational
Microsoft-Windows-Narrator/Diagnostic
Microsoft-Windows-NetShell/Performance
Microsoft-Windows-Network-and-Sharing-Center/Diagnostic
```

```
Microsoft-Windows-NetworkAccessProtection/Operational
Microsoft-Windows-NetworkAccessProtection/WHC
Microsoft-Windows-NetworkLocationWizard/Operational
Microsoft-Windows-NetworkProfile/Diagnostic
Microsoft-Windows-NetworkProfile/Operational
Microsoft-Windows-Networking-Correlation/Diagnostic
Microsoft-Windows-NlaSvc/Diagnostic
Microsoft-Windows-NlaSvc/Operational
Microsoft-Windows-OLEACC/Debug
Microsoft-Windows-OLEACC/Diagnostic
Microsoft-Windows-OOBE-Machine/Diagnostic
Microsoft-Windows-OneX/Diagnostic
Microsoft-Windows-OobeLdr/Analytic
Microsoft-Windows-PCI/Diagnostic
Microsoft-Windows-PortableDeviceSyncProvider/Analytic
Microsoft-Windows-PowerCfg/Diagnostic
Microsoft-Windows-PowerCpl/Diagnostic
Microsoft-Windows-PowerEfficiencyDiagnostics/Diagnostic
Microsoft-Windows-PowerShell/Analytic
Microsoft-Windows-PowerShell/Operational
Microsoft-Windows-PrimaryNetworkIcon/Performance
Microsoft-Windows-PrintService/Admin
Microsoft-Windows-PrintService/Debug
Microsoft-Windows-PrintService/Operational
Microsoft-Windows-QoS-Pacer/Diagnostic
Microsoft-Windows-RPC-Proxy/Debug
Microsoft-Windows-RPC/Debug
Microsoft-Windows-RPC/EEInfo
Microsoft-Windows-ReliabilityAnalysisComponent/
Operational
Microsoft-Windows-RemoteApp and Desktop Connections/Admin
Microsoft-Windows-Remotefs-UTProvider/Diagnostic
Microsoft-Windows-Resource-Exhaustion-Detector/
Operational
Microsoft-Windows-ResourcePublication/Tracing
Microsoft-Windows-RestartManager/Operational
Microsoft-Windows-Security-Audit-Configuration-Client/
Diagnostic
Microsoft-Windows-Security-Audit-Configuration-Client/
Operational
Microsoft-Windows-Security-Configuration-Wizard/
Diagnostic
Microsoft-Windows-Security-Configuration-Wizard/
Operational
Microsoft-Windows-Security-SPP/Perf
Microsoft-Windows-Sens/Debug
Microsoft-Windows-ServerManager/Analytic
```

```
Microsoft-Windows-ServerManager/Operational
Microsoft-Windows-ServiceReportingApi/Debug
Microsoft-Windows-Services-Svchost/Diagnostic
Microsoft-Windows-Services/Diagnostic
Microsoft-Windows-Setup/Analytic
Microsoft-Windows-SetupCl/Analytic
Microsoft-Windows-SetupQueue/Analytic
Microsoft-Windows-SetupUGC/Analytic
Microsoft-Windows-Shell-AuthUI-BootAnim/Diagnostic
Microsoft-Windows-Shell-AuthUI-Common/Diagnostic
Microsoft-Windows-Shell-AuthUI-CredUI/Diagnostic
Microsoft-Windows-Shell-AuthUI-Logon/Diagnostic
Microsoft-Windows-Shell-AuthUI-PasswordProvider/
Diagnostic
Microsoft-Windows-Shell-AuthUI-Shutdown/Diagnostic
Microsoft-Windows-Shell-Core/Diagnostic
Microsoft-Windows-Shell-DefaultPrograms/Diagnostic
Microsoft-Windows-Shell-Shwebsvc
Microsoft-Windows-Shell-ZipFolder/Diagnostic
Microsoft-Windows-Shsvcs/Diagnostic
Microsoft-Windows-StorDiag/Operational
Microsoft-Windows-StorPort/Operational
Microsoft-Windows-Subsys-Csr/Operational
Microsoft-Windows-Subsys-SMSS/Operational
Microsoft-Windows-Sysprep/Analytic
Microsoft-Windows-TCPIP/Diagnostic
Microsoft-Windows-TSF-msctf/Debug
Microsoft-Windows-TSF-msctf/Diagnostic
Microsoft-Windows-TSF-msutb/Debug
Microsoft-Windows-TSF-msutb/Diagnostic
Microsoft-Windows-TZUtil/Operational
Microsoft-Windows-TaskScheduler/Debug
Microsoft-Windows-TaskScheduler/Diagnostic
Microsoft-Windows-TaskScheduler/Operational
Microsoft-Windows-TaskbarCPL/Diagnostic
Microsoft-Windows-TerminalServices-ClientUSBDevices/
Admin
Microsoft-Windows-TerminalServices-ClientUSBDevices/
Analytic
Microsoft-Windows-TerminalServices-ClientUSBDevices/
Debug
Microsoft-Windows-TerminalServices-ClientUSBDevices/
Operational
Microsoft-Windows-TerminalServices-LocalSessionManager/
Admin
Microsoft-Windows-TerminalServices-LocalSessionManager/
Analytic
```

```
Microsoft-Windows-TerminalServices-LocalSessionManager/
Debug
Microsoft-Windows-TerminalServices-LocalSessionManager/
Operational
Microsoft-Windows-TerminalServices-PnPDevices/Admin
Microsoft-Windows-TerminalServices-PnPDevices/Analytic
Microsoft-Windows-TerminalServices-PnPDevices/Debug
Microsoft-Windows-TerminalServices-PnPDevices/
Operational
Microsoft-Windows-TerminalServices-RDPClient/Analytic
Microsoft-Windows-TerminalServices-RDPClient/Debug
Microsoft-Windows-TerminalServices-RDPClient/Operational
Microsoft-Windows-TerminalServices-RdpSoundDriver/
Capture
Microsoft-Windows-TerminalServices-RdpSoundDriver/
Playback
Microsoft-Windows-TerminalServices-
RemoteConnectionManager/Admin
Microsoft-Windows-TerminalServices-
RemoteConnectionManager/Analytic
Microsoft-Windows-TerminalServices-
RemoteConnection Manager/Debug
Microsoft-Windows-TerminalServices-
RemoteConnection Manager/Operational
Microsoft-Windows-ThemeCPL/Diagnostic
Microsoft-Windows-ThemeUI/Diagnostic
Microsoft-Windows-TunnelDriver
Microsoft-Windows-UAC-FileVirtualization/Operational
Microsoft-Windows-UAC/Operational
Microsoft-Windows-UIAnimation/Diagnostic
Microsoft-Windows-UIAutomationCore/Debug
Microsoft-Windows-UIAutomationCore/Diagnostic
Microsoft-Windows-UIAutomationCore/Perf
Microsoft-Windows-UIRibbon/Diagnostic
Microsoft-Windows-USB-USBHUB/Diagnostic
Microsoft-Windows-USB-USBPORT/Diagnostic
Microsoft-Windows-User Control Panel Performance/
Diagnostic
Microsoft-Windows-User Profile Service/Diagnostic
Microsoft-Windows-User Profile Service/Operational
Microsoft-Windows-User-Loader/Analytic
Microsoft-Windows-UserModePowerService/Diagnostic
Microsoft-Windows-UserPnp/DeviceMetadata/Debug
Microsoft-Windows-UserPnp/DeviceNotifications
Microsoft-Windows-UserPnp/Performance
Microsoft-Windows-UserPnp/SchedulerOperations
Microsoft-Windows-UxTheme/Diagnostic
```

```
Microsoft-Windows-VAN/Diagnostic
Microsoft-Windows-VDRVROOT/Operational
Microsoft-Windows-VHDMP/Operational
Microsoft-Windows-VolumeControl/Performance
Microsoft-Windows-VolumeSnapshot-Driver/Operational
Microsoft-Windows-WABSyncProvider/Analytic
Microsoft-Windows-WER-Diag/Operational
Microsoft-Windows-WFP/Analytic
Microsoft-Windows-WFP/Operational
Microsoft-Windows-WMI-Activity/Trace
Microsoft-Windows-WUSA/Debug
Microsoft-Windows-WWAN-NDISUIO-EVENTS/Diagnostic
Microsoft-Windows-WebIO-NDF/Diagnostic
Microsoft-Windows-WebIO/Diagnostic
Microsoft-Windows-WebServices/Tracing
Microsoft-Windows-Win32k/Concurrency
Microsoft-Windows-Win32k/Power
Microsoft-Windows-Win32k/Render
Microsoft-Windows-Win32k/Tracing
Microsoft-Windows-Win32k/UIPI
Microsoft-Windows-WinHTTP-NDF/Diagnostic
Microsoft-Windows-WinHttp/Diagnostic
Microsoft-Windows-WinINet/Analytic
Microsoft-Windows-WinRM/Analytic
Microsoft-Windows-WinRM/Debug
Microsoft-Windows-WinRM/Operational
Microsoft-Windows-Windeploy/Analytic
Microsoft-Windows-Windows Firewall With Advanced Security/
ConnectionSecurity
Microsoft-Windows-Windows Firewall With Advanced Security/
ConnectionSecurityVerbose
Microsoft-Windows-Windows Firewall With Advanced Security/
Firewall
Microsoft-Windows-Windows Firewall With Advanced Security/
FirewallVerbose
Microsoft-Windows-WindowsColorSystem/Debug
Microsoft-Windows-WindowsColorSystem/Operational
Microsoft-Windows-WindowsUpdateClient/Operational
Microsoft-Windows-Wininit/Diagnostic
Microsoft-Windows-Winlogon/Diagnostic
Microsoft-Windows-Winlogon/Operational
Microsoft-Windows-Winsock-AFD/Operational
Microsoft-Windows-Winsock-WS2HELP/Operational
Microsoft-Windows-Winsrv/Analytic
Microsoft-Windows-Wired-AutoConfig/Diagnostic
Microsoft-Windows-Wired-AutoConfig/Operational
Microsoft-Windows-Wordpad/Admin
```

```
Microsoft-Windows-Wordpad/Debug
Microsoft-Windows-Wordpad/Diagnostic
Microsoft-Windows-ntshrui
Microsoft-Windows-osk/Diagnostic
Microsoft-Windows-stobject/Diagnostic
Security
Setup
System
TabletPC_InputPanel_Channel
Windows PowerShell
microsoft-windows-RemoteDesktopServices-
RemoteDesktopSessionManager/Admin
```

Index

Note: Page numbers followed by *f* indicate figures and *t* indicate table.